Hayate the Comb

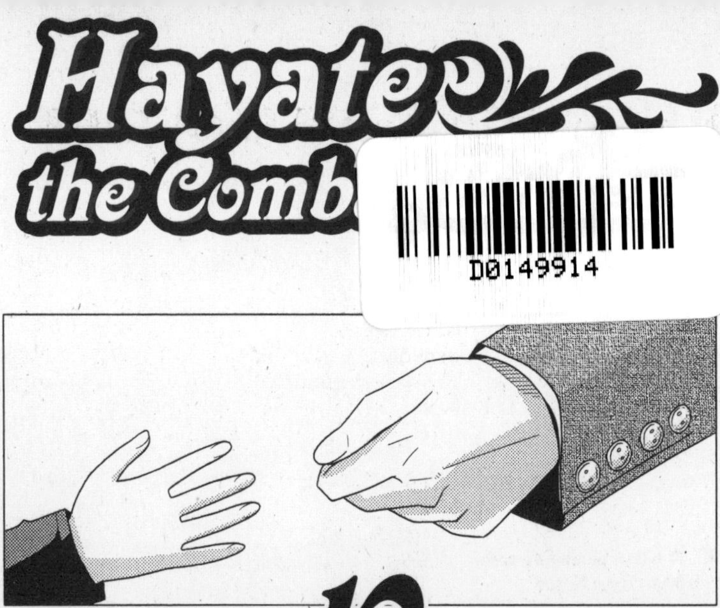

10

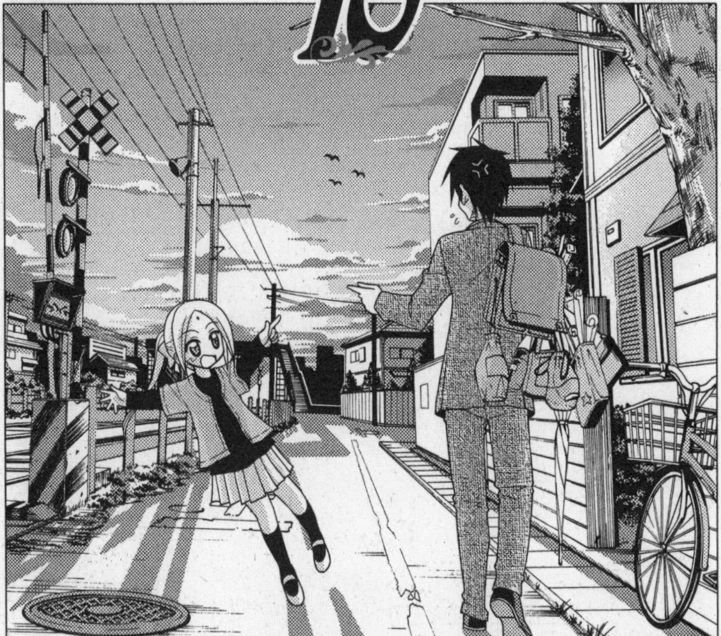

KENJIRO HATA

CONTENTS

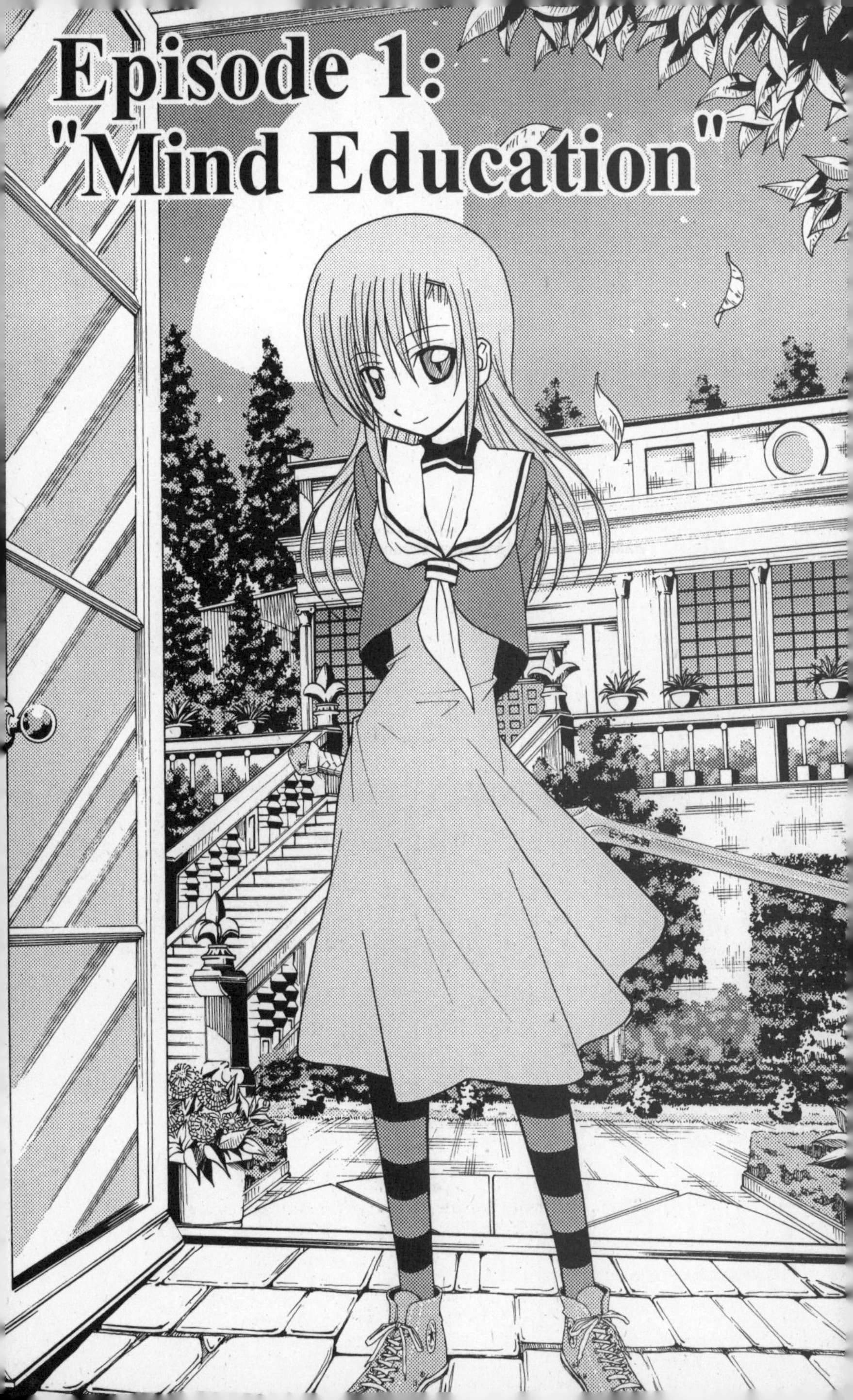
Episode 1:
"Mind Education"

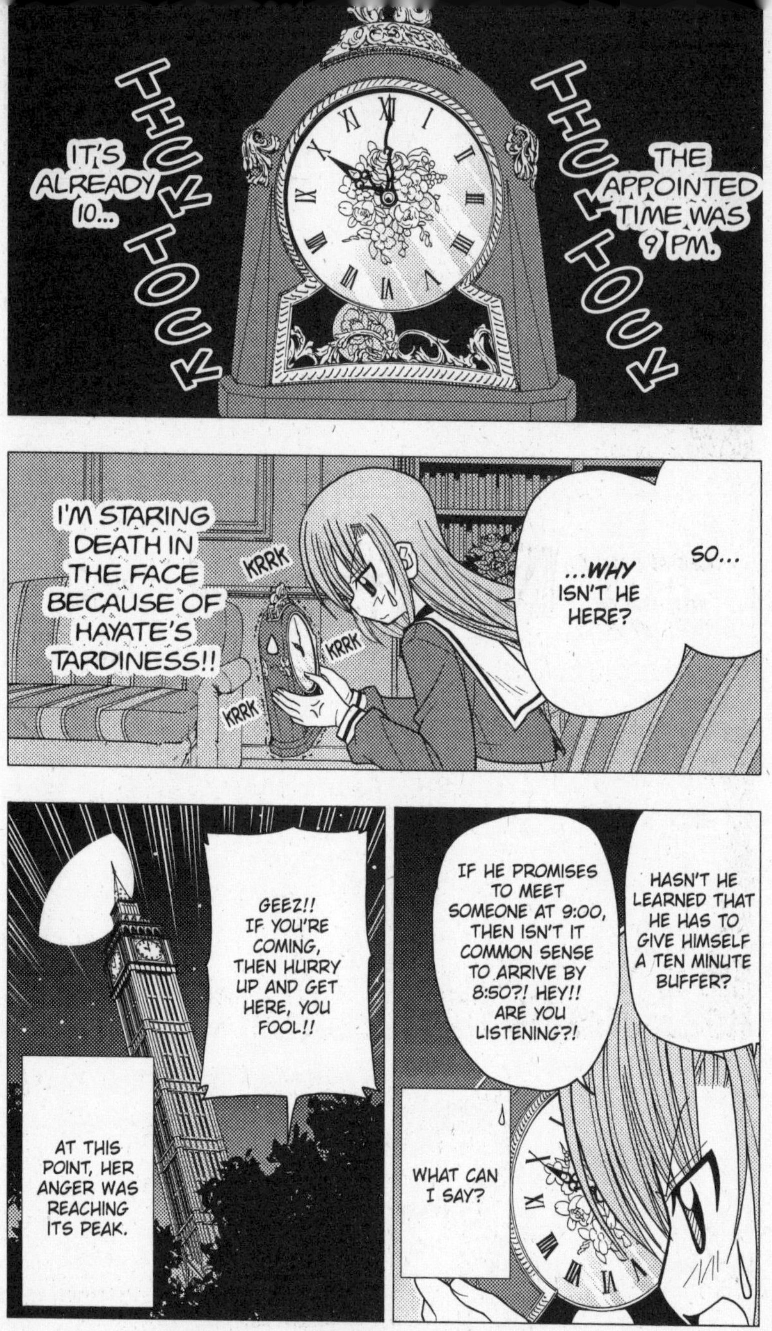
THICK TOCK
THE APPOINTED TIME WAS 9 PM.
IT'S ALREADY 10...
THICK TOCK
SO...
...WHY ISN'T HE HERE?
KRRK
KRRK
KRRK
I'M STARING DEATH IN THE FACE BECAUSE OF HAYATE'S TARDINESS!!
HASN'T HE LEARNED THAT HE HAS TO GIVE HIMSELF A TEN MINUTE BUFFER?
IF HE PROMISES TO MEET SOMEONE AT 9:00, THEN ISN'T IT COMMON SENSE TO ARRIVE BY 8:50?! HEY!! ARE YOU LISTENING?!
WHAT CAN I SAY?
GEEZ!! IF YOU'RE COMING, THEN HURRY UP AND GET HERE, YOU FOOL!!
AT THIS POINT, HER ANGER WAS REACHING ITS PEAK.

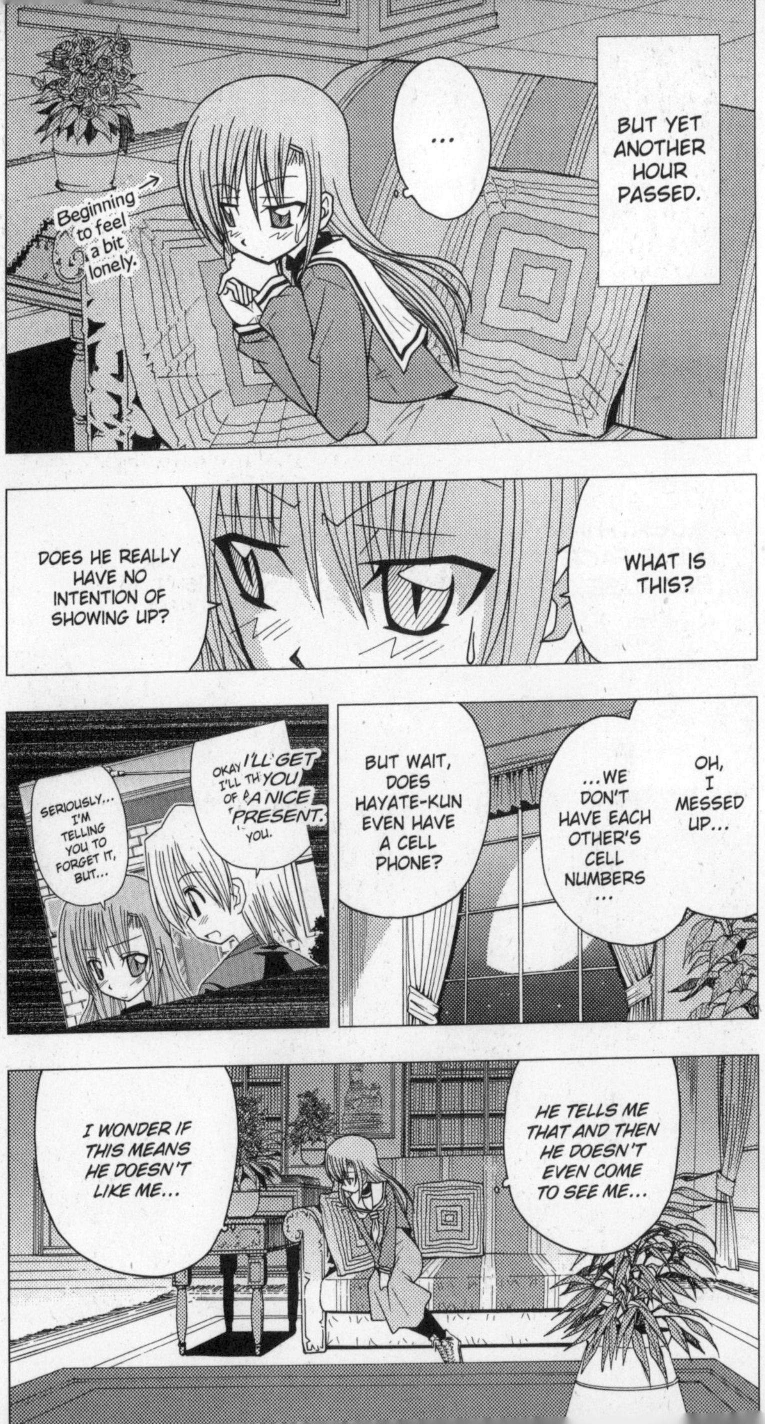
BUT YET ANOTHER HOUR PASSED.
...
Beginning to feel a bit lonely.
WHAT IS THIS?
DOES HE REALLY HAVE NO INTENTION OF SHOWING UP?
OH, I MESSED UP...
...WE DON'T HAVE EACH OTHER'S CELL NUMBERS ...
BUT WAIT, DOES HAYATE-KUN EVEN HAVE A CELL PHONE?
I'LL GET YOU A NICE PRESENT.
SERIOUSLY... I'M TELLING YOU TO FORGET IT, BUT...
HE TELLS ME THAT AND THEN HE DOESN'T EVEN COME TO SEE ME...
I WONDER IF THIS MEANS HE DOESN'T LIKE ME...

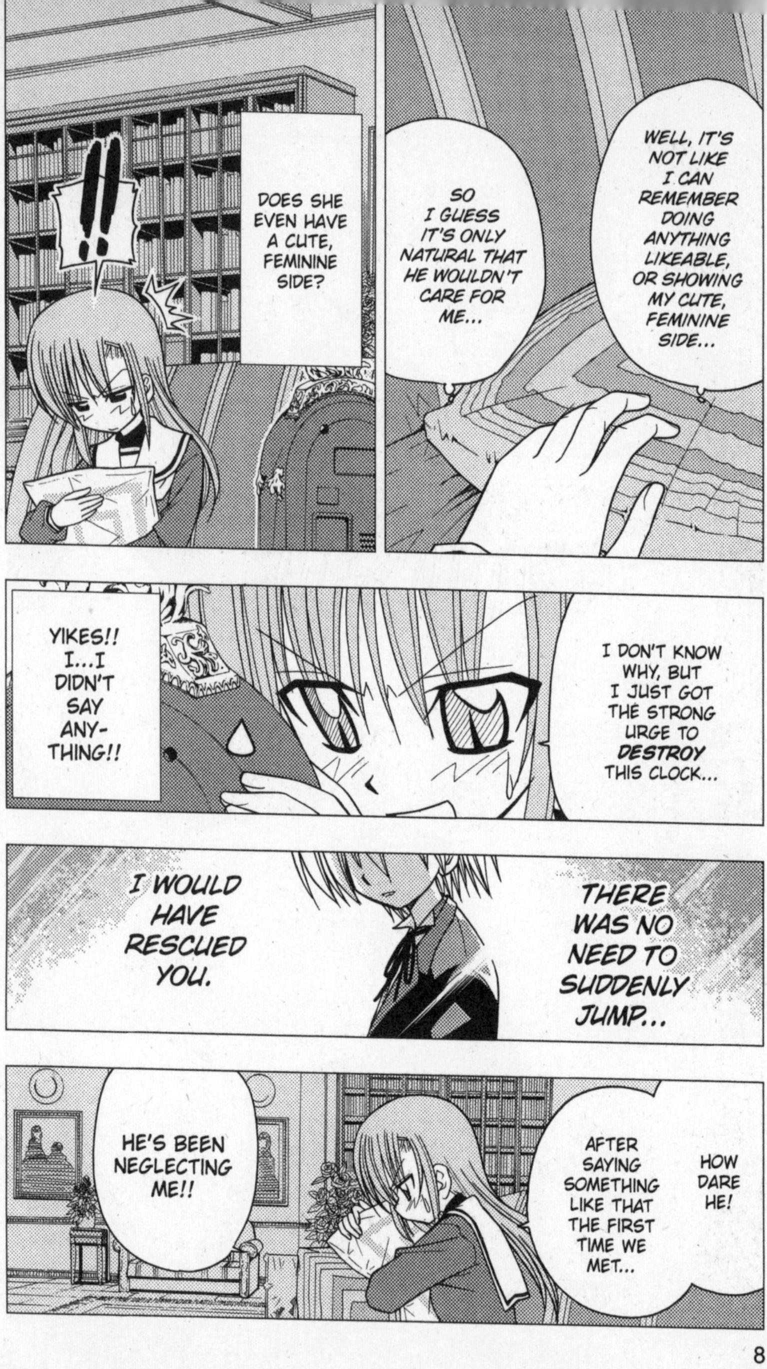
WELL, IT'S NOT LIKE I CAN REMEMBER DOING ANYTHING LIKEABLE, OR SHOWING MY CUTE, FEMININE SIDE...
SO I GUESS IT'S ONLY NATURAL THAT HE WOULDN'T CARE FOR ME...
DOES SHE EVEN HAVE A CUTE, FEMININE SIDE?
!!
I DON'T KNOW WHY, BUT I JUST GOT THE STRONG URGE TO ***DESTROY*** THIS CLOCK...
YIKES!! I...I DIDN'T SAY ANYTHING!!
THERE WAS NO NEED TO SUDDENLY JUMP...
I WOULD HAVE RESCUED YOU.
HOW DARE HE!
AFTER SAYING SOMETHING LIKE THAT THE FIRST TIME WE MET...
HE'S BEEN NEGLECTING ME!!

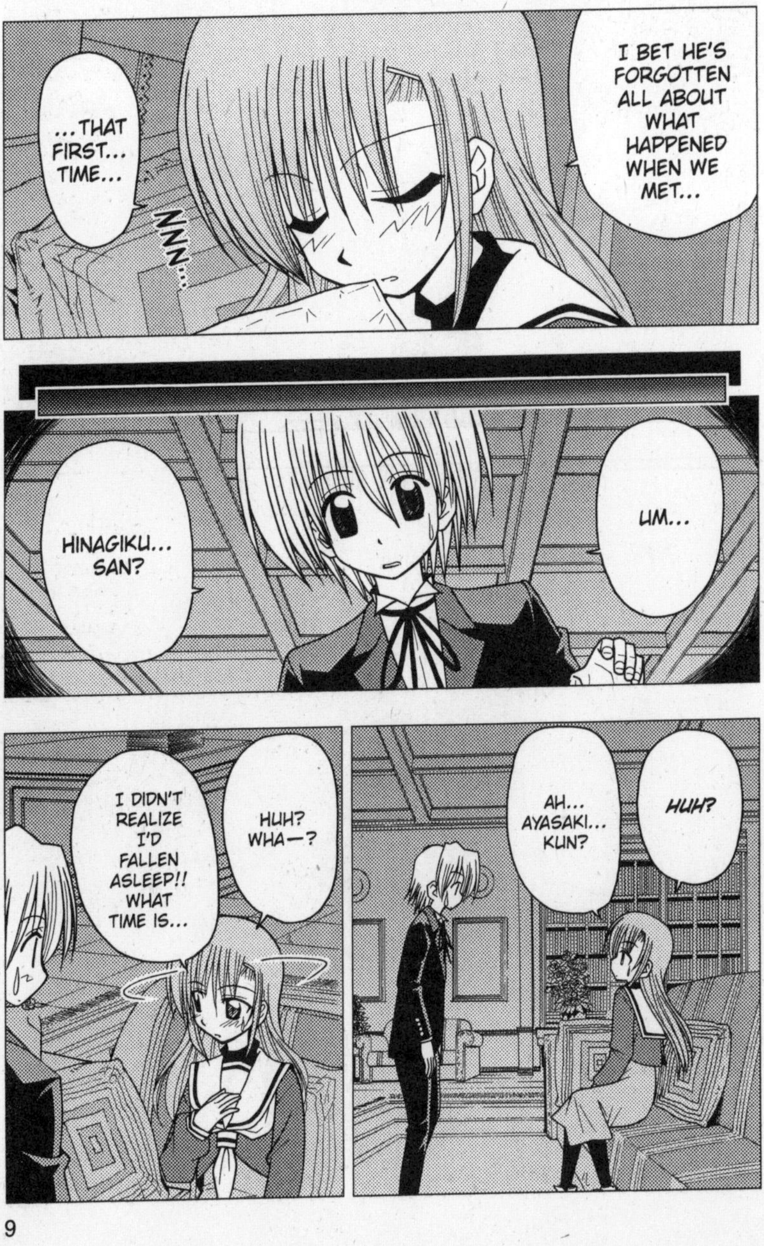
I BET HE'S FORGOTTEN ALL ABOUT WHAT HAPPENED WHEN WE MET...
...THAT FIRST... TIME...
NNN...
UM...
HINAGIKU... SAN?
HUH?
AH... AYASAKI... KUN?
HUH? WHA—?
I DIDN'T REALIZE I'D FALLEN ASLEEP!! WHAT TIME IS...

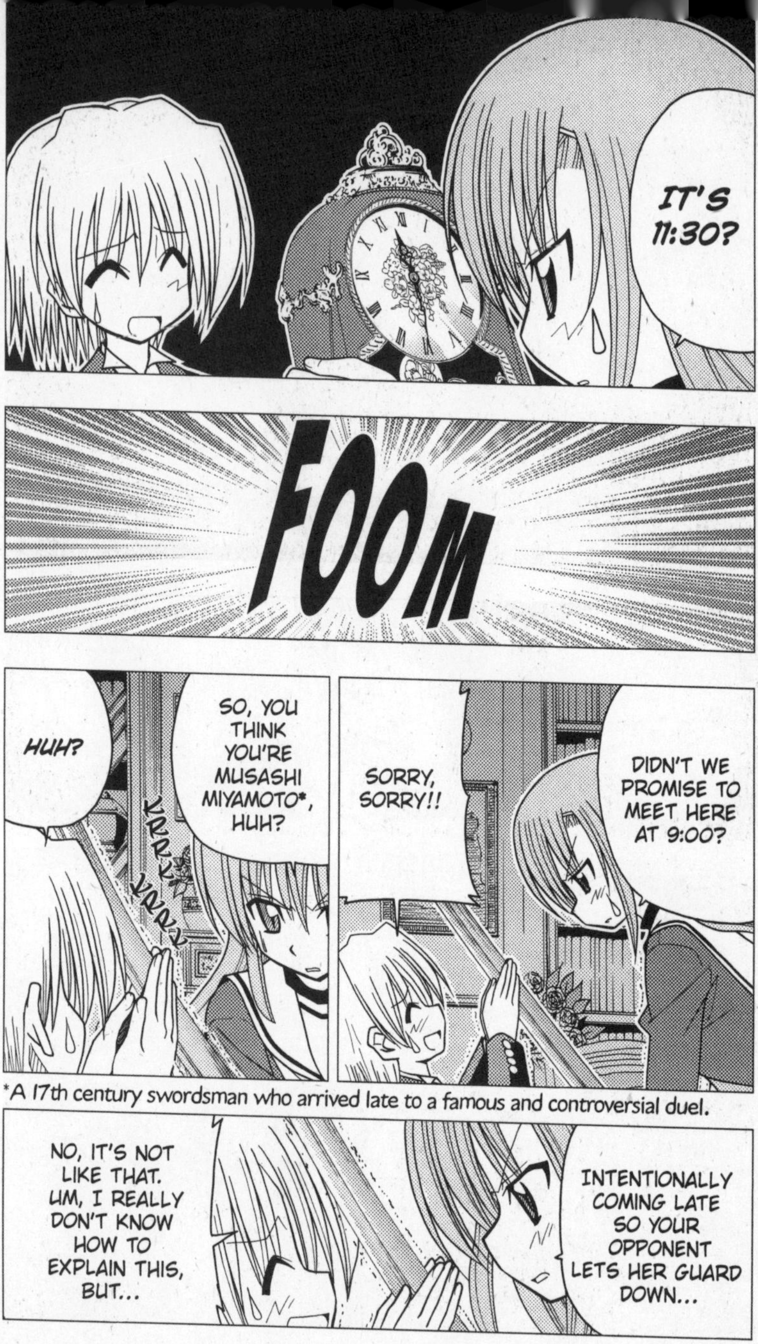
IT'S 11:30?
FOOM
DIDN'T WE PROMISE TO MEET HERE AT 9:00?
SORRY, SORRY!!
SO, YOU THINK YOU'RE MUSASHI MIYAMOTO*, HUH?
KRRR KRRR
HUH?
INTENTIONALLY COMING LATE SO YOUR OPPONENT LETS HER GUARD DOWN...
NO, IT'S NOT LIKE THAT. UM, I REALLY DON'T KNOW HOW TO EXPLAIN THIS, BUT...

*A 17th century swordsman who arrived late to a famous and controversial duel.

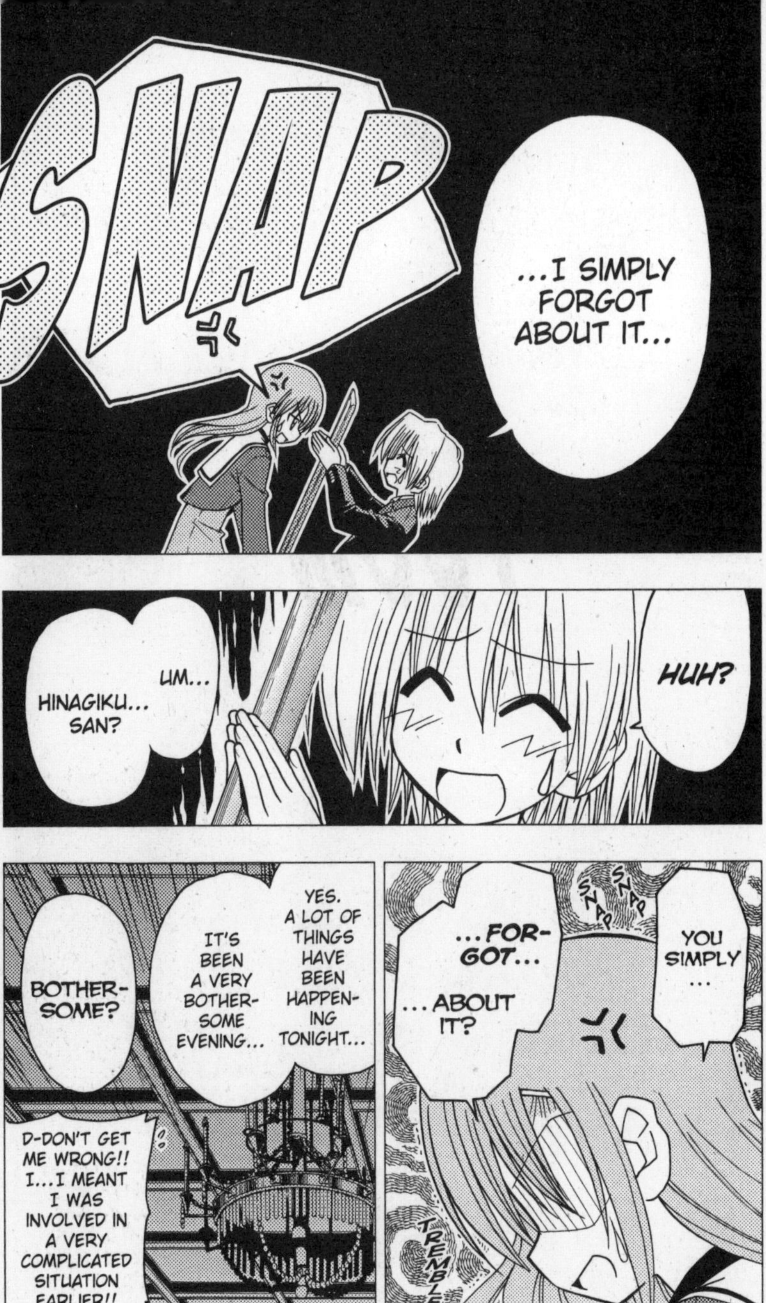
...I SIMPLY FORGOT ABOUT IT...
SNAP
HUH?
UM...
HINAGIKU... SAN?
YOU SIMPLY ...
SNAP SNAP
...FOR-GOT...
...ABOUT IT?
TREMBLE
YES. A LOT OF THINGS HAVE BEEN HAPPEN-ING TONIGHT...
IT'S BEEN A VERY BOTHER-SOME EVENING...
BOTHER-SOME?
D-DON'T GET ME WRONG!! I...I MEANT I WAS INVOLVED IN A VERY COMPLICATED SITUATION EARLIER!!

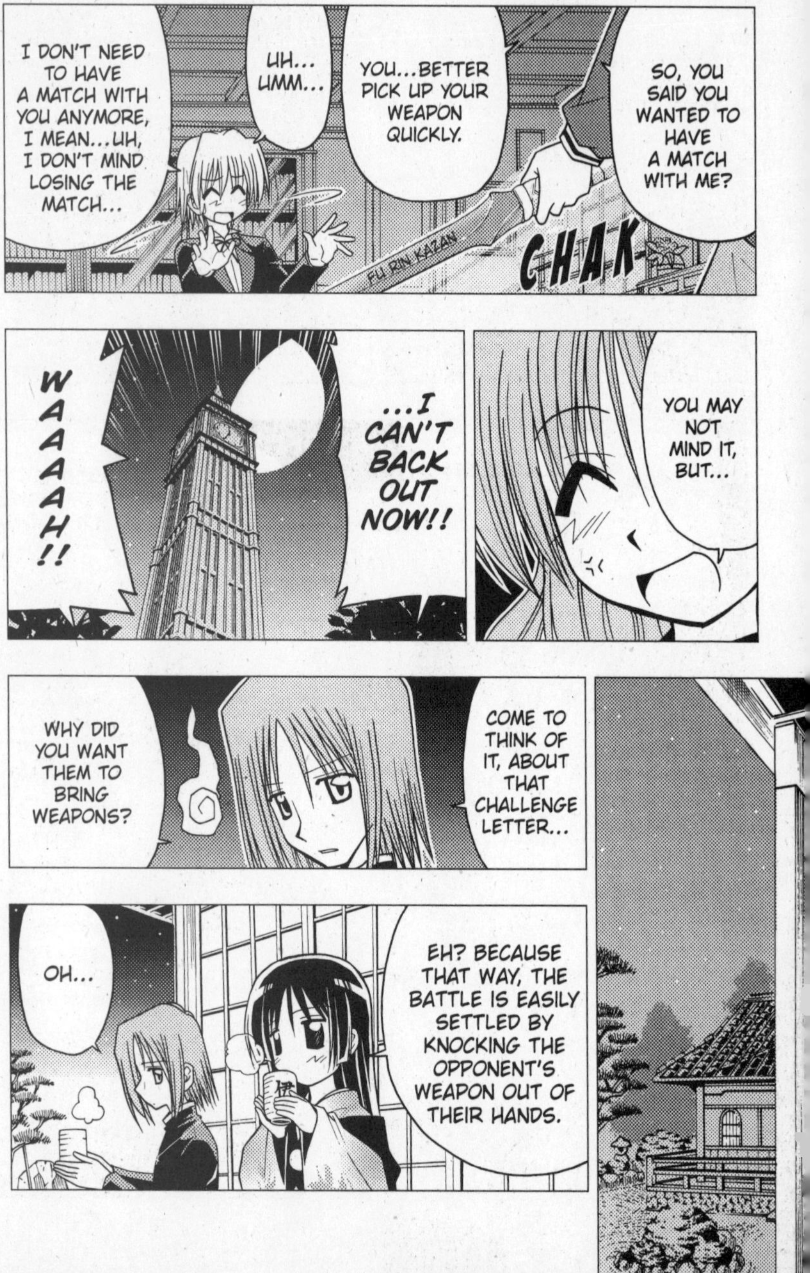
SO, YOU SAID YOU WANTED TO HAVE A MATCH WITH ME?
YOU...BETTER PICK UP YOUR WEAPON QUICKLY.
CHAK
FU RIN KAZAN
UH... UMM...
I DON'T NEED TO HAVE A MATCH WITH YOU ANYMORE, I MEAN...UH, I DON'T MIND LOSING THE MATCH...
YOU MAY NOT MIND IT, BUT...
...I CAN'T BACK OUT NOW!!
WAAAAAH!!
COME TO THINK OF IT, ABOUT THAT CHALLENGE LETTER...
WHY DID YOU WANT THEM TO BRING WEAPONS?
EH? BECAUSE THAT WAY, THE BATTLE IS EASILY SETTLED BY KNOCKING THE OPPONENT'S WEAPON OUT OF THEIR HANDS.
OH...

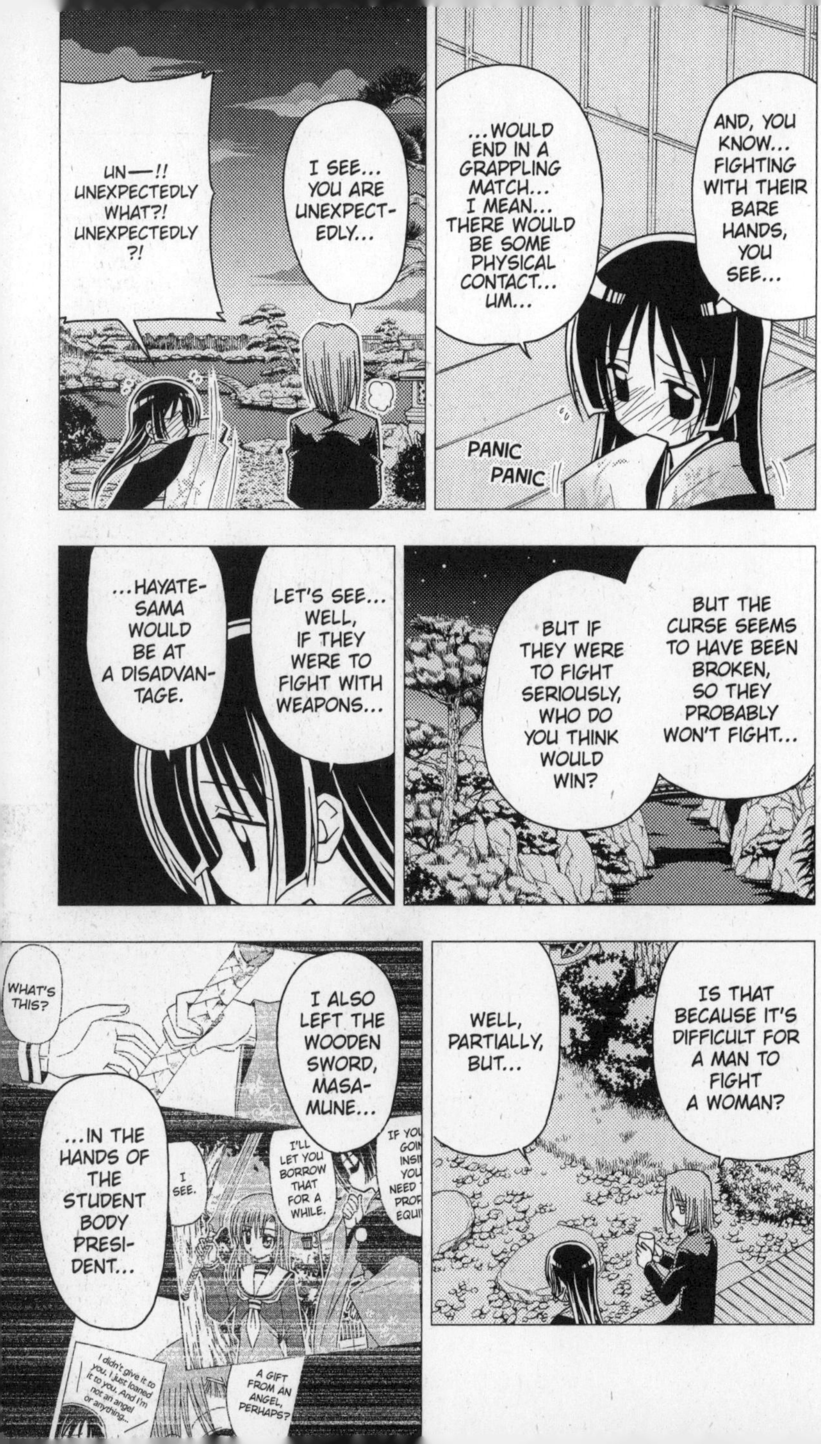
AND, YOU KNOW... FIGHTING WITH THEIR BARE HANDS, YOU SEE...
...WOULD END IN A GRAPPLING MATCH... I MEAN... THERE WOULD BE SOME PHYSICAL CONTACT... UM...
PANIC PANIC
I SEE... YOU ARE UNEXPECT-EDLY...
UN—!! UNEXPECTEDLY WHAT?! UNEXPECTEDLY ?!
BUT THE CURSE SEEMS TO HAVE BEEN BROKEN, SO THEY PROBABLY WON'T FIGHT...
BUT IF THEY WERE TO FIGHT SERIOUSLY, WHO DO YOU THINK WOULD WIN?
LET'S SEE... WELL, IF THEY WERE TO FIGHT WITH WEAPONS...
...HAYATE-SAMA WOULD BE AT A DISADVAN-TAGE.
IS THAT BECAUSE IT'S DIFFICULT FOR A MAN TO FIGHT A WOMAN?
WELL, PARTIALLY, BUT...
I ALSO LEFT THE WOODEN SWORD, MASA-MUNE...
WHAT'S THIS?
I'LL LET YOU BORROW THAT FOR A WHILE.
I SEE.
...IN THE HANDS OF THE STUDENT BODY PRESI-DENT...
A GIFT FROM AN ANGEL, PERHAPS?
I didn't give it to you, I just loaned it to you. And I'm not an angel or anything...

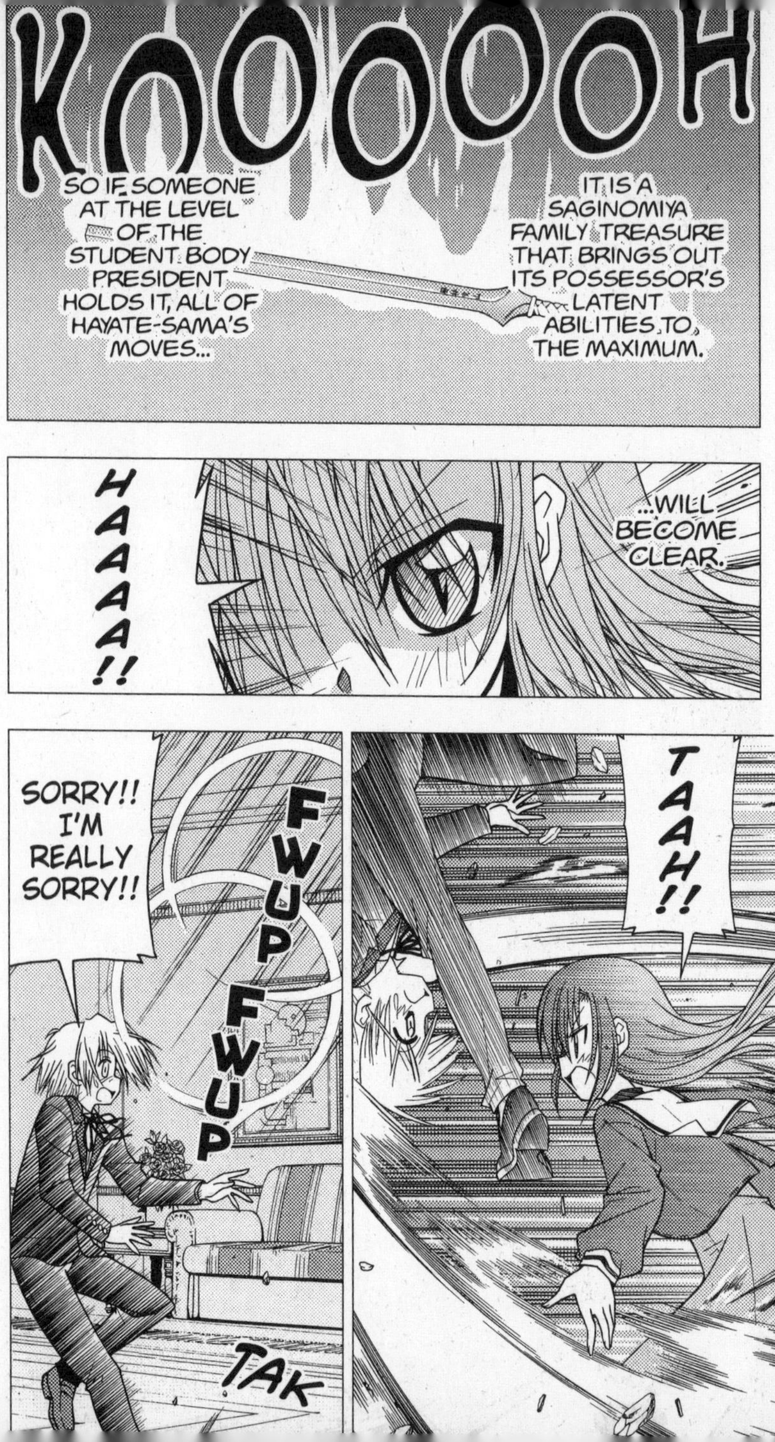
KOOOOOH
IT IS A SAGINOMIYA FAMILY TREASURE THAT BRINGS OUT ITS POSSESSOR'S LATENT ABILITIES TO THE MAXIMUM.
SO IF SOMEONE AT THE LEVEL OF THE STUDENT BODY PRESIDENT HOLDS IT, ALL OF HAYATE-SAMA'S MOVES...
...WILL BECOME CLEAR.
HAAAAA!!
TAAH!!
SORRY!! I'M REALLY SORRY!!
FWUP FWUP
TAK

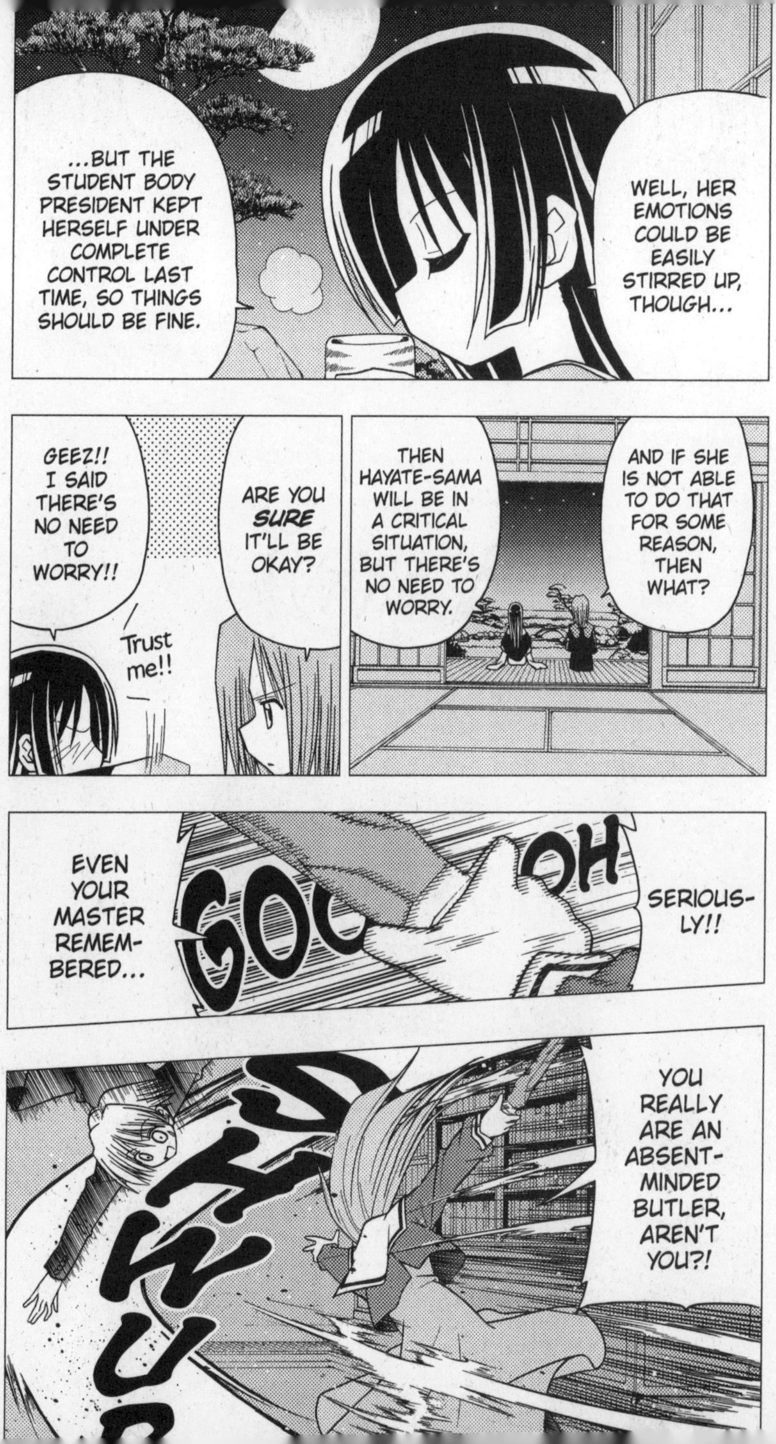
WELL, HER EMOTIONS COULD BE EASILY STIRRED UP, THOUGH...
...BUT THE STUDENT BODY PRESIDENT KEPT HERSELF UNDER COMPLETE CONTROL LAST TIME, SO THINGS SHOULD BE FINE.
AND IF SHE IS NOT ABLE TO DO THAT FOR SOME REASON, THEN WHAT?
THEN HAYATE-SAMA WILL BE IN A CRITICAL SITUATION, BUT THERE'S NO NEED TO WORRY.
ARE YOU *SURE* IT'LL BE OKAY?
GEEZ!! I SAID THERE'S NO NEED TO WORRY!!
Trust me!!
SERIOUS-LY!!
EVEN YOUR MASTER REMEM-BERED...
YOU REALLY ARE AN ABSENT-MINDED BUTLER, AREN'T YOU?!

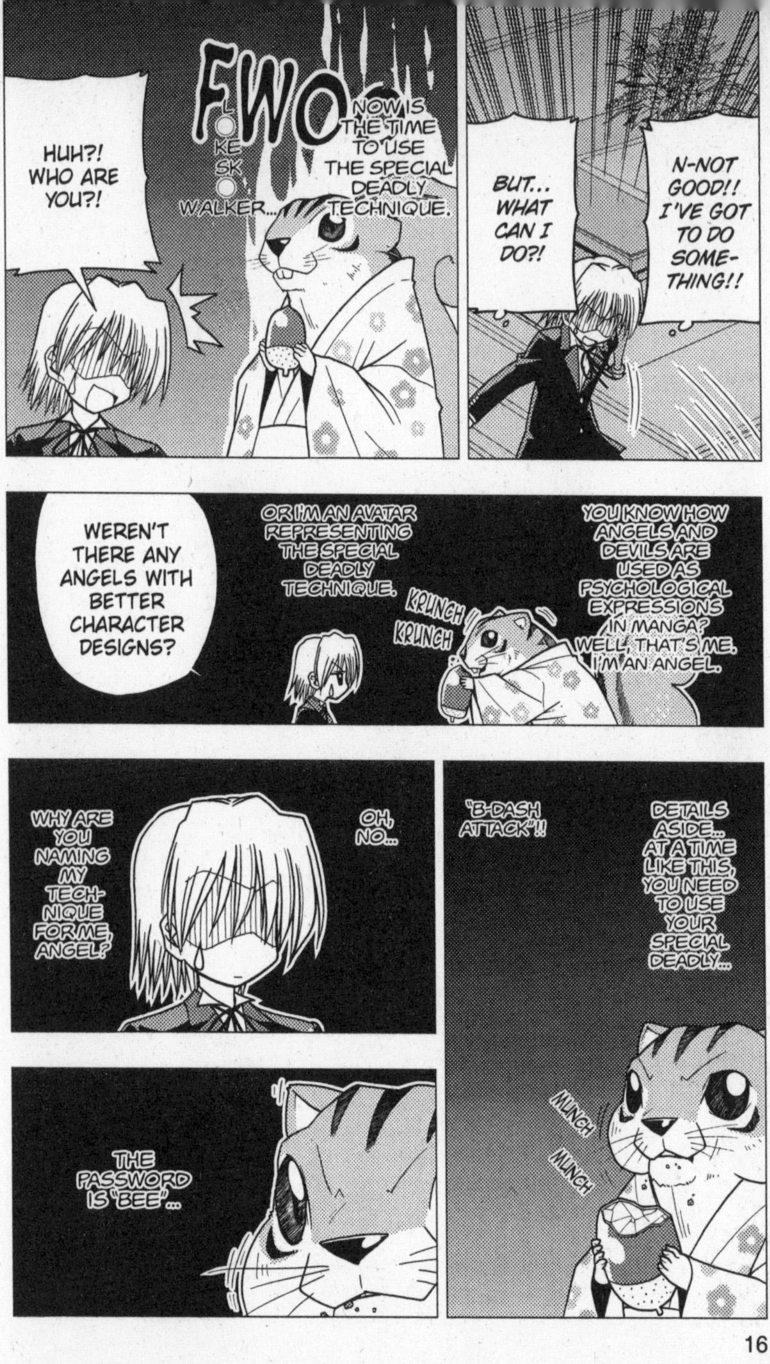
N-NOT GOOD!! I'VE GOT TO DO SOMETHING!!
BUT... WHAT CAN I DO?!
NOW IS THE TIME TO USE THE SPECIAL DEADLY TECHNIQUE.
FWO
L○KE SK○ WALKER...
HUH?! WHO ARE YOU?!
YOU KNOW HOW ANGELS AND DEVILS ARE USED AS PSYCHOLOGICAL EXPRESSIONS IN MANGA? WELL, THAT'S ME. I'M AN ANGEL.
KRUNCH KRUNCH
OR I'M AN AVATAR REPRESENTING THE SPECIAL DEADLY TECHNIQUE.
WEREN'T THERE ANY ANGELS WITH BETTER CHARACTER DESIGNS?
DETAILS ASIDE... AT A TIME LIKE THIS, YOU NEED TO USE YOUR SPECIAL DEADLY...
"B-DASH ATTACK"!!
MUNCH MUNCH
OH, NO...
WHY ARE YOU NAMING MY TECHNIQUE FOR ME, ANGEL?
THE PASSWORD IS "BEE"...

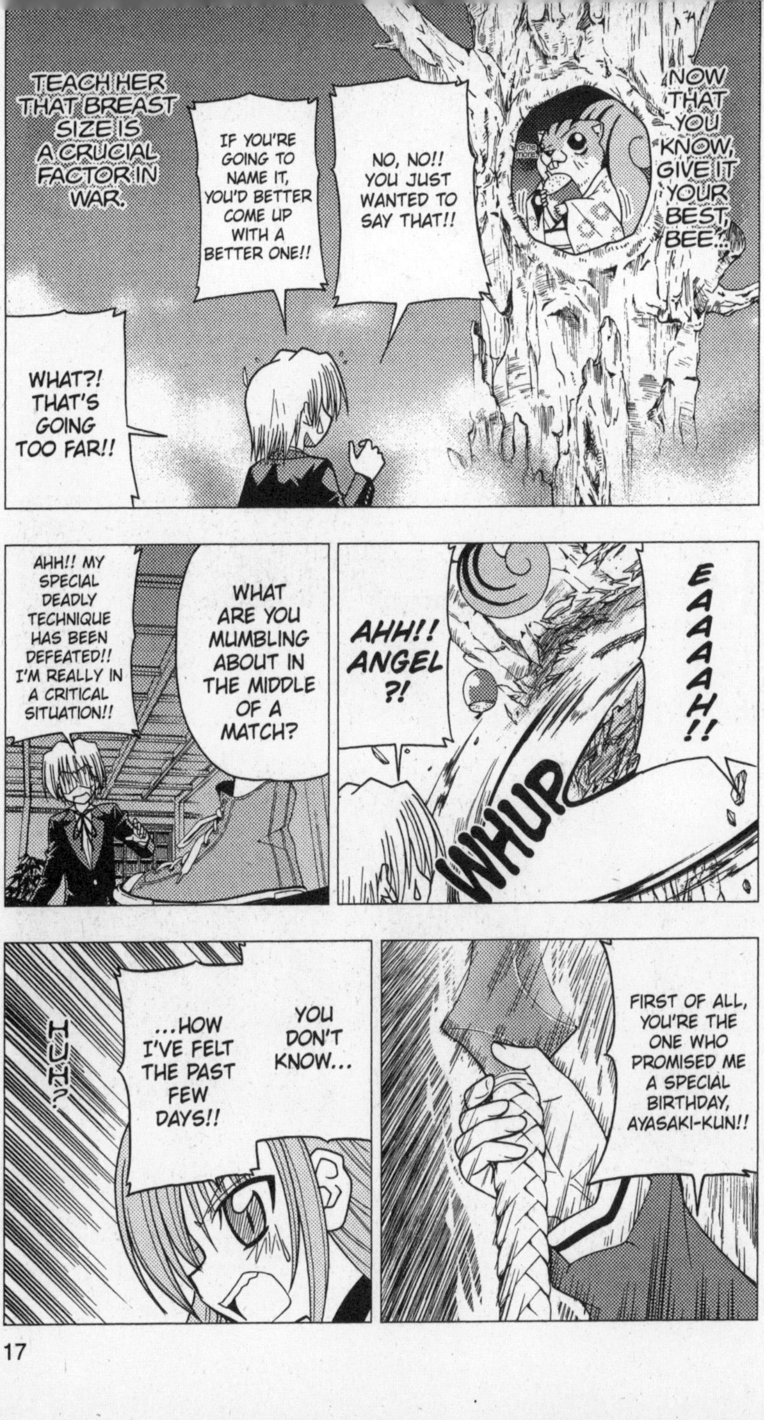
NOW THAT YOU KNOW, GIVE IT YOUR BEST, BEE...
One more.
NO, NO!! YOU JUST WANTED TO SAY THAT!!
IF YOU'RE GOING TO NAME IT, YOU'D BETTER COME UP WITH A BETTER ONE!!
TEACH HER THAT BREAST SIZE IS A CRUCIAL FACTOR IN WAR.
WHAT?! THAT'S GOING TOO FAR!!
EAAAAAH!!
AHH!! ANGEL ?!
WHUP
WHAT ARE YOU MUMBLING ABOUT IN THE MIDDLE OF A MATCH?
AHH!! MY SPECIAL DEADLY TECHNIQUE HAS BEEN DEFEATED!! I'M REALLY IN A CRITICAL SITUATION!!
FIRST OF ALL, YOU'RE THE ONE WHO PROMISED ME A SPECIAL BIRTHDAY, AYASAKI-KUN!!
YOU DON'T KNOW...
...HOW I'VE FELT THE PAST FEW DAYS!!
HUH?!

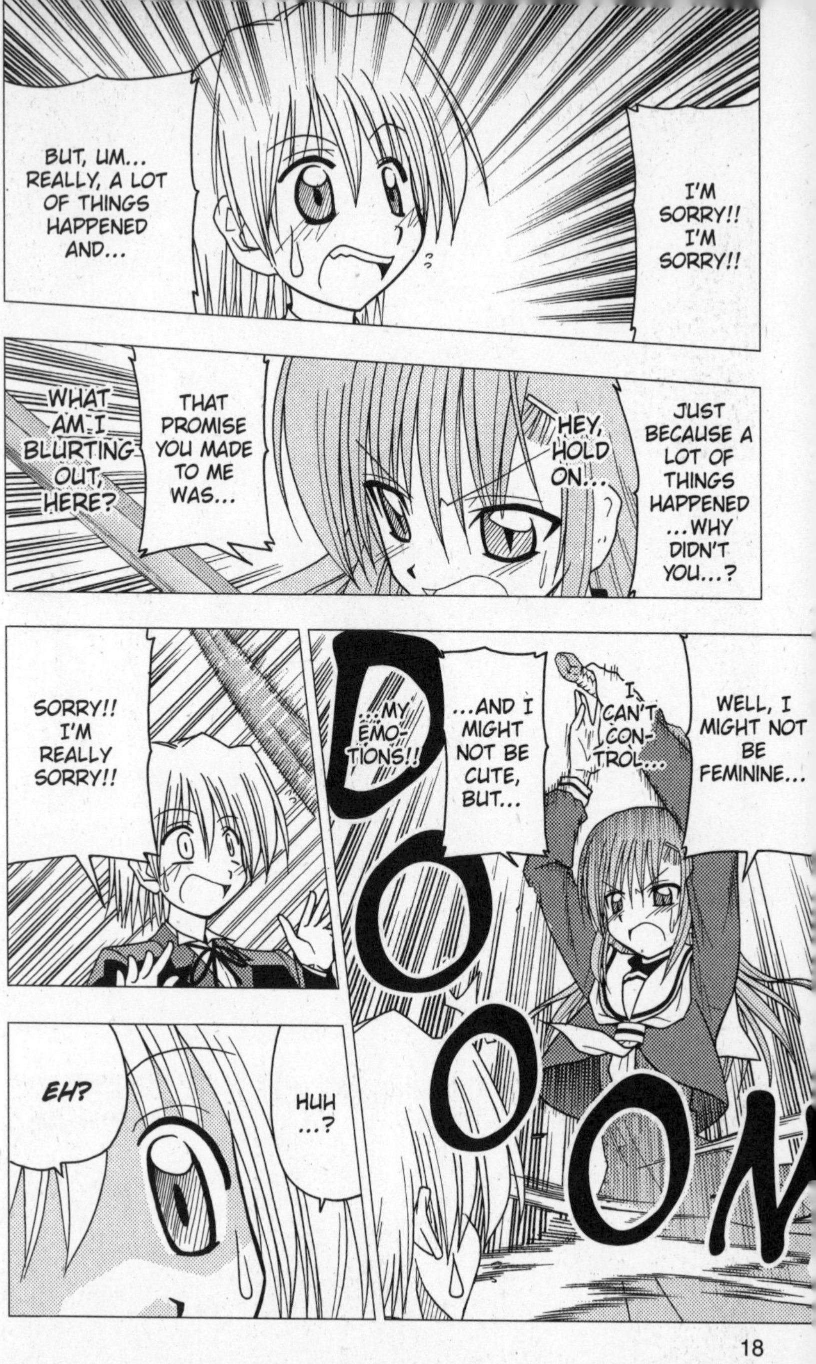
I'M SORRY!! I'M SORRY!!
BUT, UM... REALLY, A LOT OF THINGS HAPPENED AND...
JUST BECAUSE A LOT OF THINGS HAPPENED ...WHY DIDN'T YOU...?
HEY, HOLD ON...
THAT PROMISE YOU MADE TO ME WAS...
WHAT AM I BLURTING OUT, HERE?
WELL, I MIGHT NOT BE FEMININE...
I CAN'T CON-TROL...
...AND I MIGHT NOT BE CUTE, BUT...
...MY EMO-TIONS!!
DOOOOOM
SORRY!! I'M REALLY SORRY!!
HUH ...?
EH?

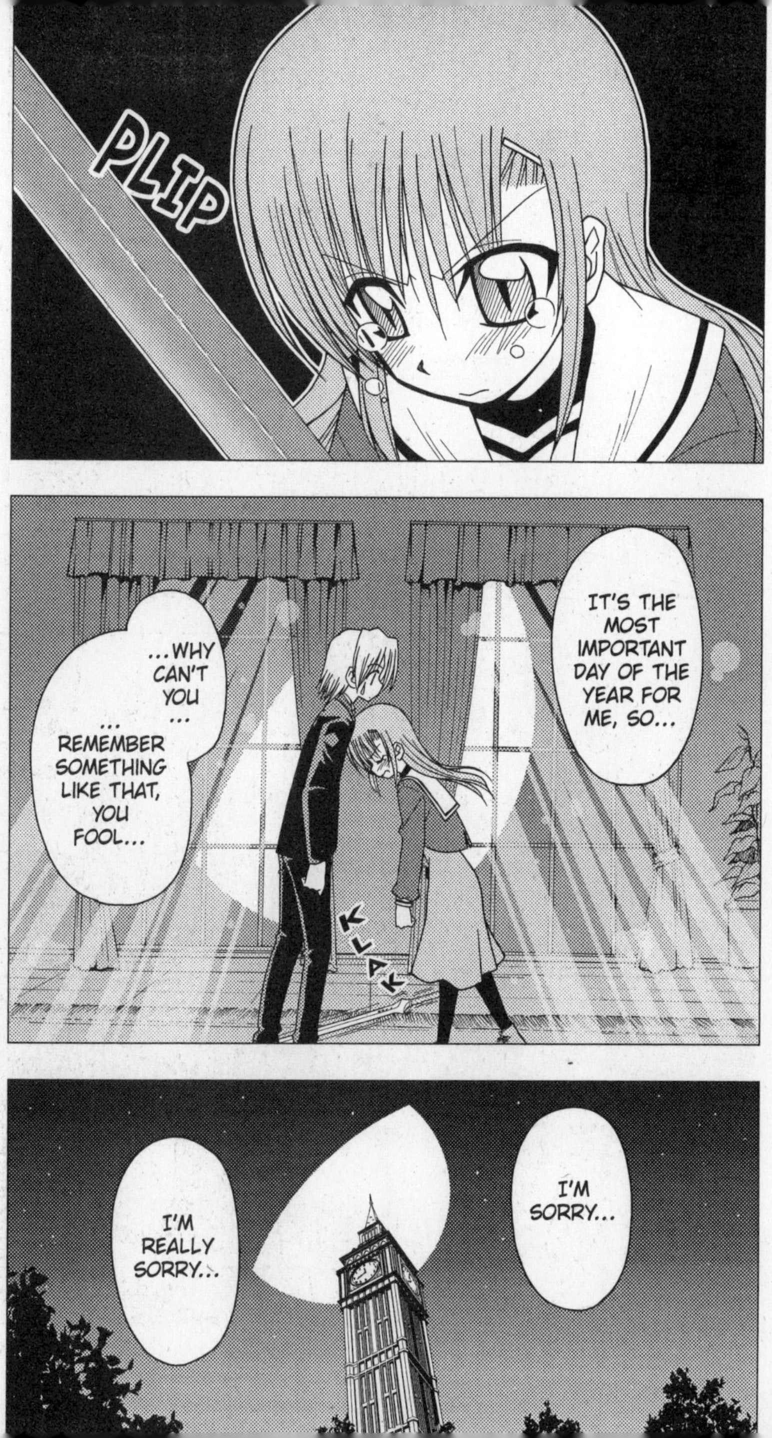
PLIP
IT'S THE MOST IMPORTANT DAY OF THE YEAR FOR ME, SO...
...WHY CAN'T YOU ... ... REMEMBER SOMETHING LIKE THAT, YOU FOOL...
KLAK
I'M SORRY...
I'M REALLY SORRY...

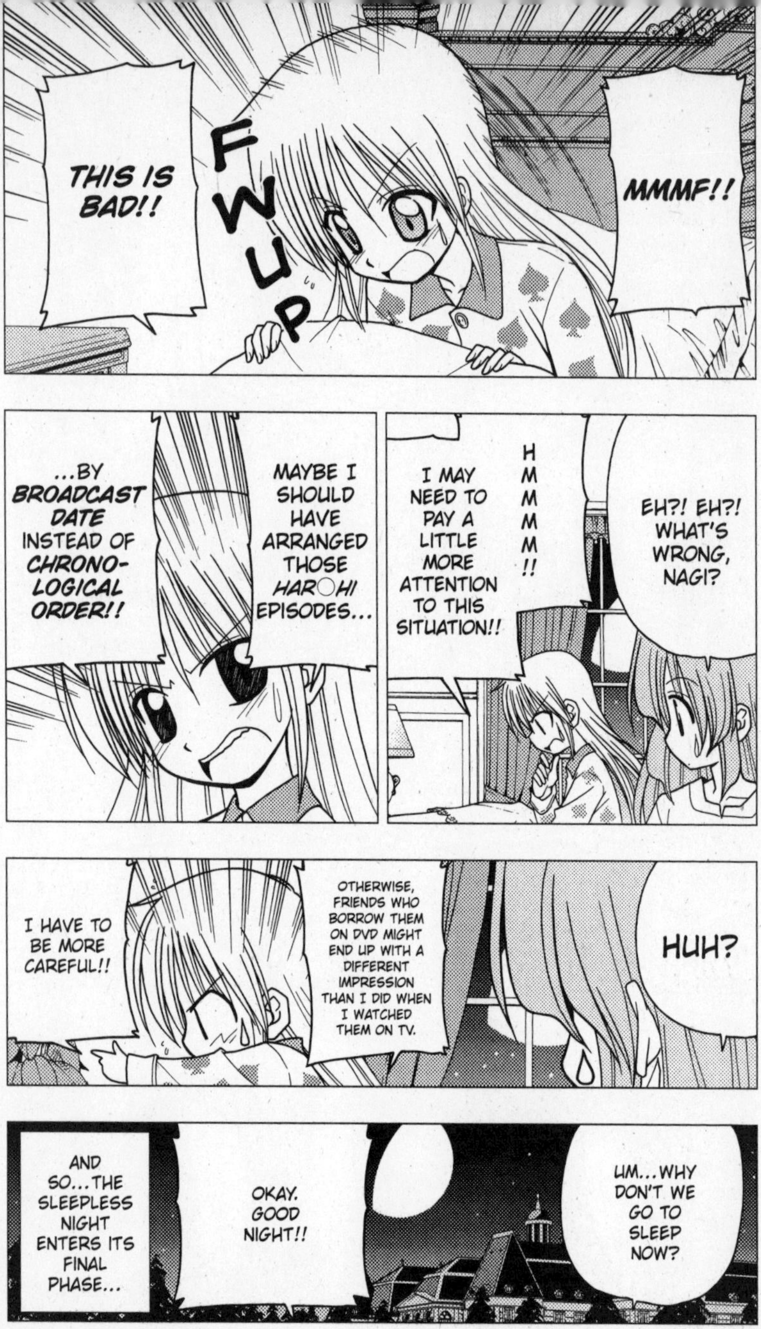
MMMF!!
FWUP
THIS IS BAD!!
EH?! EH?! WHAT'S WRONG, NAGI?
HMMMMM!!
I MAY NEED TO PAY A LITTLE MORE ATTENTION TO THIS SITUATION!!
MAYBE I SHOULD HAVE ARRANGED THOSE HAR○HI EPISODES...
...BY BROADCAST DATE INSTEAD OF CHRONOLOGICAL ORDER!!
HUH?
OTHERWISE, FRIENDS WHO BORROW THEM ON DVD MIGHT END UP WITH A DIFFERENT IMPRESSION THAN I DID WHEN I WATCHED THEM ON TV.
I HAVE TO BE MORE CAREFUL!!
UM...WHY DON'T WE GO TO SLEEP NOW?
OKAY. GOOD NIGHT!!
AND SO...THE SLEEPLESS NIGHT ENTERS ITS FINAL PHASE...

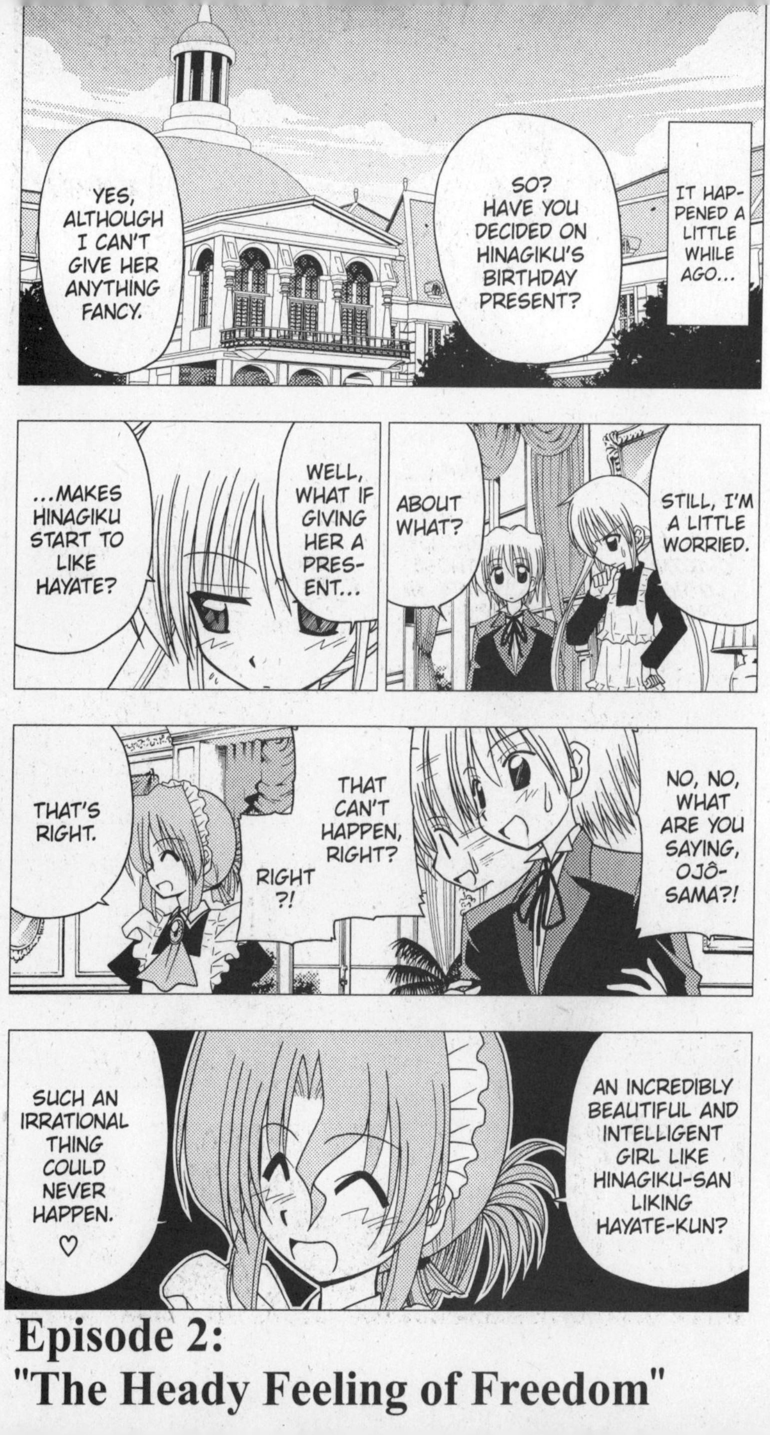
IT HAPPENED A LITTLE WHILE AGO...
SO? HAVE YOU DECIDED ON HINAGIKU'S BIRTHDAY PRESENT?
YES, ALTHOUGH I CAN'T GIVE HER ANYTHING FANCY.
STILL, I'M A LITTLE WORRIED.
ABOUT WHAT?
WELL, WHAT IF GIVING HER A PRESENT...
...MAKES HINAGIKU START TO LIKE HAYATE?
NO, NO, WHAT ARE YOU SAYING, OJÔ-SAMA?!
THAT CAN'T HAPPEN, RIGHT?
RIGHT ?!
THAT'S RIGHT.
AN INCREDIBLY BEAUTIFUL AND INTELLIGENT GIRL LIKE HINAGIKU-SAN LIKING HAYATE-KUN?
SUCH AN IRRATIONAL THING COULD NEVER HAPPEN. ♡

Episode 2: "The Heady Feeling of Freedom"

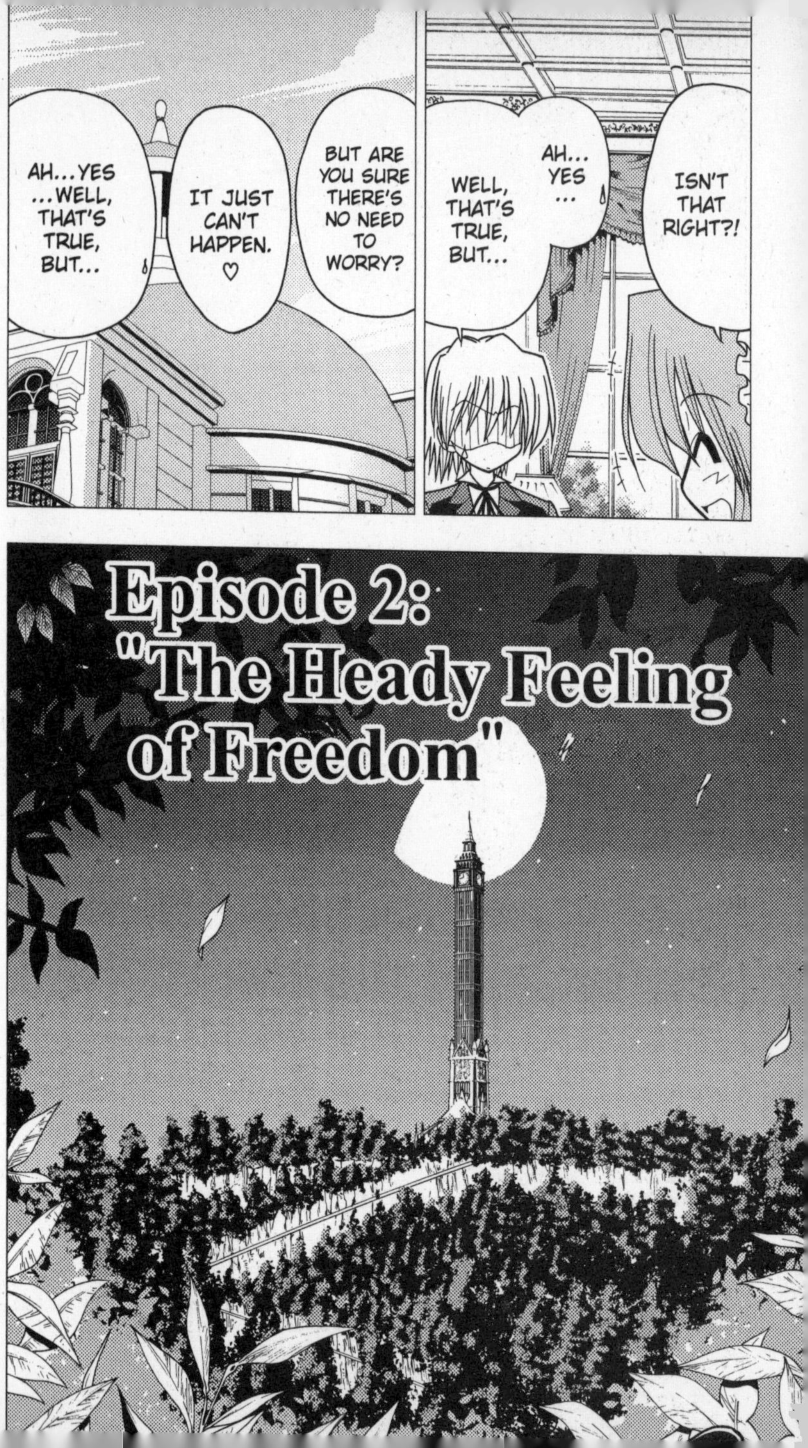
ISN'T THAT RIGHT?!
AH... YES ...
WELL, THAT'S TRUE, BUT...
BUT ARE YOU SURE THERE'S NO NEED TO WORRY?
IT JUST CAN'T HAPPEN. ♡
AH...YES ...WELL, THAT'S TRUE, BUT...
Episode 2: "The Heady Feeling of Freedom"

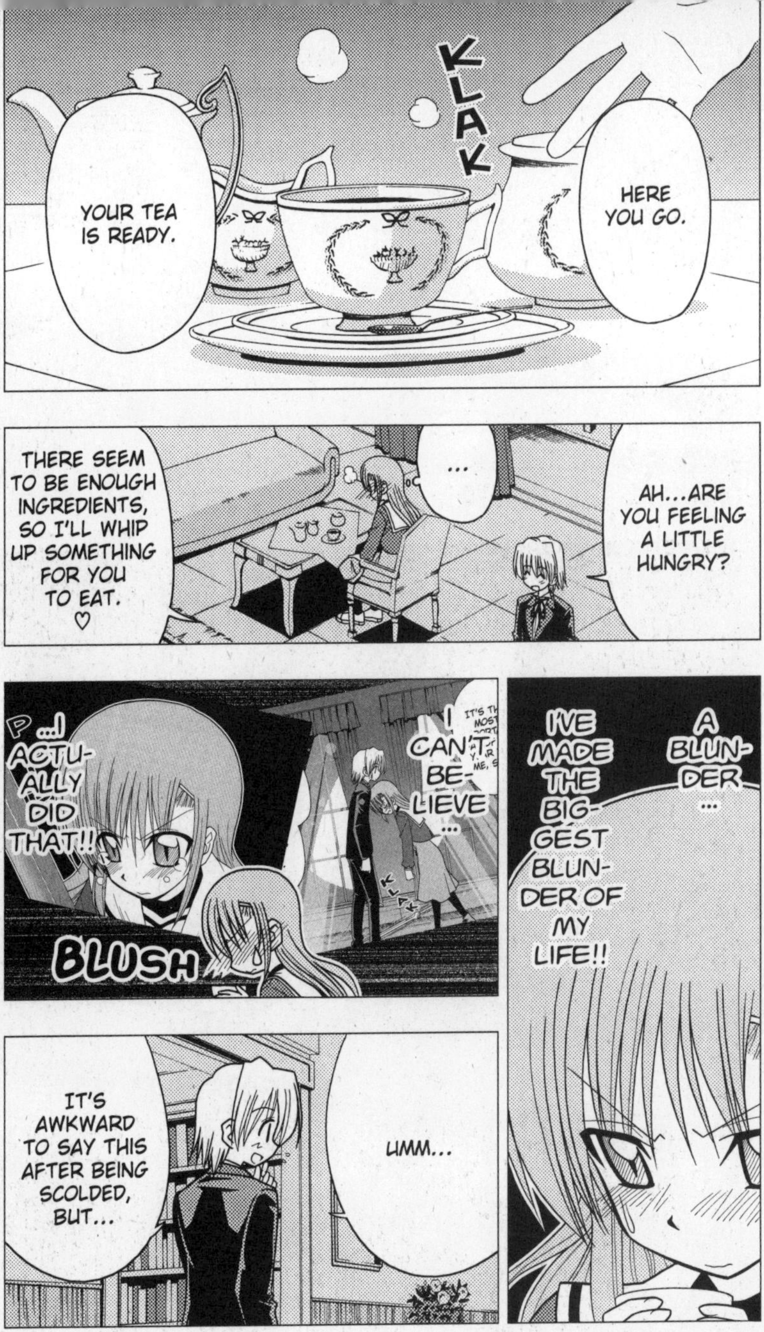
HERE YOU GO.
KLAK
YOUR TEA IS READY.
AH...ARE YOU FEELING A LITTLE HUNGRY?
...
THERE SEEM TO BE ENOUGH INGREDIENTS, SO I'LL WHIP UP SOMETHING FOR YOU TO EAT. ♡
A BLUNDER...
I'VE MADE THE BIGGEST BLUNDER OF MY LIFE!!
I CAN'T BELIEVE...
KLAK
P...I ACTUALLY DID THAT!!
BLUSH
UMM...
IT'S AWKWARD TO SAY THIS AFTER BEING SCOLDED, BUT...

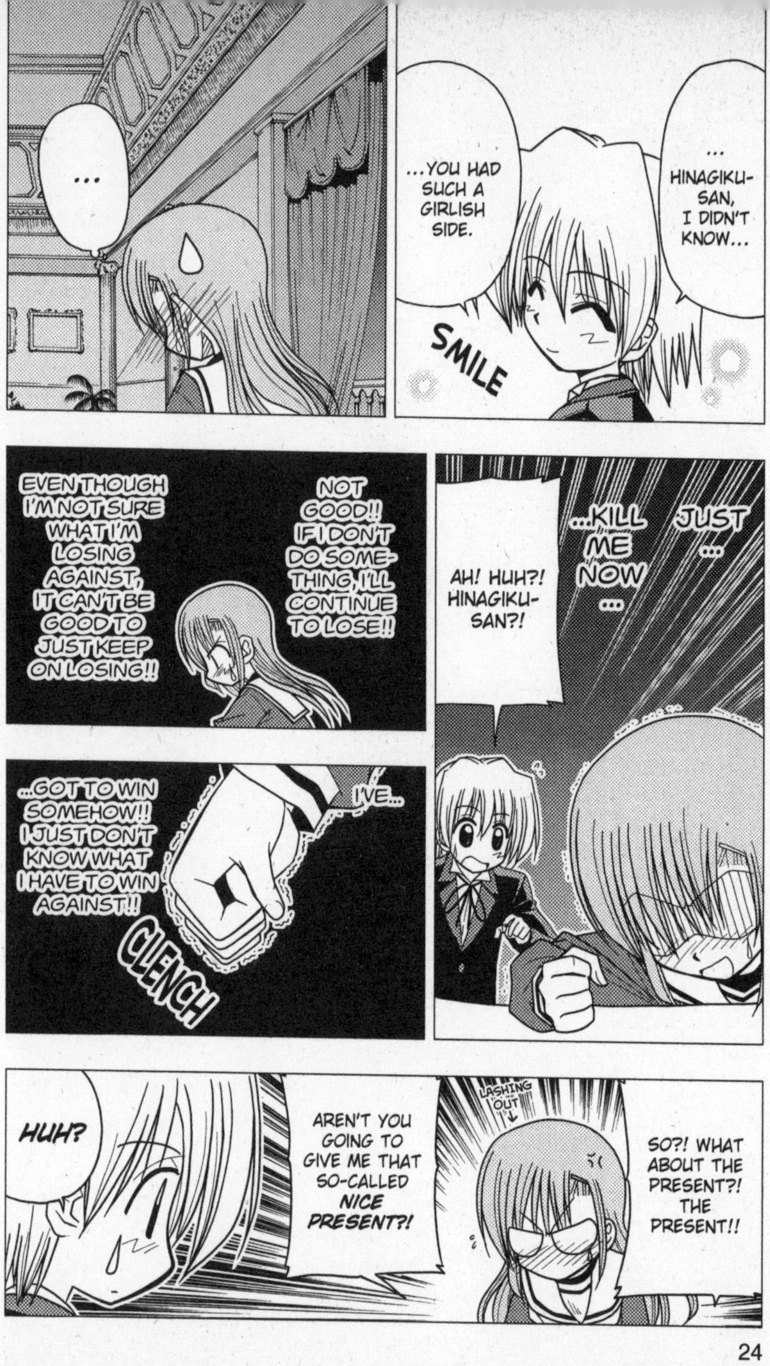
... HINAGIKU-SAN, I DIDN'T KNOW...
...YOU HAD SUCH A GIRLISH SIDE.
SMILE
...
JUST...
...KILL ME NOW...
AH! HUH?! HINAGIKU-SAN?!
NOT GOOD!! IF I DON'T DO SOMETHING, I'LL CONTINUE TO LOSE!!
EVEN THOUGH I'M NOT SURE WHAT I'M LOSING AGAINST, IT CAN'T BE GOOD TO JUST KEEP ON LOSING!!
I'VE...
...GOT TO WIN SOMEHOW!! I JUST DON'T KNOW WHAT I HAVE TO WIN AGAINST!!
CLENCH
LASHING OUT
SO?! WHAT ABOUT THE PRESENT?! THE PRESENT!!
AREN'T YOU GOING TO GIVE ME THAT SO-CALLED ***NICE PRESENT?!***
HUH?

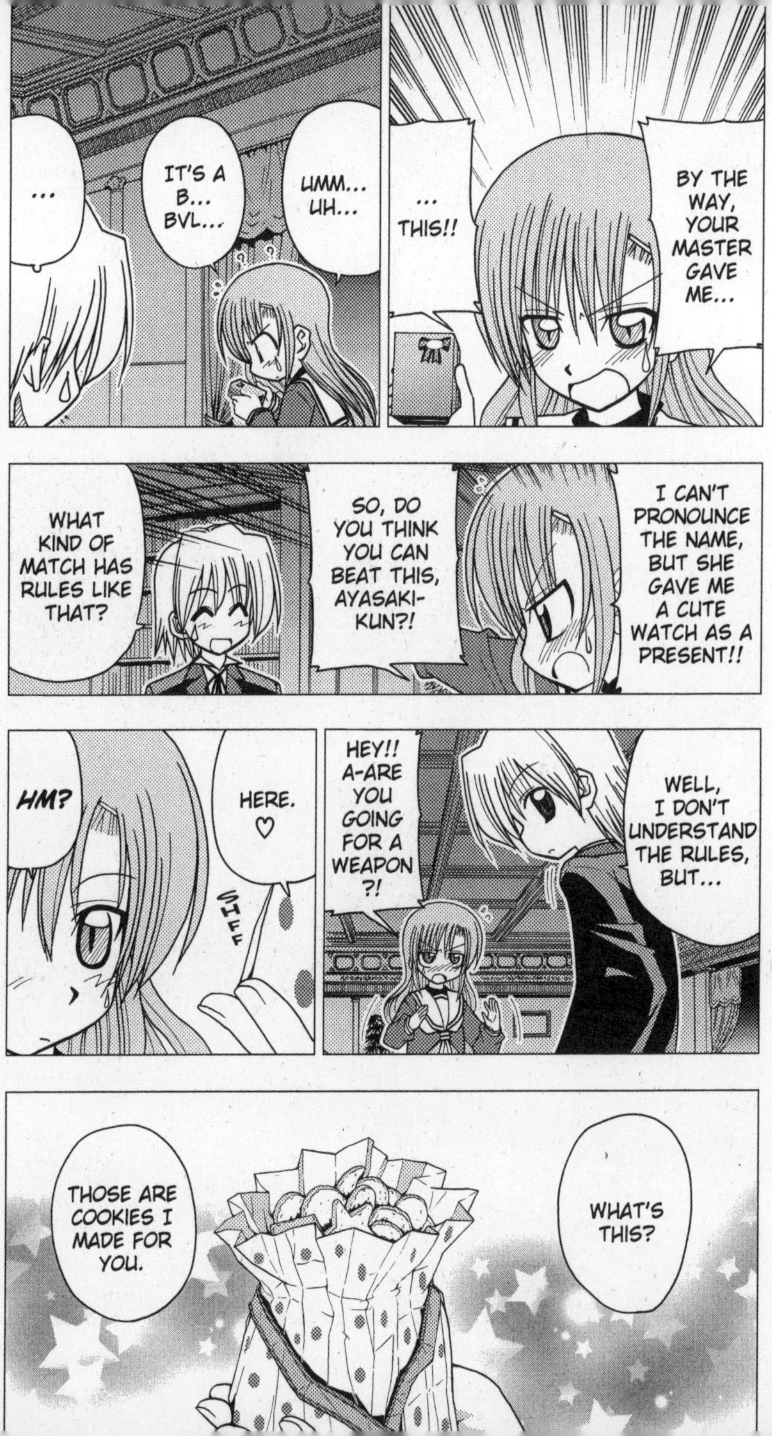
BY THE WAY, YOUR MASTER GAVE ME...
... THIS!!
UMM... UH...
IT'S A B... BVL...
...
I CAN'T PRONOUNCE THE NAME, BUT SHE GAVE ME A CUTE WATCH AS A PRESENT!!
SO, DO YOU THINK YOU CAN BEAT THIS, AYASAKI-KUN?!
WHAT KIND OF MATCH HAS RULES LIKE THAT?
WELL, I DON'T UNDERSTAND THE RULES, BUT...
HEY!! A-ARE YOU GOING FOR A WEAPON ?!
HERE. ♡
SHFF
HM?
WHAT'S THIS?
THOSE ARE COOKIES I MADE FOR YOU.

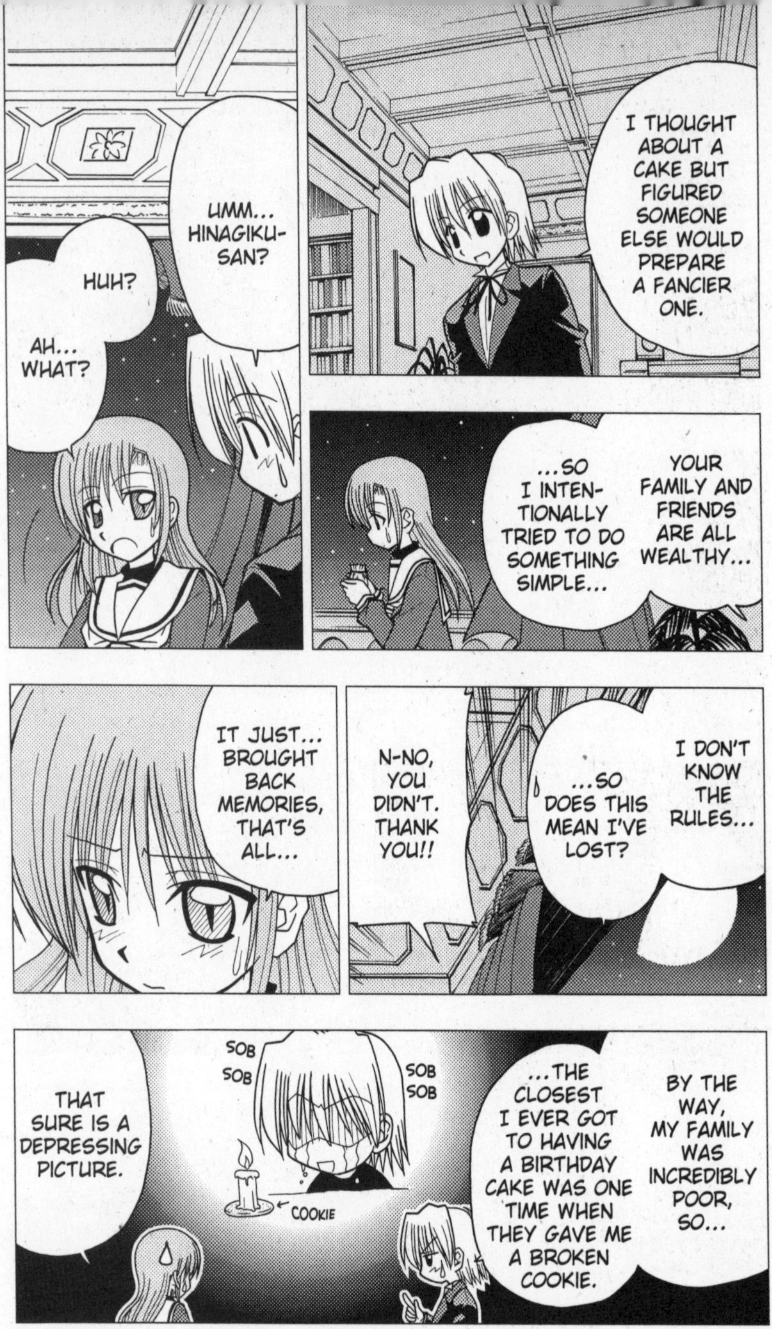
I THOUGHT ABOUT A CAKE BUT FIGURED SOMEONE ELSE WOULD PREPARE A FANCIER ONE.
YOUR FAMILY AND FRIENDS ARE ALL WEALTHY...
...SO I INTEN-TIONALLY TRIED TO DO SOMETHING SIMPLE...
UMM... HINAGIKU-SAN?
HUH?
AH... WHAT?
I DON'T KNOW THE RULES...
...SO DOES THIS MEAN I'VE LOST?
N-NO, YOU DIDN'T. THANK YOU!!
IT JUST... BROUGHT BACK MEMORIES, THAT'S ALL...
BY THE WAY, MY FAMILY WAS INCREDIBLY POOR, SO...
...THE CLOSEST I EVER GOT TO HAVING A BIRTHDAY CAKE WAS ONE TIME WHEN THEY GAVE ME A BROKEN COOKIE.
SOB SOB
COOKIE
SOB SOB
THAT SURE IS A DEPRESSING PICTURE.

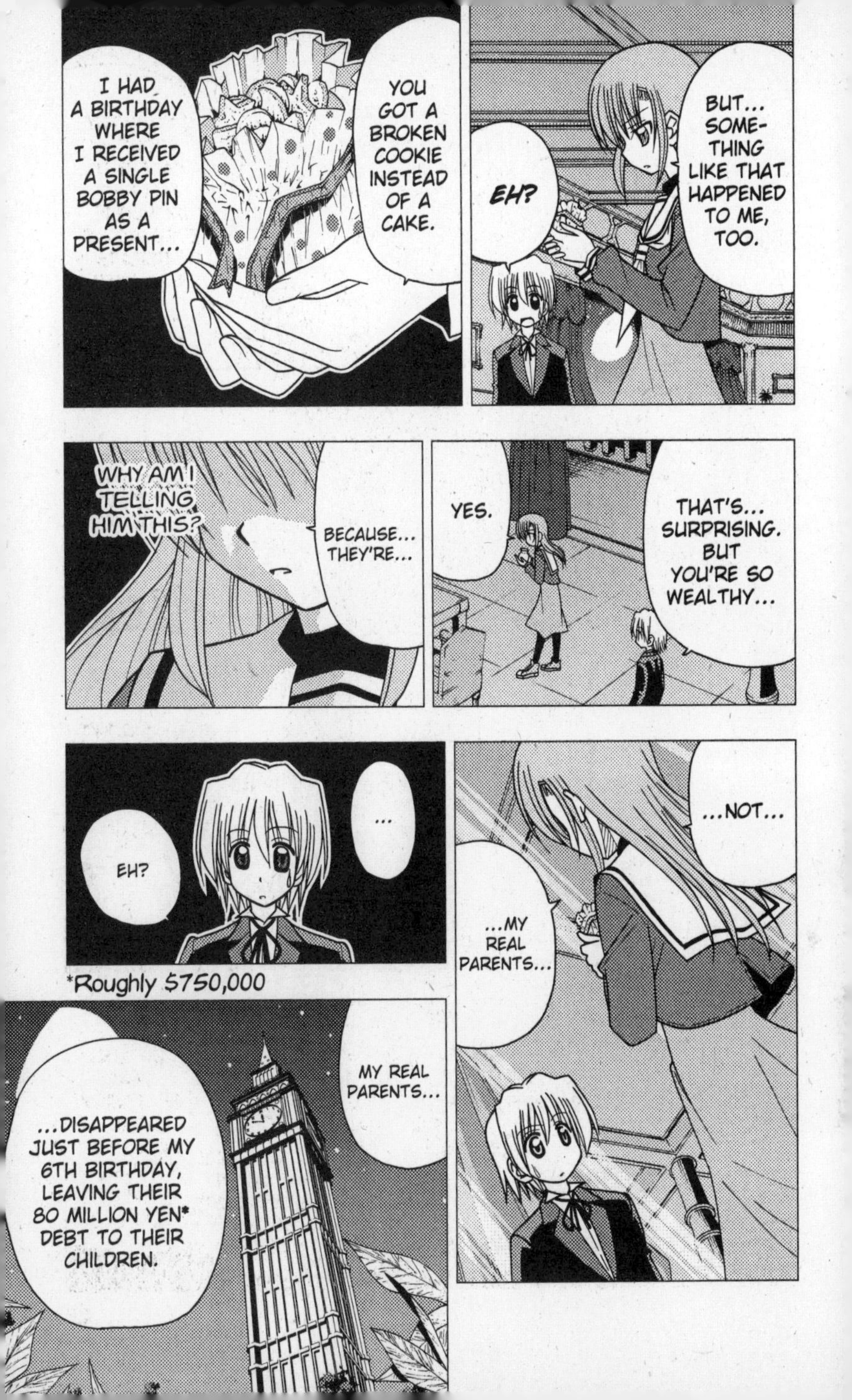
BUT... SOME-THING LIKE THAT HAPPENED TO ME, TOO.
EH?
YOU GOT A BROKEN COOKIE INSTEAD OF A CAKE.
I HAD A BIRTHDAY WHERE I RECEIVED A SINGLE BOBBY PIN AS A PRESENT...
THAT'S... SURPRISING. BUT YOU'RE SO WEALTHY...
YES.
BECAUSE... THEY'RE...
WHY AM I TELLING HIM THIS?
...NOT...
...MY REAL PARENTS...
...
EH?
*Roughly $750,000
MY REAL PARENTS...
...DISAPPEARED JUST BEFORE MY 6TH BIRTHDAY, LEAVING THEIR 80 MILLION YEN* DEBT TO THEIR CHILDREN.

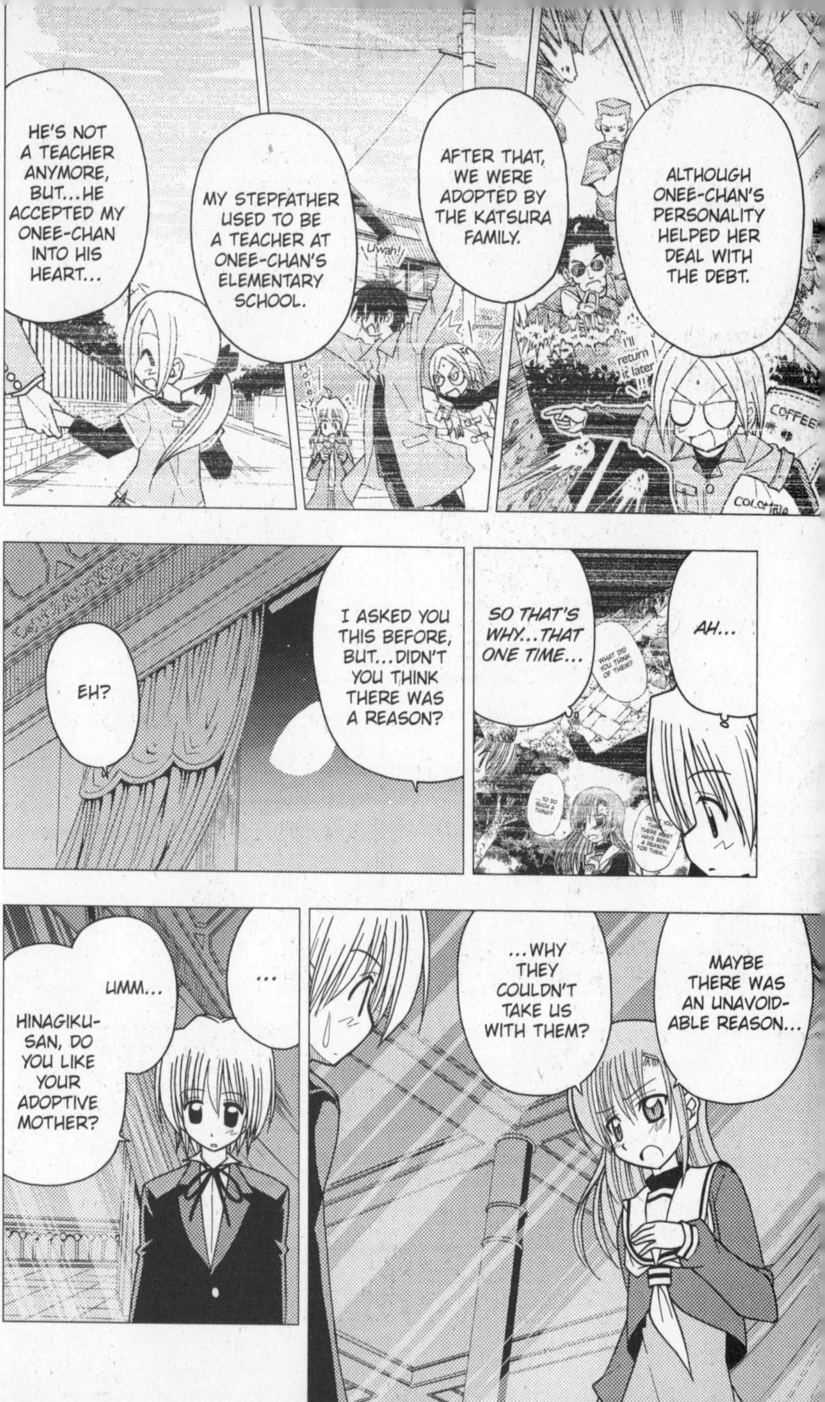
ALTHOUGH ONEE-CHAN'S PERSONALITY HELPED HER DEAL WITH THE DEBT.
I'll return it later!!
COFFEE
AFTER THAT, WE WERE ADOPTED BY THE KATSURA FAMILY.
You promised
Uwah!!
Honey
MY STEPFATHER USED TO BE A TEACHER AT ONEE-CHAN'S ELEMENTARY SCHOOL.
HE'S NOT A TEACHER ANYMORE, BUT...HE ACCEPTED MY ONEE-CHAN INTO HIS HEART...
AH...
SO THAT'S WHY...THAT ONE TIME...
WHAT DID YOU THINK OF THEM?
THERE MUST HAVE BEEN A REASON FOR THEM...
...TO DO SUCH A THING?
I ASKED YOU THIS BEFORE, BUT...DIDN'T YOU THINK THERE WAS A REASON?
EH?
MAYBE THERE WAS AN UNAVOID-ABLE REASON...
...WHY THEY COULDN'T TAKE US WITH THEM?
...
UMM...
HINAGIKU-SAN, DO YOU LIKE YOUR ADOPTIVE MOTHER?

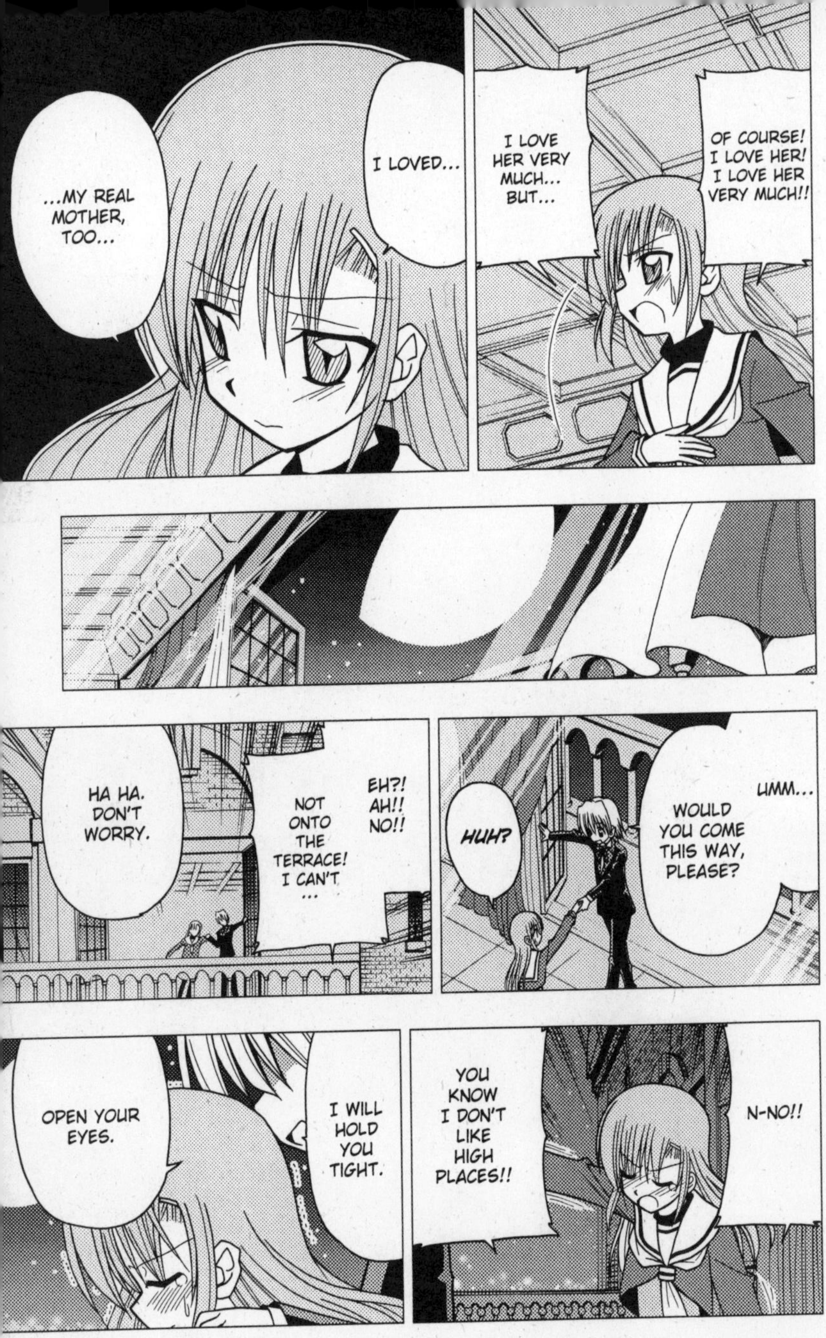
OF COURSE! I LOVE HER! I LOVE HER VERY MUCH!!
I LOVE HER VERY MUCH... BUT...
I LOVED...
...MY REAL MOTHER, TOO...
UMM...
WOULD YOU COME THIS WAY, PLEASE?
HUH?
EH?! AH!! NO!!
NOT ONTO THE TERRACE! I CAN'T ...
HA HA. DON'T WORRY.
N-NO!!
YOU KNOW I DON'T LIKE HIGH PLACES!!
I WILL HOLD YOU TIGHT.
OPEN YOUR EYES.

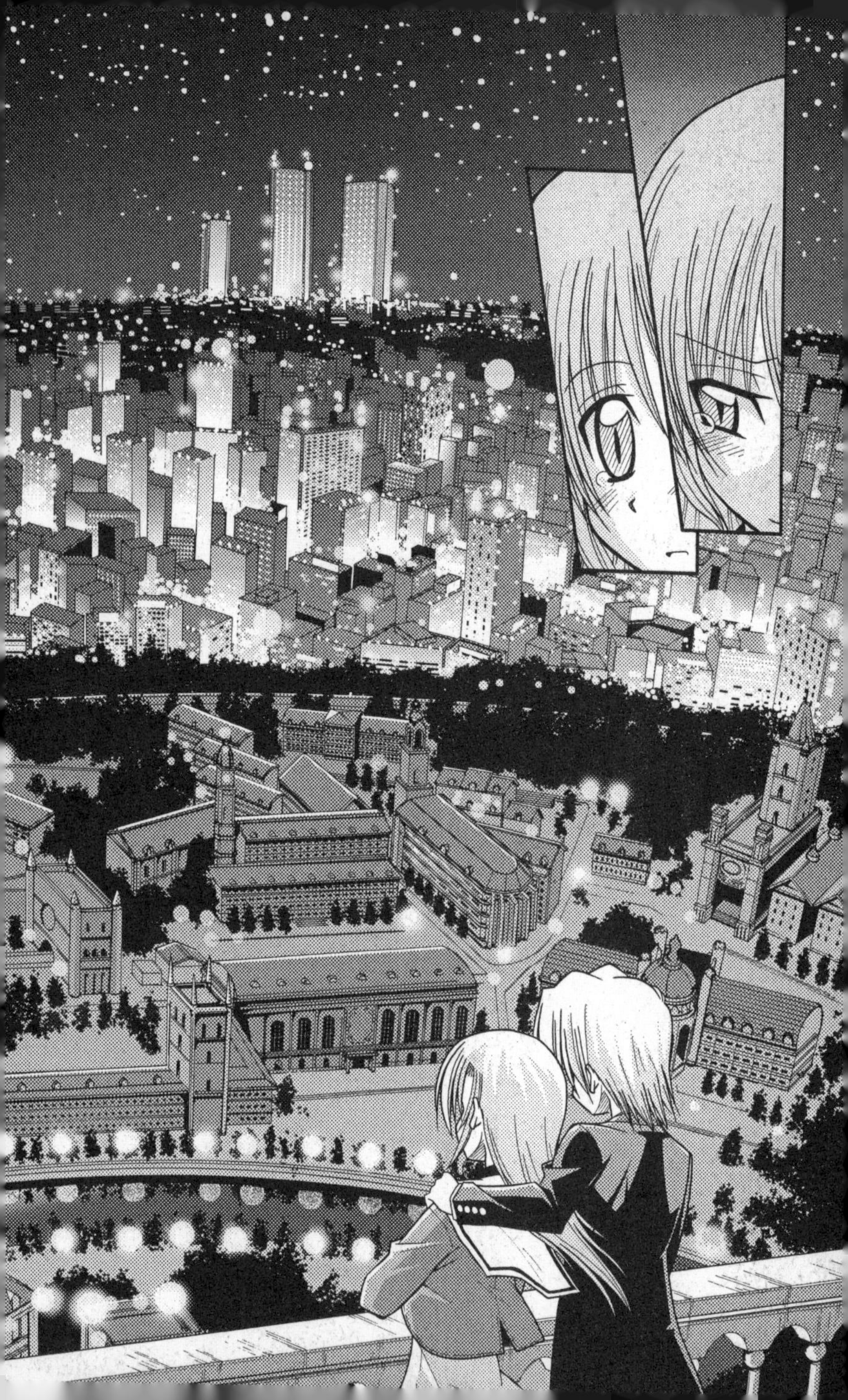

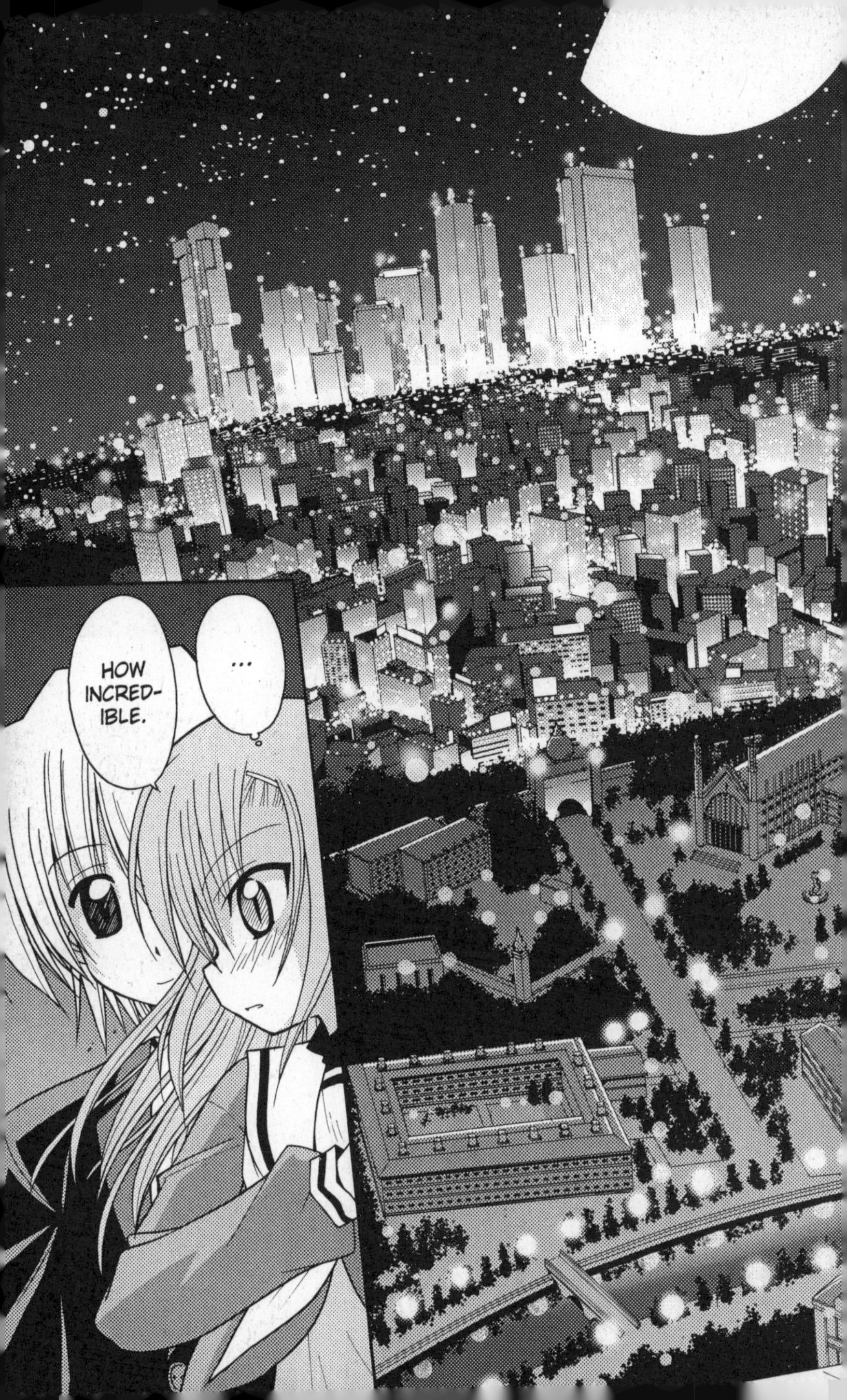
...
HOW INCRED-IBLE.

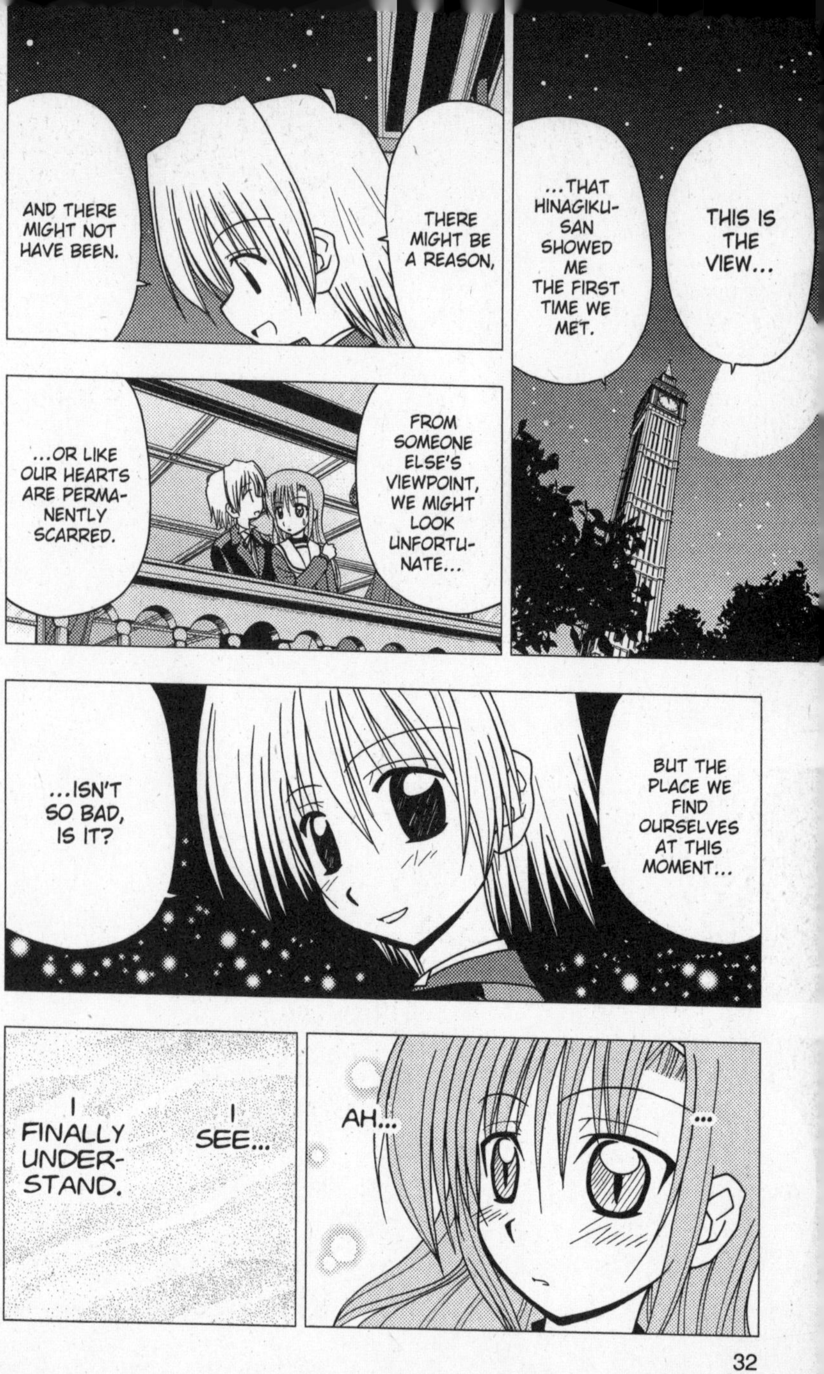

THIS IS THE VIEW...
...THAT HINAGIKU-SAN SHOWED ME THE FIRST TIME WE MET.
THERE MIGHT BE A REASON,
AND THERE MIGHT NOT HAVE BEEN.
FROM SOMEONE ELSE'S VIEWPOINT, WE MIGHT LOOK UNFORTUNATE...
...OR LIKE OUR HEARTS ARE PERMANENTLY SCARRED.
BUT THE PLACE WE FIND OURSELVES AT THIS MOMENT...
...ISN'T SO BAD, IS IT?
...
AH...
I SEE...
I FINALLY UNDERSTAND.

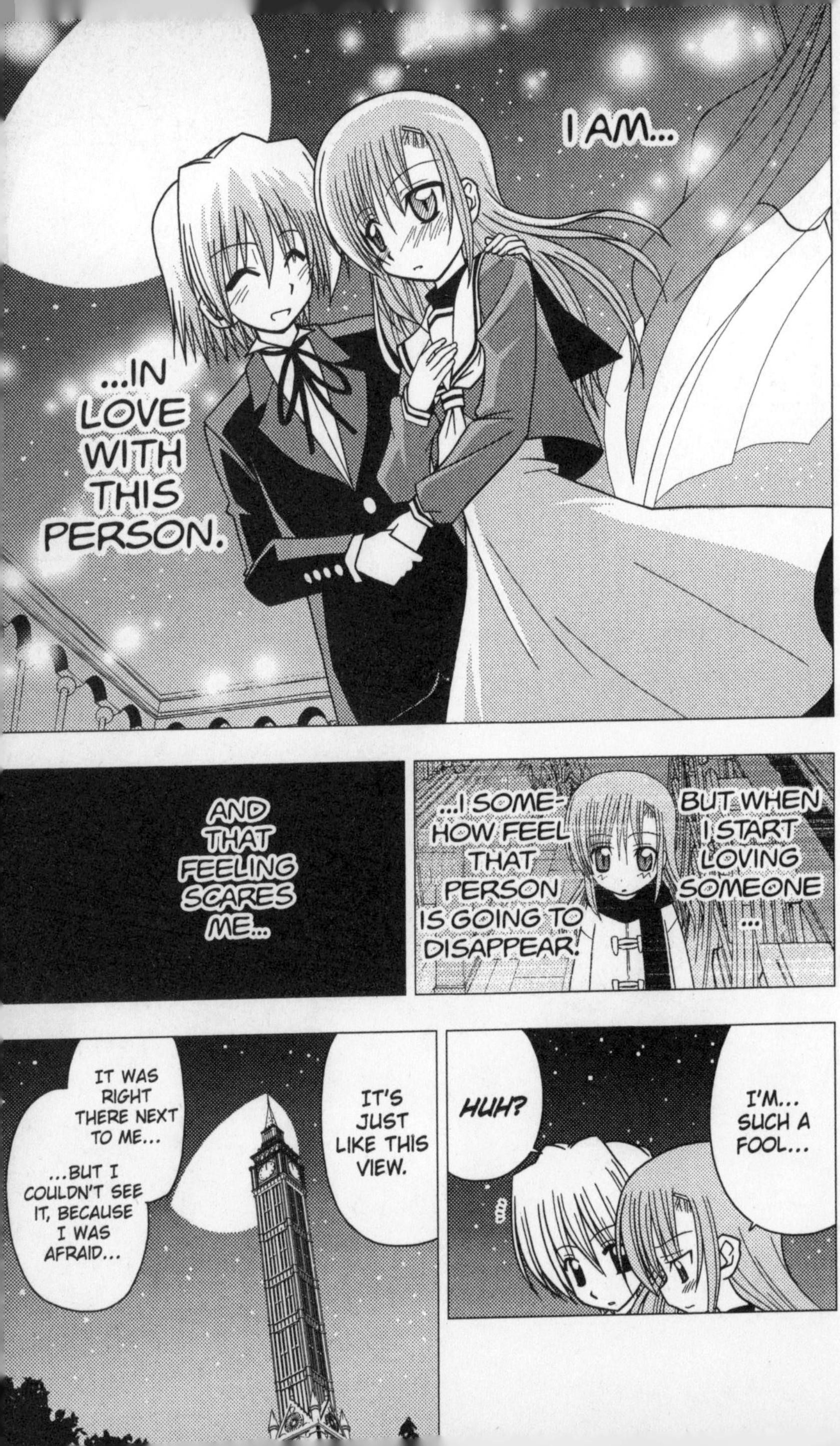
I AM...
...IN LOVE WITH THIS PERSON.
BUT WHEN I START LOVING SOMEONE...
...I SOME-HOW FEEL THAT PERSON IS GOING TO DISAPPEAR.
AND THAT FEELING SCARES ME...
I'M... SUCH A FOOL...
HUH?
IT'S JUST LIKE THIS VIEW.
IT WAS RIGHT THERE NEXT TO ME...
...BUT I COULDN'T SEE IT, BECAUSE I WAS AFRAID...

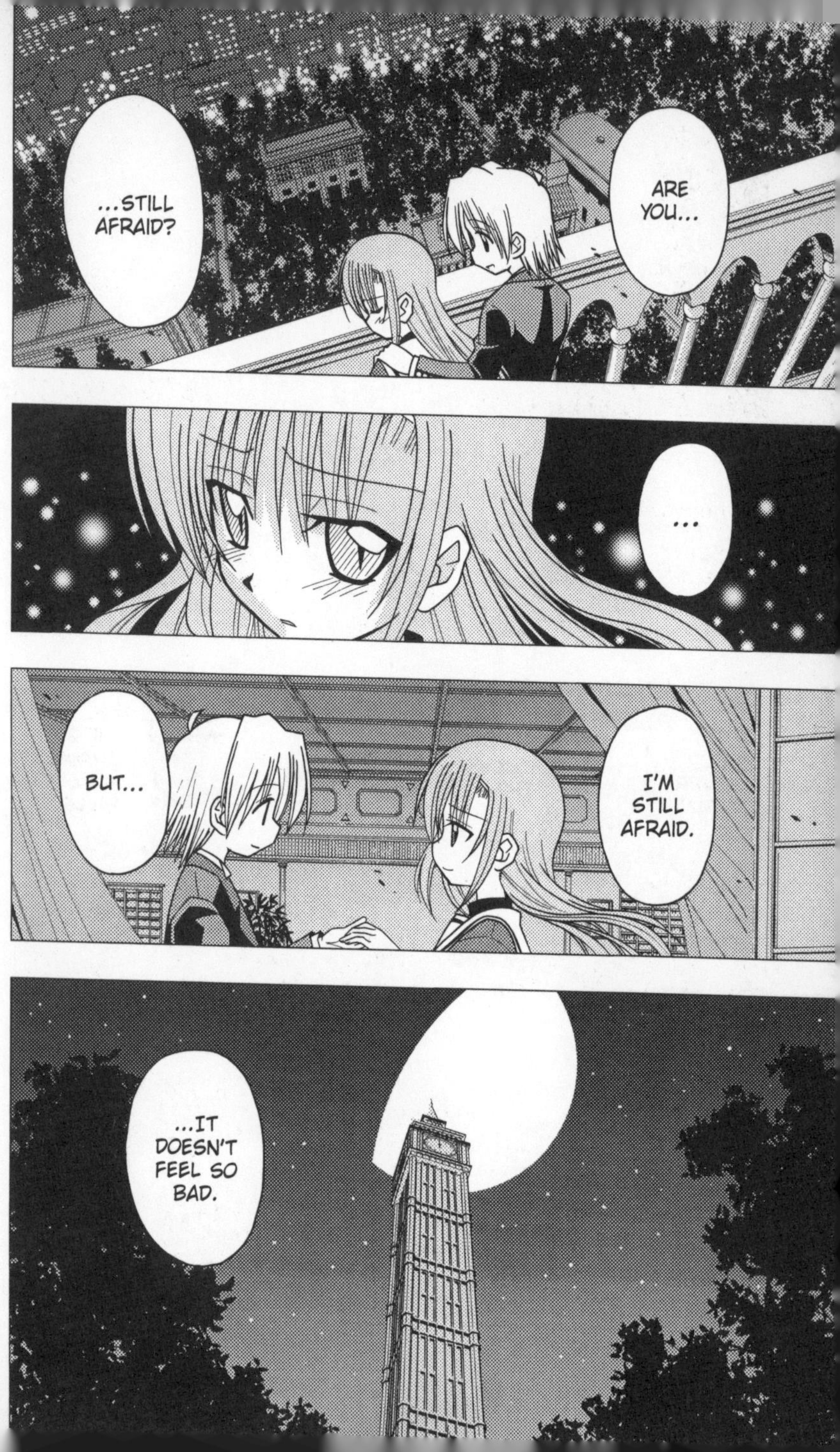
ARE YOU...
...STILL AFRAID?
...
I'M STILL AFRAID.
BUT...
...IT DOESN'T FEEL SO BAD.

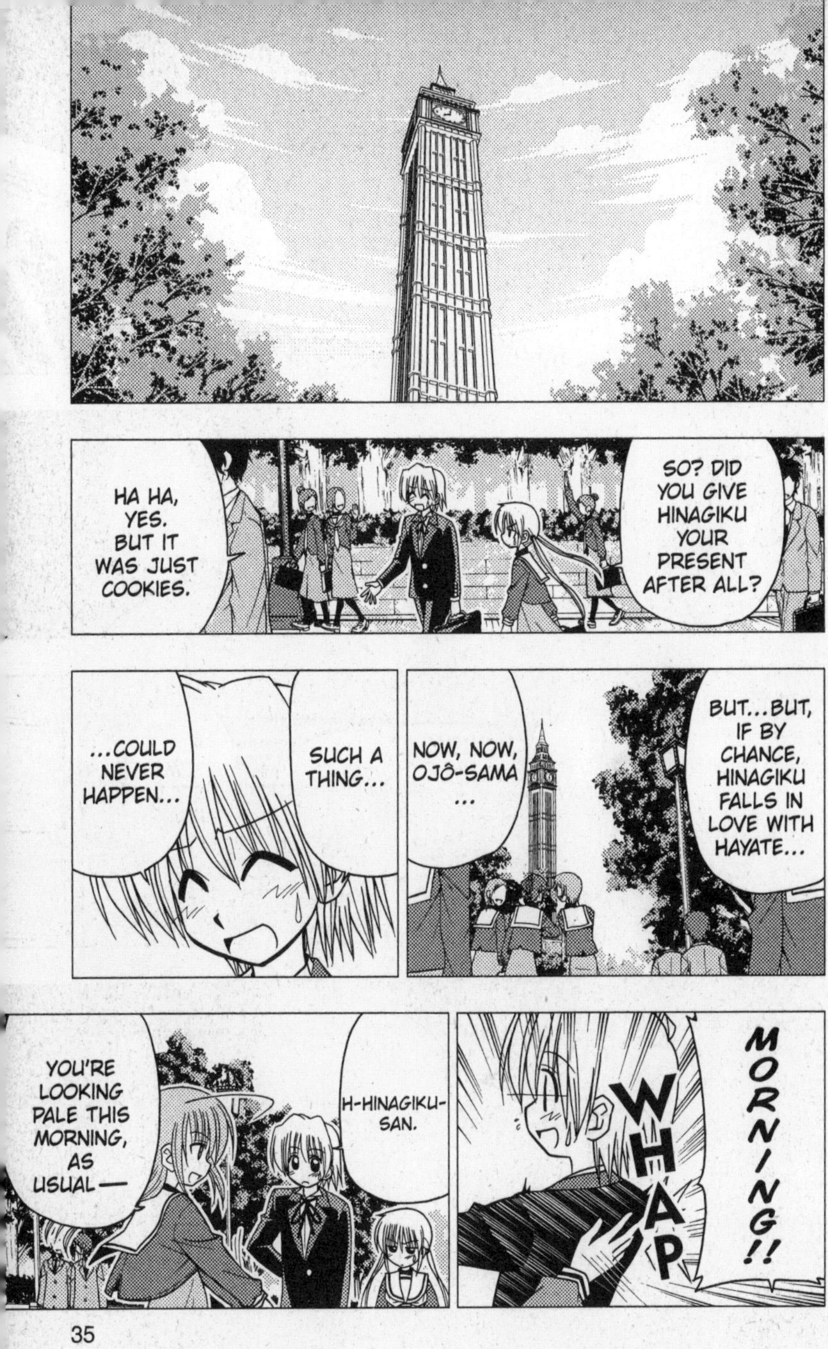
SO? DID YOU GIVE HINAGIKU YOUR PRESENT AFTER ALL?
HA HA, YES. BUT IT WAS JUST COOKIES.
BUT...BUT, IF BY CHANCE, HINAGIKU FALLS IN LOVE WITH HAYATE...
NOW, NOW, OJÔ-SAMA...
SUCH A THING...
...COULD NEVER HAPPEN...
MORNING!!
WHAP
H-HINAGIKU-SAN.
YOU'RE LOOKING PALE THIS MORNING, AS USUAL—

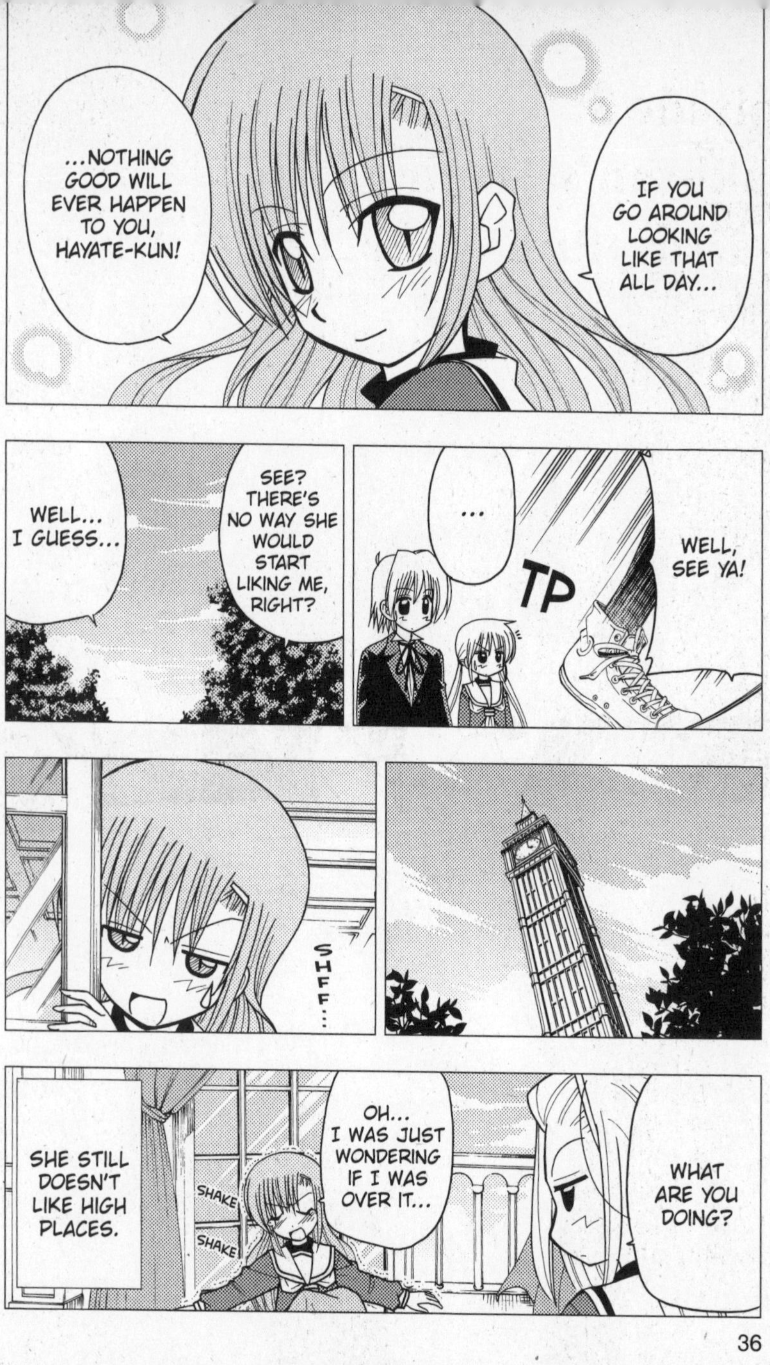
IF YOU GO AROUND LOOKING LIKE THAT ALL DAY...
...NOTHING GOOD WILL EVER HAPPEN TO YOU, HAYATE-KUN!
WELL, SEE YA!
TP
...
SEE? THERE'S NO WAY SHE WOULD START LIKING ME, RIGHT?
WELL... I GUESS...
SHFF...
WHAT ARE YOU DOING?
OH... I WAS JUST WONDERING IF I WAS OVER IT...
SHAKE
SHAKE
SHE STILL DOESN'T LIKE HIGH PLACES.

Episode 3: "Saki-san's Trifling Personal Errand (Warring Rival Episode)"

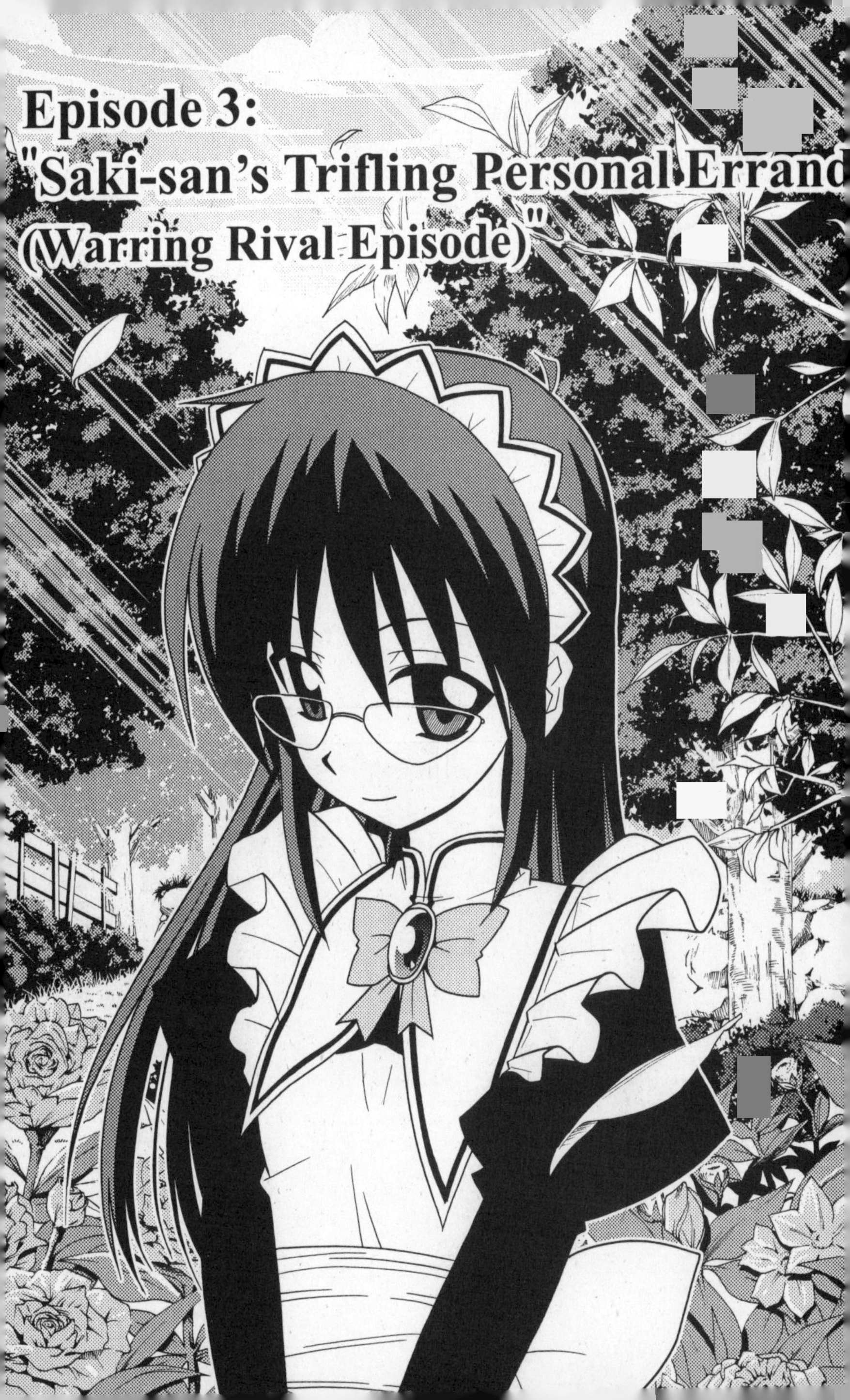

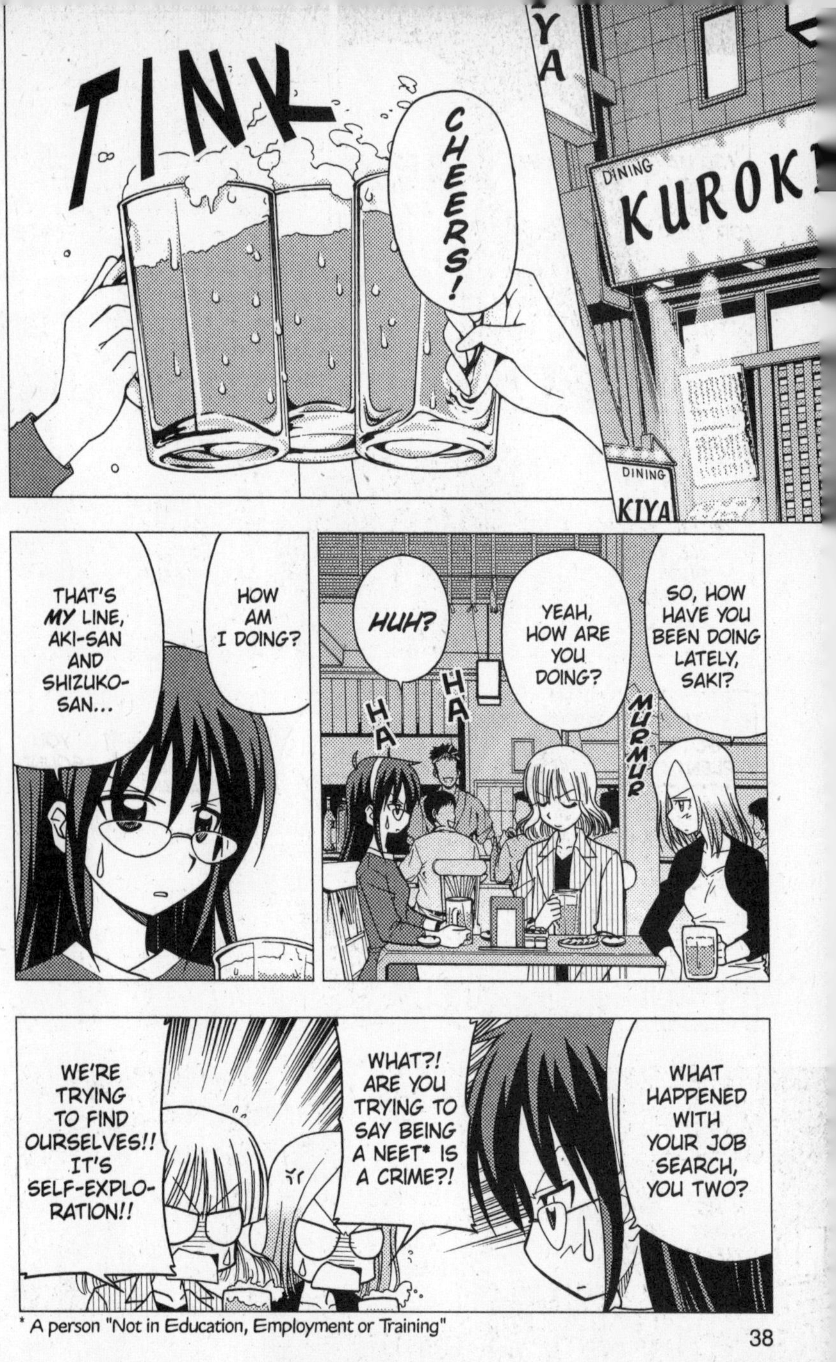
YA
DINING KUROKI
CHEERS!
TINK
DINING KIYA
SO, HOW HAVE YOU BEEN DOING LATELY, SAKI?
MURMUR
YEAH, HOW ARE YOU DOING?
HA HA
HUH?
HOW AM I DOING?
THAT'S MY LINE, AKI-SAN AND SHIZUKO-SAN...
WHAT HAPPENED WITH YOUR JOB SEARCH, YOU TWO?
WHAT?! ARE YOU TRYING TO SAY BEING A NEET* IS A CRIME?!
WE'RE TRYING TO FIND OURSELVES!! IT'S SELF-EXPLORATION!!

* A person "Not in Education, Employment or Training"

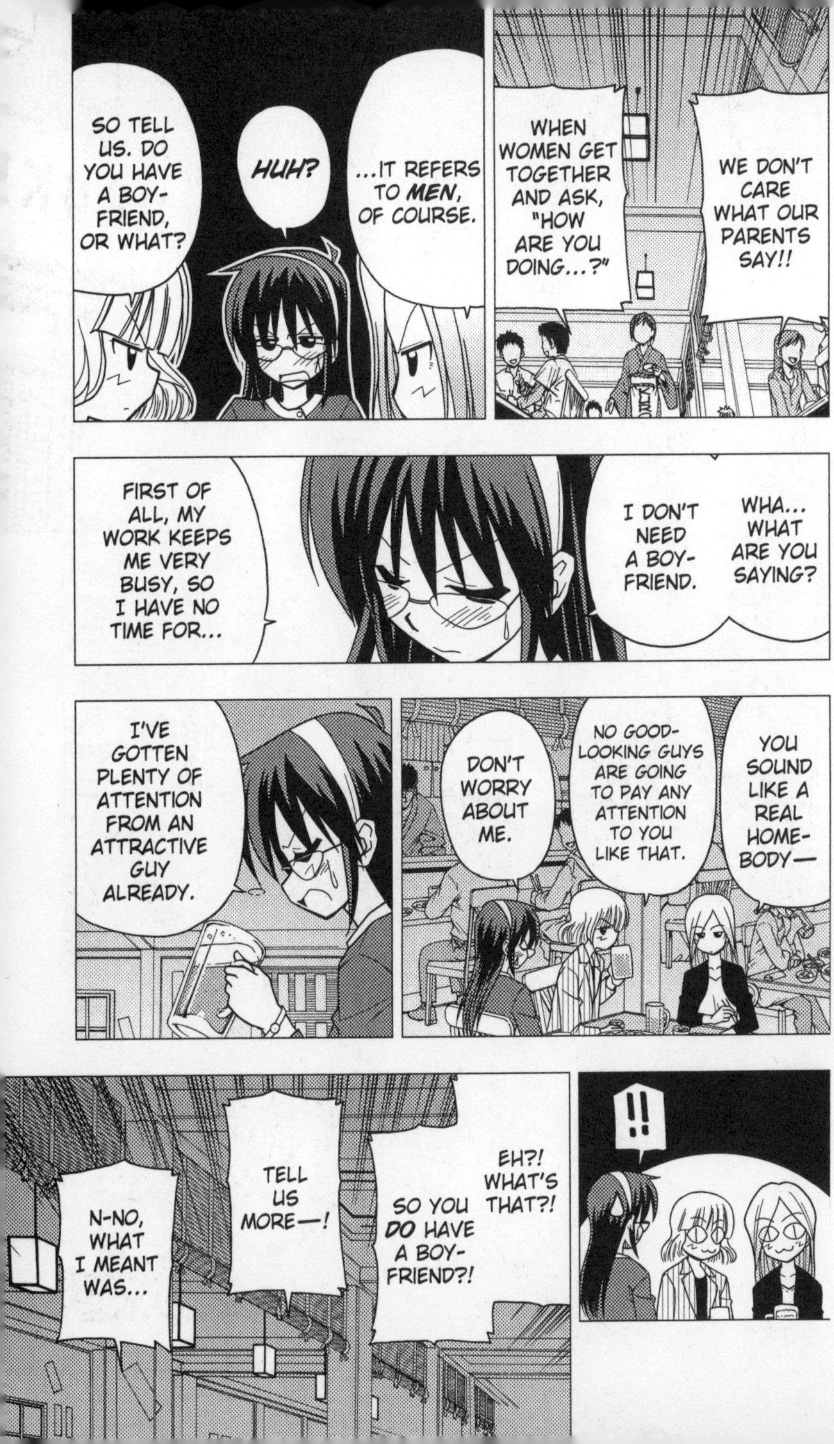
WE DON'T CARE WHAT OUR PARENTS SAY!!
WHEN WOMEN GET TOGETHER AND ASK, "HOW ARE YOU DOING...?"
...IT REFERS TO *MEN*, OF COURSE.
HUH?
SO TELL US. DO YOU HAVE A BOY-FRIEND, OR WHAT?
WHA... WHAT ARE YOU SAYING?
I DON'T NEED A BOY-FRIEND.
FIRST OF ALL, MY WORK KEEPS ME VERY BUSY, SO I HAVE NO TIME FOR...
YOU SOUND LIKE A REAL HOME-BODY—
NO GOOD-LOOKING GUYS ARE GOING TO PAY ANY ATTENTION TO YOU LIKE THAT.
DON'T WORRY ABOUT ME.
I'VE GOTTEN PLENTY OF ATTENTION FROM AN ATTRACTIVE GUY ALREADY.
!!
EH?! WHAT'S THAT?!
SO YOU *DO* HAVE A BOY-FRIEND?!
TELL US MORE—!
N-NO, WHAT I MEANT WAS...

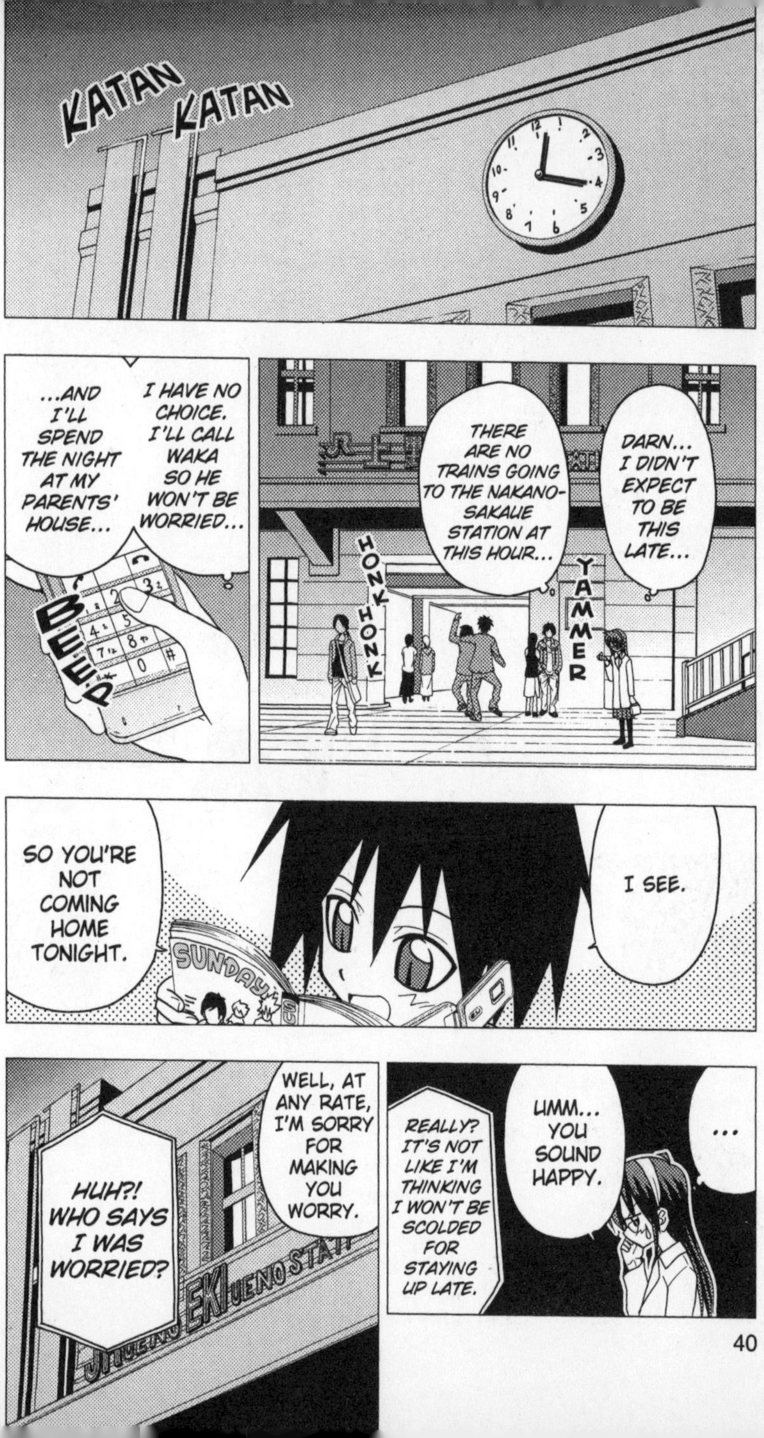
KATAN KATAN
DARN... I DIDN'T EXPECT TO BE THIS LATE...
THERE ARE NO TRAINS GOING TO THE NAKANO-SAKAUE STATION AT THIS HOUR...
YAMMER
HONK HONK
I HAVE NO CHOICE. I'LL CALL WAKA SO HE WON'T BE WORRIED...
...AND I'LL SPEND THE NIGHT AT MY PARENTS' HOUSE...
BEEP
I SEE.
SO YOU'RE NOT COMING HOME TONIGHT.
SUNDAY
...
UMM... YOU SOUND HAPPY.
REALLY? IT'S NOT LIKE I'M THINKING I WON'T BE SCOLDED FOR STAYING UP LATE.
WELL, AT ANY RATE, I'M SORRY FOR MAKING YOU WORRY.
HUH?! WHO SAYS I WAS WORRIED?
EKI UENO STATI

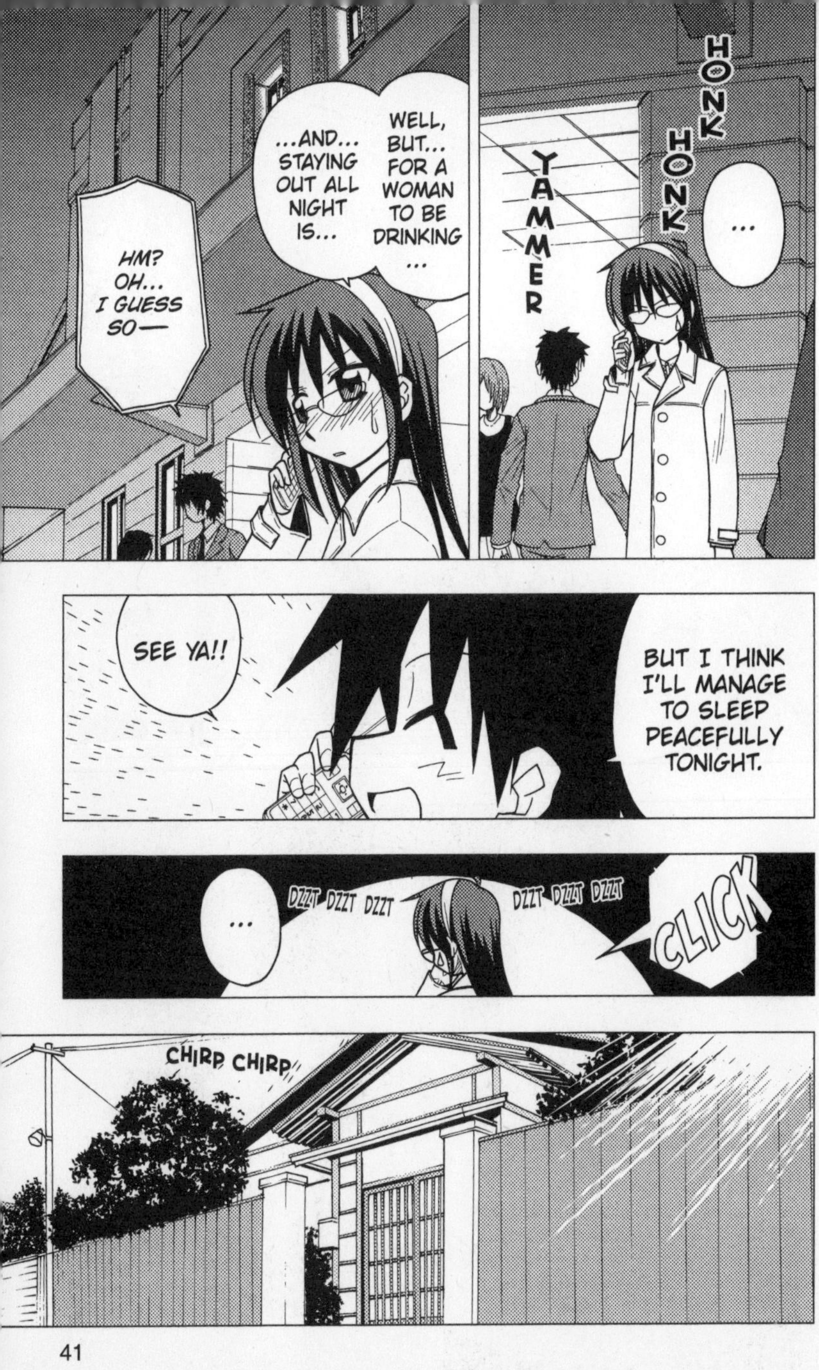
HONK HONK
YAMMER
...
WELL, BUT... FOR A WOMAN TO BE DRINKING...
...AND... STAYING OUT ALL NIGHT IS...
HM? OH... I GUESS SO—
BUT I THINK I'LL MANAGE TO SLEEP PEACEFULLY TONIGHT.
SEE YA!!
CLICK
DZZT DZZT DZZT
DZZT DZZT DZZT
...
CHIRP CHIRP

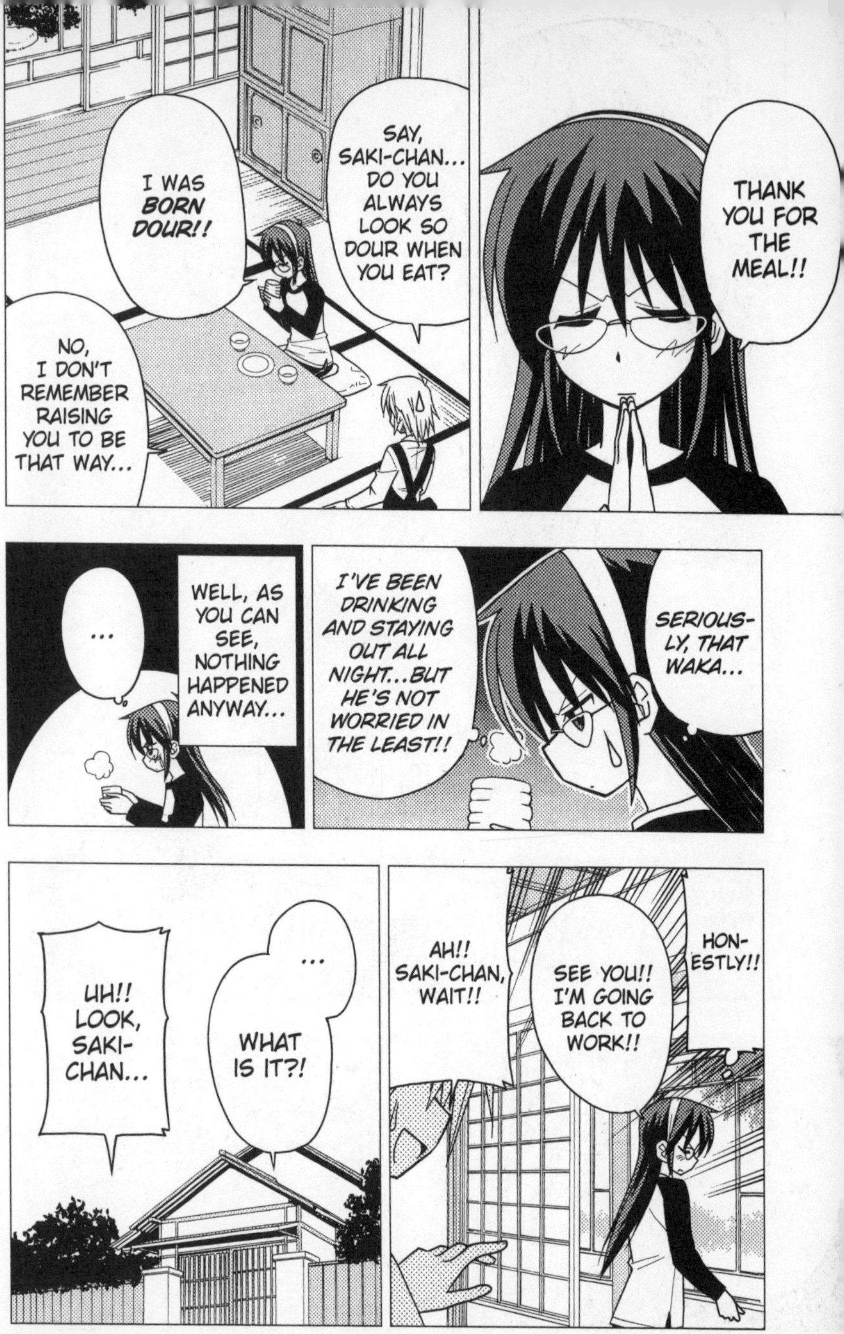
THANK YOU FOR THE MEAL!!
SAY, SAKI-CHAN... DO YOU ALWAYS LOOK SO DOUR WHEN YOU EAT?
I WAS BORN DOUR!!
NO, I DON'T REMEMBER RAISING YOU TO BE THAT WAY...
SERIOUS-LY, THAT WAKA...
I'VE BEEN DRINKING AND STAYING OUT ALL NIGHT...BUT HE'S NOT WORRIED IN THE LEAST!!
WELL, AS YOU CAN SEE, NOTHING HAPPENED ANYWAY...
...
HON-ESTLY!!
SEE YOU!! I'M GOING BACK TO WORK!!
AH!! SAKI-CHAN, WAIT!!
...
WHAT IS IT?!
UH!! LOOK, SAKI-CHAN...

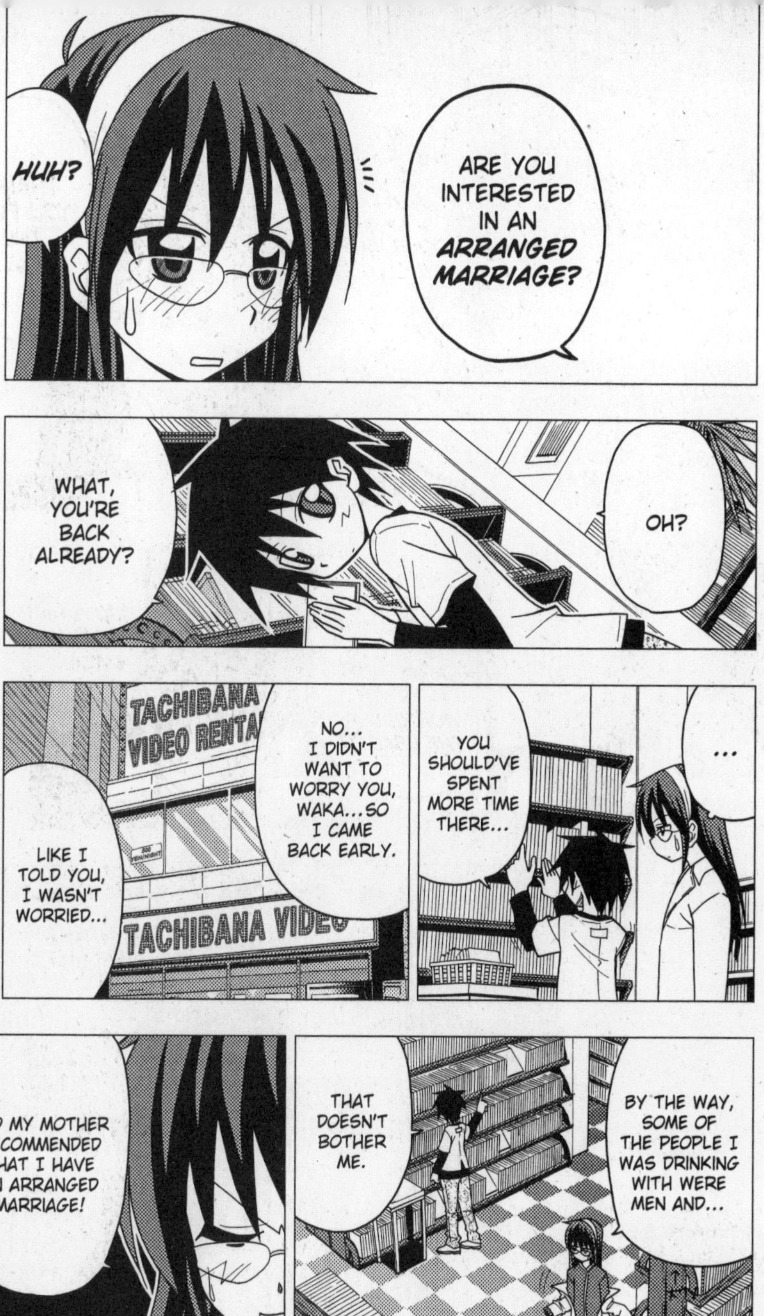
ARE YOU INTERESTED IN AN ***ARRANGED MARRIAGE?***
HUH?
OH?
WHAT, YOU'RE BACK ALREADY?
...
YOU SHOULD'VE SPENT MORE TIME THERE...
TACHIBANA VIDEO RENTA
NO... I DIDN'T WANT TO WORRY YOU, WAKA...SO I CAME BACK EARLY.
LIKE I TOLD YOU, I WASN'T WORRIED...
TACHIBANA VIDEO
BY THE WAY, SOME OF THE PEOPLE I WAS DRINKING WITH WERE MEN AND...
THAT DOESN'T BOTHER ME.
AND MY MOTHER RECOMMENDED THAT I HAVE AN ARRANGED MARRIAGE!

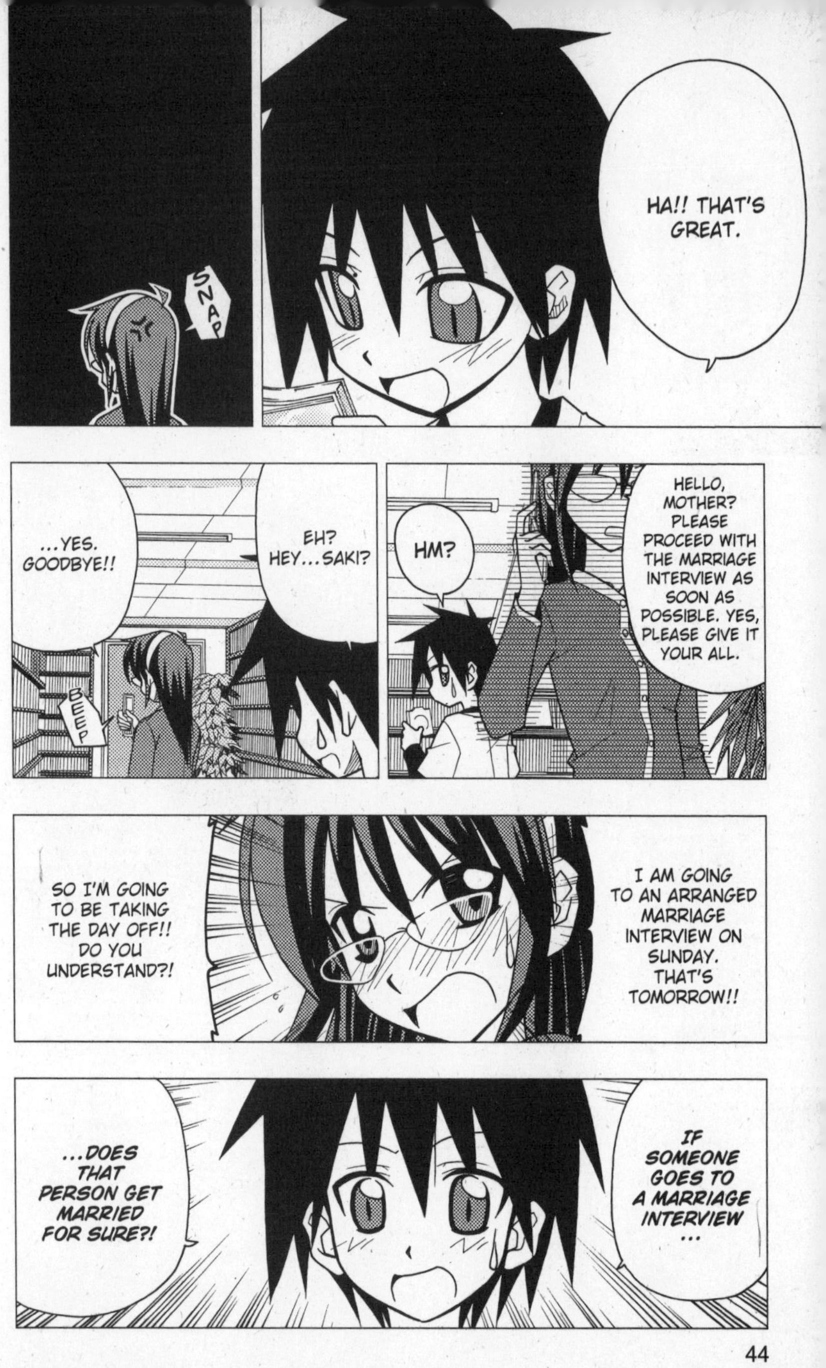

HA!! THAT'S GREAT.
SNAP
HELLO, MOTHER? PLEASE PROCEED WITH THE MARRIAGE INTERVIEW AS SOON AS POSSIBLE. YES, PLEASE GIVE IT YOUR ALL.
HM?
EH? HEY...SAKI?
...YES. GOODBYE!!
BEEP
I AM GOING TO AN ARRANGED MARRIAGE INTERVIEW ON SUNDAY. THAT'S TOMORROW!!
SO I'M GOING TO BE TAKING THE DAY OFF!! DO YOU UNDERSTAND?!
IF SOMEONE GOES TO A MARRIAGE INTERVIEW ...
...DOES THAT PERSON GET MARRIED FOR SURE?!

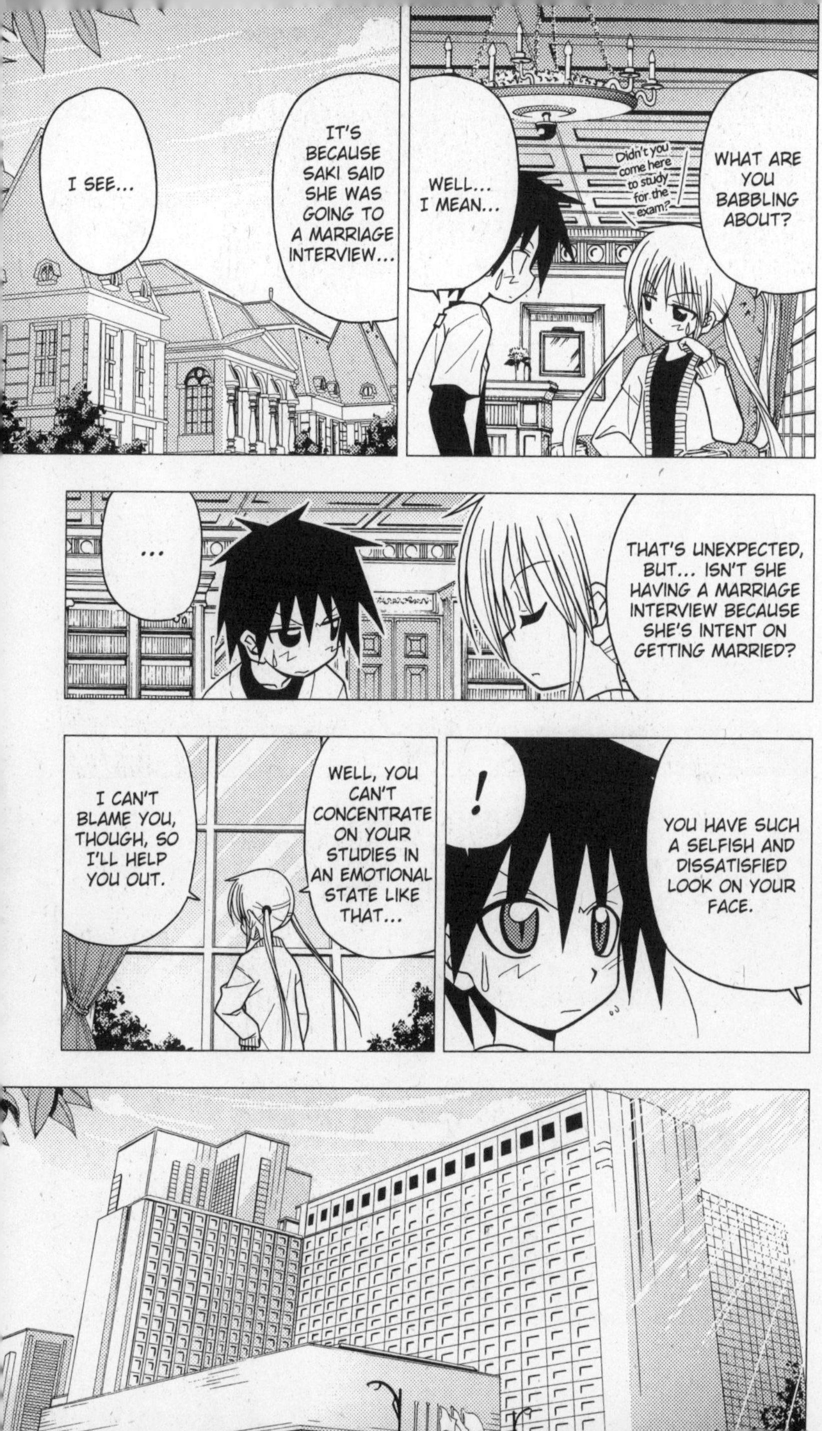
WHAT ARE YOU BABBLING ABOUT?
Didn't you come here to study for the exam?
WELL... I MEAN...
IT'S BECAUSE SAKI SAID SHE WAS GOING TO A MARRIAGE INTERVIEW...
I SEE...
THAT'S UNEXPECTED, BUT... ISN'T SHE HAVING A MARRIAGE INTERVIEW BECAUSE SHE'S INTENT ON GETTING MARRIED?
...
YOU HAVE SUCH A SELFISH AND DISSATISFIED LOOK ON YOUR FACE.
!
WELL, YOU CAN'T CONCENTRATE ON YOUR STUDIES IN AN EMOTIONAL STATE LIKE THAT...
I CAN'T BLAME YOU, THOUGH, SO I'LL HELP YOU OUT.

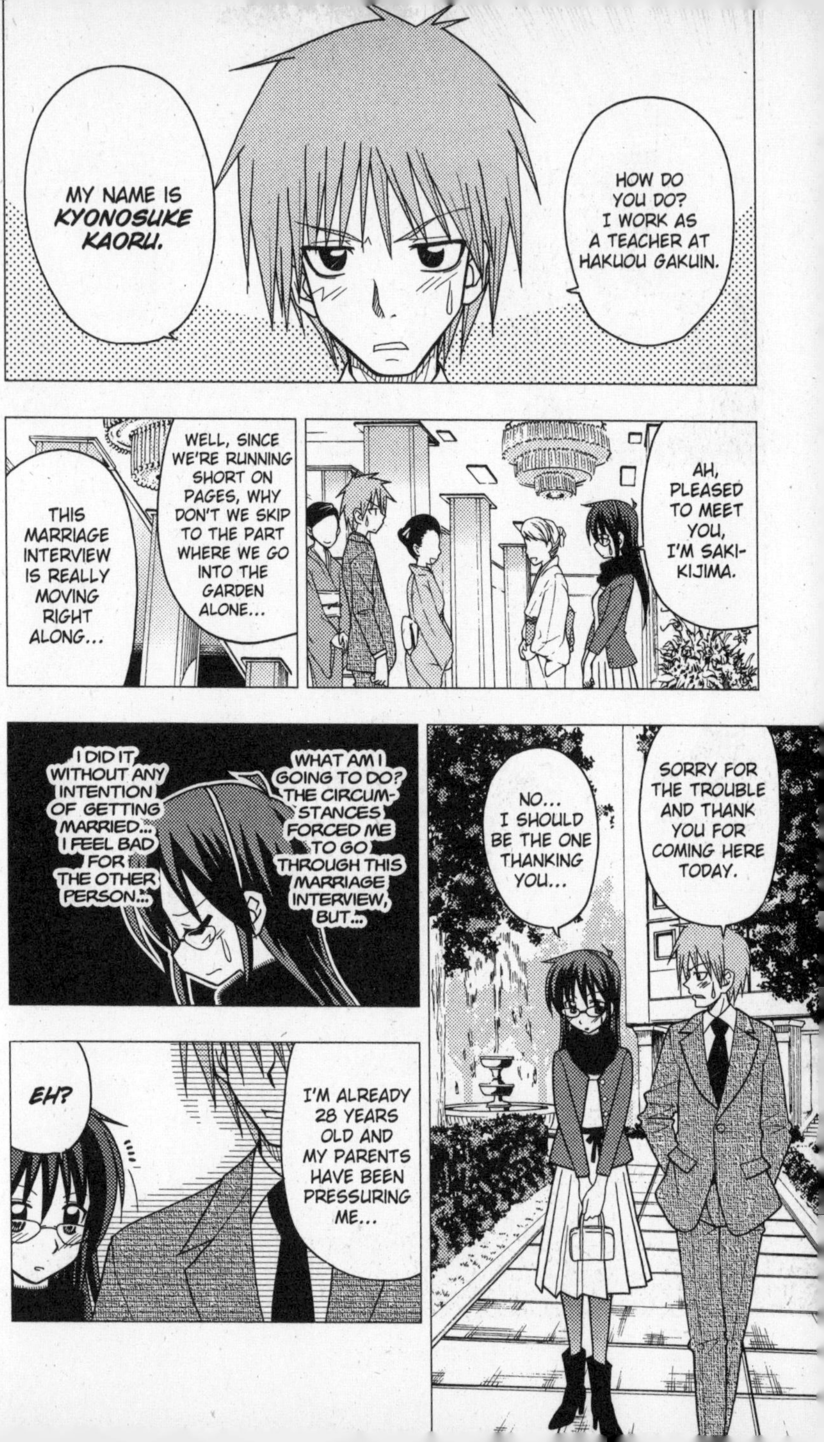
HOW DO YOU DO? I WORK AS A TEACHER AT HAKUOU GAKUIN.
MY NAME IS *KYONOSUKE KAORU.*
AH, PLEASED TO MEET YOU, I'M SAKI-KIJIMA.
WELL, SINCE WE'RE RUNNING SHORT ON PAGES, WHY DON'T WE SKIP TO THE PART WHERE WE GO INTO THE GARDEN ALONE...
THIS MARRIAGE INTERVIEW IS REALLY MOVING RIGHT ALONG...
SORRY FOR THE TROUBLE AND THANK YOU FOR COMING HERE TODAY.
NO... I SHOULD BE THE ONE THANKING YOU...
WHAT AM I GOING TO DO? THE CIRCUM-STANCES FORCED ME TO GO THROUGH THIS MARRIAGE INTERVIEW, BUT...
I DID IT WITHOUT ANY INTENTION OF GETTING MARRIED... I FEEL BAD FOR THE OTHER PERSON...
I'M ALREADY 28 YEARS OLD AND MY PARENTS HAVE BEEN PRESSURING ME...
EH?

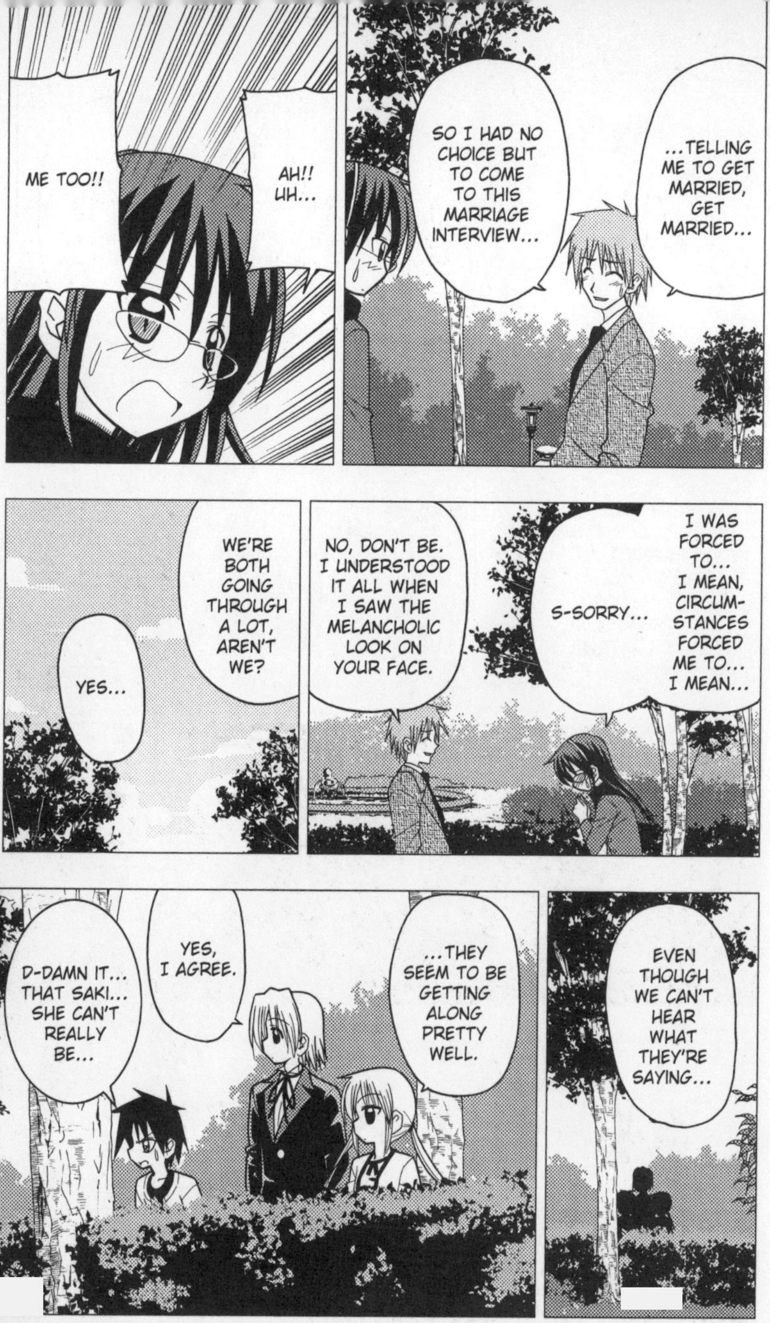
...TELLING ME TO GET MARRIED, GET MARRIED...
SO I HAD NO CHOICE BUT TO COME TO THIS MARRIAGE INTERVIEW...
AH!! UH...
ME TOO!!
I WAS FORCED TO... I MEAN, CIRCUM-STANCES FORCED ME TO... I MEAN...
S-SORRY...
NO, DON'T BE. I UNDERSTOOD IT ALL WHEN I SAW THE MELANCHOLIC LOOK ON YOUR FACE.
WE'RE BOTH GOING THROUGH A LOT, AREN'T WE?
YES...
EVEN THOUGH WE CAN'T HEAR WHAT THEY'RE SAYING...
...THEY SEEM TO BE GETTING ALONG PRETTY WELL.
YES, I AGREE.
D-DAMN IT... THAT SAKI... SHE CAN'T REALLY BE...

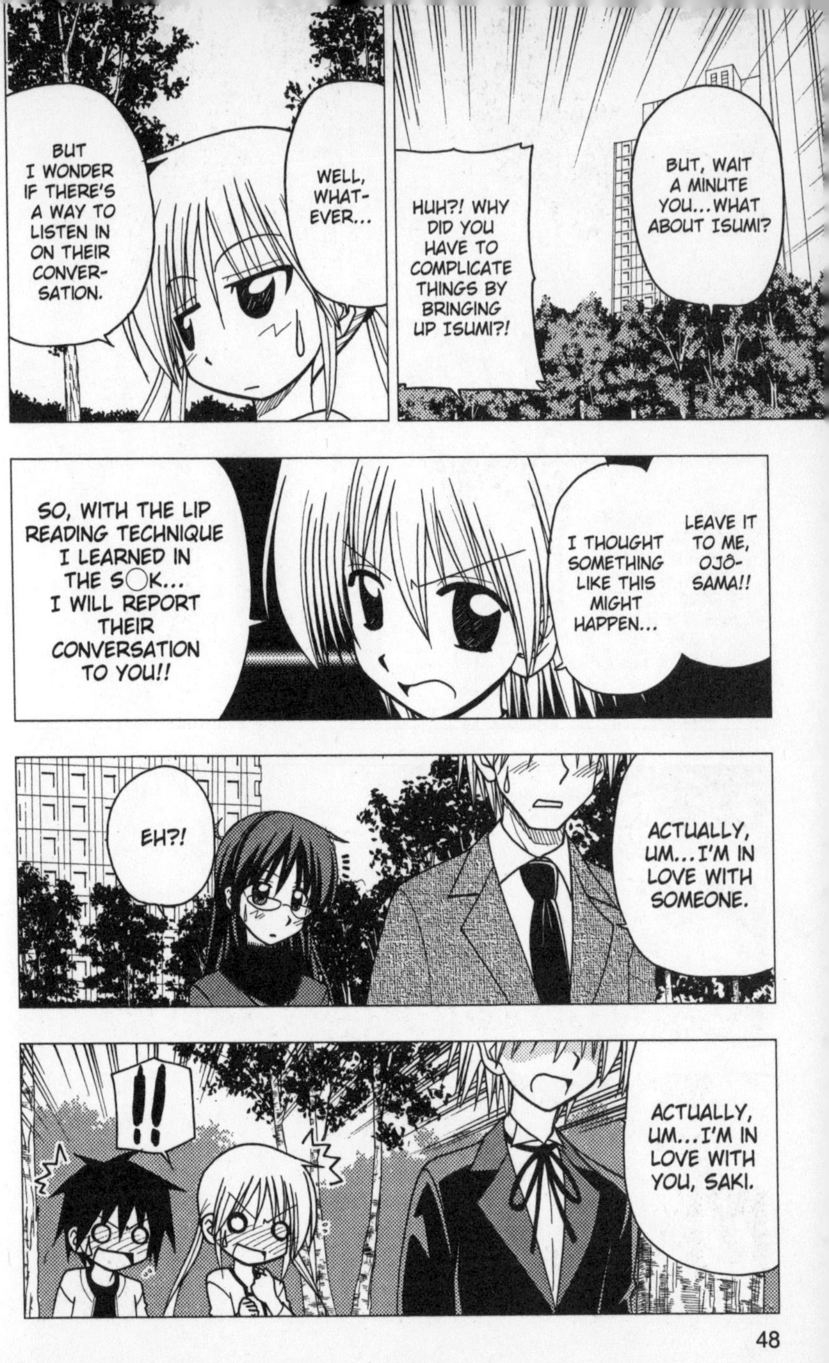
BUT, WAIT A MINUTE YOU...WHAT ABOUT ISUMI?
HUH?! WHY DID YOU HAVE TO COMPLICATE THINGS BY BRINGING UP ISUMI?!
WELL, WHAT-EVER...
BUT I WONDER IF THERE'S A WAY TO LISTEN IN ON THEIR CONVER-SATION.
LEAVE IT TO ME, OJÔ-SAMA!!
I THOUGHT SOMETHING LIKE THIS MIGHT HAPPEN...
SO, WITH THE LIP READING TECHNIQUE I LEARNED IN THE S◯K... I WILL REPORT THEIR CONVERSATION TO YOU!!
ACTUALLY, UM...I'M IN LOVE WITH SOMEONE.
EH?!
ACTUALLY, UM...I'M IN LOVE WITH YOU, SAKI.
!!

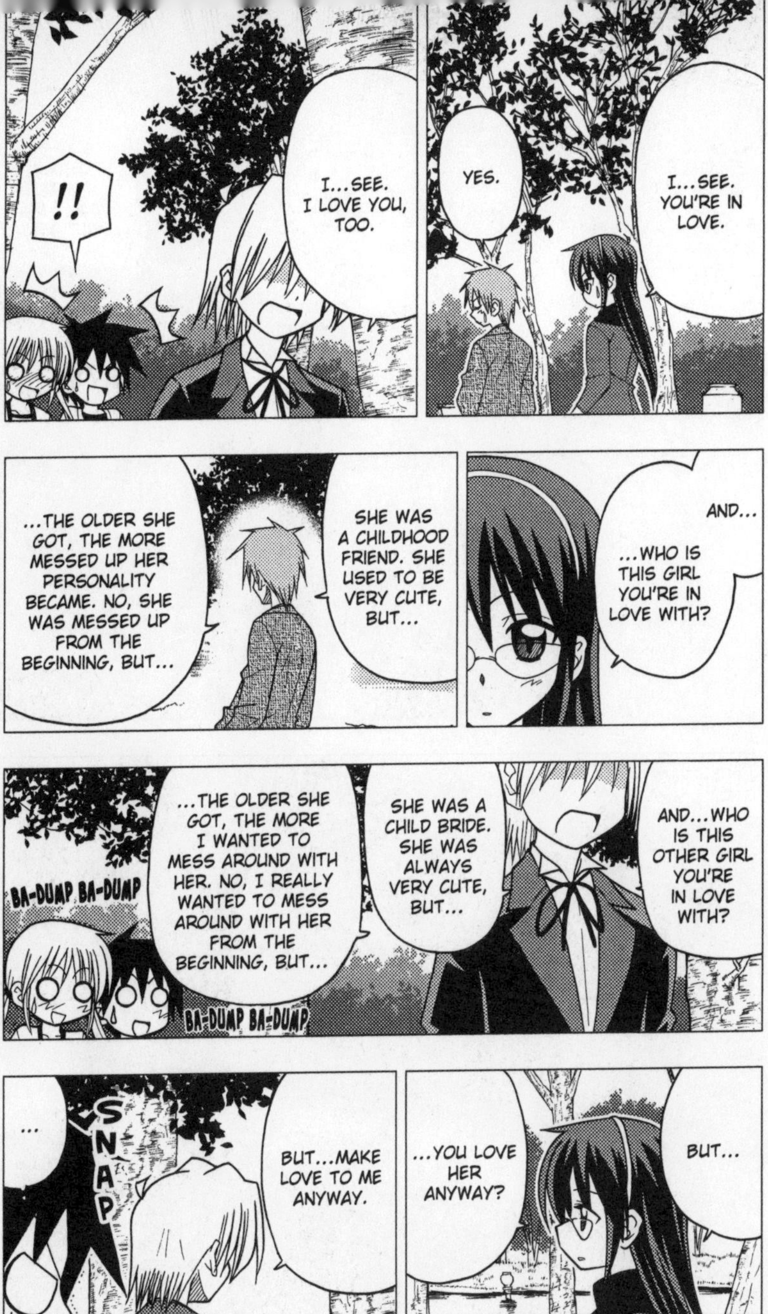
I...SEE. YOU'RE IN LOVE.
YES.
I...SEE. I LOVE YOU, TOO.
!!
AND...
...WHO IS THIS GIRL YOU'RE IN LOVE WITH?
SHE WAS A CHILDHOOD FRIEND. SHE USED TO BE VERY CUTE, BUT...
...THE OLDER SHE GOT, THE MORE MESSED UP HER PERSONALITY BECAME. NO, SHE WAS MESSED UP FROM THE BEGINNING, BUT...
AND...WHO IS THIS OTHER GIRL YOU'RE IN LOVE WITH?
SHE WAS A CHILD BRIDE. SHE WAS ALWAYS VERY CUTE, BUT...
...THE OLDER SHE GOT, THE MORE I WANTED TO MESS AROUND WITH HER. NO, I REALLY WANTED TO MESS AROUND WITH HER FROM THE BEGINNING, BUT...
BA-DUMP BA-DUMP
BA-DUMP BA-DUMP
BUT...
...YOU LOVE HER ANYWAY?
BUT...MAKE LOVE TO ME ANYWAY.
SNAP
...

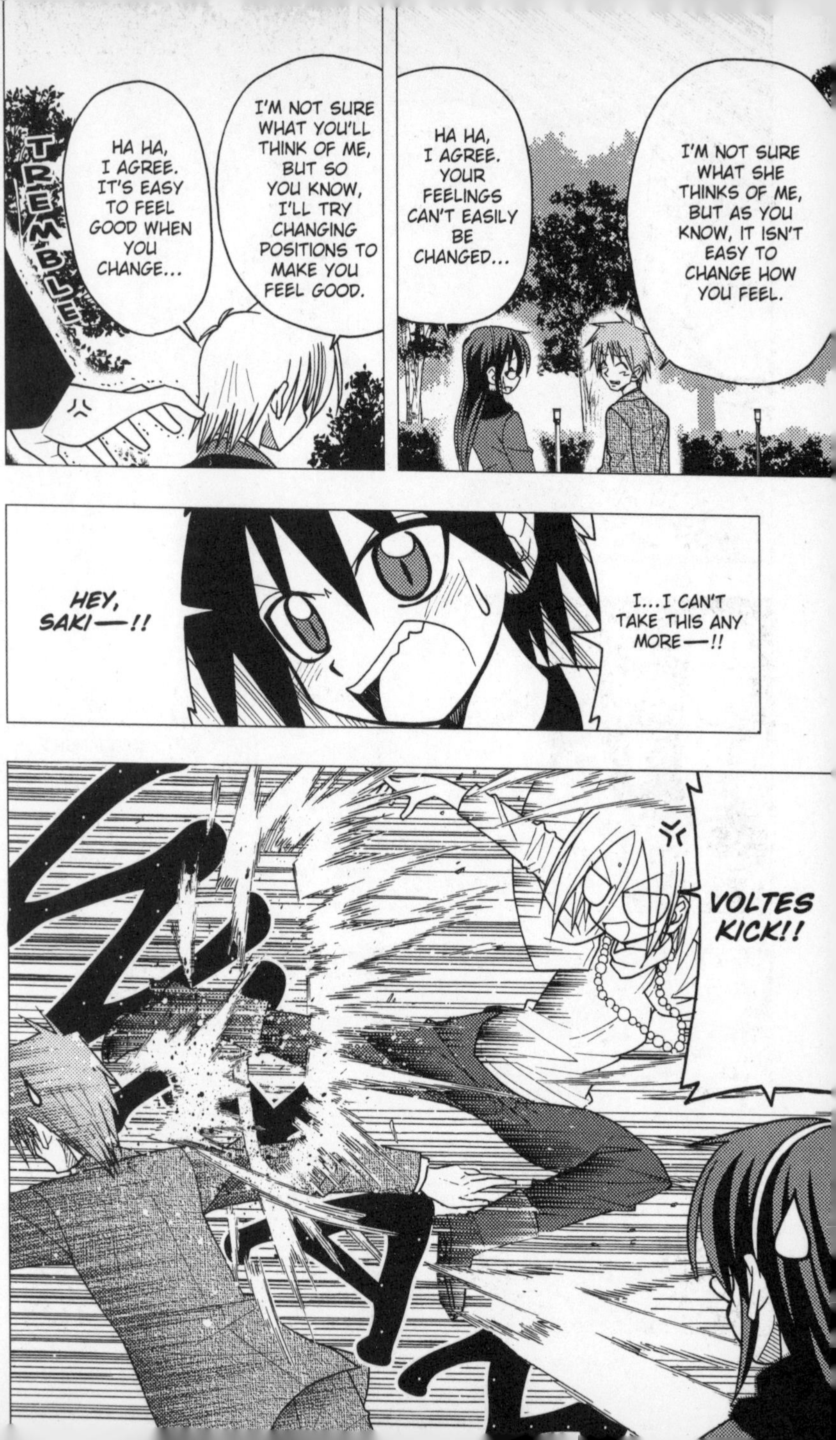
I'M NOT SURE WHAT SHE THINKS OF ME, BUT AS YOU KNOW, IT ISN'T EASY TO CHANGE HOW YOU FEEL.
HA HA, I AGREE. YOUR FEELINGS CAN'T EASILY BE CHANGED...
I'M NOT SURE WHAT YOU'LL THINK OF ME, BUT SO YOU KNOW, I'LL TRY CHANGING POSITIONS TO MAKE YOU FEEL GOOD.
HA HA, I AGREE. IT'S EASY TO FEEL GOOD WHEN YOU CHANGE...
TREMBLE
I...I CAN'T TAKE THIS ANY MORE—!!
HEY, SAKI—!!
VOLTES KICK!!

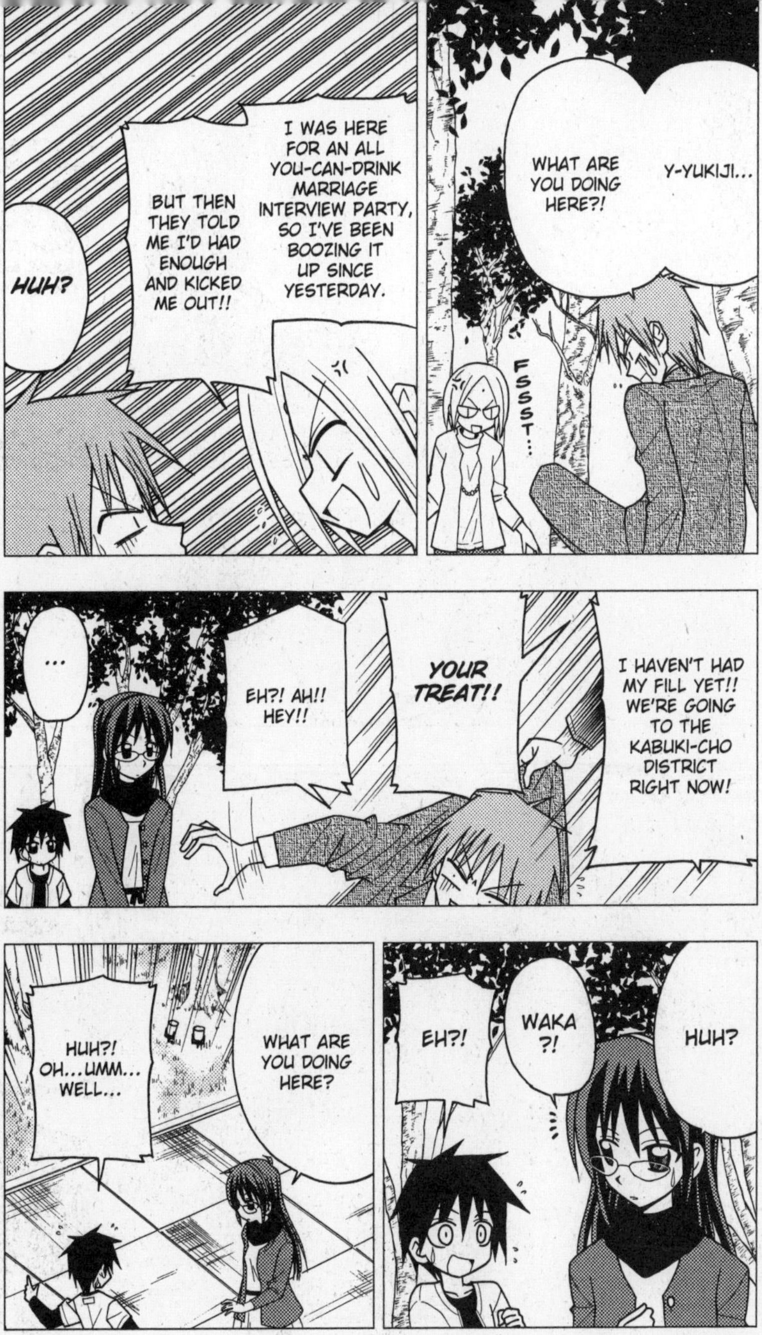
Y-YUKIJI...
WHAT ARE YOU DOING HERE?!
FSSST...
I WAS HERE FOR AN ALL YOU-CAN-DRINK MARRIAGE INTERVIEW PARTY, SO I'VE BEEN BOOZING IT UP SINCE YESTERDAY.
BUT THEN THEY TOLD ME I'D HAD ENOUGH AND KICKED ME OUT!!
HUH?
I HAVEN'T HAD MY FILL YET!! WE'RE GOING TO THE KABUKI-CHO DISTRICT RIGHT NOW!
YOUR TREAT!!
EH?! AH!! HEY!!
...
HUH?
WAKA ?!
EH?!
WHAT ARE YOU DOING HERE?
HUH?! OH...UMM... WELL...

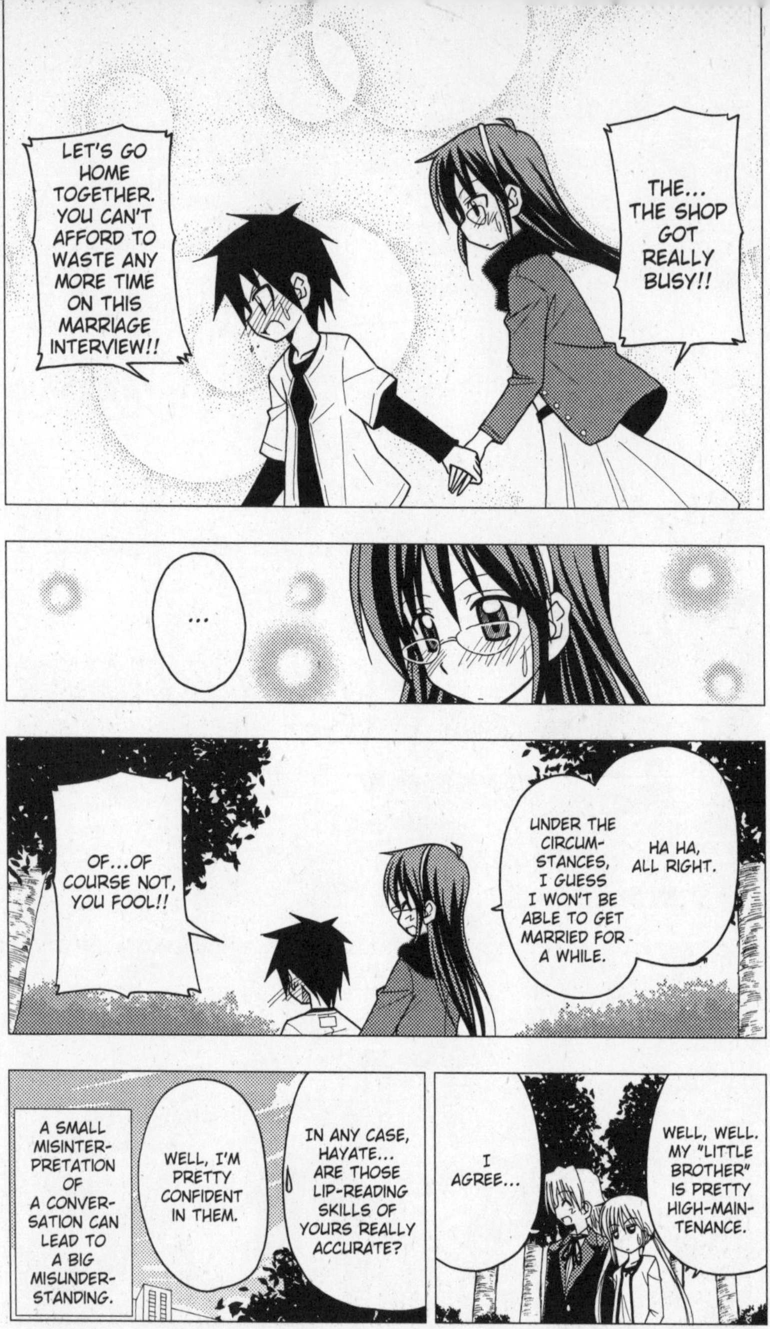
THE... THE SHOP GOT REALLY BUSY!!
LET'S GO HOME TOGETHER. YOU CAN'T AFFORD TO WASTE ANY MORE TIME ON THIS MARRIAGE INTERVIEW!!
...
HA HA, ALL RIGHT.
UNDER THE CIRCUM-STANCES, I GUESS I WON'T BE ABLE TO GET MARRIED FOR A WHILE.
OF...OF COURSE NOT, YOU FOOL!!
WELL, WELL. MY "LITTLE BROTHER" IS PRETTY HIGH-MAIN-TENANCE.
I AGREE...
IN ANY CASE, HAYATE... ARE THOSE LIP-READING SKILLS OF YOURS REALLY ACCURATE?
WELL, I'M PRETTY CONFIDENT IN THEM.
A SMALL MISINTER-PRETATION OF A CONVER-SATION CAN LEAD TO A BIG MISUNDER-STANDING.

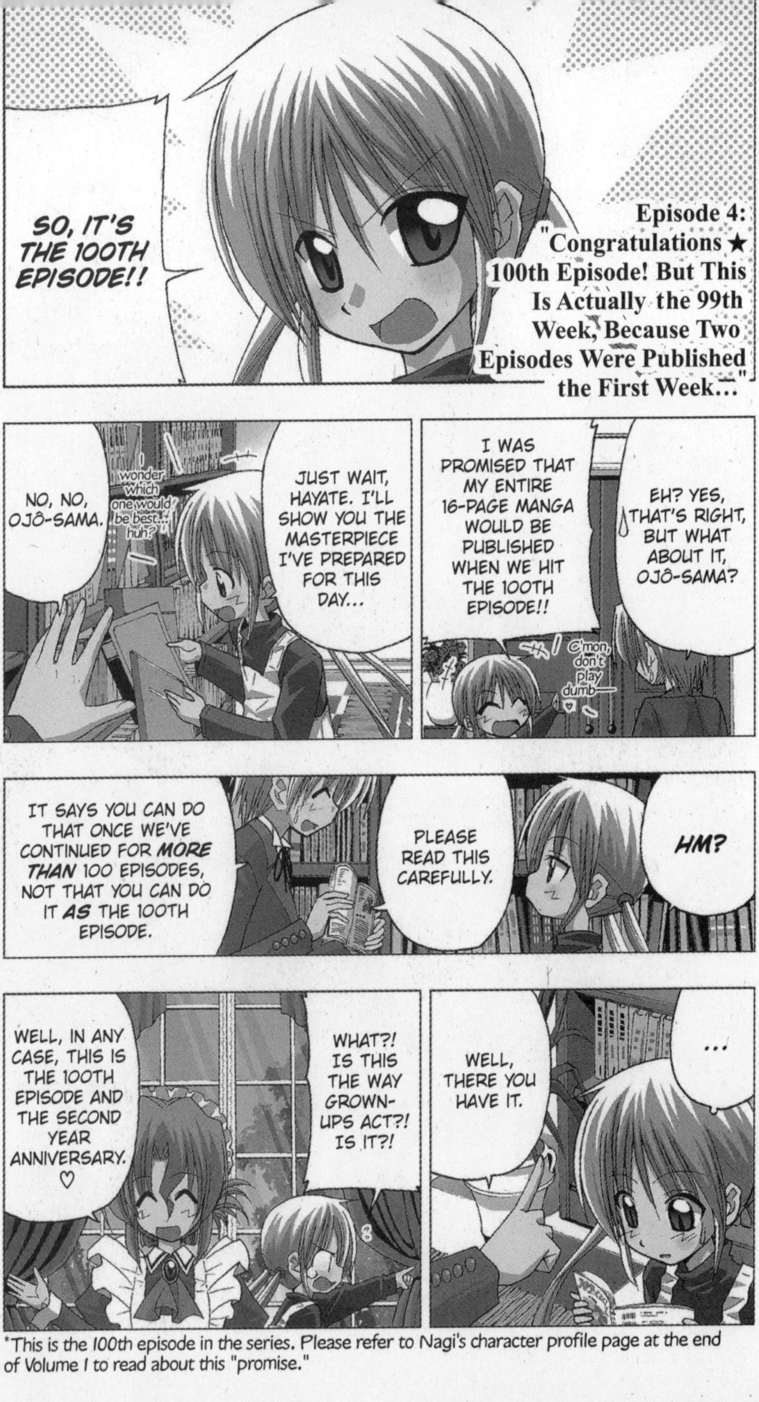
Episode 4: "Congratulations ★ 100th Episode! But This Is Actually the 99th Week, Because Two Episodes Were Published the First Week..."
SO, IT'S THE 100TH EPISODE!!
EH? YES, THAT'S RIGHT, BUT WHAT ABOUT IT, OJÔ-SAMA?
I WAS PROMISED THAT MY ENTIRE 16-PAGE MANGA WOULD BE PUBLISHED WHEN WE HIT THE 100TH EPISODE!!
C'mon, don't play dumb— ♡
JUST WAIT, HAYATE. I'LL SHOW YOU THE MASTERPIECE I'VE PREPARED FOR THIS DAY...
wonder which one would be best... huh?
NO, NO, OJÔ-SAMA.
HM?
PLEASE READ THIS CAREFULLY.
IT SAYS YOU CAN DO THAT ONCE WE'VE CONTINUED FOR MORE THAN 100 EPISODES, NOT THAT YOU CAN DO IT AS THE 100TH EPISODE.
...
WELL, THERE YOU HAVE IT.
WHAT?! IS THIS THE WAY GROWN-UPS ACT?! IS IT?!
WELL, IN ANY CASE, THIS IS THE 100TH EPISODE AND THE SECOND YEAR ANNIVERSARY. ♡

*This is the 100th episode in the series. Please refer to Nagi's character profile page at the end of Volume 1 to read about this "promise."

But This Is Actually the 99th Published the First Week..."

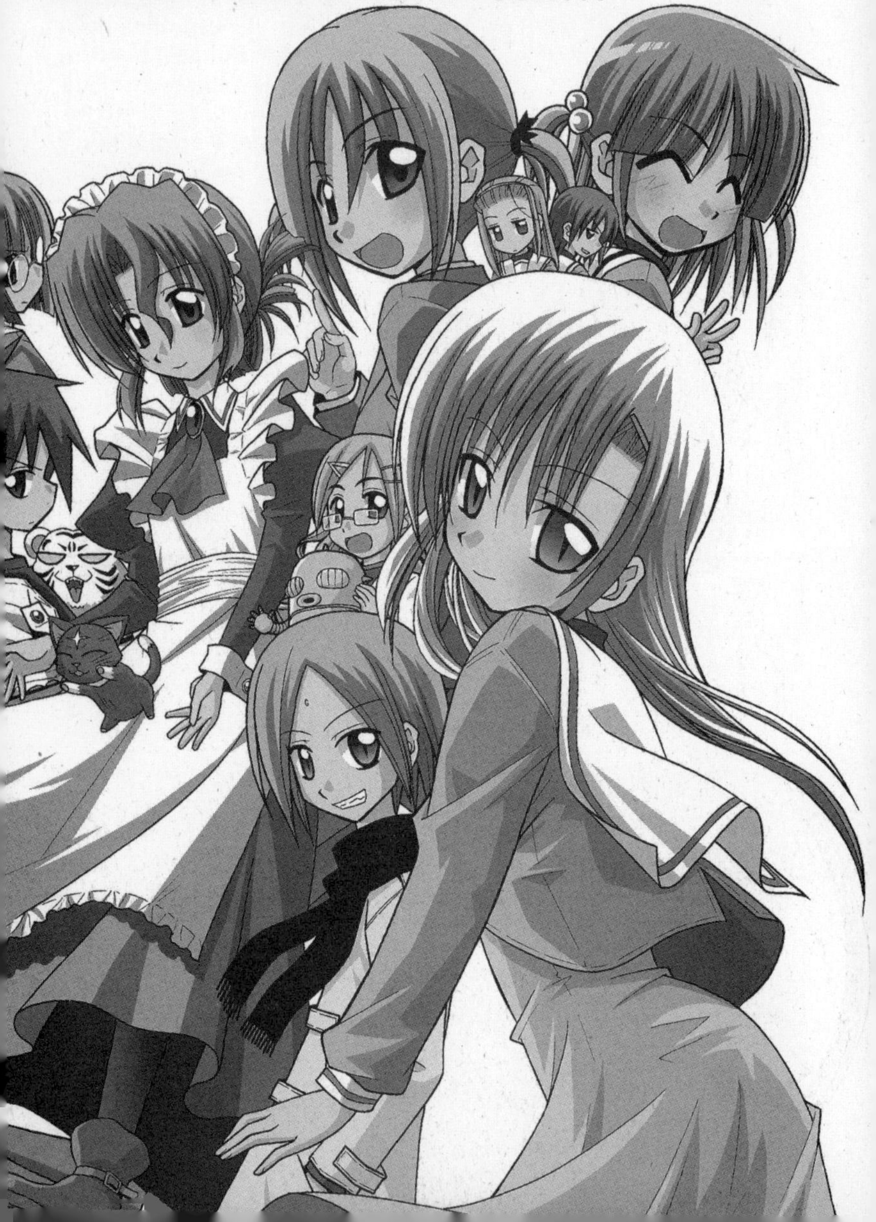

Episode 4:
"Congratulations ★100th Episode! Week, Because Two Episodes Were

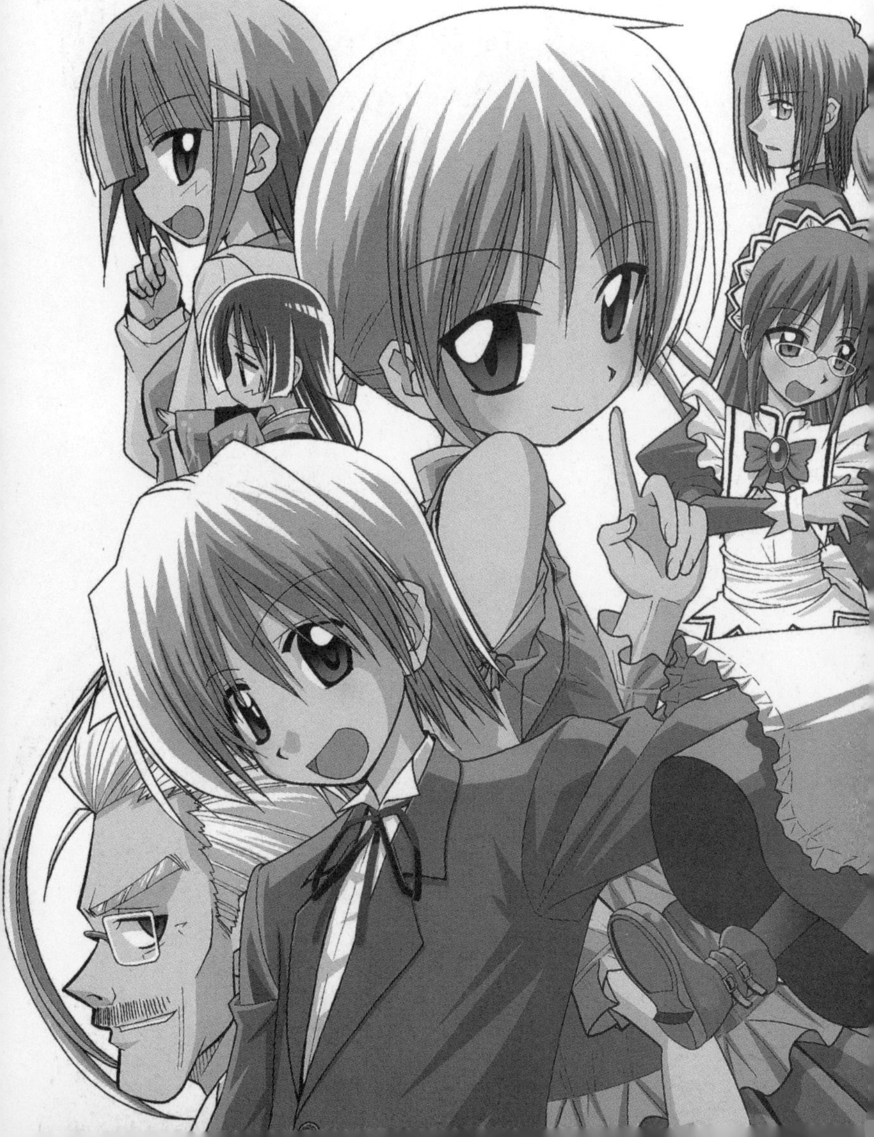

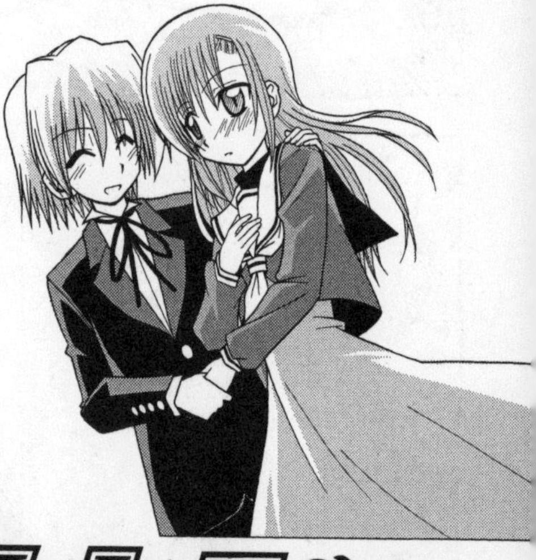

ハヤテのごとく!
Hayate the combat butler

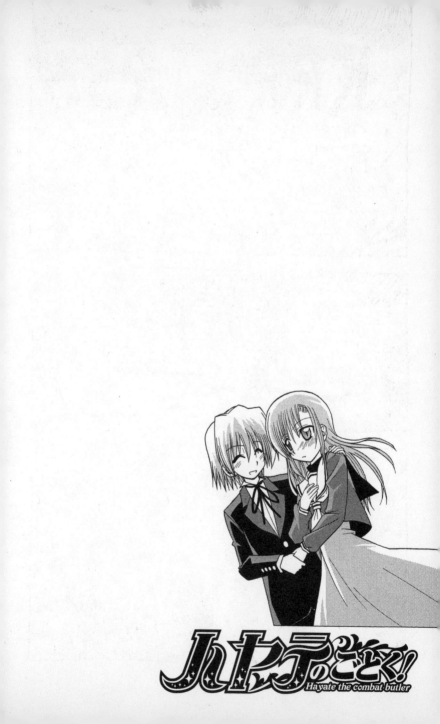

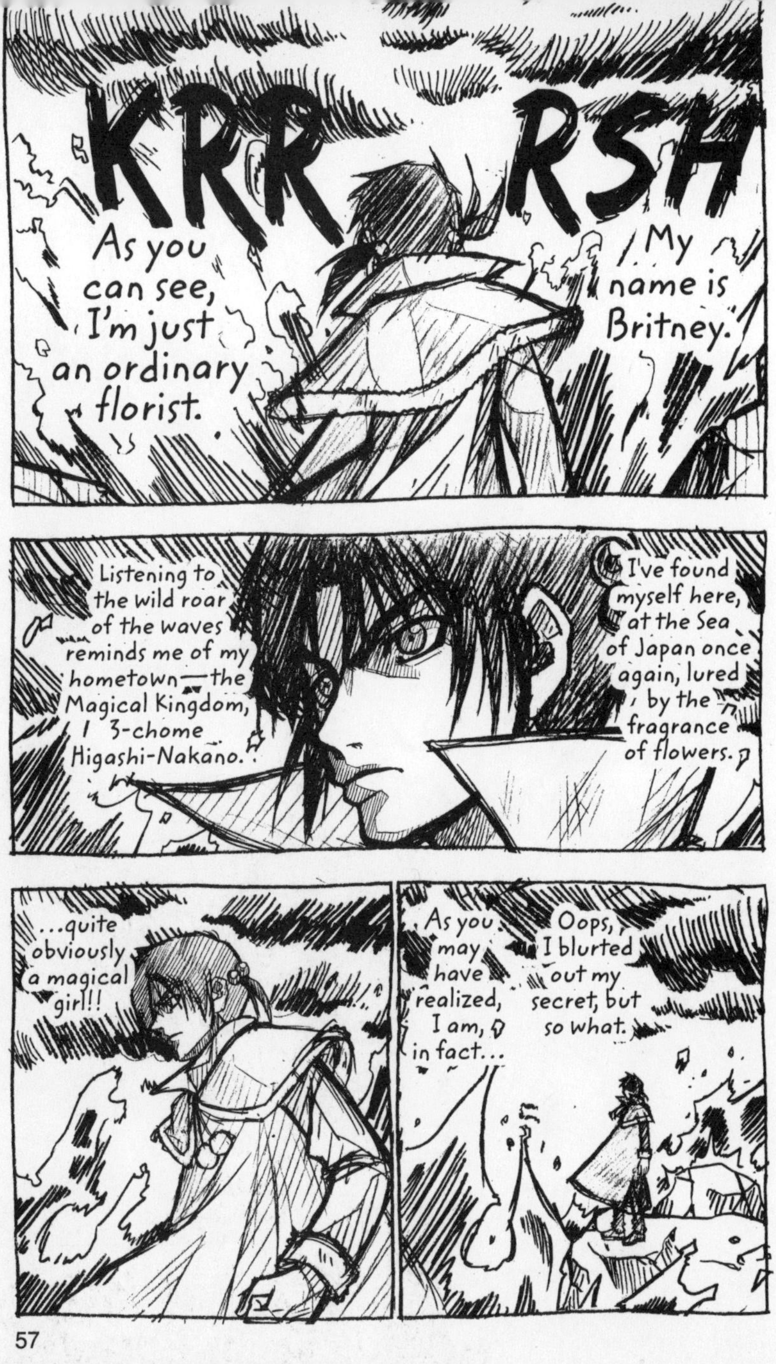

KRR RSH
My name is Britney.
As you can see, I'm just an ordinary florist.
I've found myself here, at the Sea of Japan once again, lured by the fragrance of flowers.
Listening to the wild roar of the waves reminds me of my hometown—the Magical Kingdom, 1 3-chome Higashi-Nakano.
Oops, I blurted out my secret, but so what.
As you may have realized, I am, in fact...
...quite obviously a magical girl!!

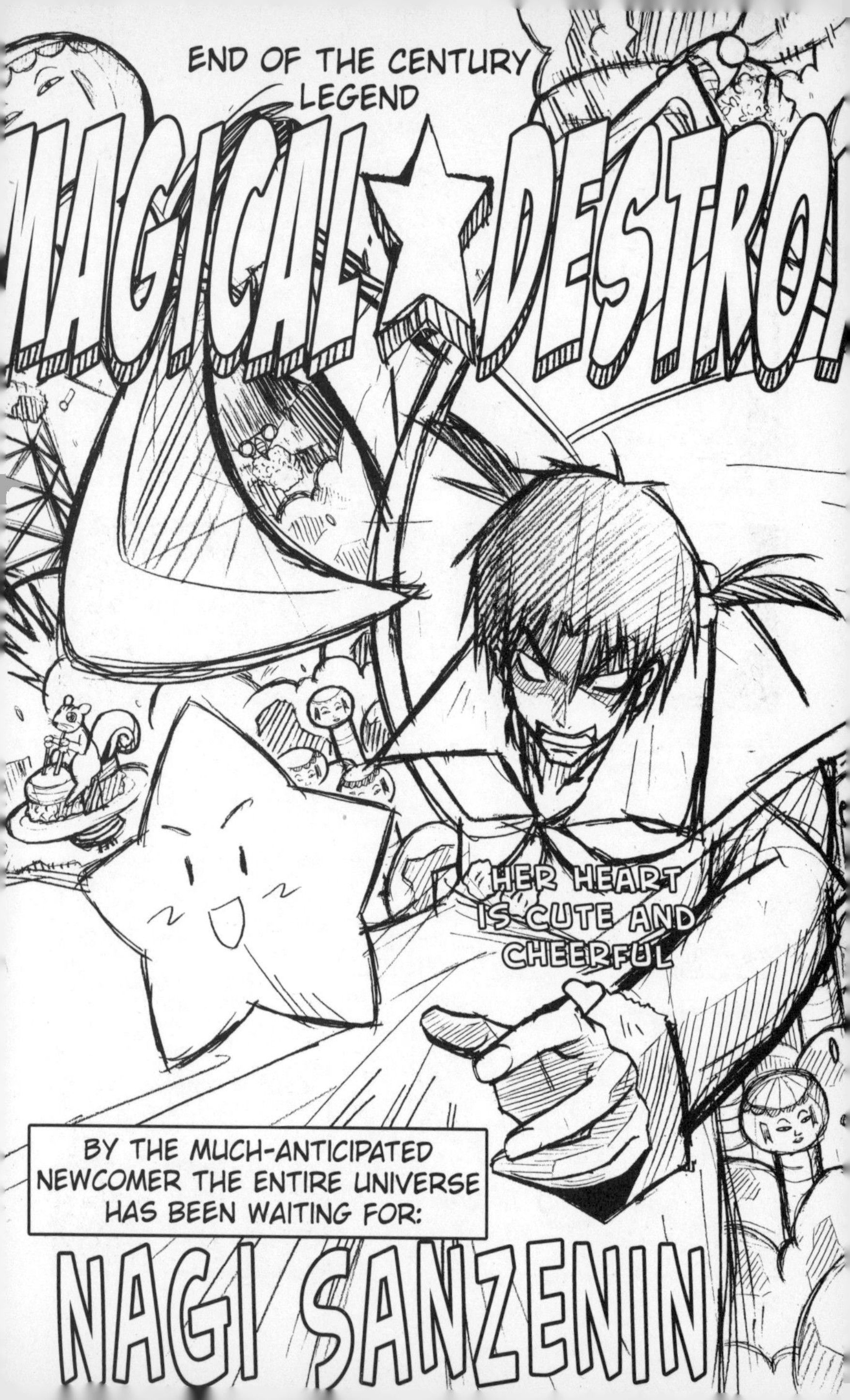
END OF THE CENTURY LEGEND
MAGICAL☆DESTRO
HER HEART IS CUTE AND CHEERFUL
BY THE MUCH-ANTICIPATED NEWCOMER THE ENTIRE UNIVERSE HAS BEEN WAITING FOR:
NAGI SANZENIN

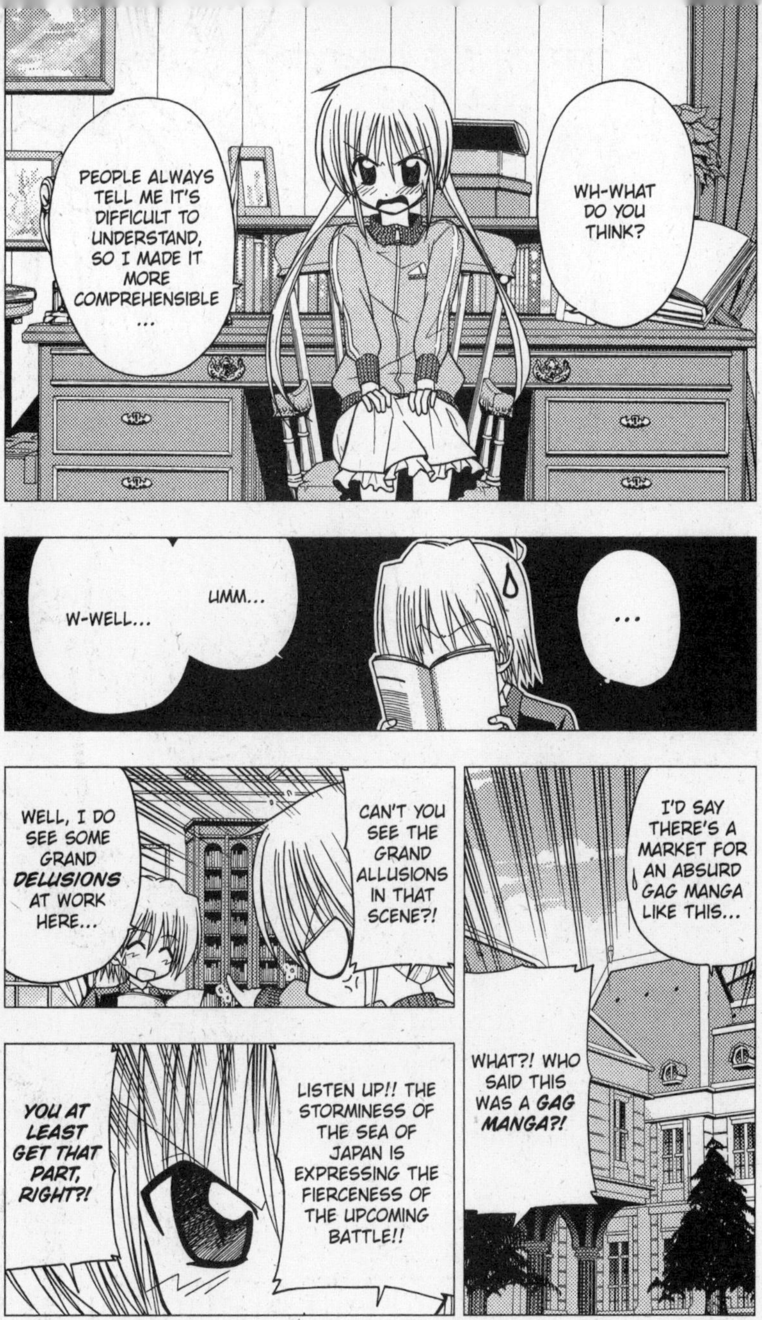
WH-WHAT DO YOU THINK?
PEOPLE ALWAYS TELL ME IT'S DIFFICULT TO UNDERSTAND, SO I MADE IT MORE COMPREHENSIBLE ...
...
UMM...
W-WELL...
I'D SAY THERE'S A MARKET FOR AN ABSURD GAG MANGA LIKE THIS...
WHAT?! WHO SAID THIS WAS A ***GAG MANGA***?!
CAN'T YOU SEE THE GRAND ALLUSIONS IN THAT SCENE?!
WELL, I DO SEE SOME GRAND ***DELUSIONS*** AT WORK HERE...
LISTEN UP!! THE STORMINESS OF THE SEA OF JAPAN IS EXPRESSING THE FIERCENESS OF THE UPCOMING BATTLE!!
YOU AT LEAST GET THAT PART, RIGHT?!

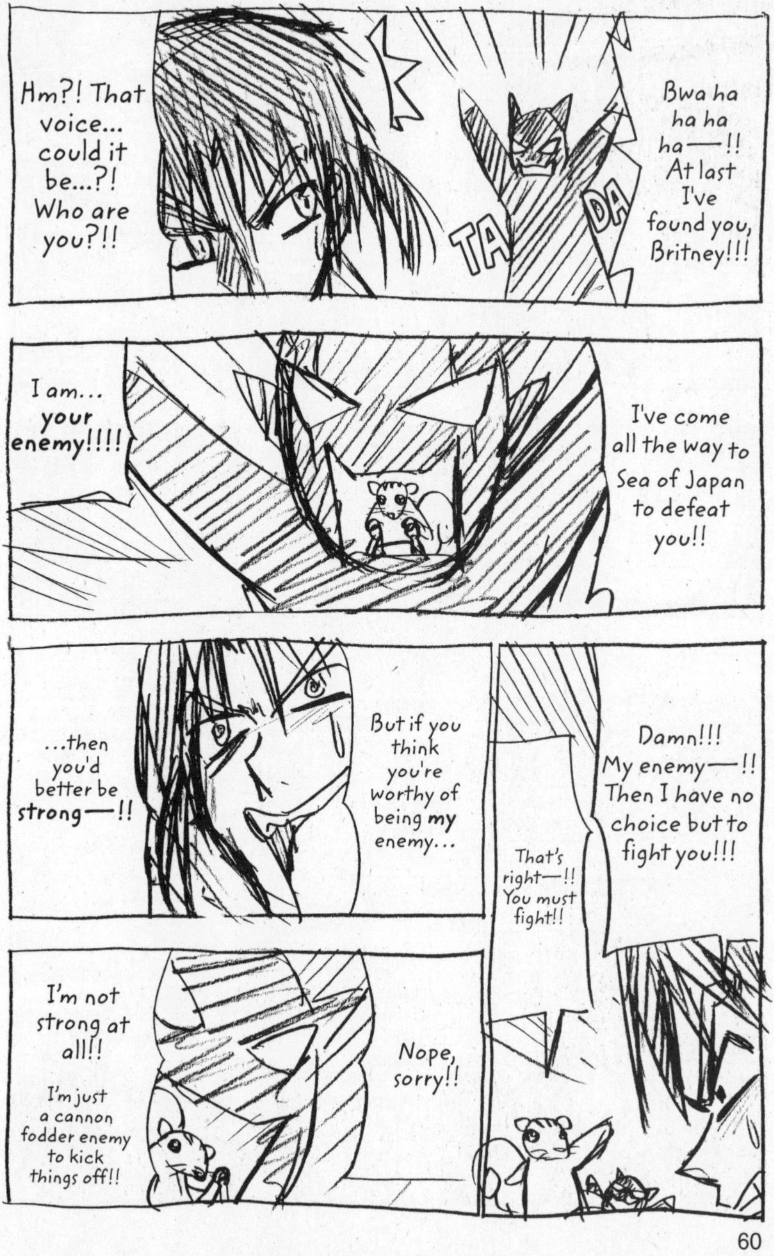
Bwa ha ha ha—!! At last I've found you, Britney!!!
TA DA
Hm?! That voice... could it be...?! Who are you?!!
I've come all the way to Sea of Japan to defeat you!!
I am... your enemy!!!!
Damn!!! My enemy—!! Then I have no choice but to fight you!!!
That's right—!! You must fight!!
But if you think you're worthy of being my enemy...
...then you'd better be strong—!!
Nope, sorry!!
I'm not strong at all!!
I'm just a cannon fodder enemy to kick things off!!

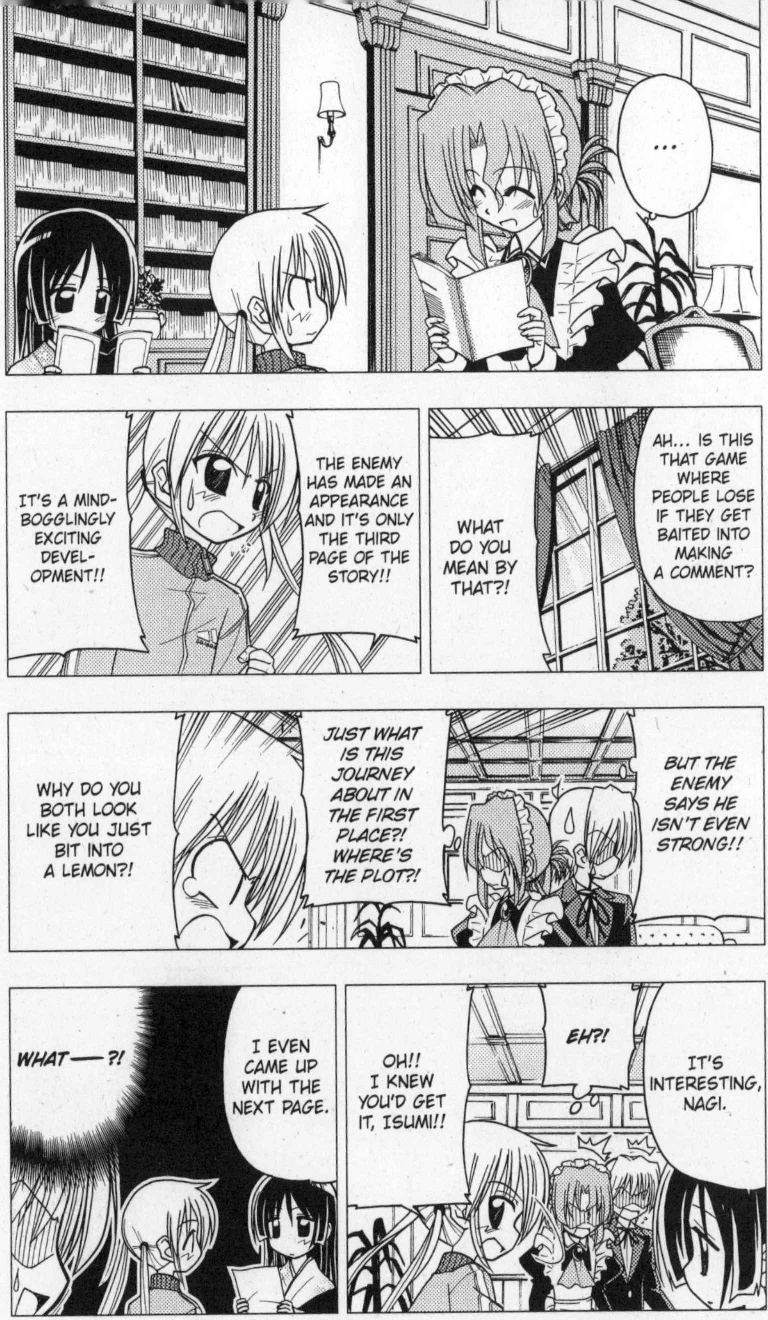
...
AH... IS THIS THAT GAME WHERE PEOPLE LOSE IF THEY GET BAITED INTO MAKING A COMMENT?
WHAT DO YOU MEAN BY THAT?!
THE ENEMY HAS MADE AN APPEARANCE AND IT'S ONLY THE THIRD PAGE OF THE STORY!!
IT'S A MIND-BOGGLINGLY EXCITING DEVEL-OPMENT!!
BUT THE ENEMY SAYS HE ISN'T EVEN STRONG!!
JUST WHAT IS THIS JOURNEY ABOUT IN THE FIRST PLACE?! WHERE'S THE PLOT?!
WHY DO YOU BOTH LOOK LIKE YOU JUST BIT INTO A LEMON?!
IT'S INTERESTING, NAGI.
EH?!
OH!! I KNEW YOU'D GET IT, ISUMI!!
I EVEN CAME UP WITH THE NEXT PAGE.
WHAT—?!

A KITTEN'S LIFE

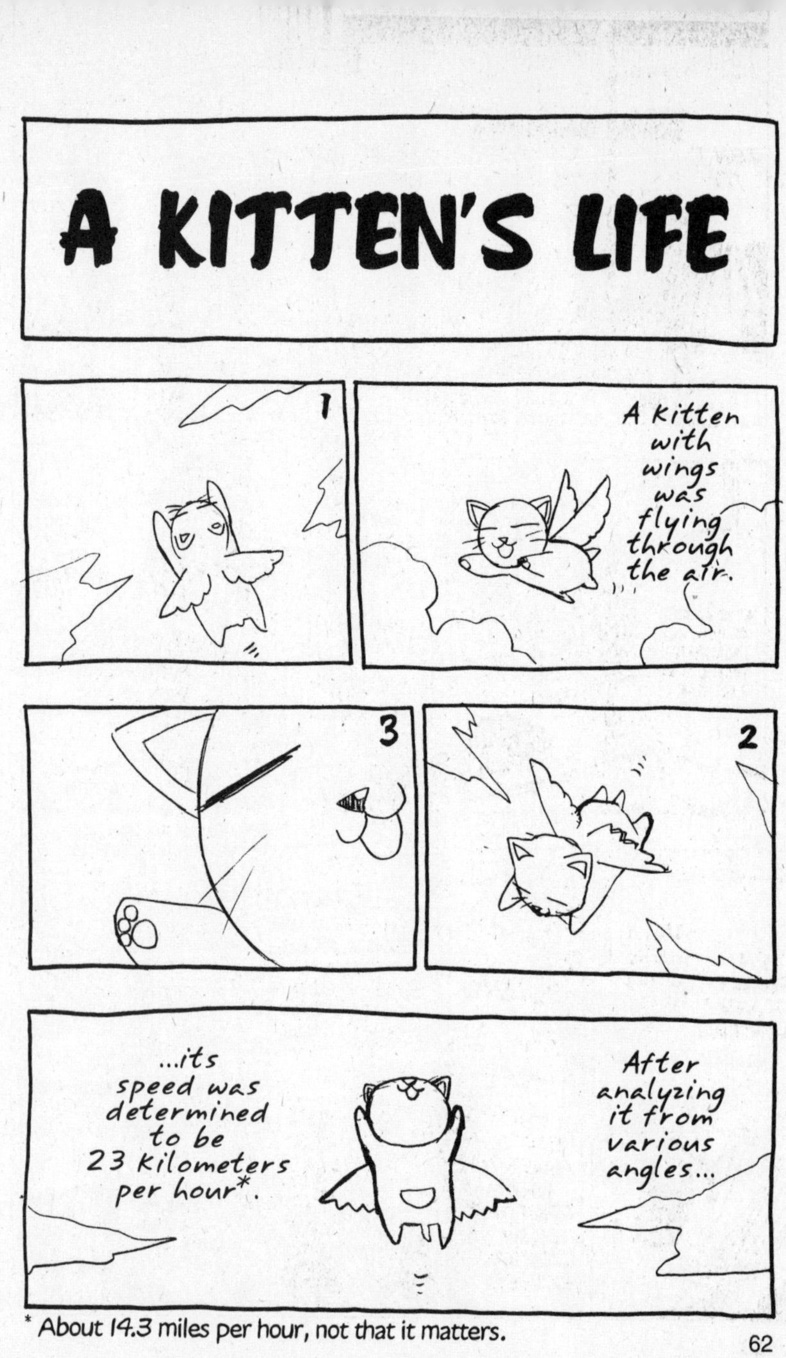
A kitten with wings was flying through the air.
1
2
3
After analyzing it from various angles...
...its speed was determined to be 23 kilometers per hour*.

* About 14.3 miles per hour, not that it matters.

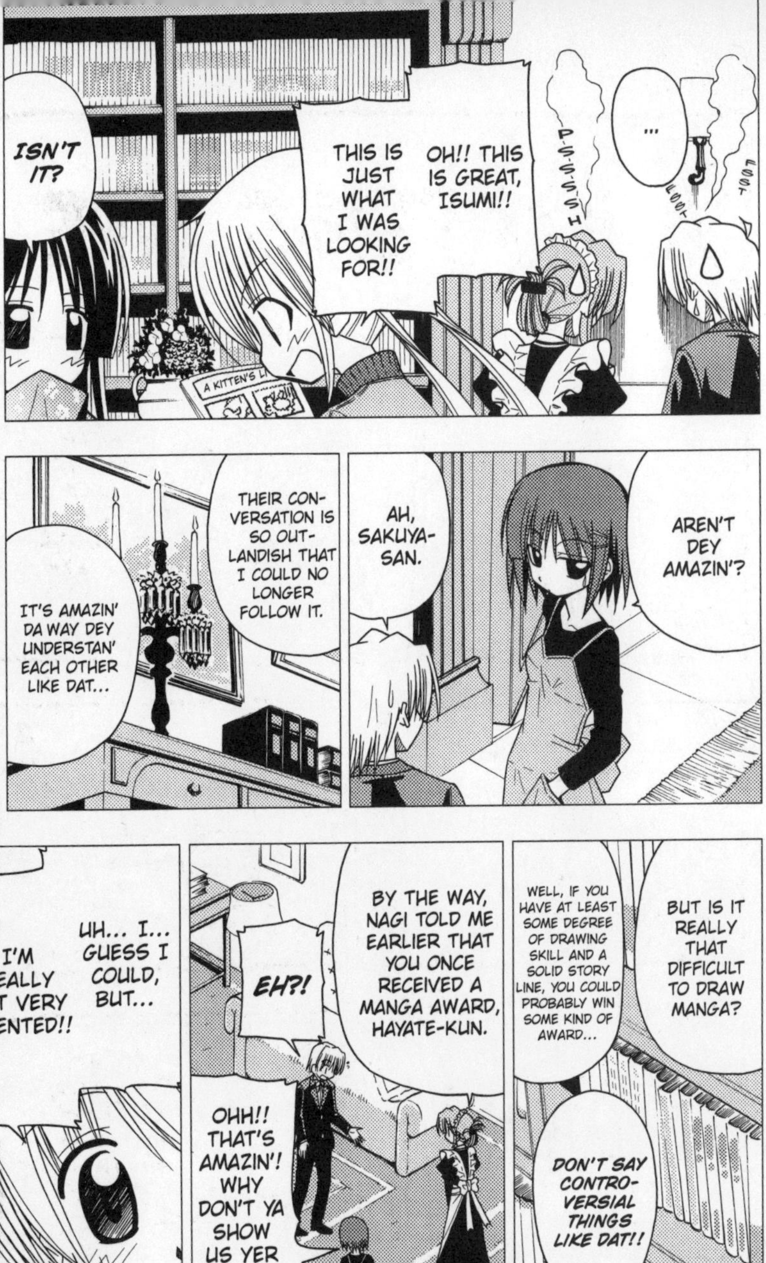
...
P-S-S-S-H
FSST
FSST
OH!! THIS IS GREAT, ISUMI!!
THIS IS JUST WHAT I WAS LOOKING FOR!!
A KITTEN'S LI
ISN'T IT?
AREN'T DEY AMAZIN'?
AH, SAKUYA-SAN.
THEIR CON-VERSATION IS SO OUT-LANDISH THAT I COULD NO LONGER FOLLOW IT.
IT'S AMAZIN' DA WAY DEY UNDERSTAN' EACH OTHER LIKE DAT...
BUT IS IT REALLY THAT DIFFICULT TO DRAW MANGA?
WELL, IF YOU HAVE AT LEAST SOME DEGREE OF DRAWING SKILL AND A SOLID STORY LINE, YOU COULD PROBABLY WIN SOME KIND OF AWARD...
DON'T SAY CONTRO-VERSIAL THINGS LIKE DAT!!
BY THE WAY, NAGI TOLD ME EARLIER THAT YOU ONCE RECEIVED A MANGA AWARD, HAYATE-KUN.
EH?!
OHH!! THAT'S AMAZIN'! WHY DON'T YA SHOW US YER SKILLS!!
UH... I... GUESS I COULD, BUT...
I'M REALLY NOT VERY TALENTED!!

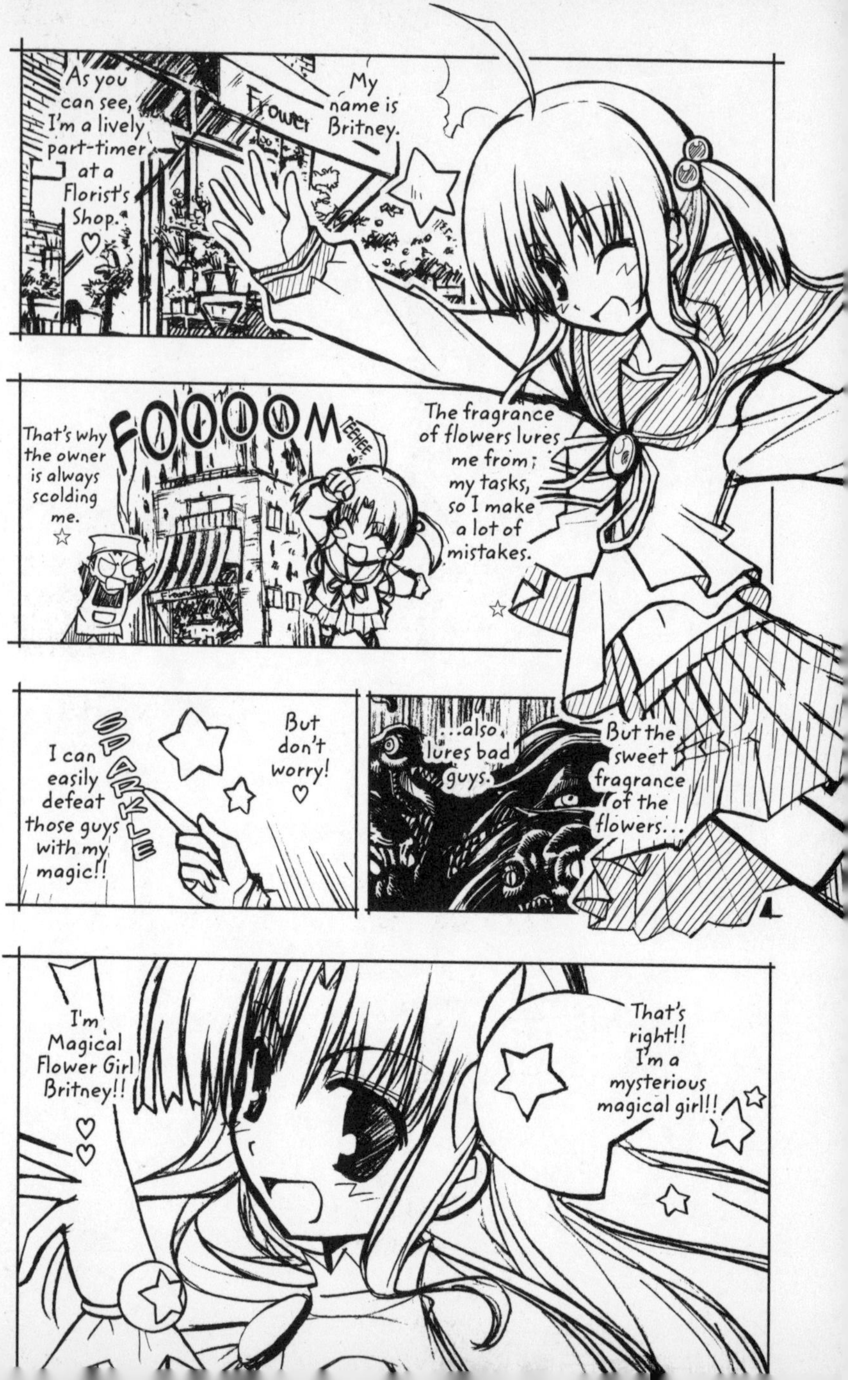
My name is Britney.
As you can see, I'm a lively part-timer at a Florist's Shop. ♡
The fragrance of flowers lures me from my tasks, so I make a lot of mistakes.
FOOOOM
TEEHEE
That's why the owner is always scolding me.
But the sweet fragrance of the flowers...
...also lures bad guys.
But don't worry! ♡
SPARKLE
I can easily defeat those guys with my magic!!
That's right!! I'm a mysterious magical girl!!
I'm Magical Flower Girl Britney!! ♡♡

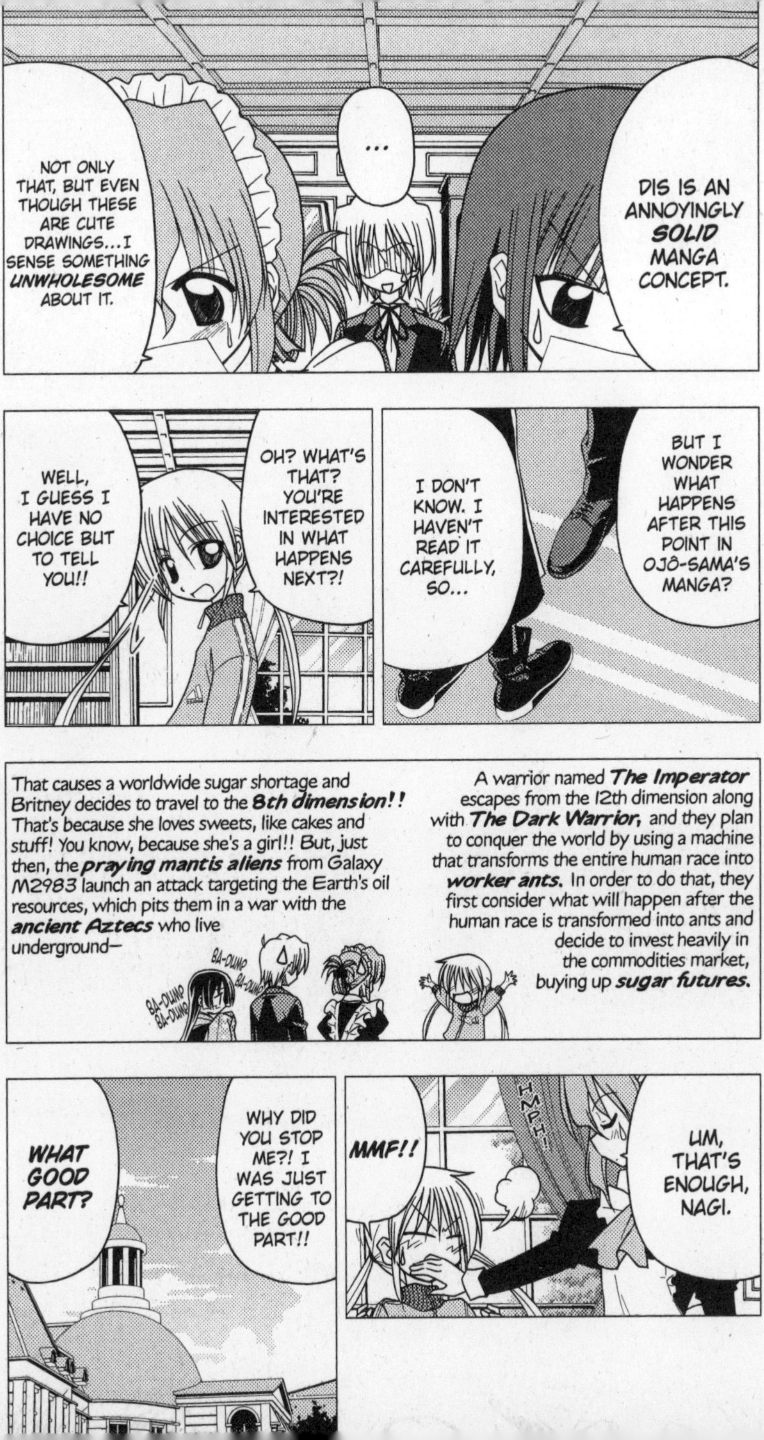
DIS IS AN ANNOYINGLY SOLID MANGA CONCEPT.
...
NOT ONLY THAT, BUT EVEN THOUGH THESE ARE CUTE DRAWINGS...I SENSE SOMETHING UNWHOLESOME ABOUT IT.
BUT I WONDER WHAT HAPPENS AFTER THIS POINT IN OJÔ-SAMA'S MANGA?
I DON'T KNOW. I HAVEN'T READ IT CAREFULLY, SO...
OH? WHAT'S THAT? YOU'RE INTERESTED IN WHAT HAPPENS NEXT?!
WELL, I GUESS I HAVE NO CHOICE BUT TO TELL YOU!!
A warrior named The Imperator escapes from the 12th dimension along with The Dark Warrior, and they plan to conquer the world by using a machine that transforms the entire human race into worker ants. In order to do that, they first consider what will happen after the human race is transformed into ants and decide to invest heavily in the commodities market, buying up sugar futures.
That causes a worldwide sugar shortage and Britney decides to travel to the 8th dimension!! That's because she loves sweets, like cakes and stuff! You know, because she's a girl!! But, just then, the praying mantis aliens from Galaxy M2983 launch an attack targeting the Earth's oil resources, which pits them in a war with the ancient Aztecs who live underground—
BA-DUMP BA-DUMP
BA-DUMP BA-DUMP
UM, THAT'S ENOUGH, NAGI.
HMPH!
MMF!!
WHY DID YOU STOP ME?! I WAS JUST GETTING TO THE GOOD PART!!
WHAT GOOD PART?

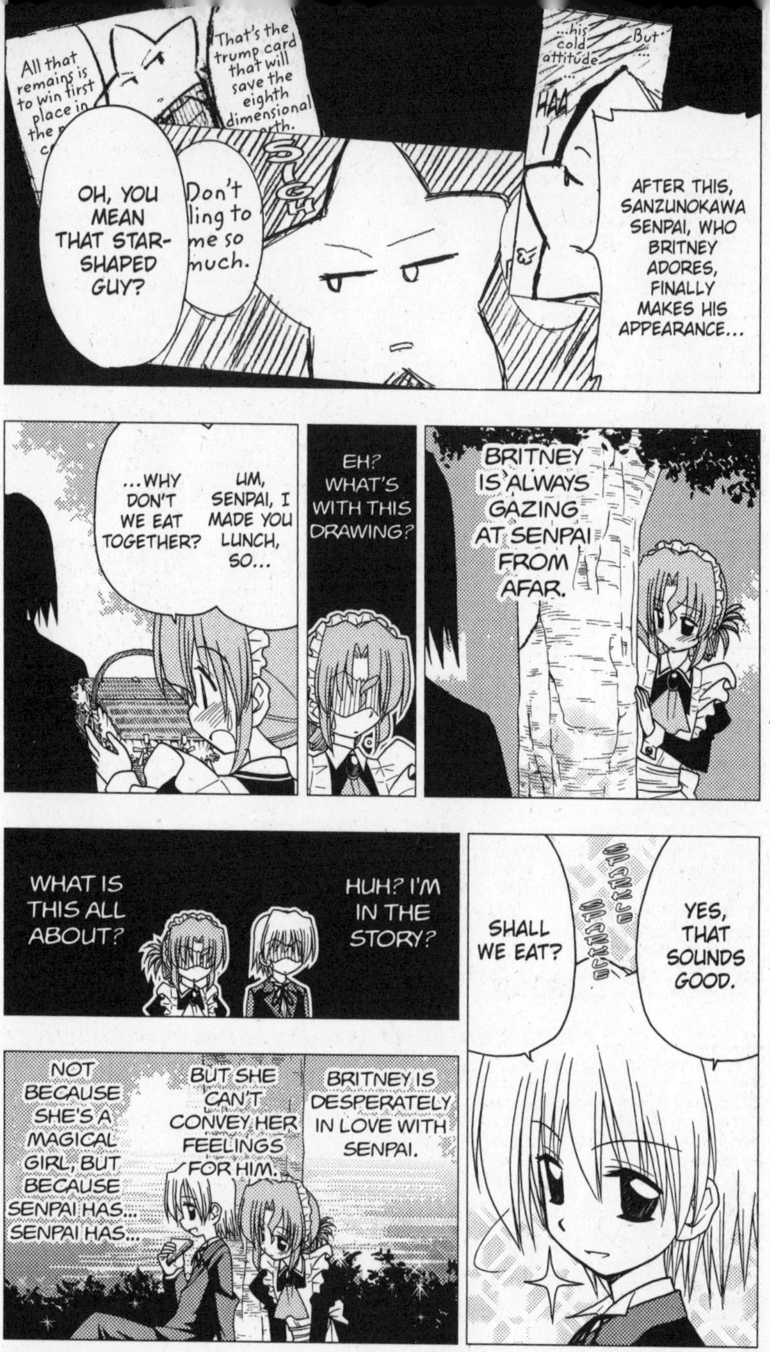
But...
...his cold attitude...
HAA
AFTER THIS, SANZUNOKAWA SENPAI, WHO BRITNEY ADORES, FINALLY MAKES HIS APPEARANCE...
SIGH
Don't cling to me so much.
That's the trump card that will save the eighth dimensional earth.
All that remains is to win first place in the
OH, YOU MEAN THAT STAR-SHAPED GUY?
BRITNEY IS ALWAYS GAZING AT SENPAI FROM AFAR.
EH? WHAT'S WITH THIS DRAWING?
UM, SENPAI, I MADE YOU LUNCH, SO...
...WHY DON'T WE EAT TOGETHER?
YES, THAT SOUNDS GOOD.
SHALL WE EAT?
HUH? I'M IN THE STORY?
WHAT IS THIS ALL ABOUT?
BRITNEY IS DESPERATELY IN LOVE WITH SENPAI.
BUT SHE CAN'T CONVEY HER FEELINGS FOR HIM.
NOT BECAUSE SHE'S A MAGICAL GIRL, BUT BECAUSE SENPAI HAS... SENPAI HAS...

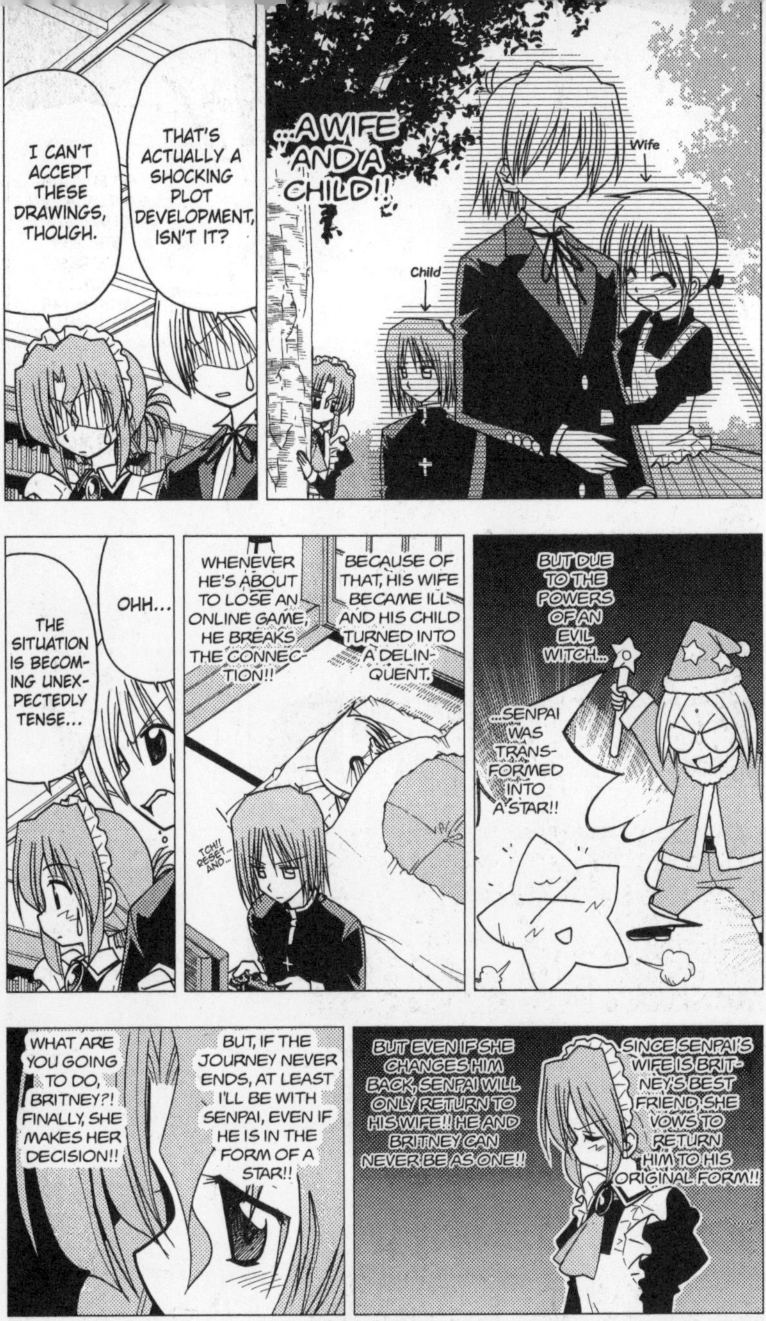

...A WIFE AND A CHILD!!
Wife
Child
THAT'S ACTUALLY A SHOCKING PLOT DEVELOPMENT, ISN'T IT?
I CAN'T ACCEPT THESE DRAWINGS, THOUGH.
BUT DUE TO THE POWERS OF AN EVIL WITCH...
...SENPAI WAS TRANSFORMED INTO A STAR!!
BECAUSE OF THAT, HIS WIFE BECAME ILL AND HIS CHILD TURNED INTO A DELINQUENT.
WHENEVER HE'S ABOUT TO LOSE AN ONLINE GAME, HE BREAKS THE CONNECTION!!
TCH!! RESET AND...
OHH...
THE SITUATION IS BECOMING UNEXPECTEDLY TENSE...
SINCE SENPAI'S WIFE IS BRITNEY'S BEST FRIEND, SHE VOWS TO RETURN HIM TO HIS ORIGINAL FORM!!
BUT EVEN IF SHE CHANGES HIM BACK, SENPAI WILL ONLY RETURN TO HIS WIFE!! HE AND BRITNEY CAN NEVER BE AS ONE!!
BUT, IF THE JOURNEY NEVER ENDS, AT LEAST I'LL BE WITH SENPAI, EVEN IF HE IS IN THE FORM OF A STAR!!
WHAT ARE YOU GOING TO DO, BRITNEY?! FINALLY, SHE MAKES HER DECISION!!

A KITTEN'S LIFE

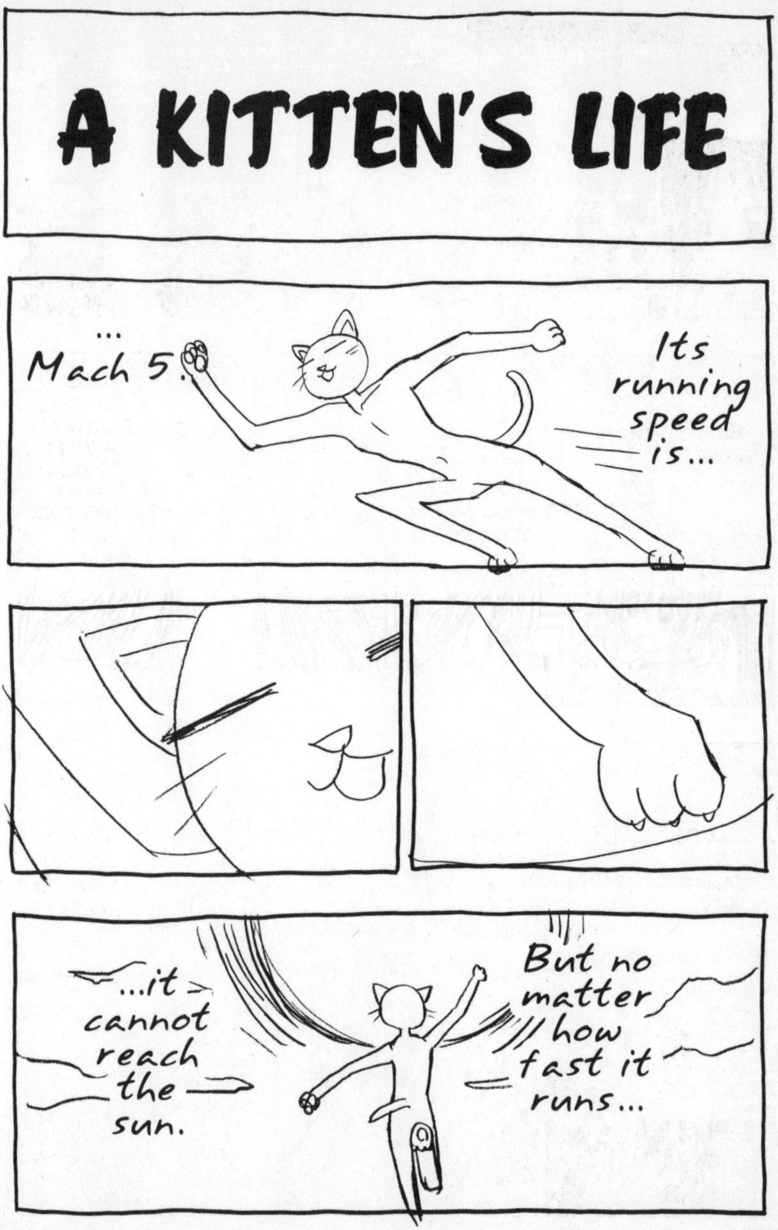
Its running speed is...
...Mach 5.
But no matter how fast it runs...
...it cannot reach the sun.

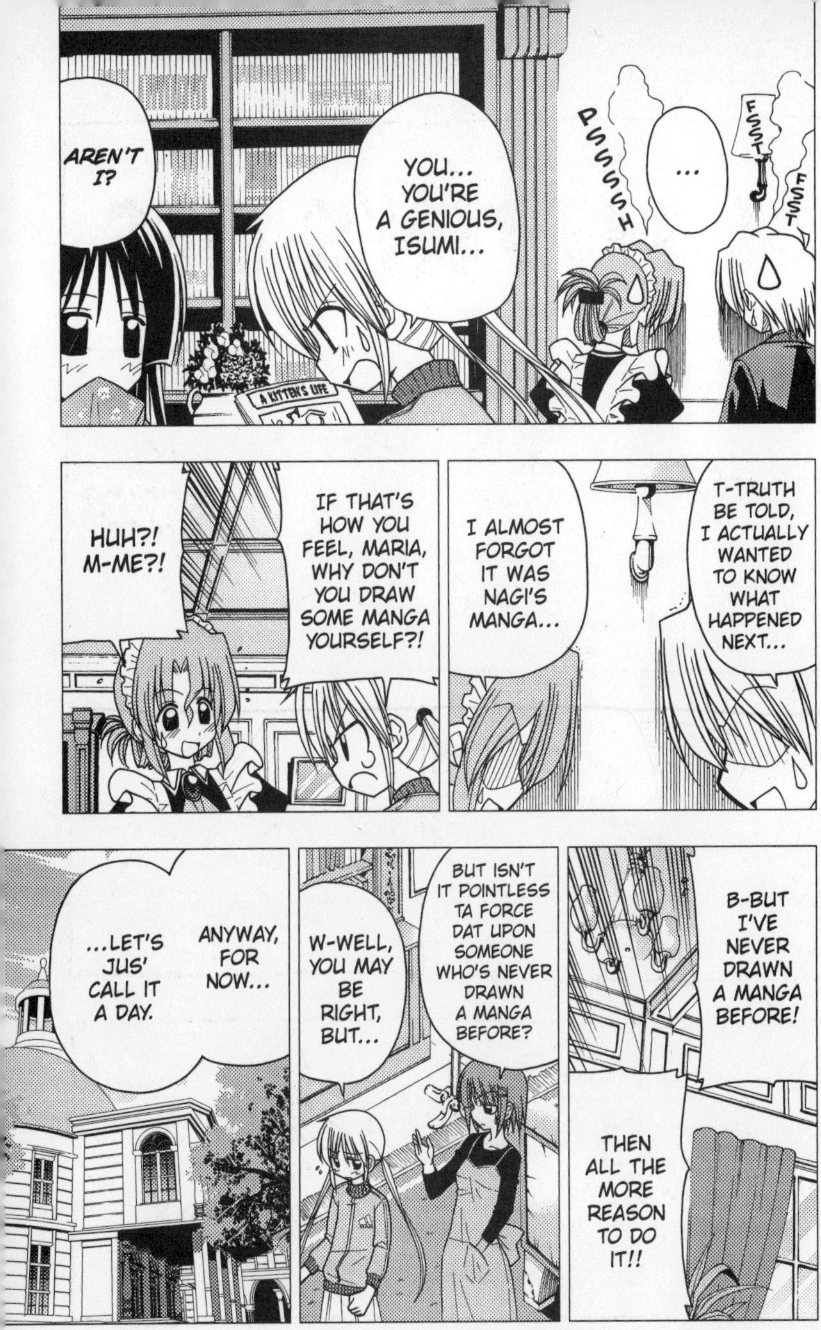
FSST
FSST
PSSSSH
...
YOU... YOU'RE A GENIOUS, ISUMI...
A KITTEN'S LIFE
AREN'T I?
T-TRUTH BE TOLD, I ACTUALLY WANTED TO KNOW WHAT HAPPENED NEXT...
I ALMOST FORGOT IT WAS NAGI'S MANGA...
IF THAT'S HOW YOU FEEL, MARIA, WHY DON'T YOU DRAW SOME MANGA YOURSELF?!
HUH?! M-ME?!
B-BUT I'VE NEVER DRAWN A MANGA BEFORE!
THEN ALL THE MORE REASON TO DO IT!!
BUT ISN'T IT POINTLESS TA FORCE DAT UPON SOMEONE WHO'S NEVER DRAWN A MANGA BEFORE?
W-WELL, YOU MAY BE RIGHT, BUT...
ANYWAY, FOR NOW...
...LET'S JUS' CALL IT A DAY.

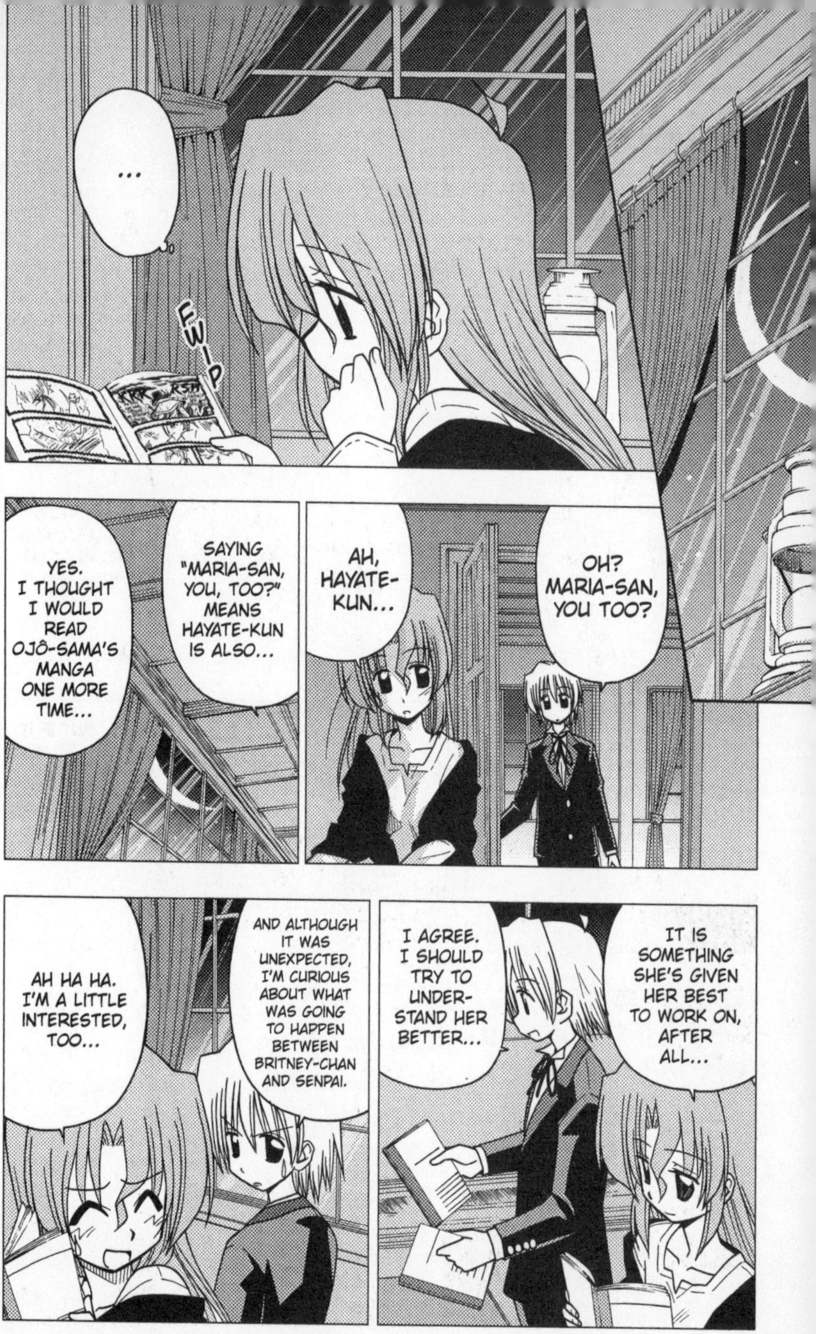
...
FWIP
OH? MARIA-SAN, YOU TOO?
AH, HAYATE-KUN...
SAYING "MARIA-SAN, YOU, TOO?" MEANS HAYATE-KUN IS ALSO...
YES. I THOUGHT I WOULD READ OJÔ-SAMA'S MANGA ONE MORE TIME...
IT IS SOMETHING SHE'S GIVEN HER BEST TO WORK ON, AFTER ALL...
I AGREE. I SHOULD TRY TO UNDER-STAND HER BETTER...
AND ALTHOUGH IT WAS UNEXPECTED, I'M CURIOUS ABOUT WHAT WAS GOING TO HAPPEN BETWEEN BRITNEY-CHAN AND SENPAI.
AH HA HA. I'M A LITTLE INTERESTED, TOO...

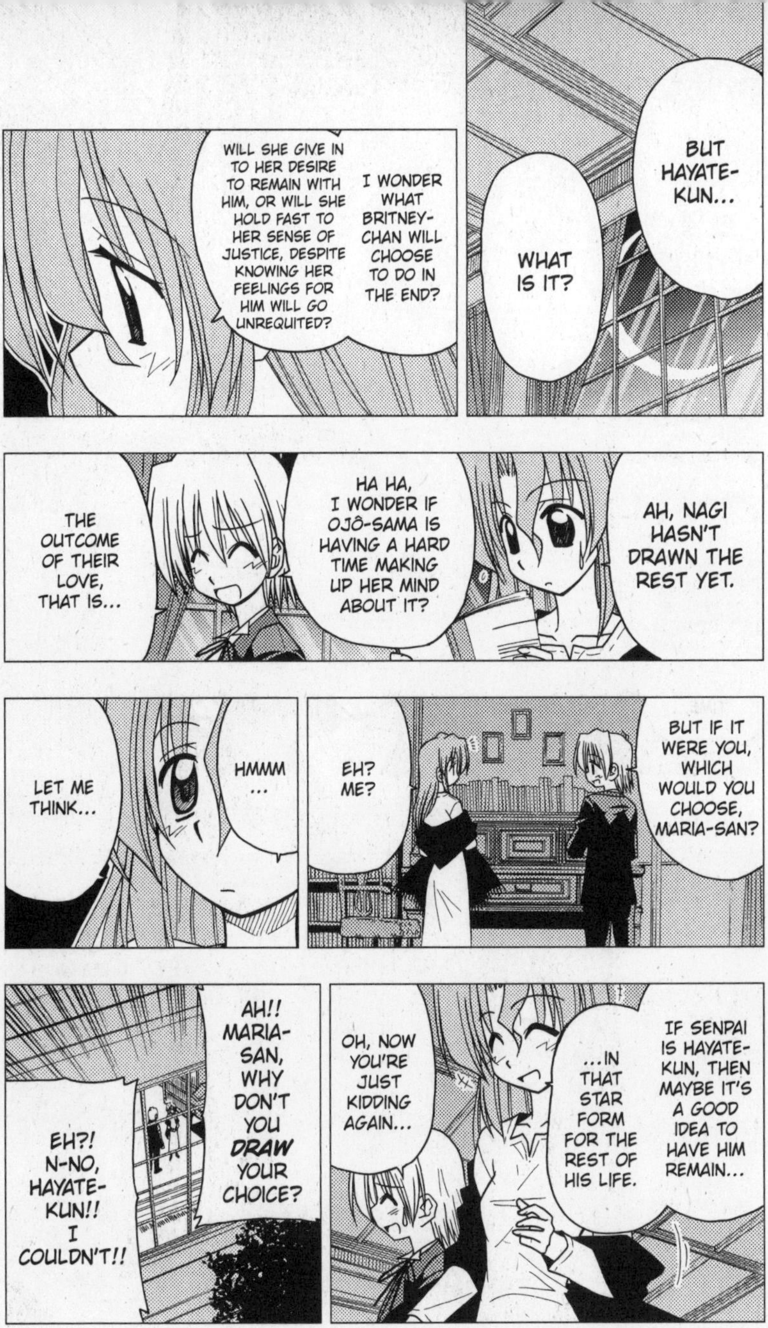
BUT HAYATE-KUN...
WHAT IS IT?
I WONDER WHAT BRITNEY-CHAN WILL CHOOSE TO DO IN THE END?
WILL SHE GIVE IN TO HER DESIRE TO REMAIN WITH HIM, OR WILL SHE HOLD FAST TO HER SENSE OF JUSTICE, DESPITE KNOWING HER FEELINGS FOR HIM WILL GO UNREQUITED?
AH, NAGI HASN'T DRAWN THE REST YET.
HA HA, I WONDER IF OJÔ-SAMA IS HAVING A HARD TIME MAKING UP HER MIND ABOUT IT?
THE OUTCOME OF THEIR LOVE, THAT IS...
BUT IF IT WERE YOU, WHICH WOULD YOU CHOOSE, MARIA-SAN?
EH? ME?
HMMM...
LET ME THINK...
IF SENPAI IS HAYATE-KUN, THEN MAYBE IT'S A GOOD IDEA TO HAVE HIM REMAIN...
...IN THAT STAR FORM FOR THE REST OF HIS LIFE.
OH, NOW YOU'RE JUST KIDDING AGAIN...
AH!! MARIA-SAN, WHY DON'T YOU *DRAW* YOUR CHOICE?
EH?! N-NO, HAYATE-KUN!! I COULDN'T!!

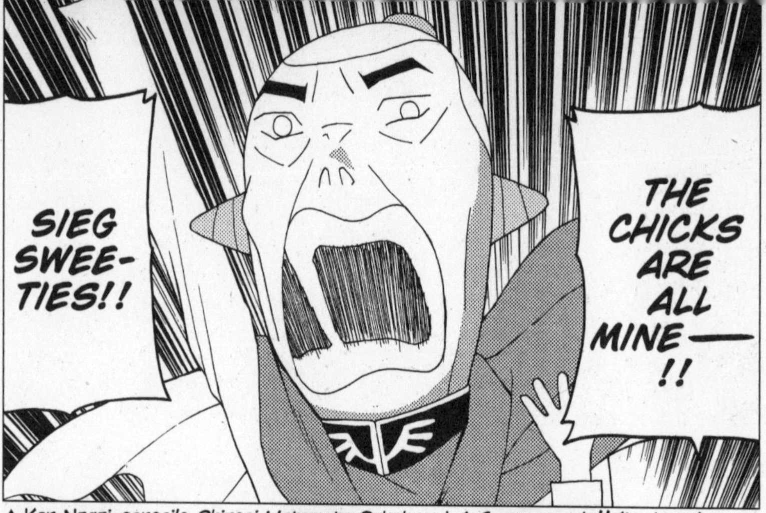
THE CHICKS ARE ALL MINE—!!
SIEG SWEETIES!!

▲ Ken Nagai-sensei's *Shinsei Motemote Oukoku* vol. 1-6 are on sale!! (in Japan)

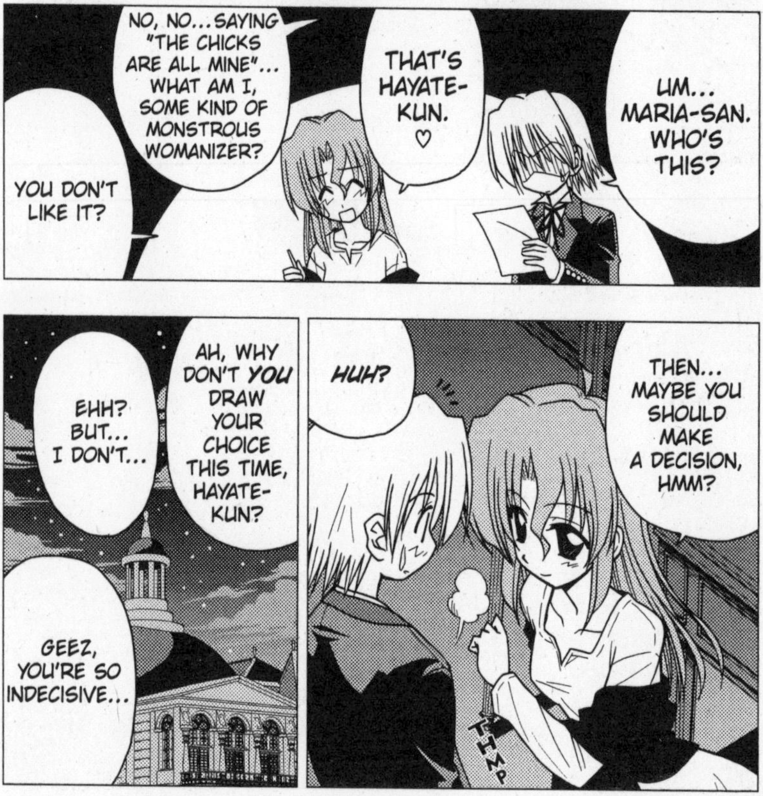
UM... MARIA-SAN. WHO'S THIS?
THAT'S HAYATE-KUN. ♡
NO, NO...SAYING "THE CHICKS ARE ALL MINE"... WHAT AM I, SOME KIND OF MONSTROUS WOMANIZER?
YOU DON'T LIKE IT?
THEN... MAYBE YOU SHOULD MAKE A DECISION, HMM?
HUH?
THMP
AH, WHY DON'T *YOU* DRAW YOUR CHOICE THIS TIME, HAYATE-KUN?
EHH? BUT... I DON'T...
GEEZ, YOU'RE SO INDECISIVE...

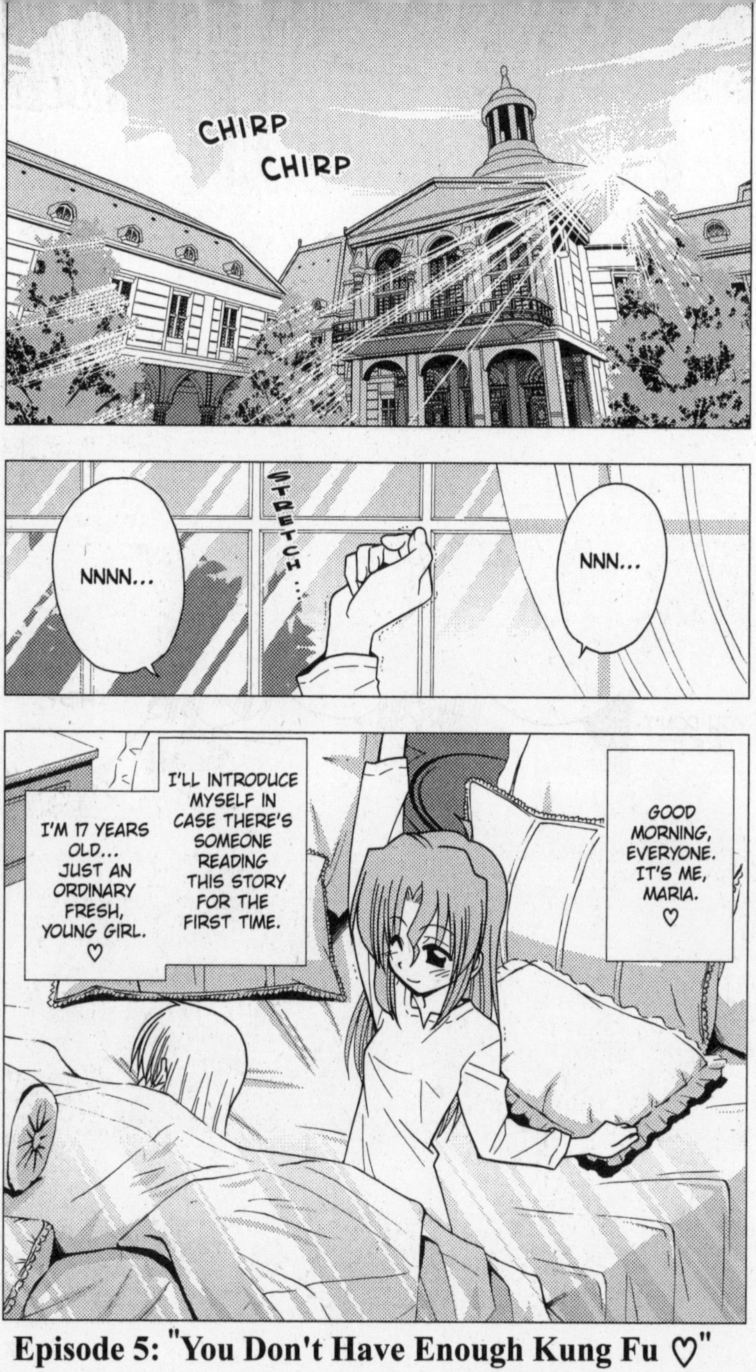
CHIRP
CHIRP
NNN...
STRETCH...
NNNN...
GOOD MORNING, EVERYONE. IT'S ME, MARIA. ♡
I'LL INTRODUCE MYSELF IN CASE THERE'S SOMEONE READING THIS STORY FOR THE FIRST TIME.
I'M 17 YEARS OLD... JUST AN ORDINARY FRESH, YOUNG GIRL. ♡

Episode 5: "You Don't Have Enough Kung Fu ♡"

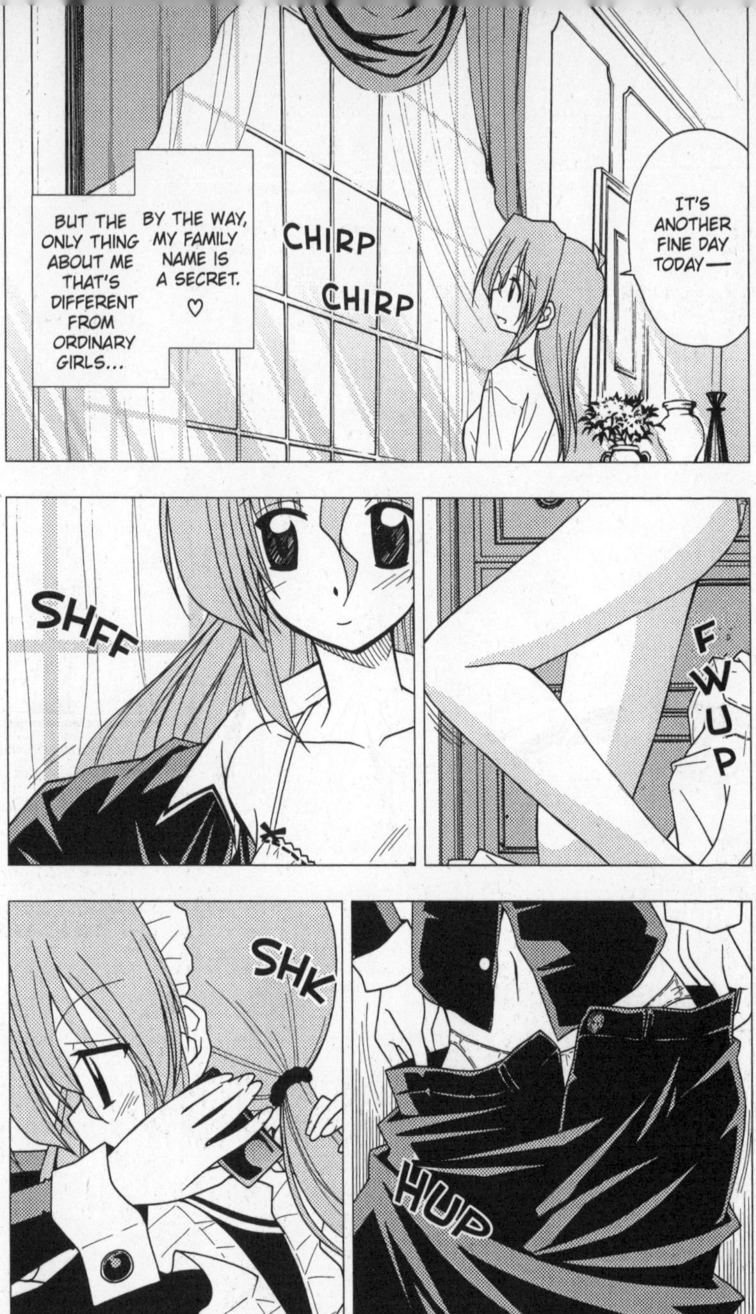
IT'S ANOTHER FINE DAY TODAY—
CHIRP
CHIRP
BY THE WAY, MY FAMILY NAME IS A SECRET. ♡
BUT THE ONLY THING ABOUT ME THAT'S DIFFERENT FROM ORDINARY GIRLS...
FWUP
SHFF
HUP
SHK

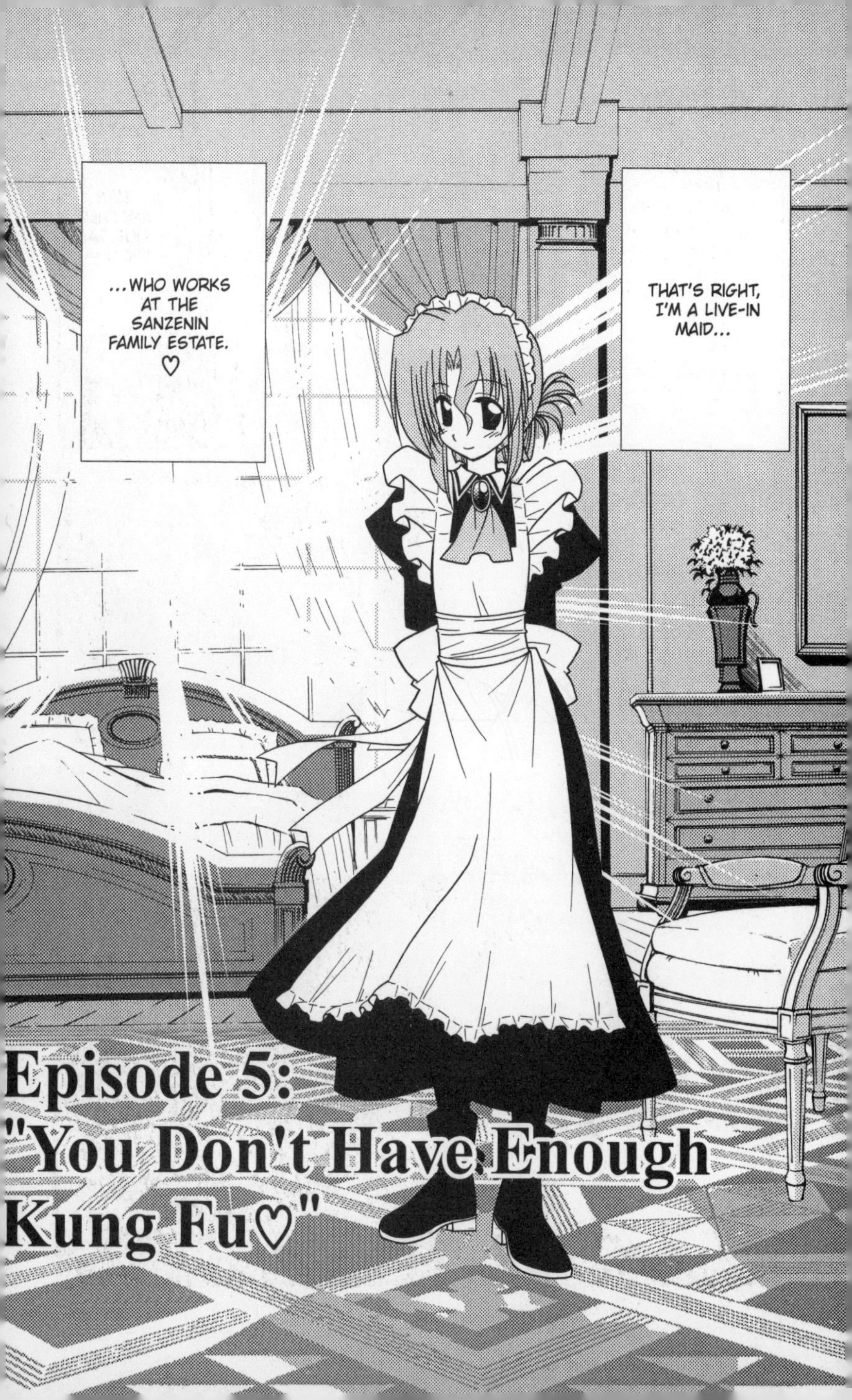
THAT'S RIGHT, I'M A LIVE-IN MAID...
...WHO WORKS AT THE SANZENIN FAMILY ESTATE. ♡

Episode 5: "You Don't Have Enough Kung Fu♡"

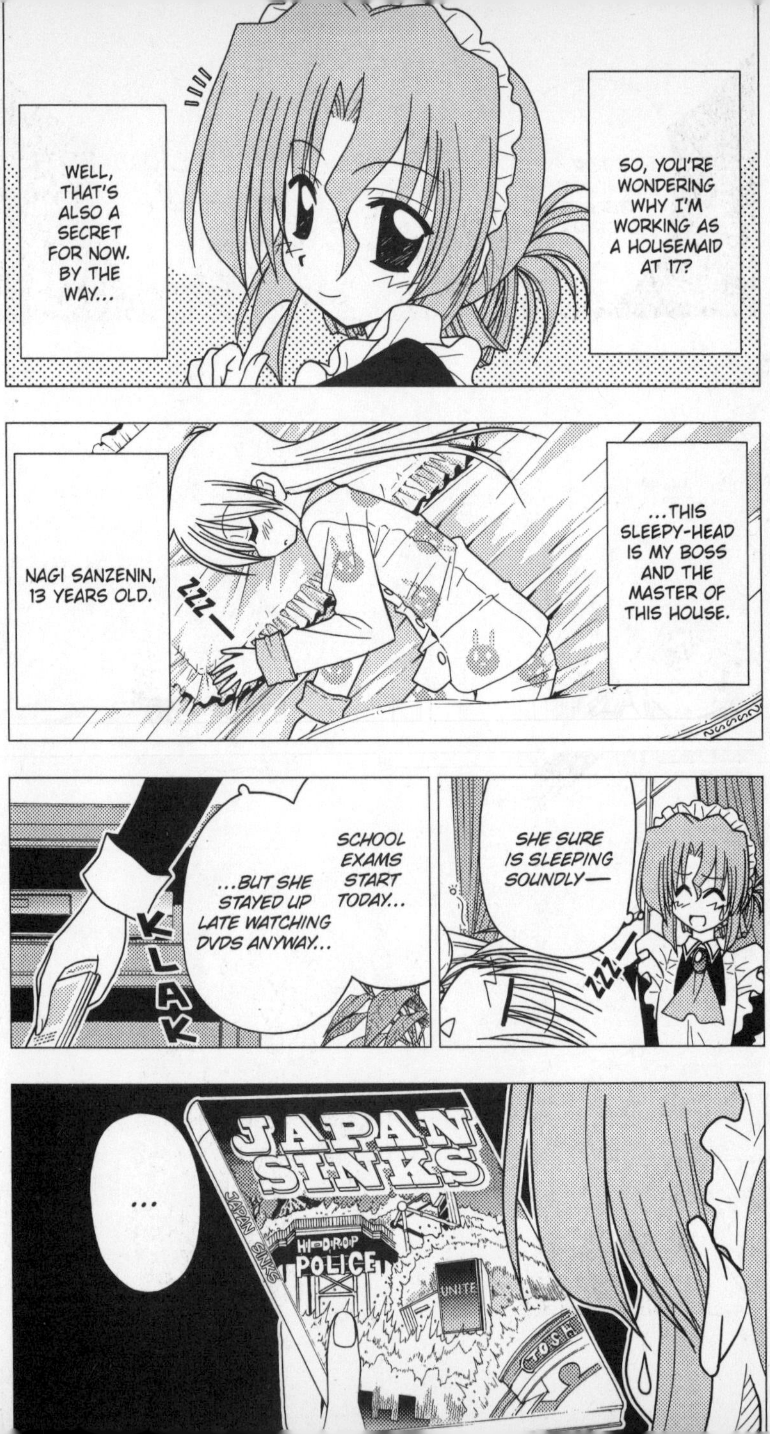
SO, YOU'RE WONDERING WHY I'M WORKING AS A HOUSEMAID AT 17?
WELL, THAT'S ALSO A SECRET FOR NOW. BY THE WAY...
...THIS SLEEPY-HEAD IS MY BOSS AND THE MASTER OF THIS HOUSE.
ZZZ—
NAGI SANZENIN, 13 YEARS OLD.
SHE SURE IS SLEEPING SOUNDLY—
ZZZ—
SCHOOL EXAMS START TODAY...
...BUT SHE STAYED UP LATE WATCHING DVDS ANYWAY...
KLAK
JAPAN SINKS
JAPAN SINKS
HI-DROP
POLICE
UNITE
...

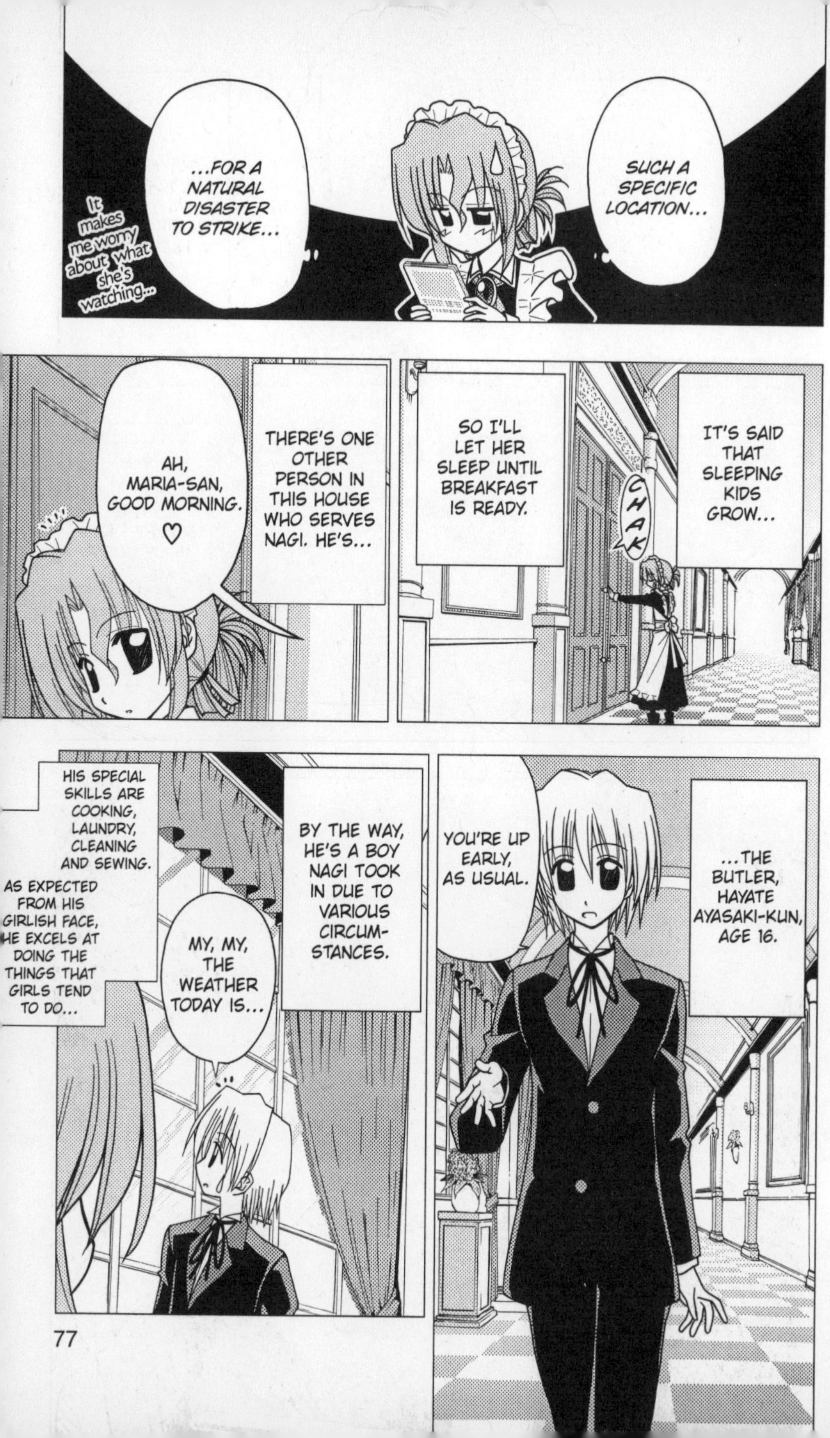
SUCH A SPECIFIC LOCATION...
...FOR A NATURAL DISASTER TO STRIKE...
It makes me worry about what she's watching...
IT'S SAID THAT SLEEPING KIDS GROW...
SO I'LL LET HER SLEEP UNTIL BREAKFAST IS READY.
CHAK
THERE'S ONE OTHER PERSON IN THIS HOUSE WHO SERVES NAGI. HE'S...
AH, MARIA-SAN, GOOD MORNING. ♡
...THE BUTLER, HAYATE AYASAKI-KUN, AGE 16.
YOU'RE UP EARLY, AS USUAL.
BY THE WAY, HE'S A BOY NAGI TOOK IN DUE TO VARIOUS CIRCUM-STANCES.
MY, MY, THE WEATHER TODAY IS...
HIS SPECIAL SKILLS ARE COOKING, LAUNDRY, CLEANING AND SEWING.
AS EXPECTED FROM HIS GIRLISH FACE, HE EXCELS AT DOING THE THINGS THAT GIRLS TEND TO DO...

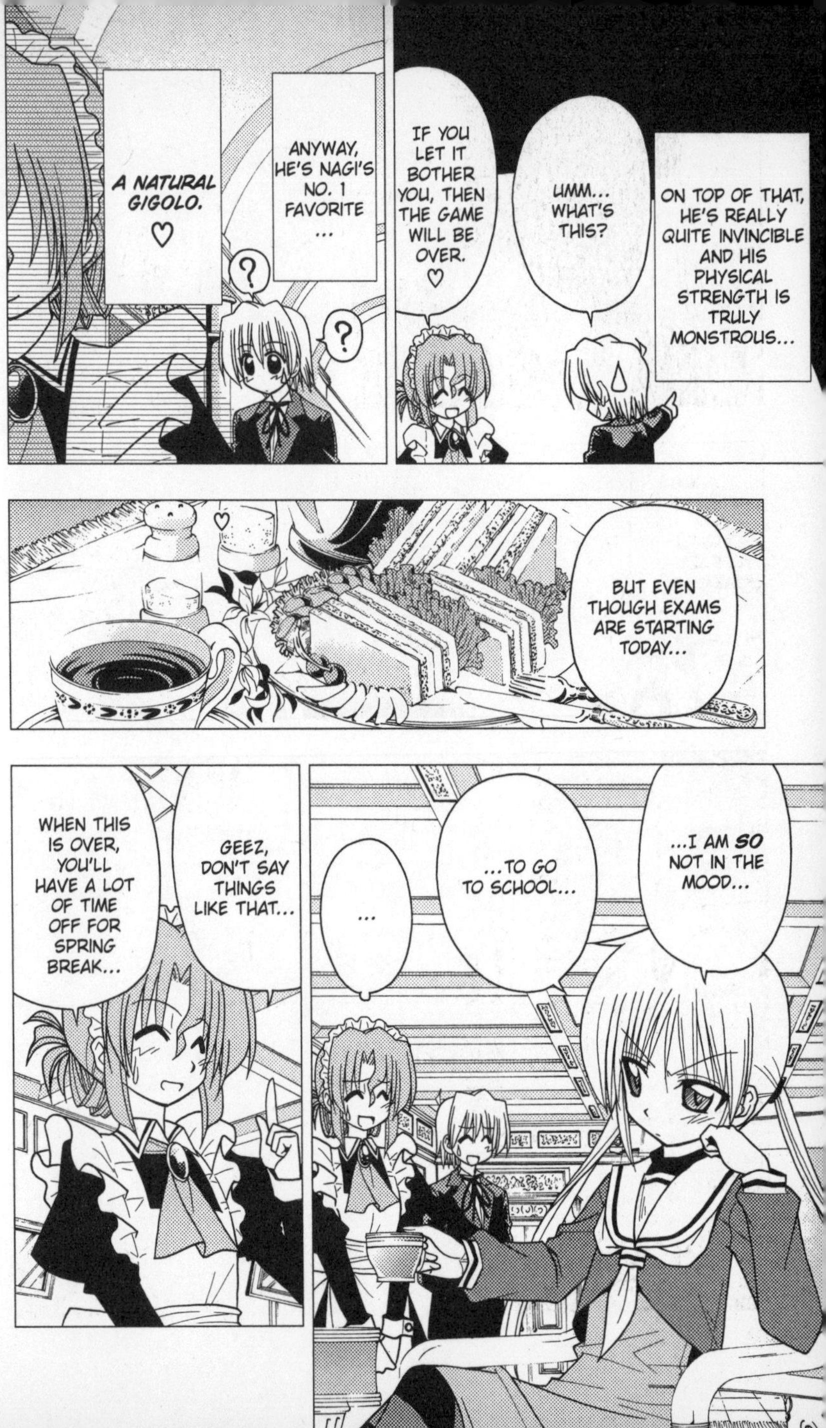
ON TOP OF THAT, HE'S REALLY QUITE INVINCIBLE AND HIS PHYSICAL STRENGTH IS TRULY MONSTROUS...
UMM... WHAT'S THIS?
IF YOU LET IT BOTHER YOU, THEN THE GAME WILL BE OVER. ♡
ANYWAY, HE'S NAGI'S NO. 1 FAVORITE ...
?
?
A NATURAL GIGOLO. ♡
BUT EVEN THOUGH EXAMS ARE STARTING TODAY...
...I AM **SO** NOT IN THE MOOD...
...TO GO TO SCHOOL...
...
GEEZ, DON'T SAY THINGS LIKE THAT...
WHEN THIS IS OVER, YOU'LL HAVE A LOT OF TIME OFF FOR SPRING BREAK...

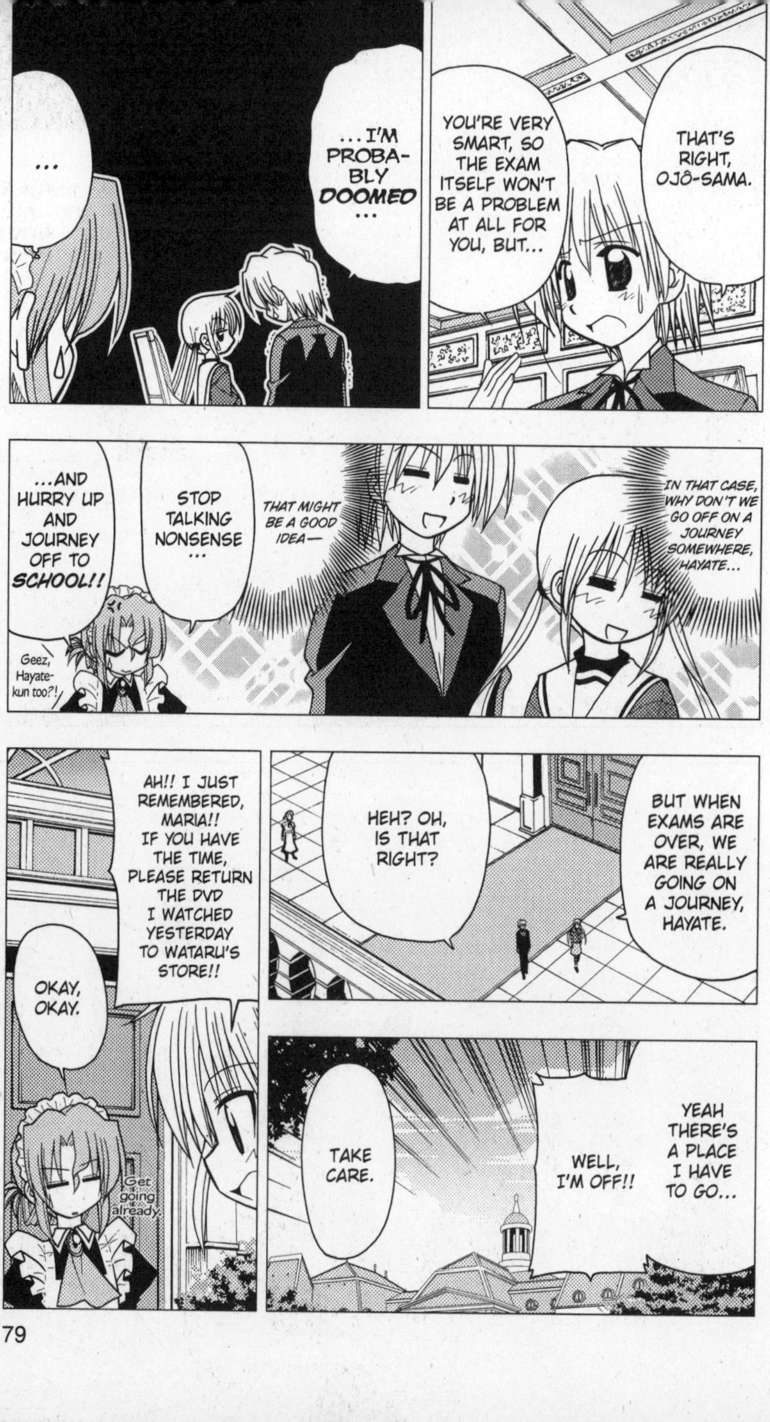
THAT'S RIGHT, OJÔ-SAMA.
YOU'RE VERY SMART, SO THE EXAM ITSELF WON'T BE A PROBLEM AT ALL FOR YOU, BUT...
...I'M PROBA-BLY DOOMED...
...
IN THAT CASE, WHY DON'T WE GO OFF ON A JOURNEY SOMEWHERE, HAYATE...
THAT MIGHT BE A GOOD IDEA—
STOP TALKING NONSENSE...
...AND HURRY UP AND JOURNEY OFF TO SCHOOL!!
Geez, Hayate-kun too?!
BUT WHEN EXAMS ARE OVER, WE ARE REALLY GOING ON A JOURNEY, HAYATE.
HEH? OH, IS THAT RIGHT?
YEAH THERE'S A PLACE I HAVE TO GO...
WELL, I'M OFF!!
TAKE CARE.
AH!! I JUST REMEMBERED, MARIA!! IF YOU HAVE THE TIME, PLEASE RETURN THE DVD I WATCHED YESTERDAY TO WATARU'S STORE!!
OKAY, OKAY.
Get going already.

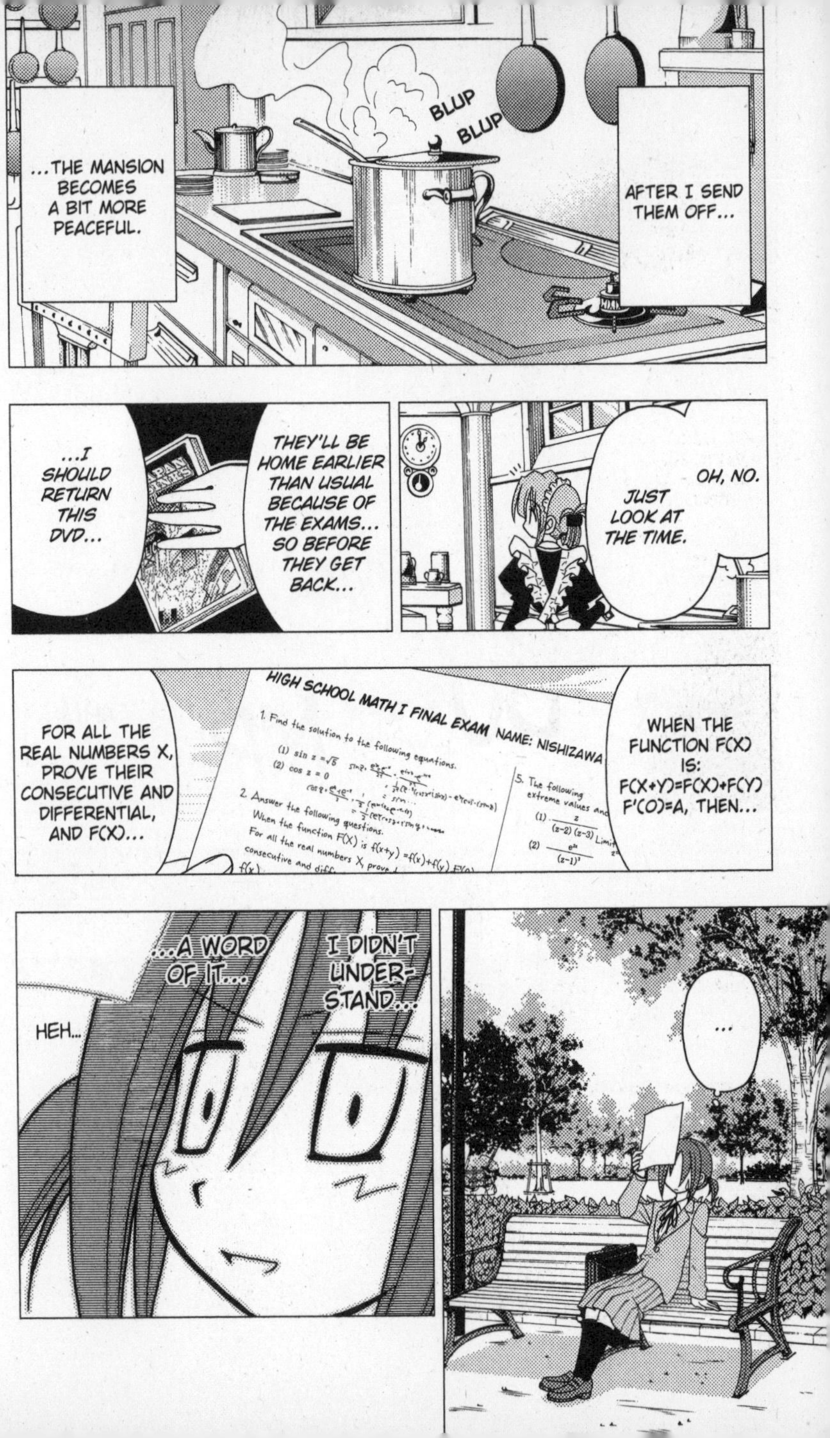
AFTER I SEND THEM OFF...
BLUP BLUP
...THE MANSION BECOMES A BIT MORE PEACEFUL.
OH, NO. JUST LOOK AT THE TIME.
THEY'LL BE HOME EARLIER THAN USUAL BECAUSE OF THE EXAMS... SO BEFORE THEY GET BACK...
...I SHOULD RETURN THIS DVD...
WHEN THE FUNCTION F(X) IS: F(X+Y)=F(X)+F(Y) F'(0)=A, THEN...
HIGH SCHOOL MATH I FINAL EXAM NAME: NISHIZAWA
1. Find the solution to the following equations.
(1) sin z = √5
(2) cos z = 0
2. Answer the following questions.
When the function F(X) is f(x+y) = f(x)+f(y)
For all the real numbers X, prove
consecutive and diff
5. The following extreme values and
FOR ALL THE REAL NUMBERS X, PROVE THEIR CONSECUTIVE AND DIFFERENTIAL, AND F(X)...
...
I DIDN'T UNDERSTAND...
...A WORD OF IT...
HEH...

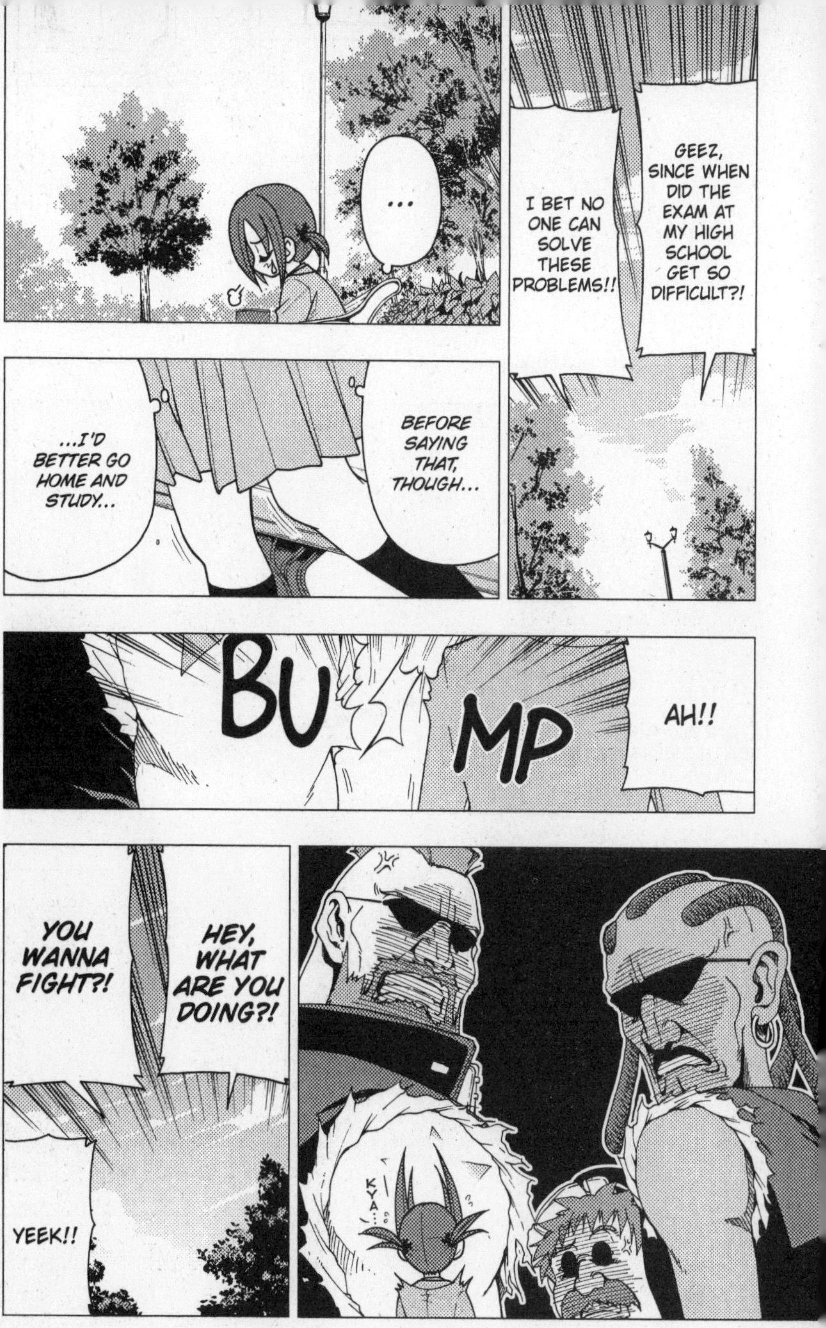
GEEZ, SINCE WHEN DID THE EXAM AT MY HIGH SCHOOL GET SO DIFFICULT?!
I BET NO ONE CAN SOLVE THESE PROBLEMS!!
...
BEFORE SAYING THAT, THOUGH...
...I'D BETTER GO HOME AND STUDY...
AH!!
BUMP
KYA...
HEY, WHAT ARE YOU DOING?!
YOU WANNA FIGHT?!
YEEK!!

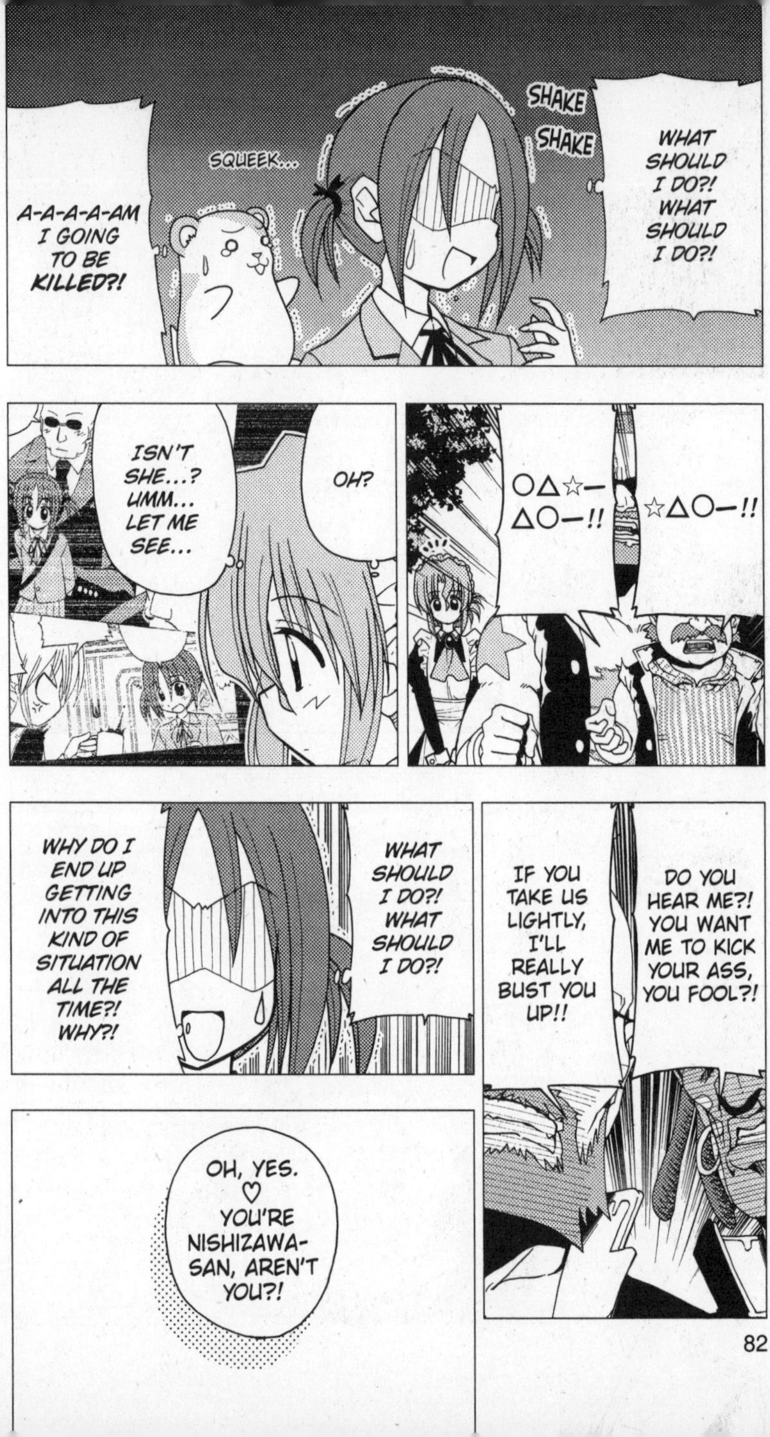
WHAT SHOULD I DO?! WHAT SHOULD I DO?!
SHAKE
SHAKE
SQUEEK...
A-A-A-A-AM I GOING TO BE KILLED?!
☆△○—!!
○△☆— △○—!!
OH?
ISN'T SHE...? UMM... LET ME SEE...
DO YOU HEAR ME?! YOU WANT ME TO KICK YOUR ASS, YOU FOOL?!
IF YOU TAKE US LIGHTLY, I'LL REALLY BUST YOU UP!!
WHAT SHOULD I DO?! WHAT SHOULD I DO?!
WHY DO I END UP GETTING INTO THIS KIND OF SITUATION ALL THE TIME?! WHY?!
OH, YES. ♡ YOU'RE NISHIZAWA-SAN, AREN'T YOU?!

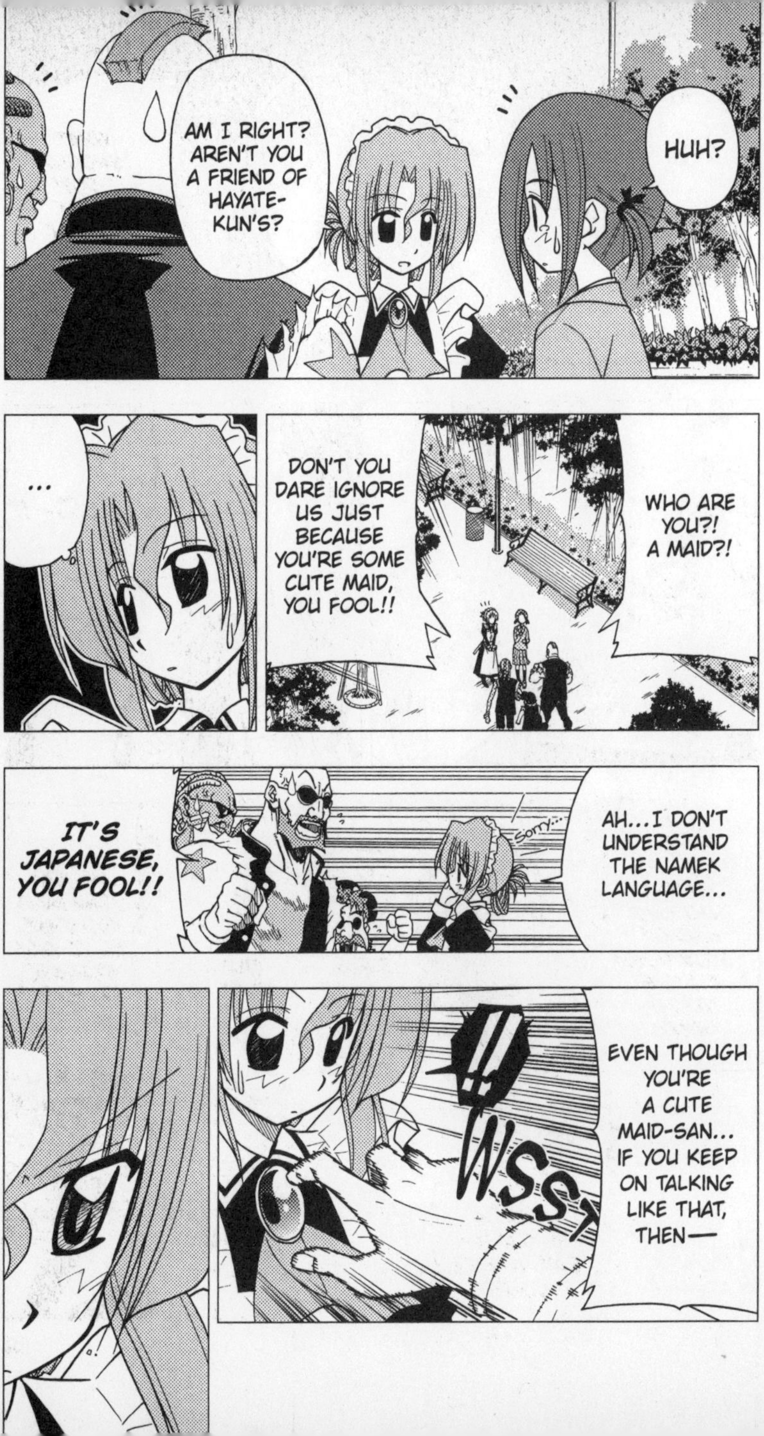
HUH?
AM I RIGHT? AREN'T YOU A FRIEND OF HAYATE-KUN'S?
WHO ARE YOU?! A MAID?!
DON'T YOU DARE IGNORE US JUST BECAUSE YOU'RE SOME CUTE MAID, YOU FOOL!!
...
AH...I DON'T UNDERSTAND THE NAMEK LANGUAGE...
Sorry...
IT'S JAPANESE, YOU FOOL!!
EVEN THOUGH YOU'RE A CUTE MAID-SAN... IF YOU KEEP ON TALKING LIKE THAT, THEN—
!!
WSST

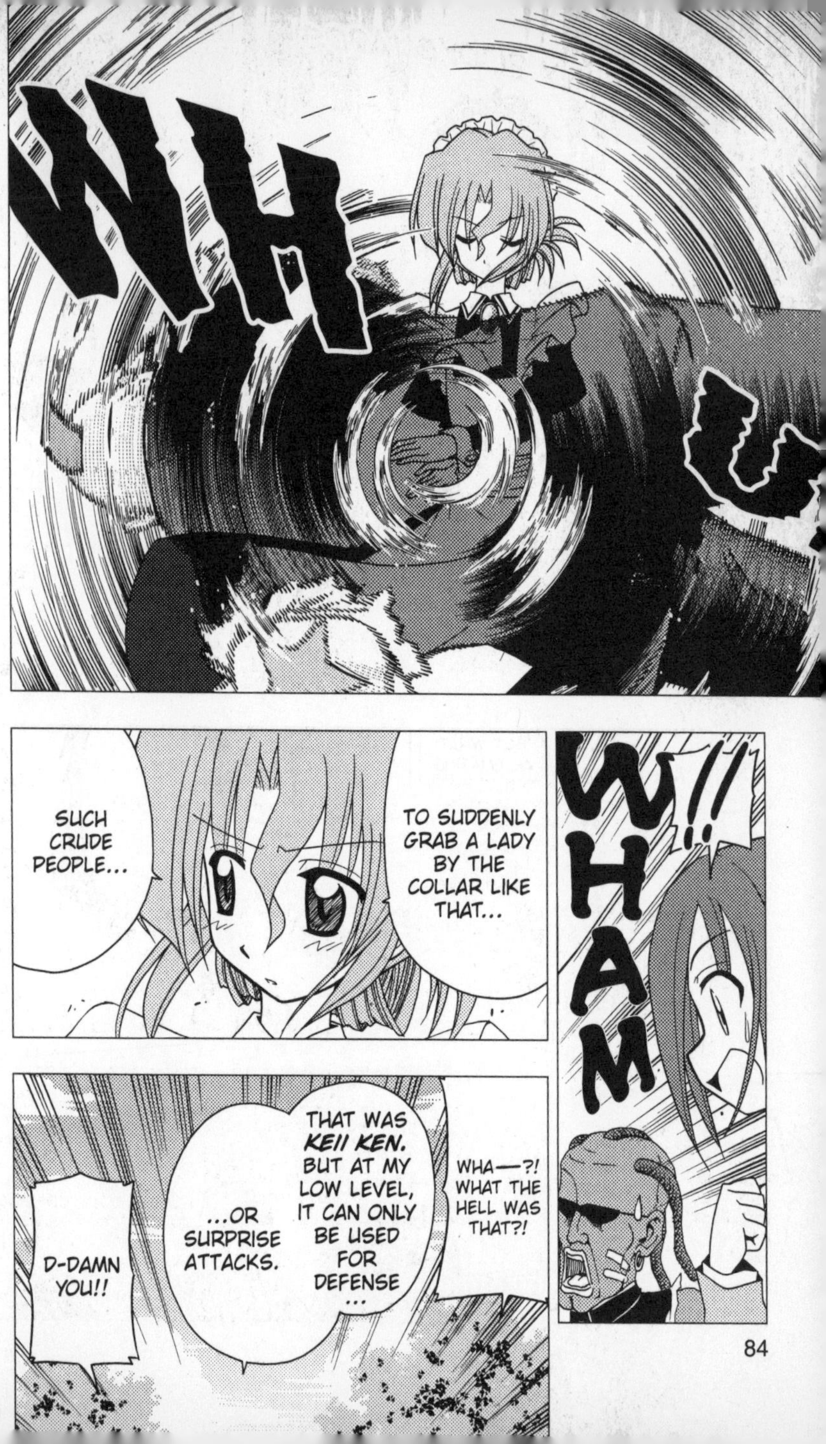
WHU
WHAM!!
TO SUDDENLY GRAB A LADY BY THE COLLAR LIKE THAT...
SUCH CRUDE PEOPLE...
WHA—?! WHAT THE HELL WAS THAT?!
THAT WAS *KEII KEN.* BUT AT MY LOW LEVEL, IT CAN ONLY BE USED FOR DEFENSE ...
...OR SURPRISE ATTACKS.
D-DAMN YOU!!

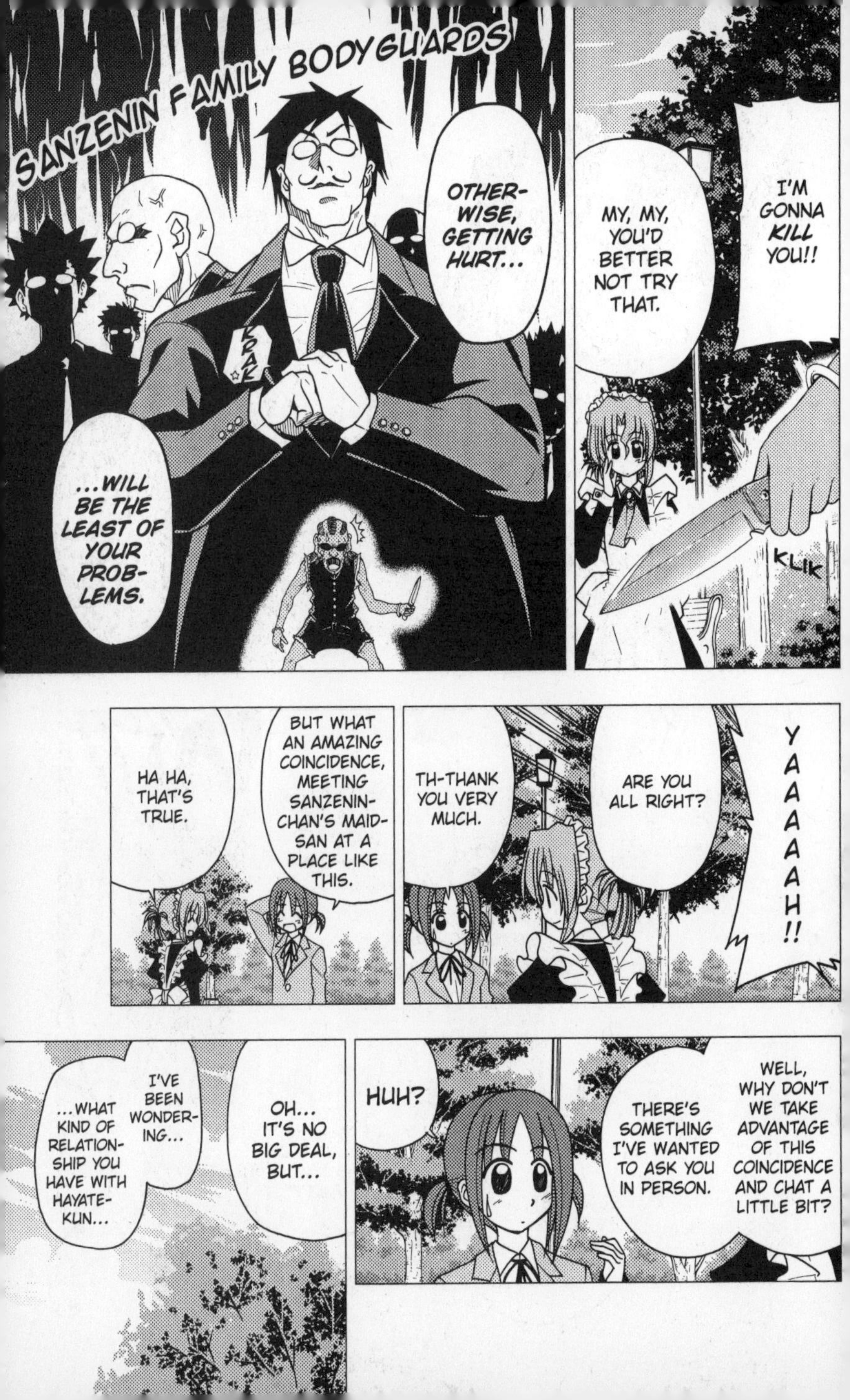
I'M GONNA KILL YOU!!
MY, MY, YOU'D BETTER NOT TRY THAT.
KLIK
SANZENIN FAMILY BODYGUARDS
OTHERWISE, GETTING HURT...
KRAK
...WILL BE THE LEAST OF YOUR PROBLEMS.
YAAAAAH!!
ARE YOU ALL RIGHT?
TH-THANK YOU VERY MUCH.
BUT WHAT AN AMAZING COINCIDENCE, MEETING SANZENIN-CHAN'S MAID-SAN AT A PLACE LIKE THIS.
HA HA, THAT'S TRUE.
WELL, WHY DON'T WE TAKE ADVANTAGE OF THIS COINCIDENCE AND CHAT A LITTLE BIT?
THERE'S SOMETHING I'VE WANTED TO ASK YOU IN PERSON.
HUH?
OH... IT'S NO BIG DEAL, BUT...
I'VE BEEN WONDERING...
...WHAT KIND OF RELATIONSHIP YOU HAVE WITH HAYATE-KUN...

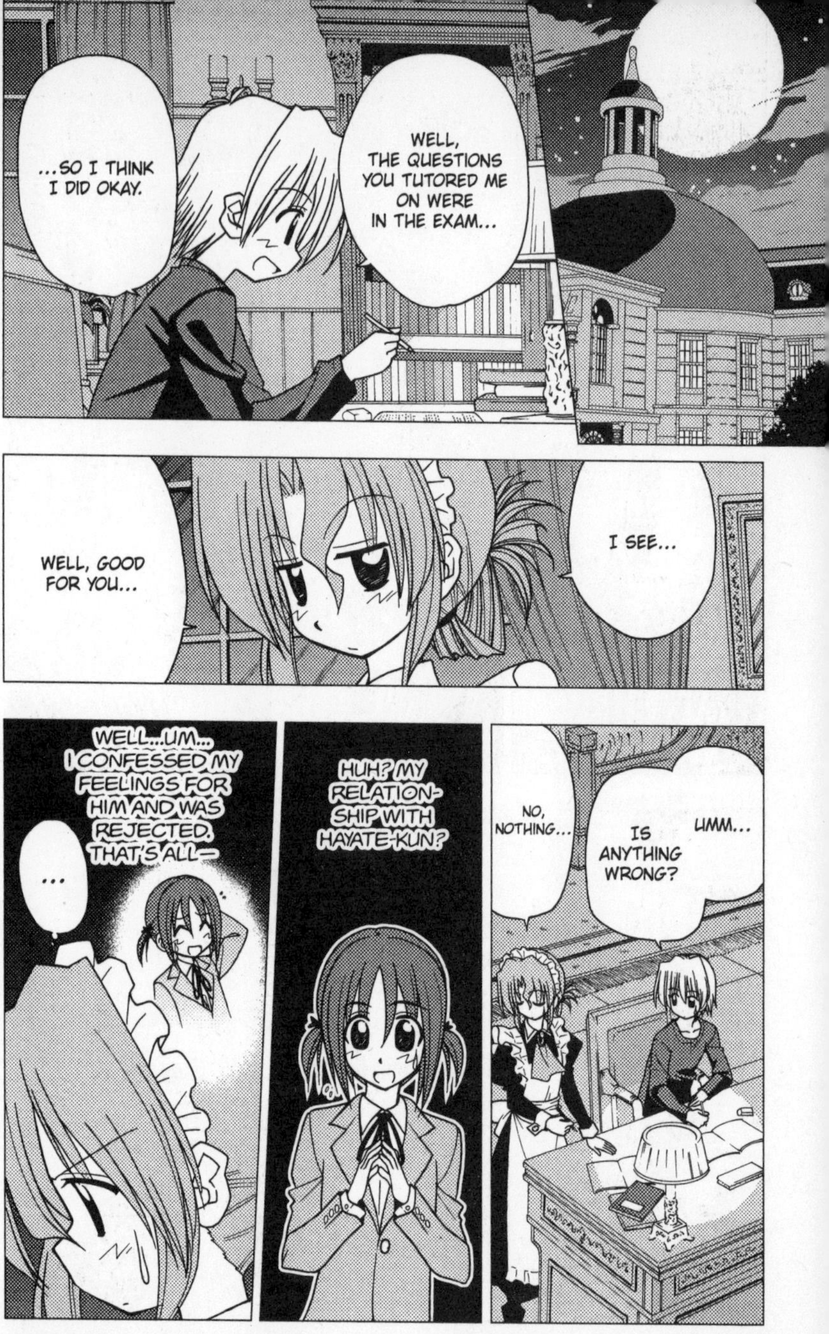
WELL, THE QUESTIONS YOU TUTORED ME ON WERE IN THE EXAM...
...SO I THINK I DID OKAY.
I SEE...
WELL, GOOD FOR YOU...
UMM...
IS ANYTHING WRONG?
NO, NOTHING...
HUH? MY RELATIONSHIP WITH HAYATE-KUN?
WELL...UM... I CONFESSED MY FEELINGS FOR HIM AND WAS REJECTED. THAT'S ALL—
...

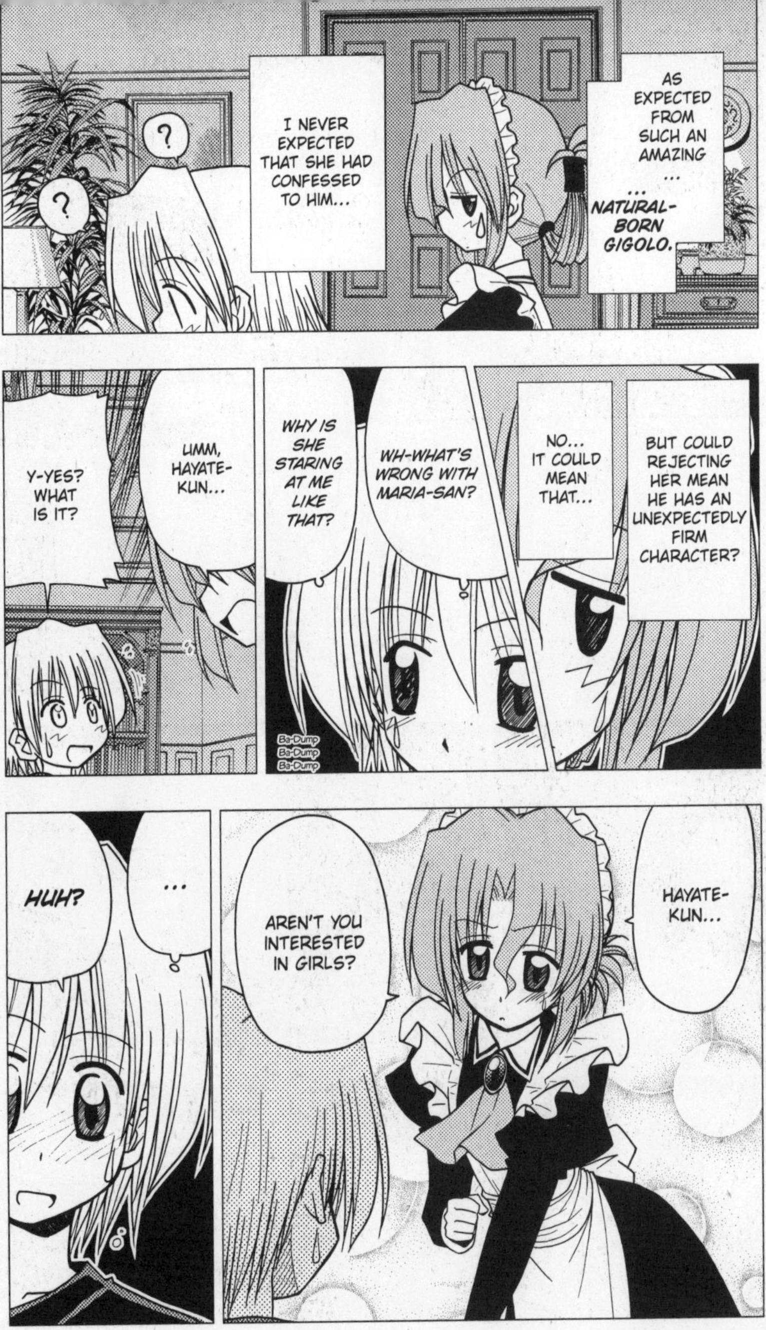
AS EXPECTED FROM SUCH AN AMAZING ... NATURAL-BORN GIGOLO.
I NEVER EXPECTED THAT SHE HAD CONFESSED TO HIM...
?
?
BUT COULD REJECTING HER MEAN HE HAS AN UNEXPECTEDLY FIRM CHARACTER?
NO... IT COULD MEAN THAT...
WH-WHAT'S WRONG WITH MARIA-SAN?
WHY IS SHE STARING AT ME LIKE THAT?
Ba-Dump Ba-Dump Ba-Dump
UMM, HAYATE-KUN...
Y-YES? WHAT IS IT?
HAYATE-KUN...
AREN'T YOU INTERESTED IN GIRLS?
...
HUH?

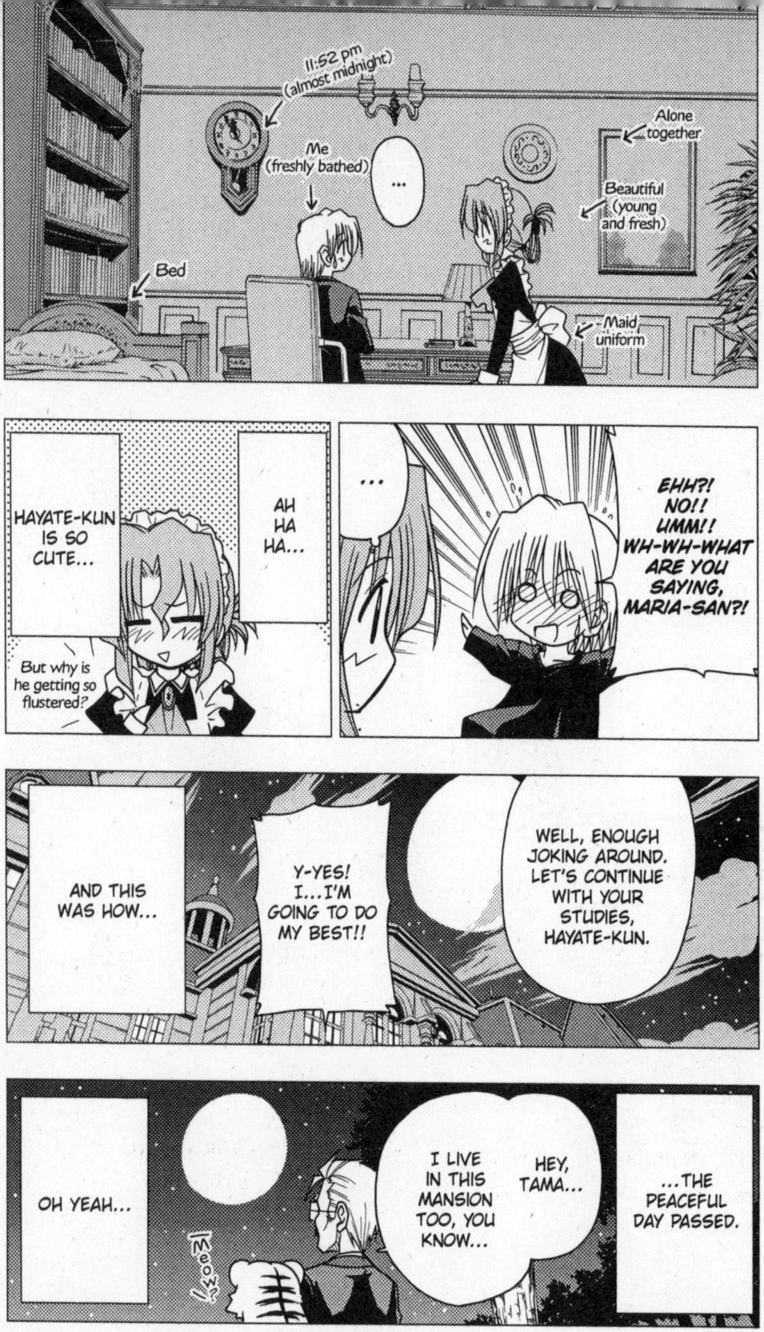

Alone together
Beautiful (young and fresh)
Maid uniform
11:52 pm (almost midnight)
...
Me (freshly bathed)
Bed
EHH?! NO!! UMM!! WH-WH-WHAT ARE YOU SAYING, MARIA-SAN?!
...
AH HA HA...
HAYATE-KUN IS SO CUTE...
But why is he getting so flustered?
WELL, ENOUGH JOKING AROUND. LET'S CONTINUE WITH YOUR STUDIES, HAYATE-KUN.
Y-YES! I...I'M GOING TO DO MY BEST!!
AND THIS WAS HOW...
...THE PEACEFUL DAY PASSED.
HEY, TAMA...
I LIVE IN THIS MANSION TOO, YOU KNOW...
OH YEAH...
Meow?

Episode 6: "Well, Amuro Had a Place to Return to, But..."

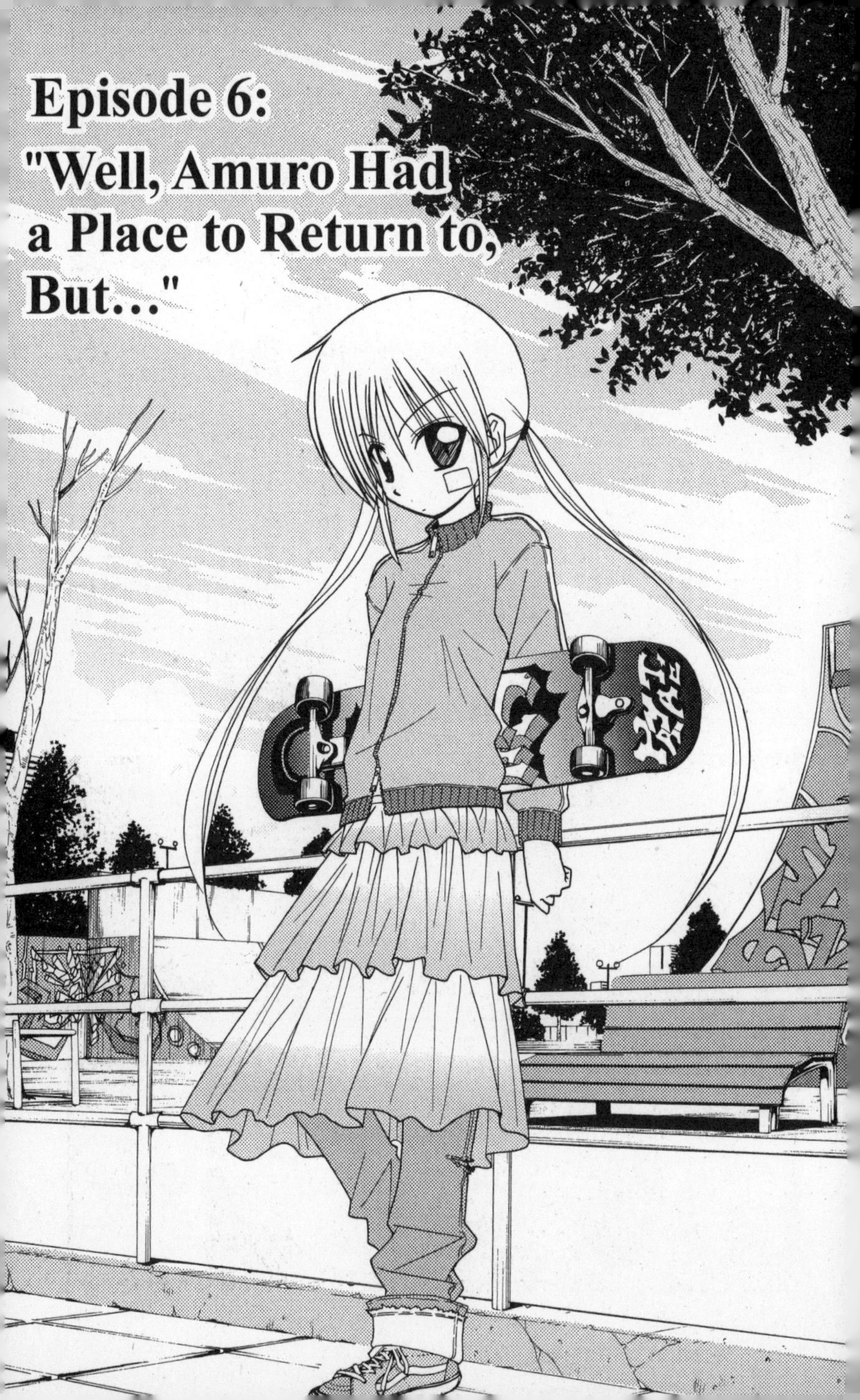

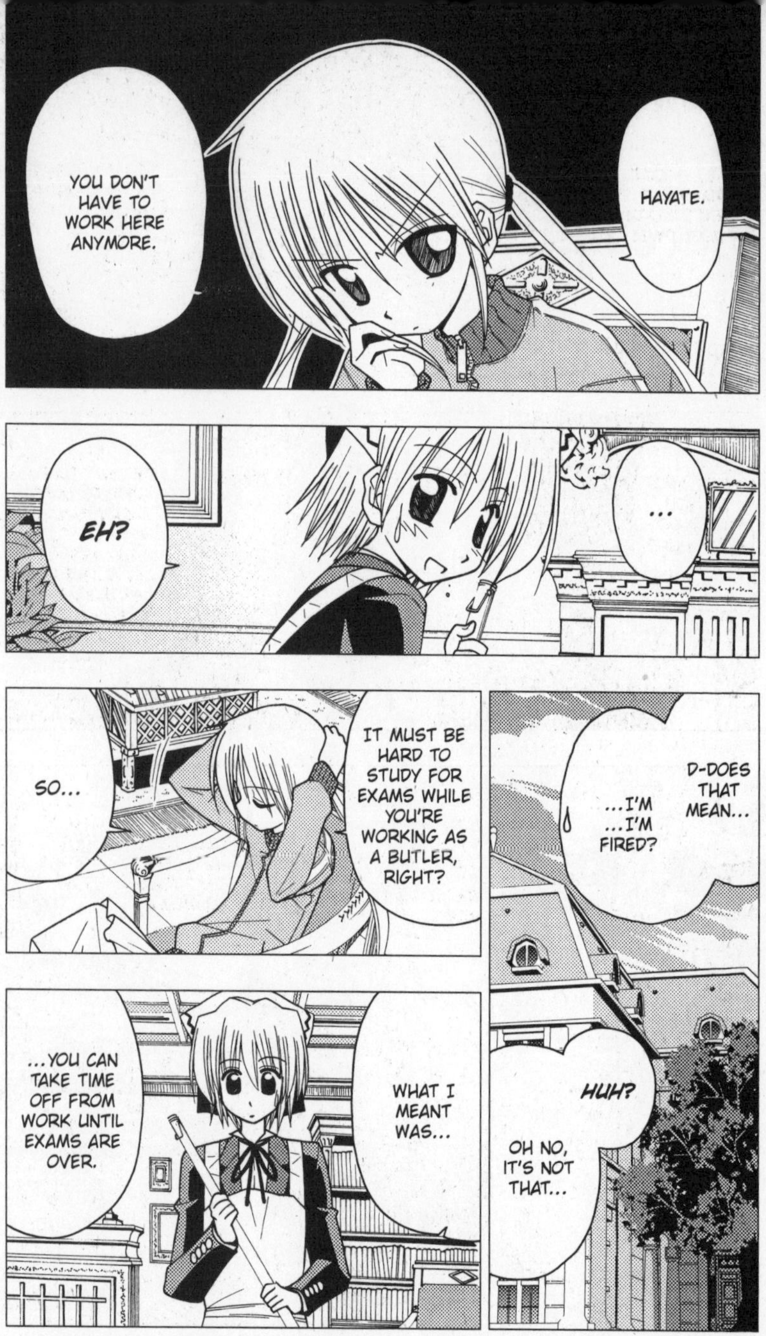
HAYATE.
YOU DON'T HAVE TO WORK HERE ANYMORE.
...
EH?
D-DOES THAT MEAN...
...I'M ...I'M FIRED?
HUH?
OH NO, IT'S NOT THAT...
IT MUST BE HARD TO STUDY FOR EXAMS WHILE YOU'RE WORKING AS A BUTLER, RIGHT?
SO...
WHAT I MEANT WAS...
...YOU CAN TAKE TIME OFF FROM WORK UNTIL EXAMS ARE OVER.

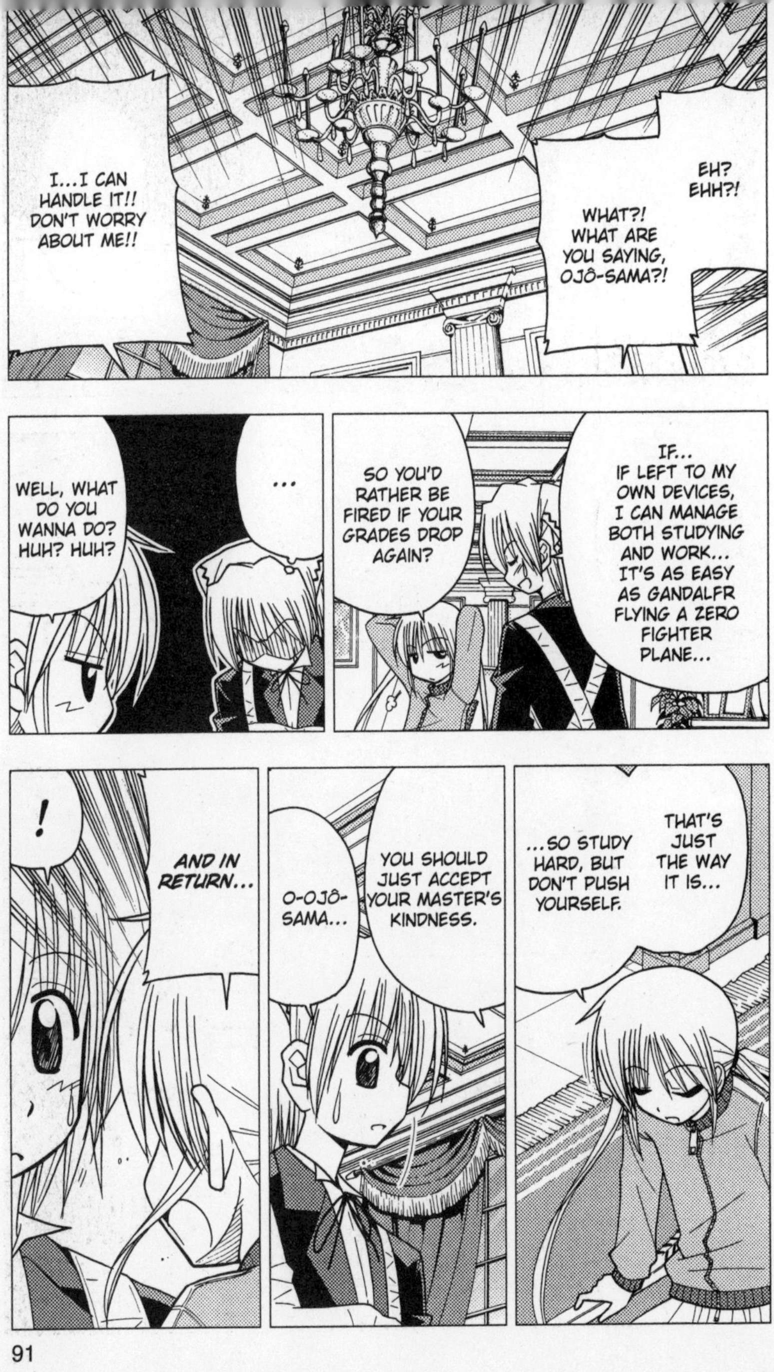
EH? EHH?!
WHAT?! WHAT ARE YOU SAYING, OJÔ-SAMA?!
I...I CAN HANDLE IT!! DON'T WORRY ABOUT ME!!
IF... IF LEFT TO MY OWN DEVICES, I CAN MANAGE BOTH STUDYING AND WORK... IT'S AS EASY AS GANDALFR FLYING A ZERO FIGHTER PLANE...
SO YOU'D RATHER BE FIRED IF YOUR GRADES DROP AGAIN?
...
WELL, WHAT DO YOU WANNA DO? HUH? HUH?
THAT'S JUST THE WAY IT IS...
...SO STUDY HARD, BUT DON'T PUSH YOURSELF.
YOU SHOULD JUST ACCEPT YOUR MASTER'S KINDNESS.
O-OJÔ-SAMA...
!
AND IN RETURN...

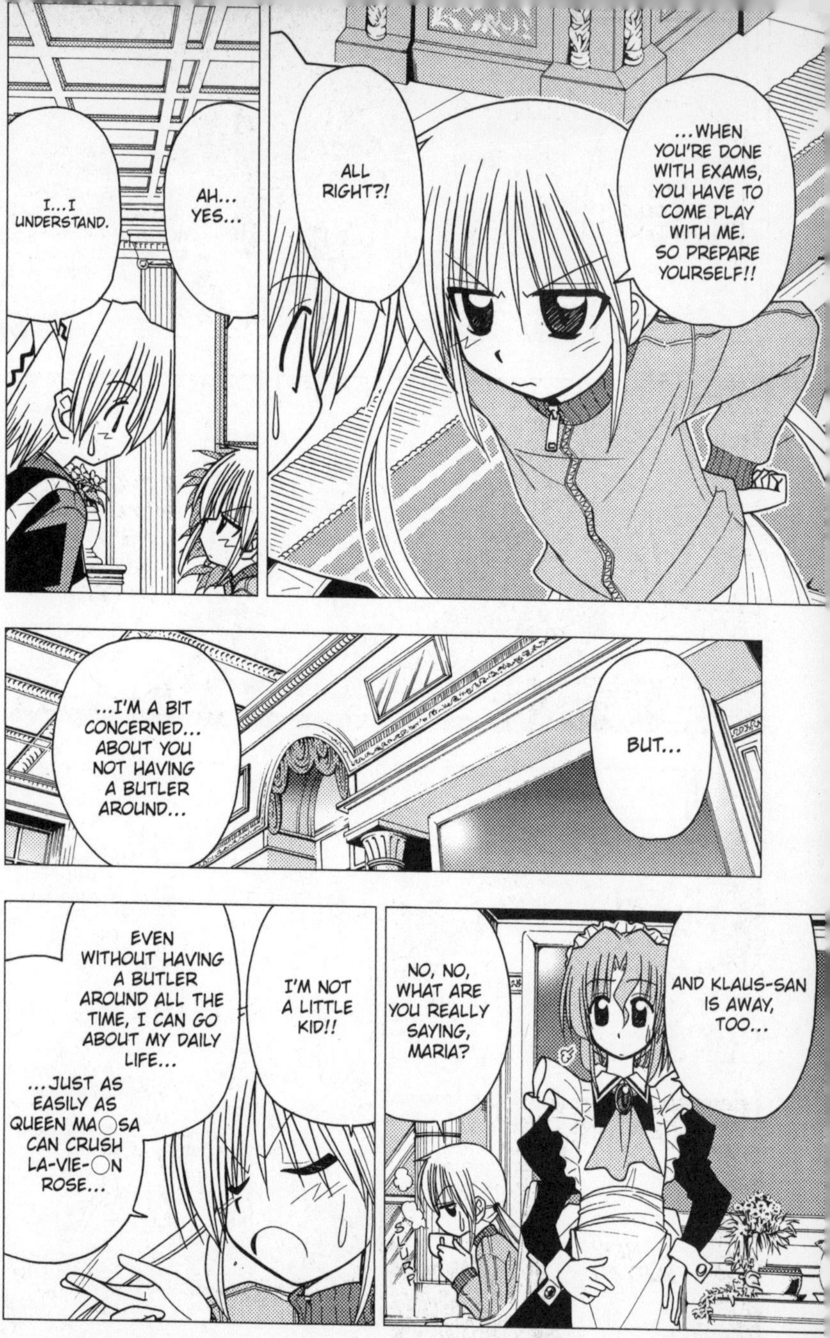
...WHEN YOU'RE DONE WITH EXAMS, YOU HAVE TO COME PLAY WITH ME. SO PREPARE YOURSELF!!
ALL RIGHT?!
AH... YES...
I...I UNDERSTAND.
BUT...
...I'M A BIT CONCERNED... ABOUT YOU NOT HAVING A BUTLER AROUND...
AND KLAUS-SAN IS AWAY, TOO...
NO, NO, WHAT ARE YOU REALLY SAYING, MARIA?
SLURP
I'M NOT A LITTLE KID!!
EVEN WITHOUT HAVING A BUTLER AROUND ALL THE TIME, I CAN GO ABOUT MY DAILY LIFE...
...JUST AS EASILY AS QUEEN MA◯SA CAN CRUSH LA-VIE-◯N ROSE...

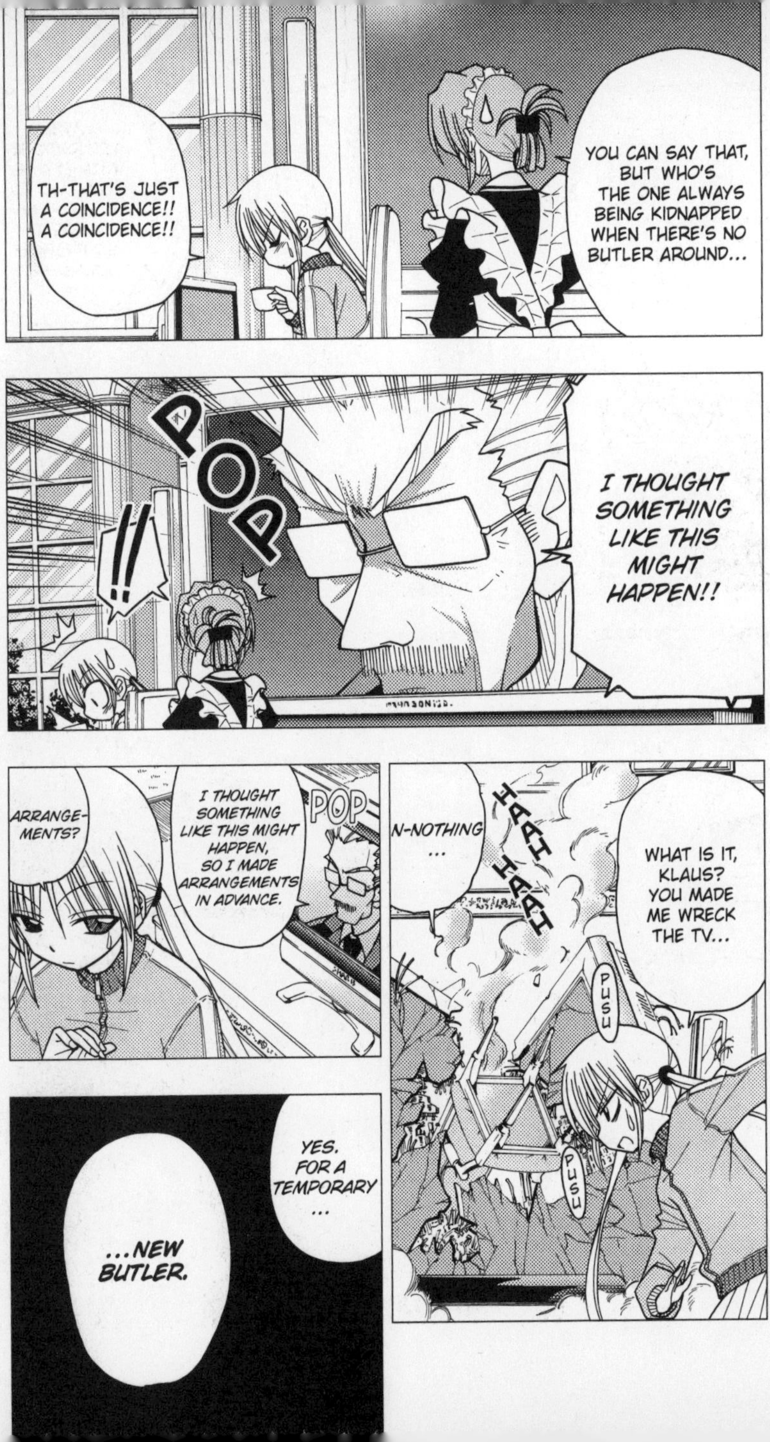
YOU CAN SAY THAT, BUT WHO'S THE ONE ALWAYS BEING KIDNAPPED WHEN THERE'S NO BUTLER AROUND...
TH-THAT'S JUST A COINCIDENCE!! A COINCIDENCE!!
I THOUGHT SOMETHING LIKE THIS MIGHT HAPPEN!!
POP
!!
WHAT IS IT, KLAUS? YOU MADE ME WRECK THE TV...
HAAH HAAH
PUSU
N-NOTHING...
PUSU
I THOUGHT SOMETHING LIKE THIS MIGHT HAPPEN, SO I MADE ARRANGEMENTS IN ADVANCE.
POP
ARRANGE-MENTS?
YES. FOR A TEMPORARY...
...NEW BUTLER.

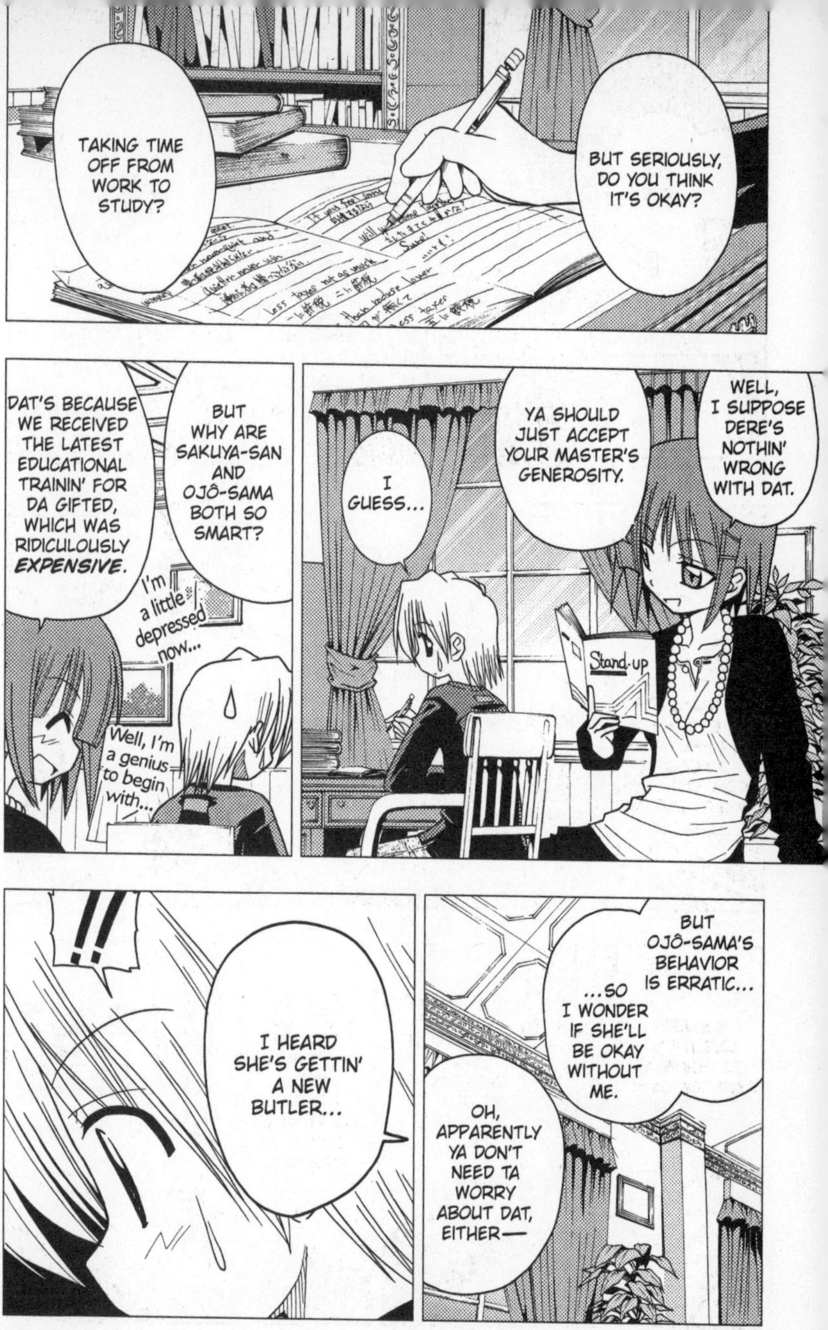
BUT SERIOUSLY, DO YOU THINK IT'S OKAY?
TAKING TIME OFF FROM WORK TO STUDY?
WELL, I SUPPOSE DERE'S NOTHIN' WRONG WITH DAT.
YA SHOULD JUST ACCEPT YOUR MASTER'S GENEROSITY.
I GUESS...
Stand-up
BUT WHY ARE SAKUYA-SAN AND OJÔ-SAMA BOTH SO SMART?
DAT'S BECAUSE WE RECEIVED THE LATEST EDUCATIONAL TRAININ' FOR DA GIFTED, WHICH WAS RIDICULOUSLY ***EXPENSIVE***.
I'm a little depressed now...
Well, I'm a genius to begin with...
BUT OJÔ-SAMA'S BEHAVIOR IS ERRATIC...
...SO I WONDER IF SHE'LL BE OKAY WITHOUT ME.
OH, APPARENTLY YA DON'T NEED TA WORRY ABOUT DAT, EITHER—
I HEARD SHE'S GETTIN' A NEW BUTLER...
!!

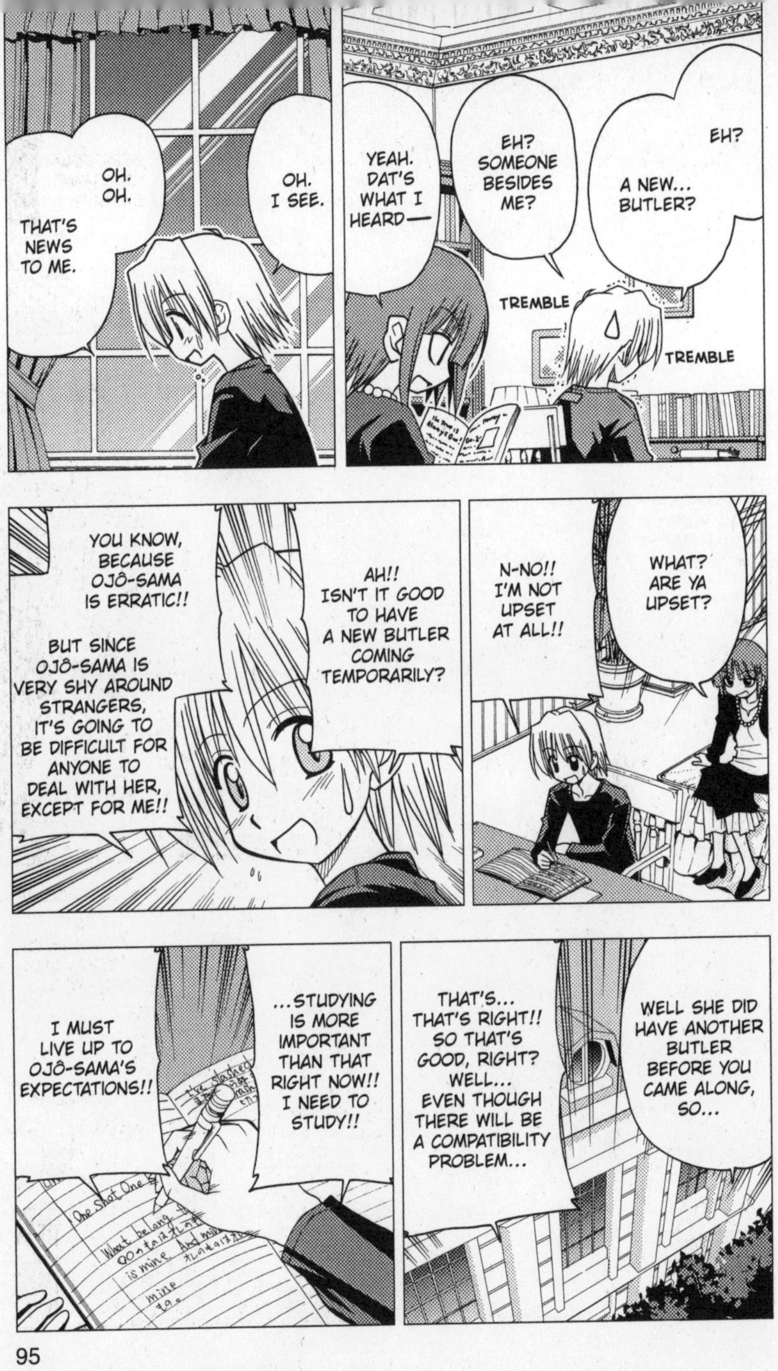
EH? A NEW... BUTLER?
EH? SOMEONE BESIDES ME?
TREMBLE
TREMBLE
YEAH. DAT'S WHAT I HEARD—
OH. I SEE.
OH. OH.
THAT'S NEWS TO ME.
WHAT? ARE YA UPSET?
N-NO!! I'M NOT UPSET AT ALL!!
AH!! ISN'T IT GOOD TO HAVE A NEW BUTLER COMING TEMPORARILY?
YOU KNOW, BECAUSE OJÔ-SAMA IS ERRATIC!!
BUT SINCE OJÔ-SAMA IS VERY SHY AROUND STRANGERS, IT'S GOING TO BE DIFFICULT FOR ANYONE TO DEAL WITH HER, EXCEPT FOR ME!!
WELL SHE DID HAVE ANOTHER BUTLER BEFORE YOU CAME ALONG, SO...
THAT'S... THAT'S RIGHT!! SO THAT'S GOOD, RIGHT? WELL... EVEN THOUGH THERE WILL BE A COMPATIBILITY PROBLEM...
...STUDYING IS MORE IMPORTANT THAN THAT RIGHT NOW!! I NEED TO STUDY!!
I MUST LIVE UP TO OJÔ-SAMA'S EXPECTATIONS!!

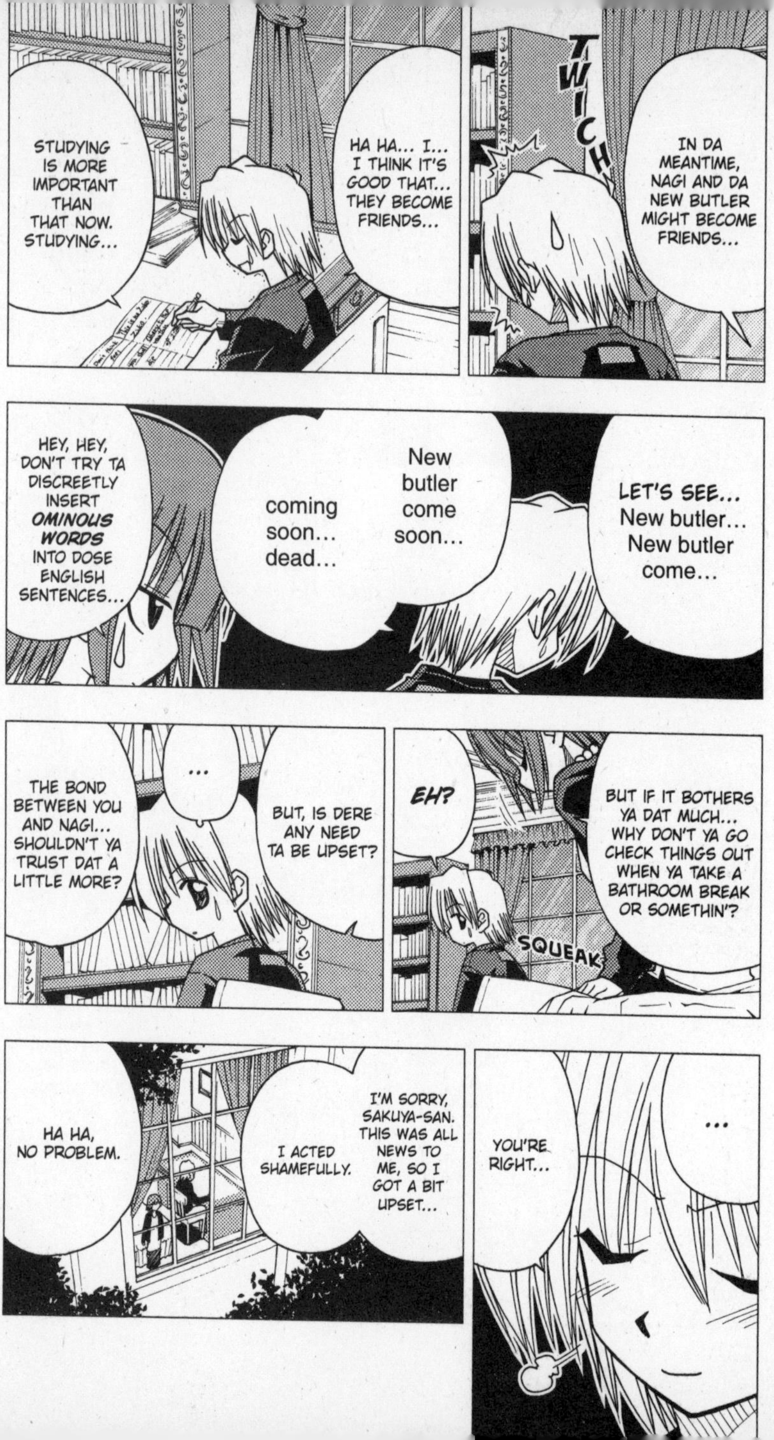
TWITCH
IN DA MEANTIME, NAGI AND DA NEW BUTLER MIGHT BECOME FRIENDS...
HA HA... I... I THINK IT'S GOOD THAT... THEY BECOME FRIENDS...
STUDYING IS MORE IMPORTANT THAN THAT NOW. STUDYING...
LET'S SEE... New butler... New butler come...
New butler come soon...
coming soon... dead...
HEY, HEY, DON'T TRY TA DISCREETLY INSERT ***OMINOUS WORDS*** INTO DOSE ENGLISH SENTENCES...
BUT IF IT BOTHERS YA DAT MUCH... WHY DON'T YA GO CHECK THINGS OUT WHEN YA TAKE A BATHROOM BREAK OR SOMETHIN'?
SQUEAK
EH?
BUT, IS DERE ANY NEED TA BE UPSET?
...
THE BOND BETWEEN YOU AND NAGI... SHOULDN'T YA TRUST DAT A LITTLE MORE?
...
YOU'RE RIGHT...
I'M SORRY, SAKUYA-SAN. THIS WAS ALL NEWS TO ME, SO I GOT A BIT UPSET...
I ACTED SHAMEFULLY.
HA HA, NO PROBLEM.

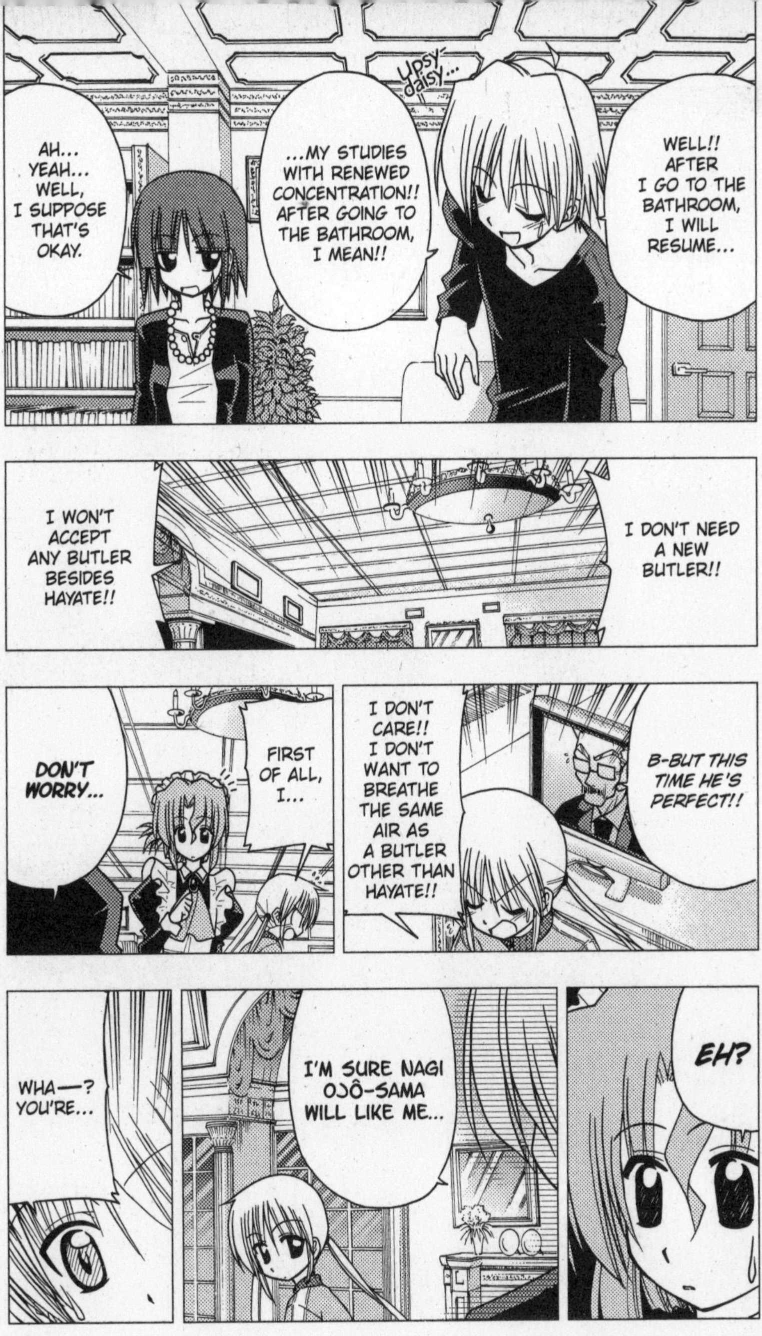
WELL!! AFTER I GO TO THE BATHROOM, I WILL RESUME...
Upsy-daisy...
...MY STUDIES WITH RENEWED CONCENTRATION!! AFTER GOING TO THE BATHROOM, I MEAN!!
AH... YEAH... WELL, I SUPPOSE THAT'S OKAY.
I DON'T NEED A NEW BUTLER!!
I WON'T ACCEPT ANY BUTLER BESIDES HAYATE!!
B-BUT THIS TIME HE'S PERFECT!!
I DON'T CARE!! I DON'T WANT TO BREATHE THE SAME AIR AS A BUTLER OTHER THAN HAYATE!!
FIRST OF ALL, I...
DON'T WORRY...
EH?
I'M SURE NAGI OJÔ-SAMA WILL LIKE ME...
WHA—? YOU'RE...

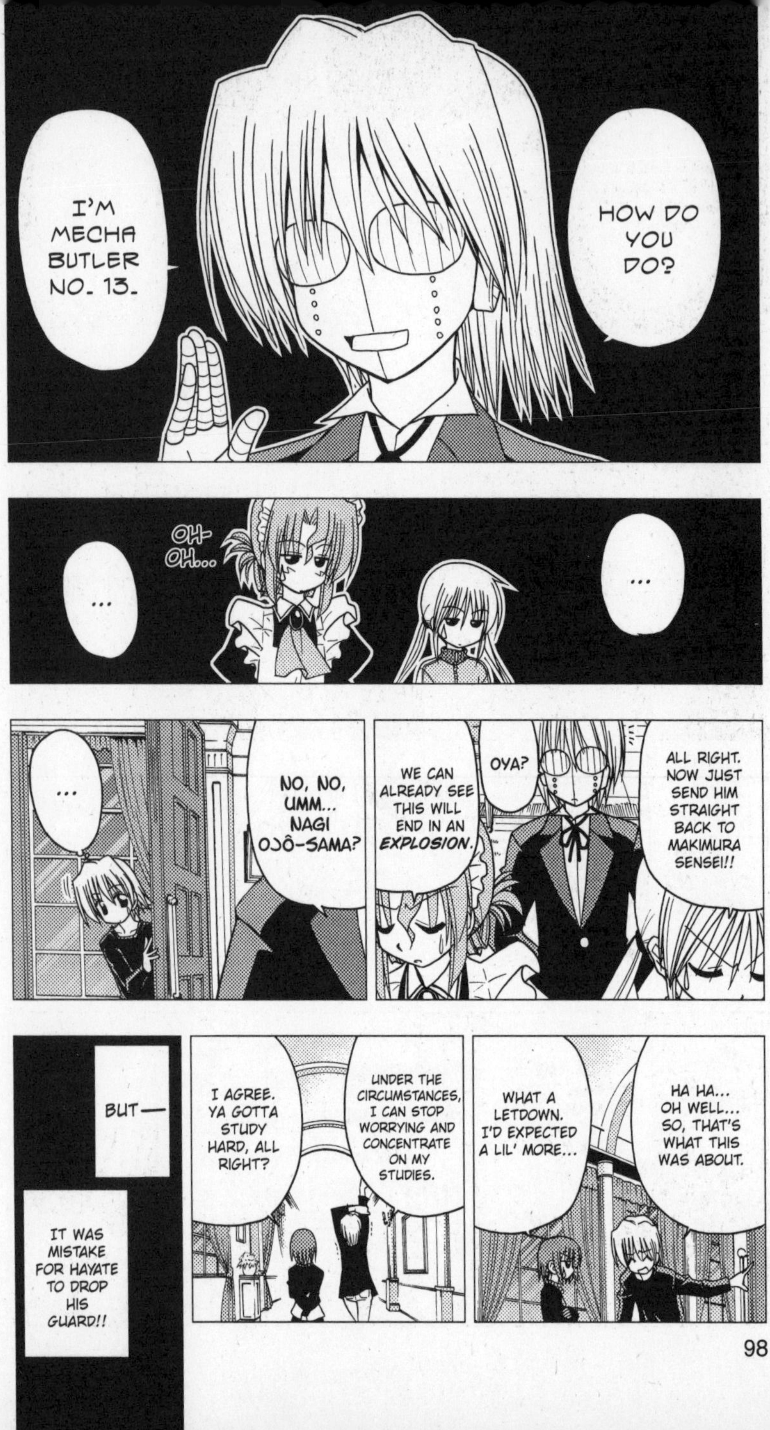
HOW DO YOU DO?
I'M MECHA BUTLER NO. 13.
...
OH-OH...
...
ALL RIGHT. NOW JUST SEND HIM STRAIGHT BACK TO MAKIMURA SENSEI!!
OYA?
WE CAN ALREADY SEE THIS WILL END IN AN *EXPLOSION*.
NO, NO, UMM... NAGI OJÔ-SAMA?
...
HA HA... OH WELL... SO, THAT'S WHAT THIS WAS ABOUT.
WHAT A LETDOWN. I'D EXPECTED A LIL' MORE...
UNDER THE CIRCUMSTANCES, I CAN STOP WORRYING AND CONCENTRATE ON MY STUDIES.
I AGREE. YA GOTTA STUDY HARD, ALL RIGHT?
BUT—
IT WAS MISTAKE FOR HAYATE TO DROP HIS GUARD!!

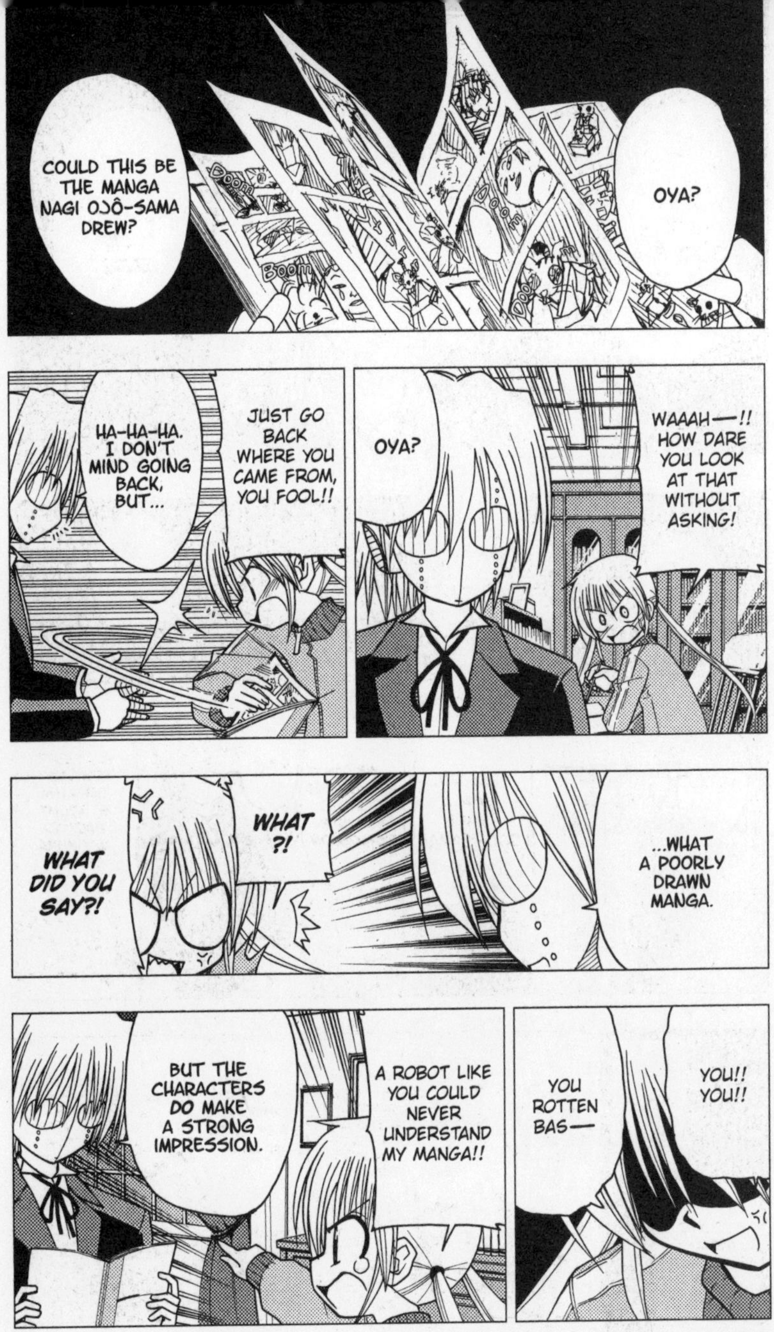
OYA?
COULD THIS BE THE MANGA NAGI OJÔ-SAMA DREW?
WAAAH—!! HOW DARE YOU LOOK AT THAT WITHOUT ASKING!
OYA?
JUST GO BACK WHERE YOU CAME FROM, YOU FOOL!!
HA-HA-HA. I DON'T MIND GOING BACK, BUT...
...WHAT A POORLY DRAWN MANGA.
WHAT ?!
WHAT DID YOU SAY?!
YOU!! YOU!!
YOU ROTTEN BAS—
A ROBOT LIKE YOU COULD NEVER UNDERSTAND MY MANGA!!
BUT THE CHARACTERS DO MAKE A STRONG IMPRESSION.

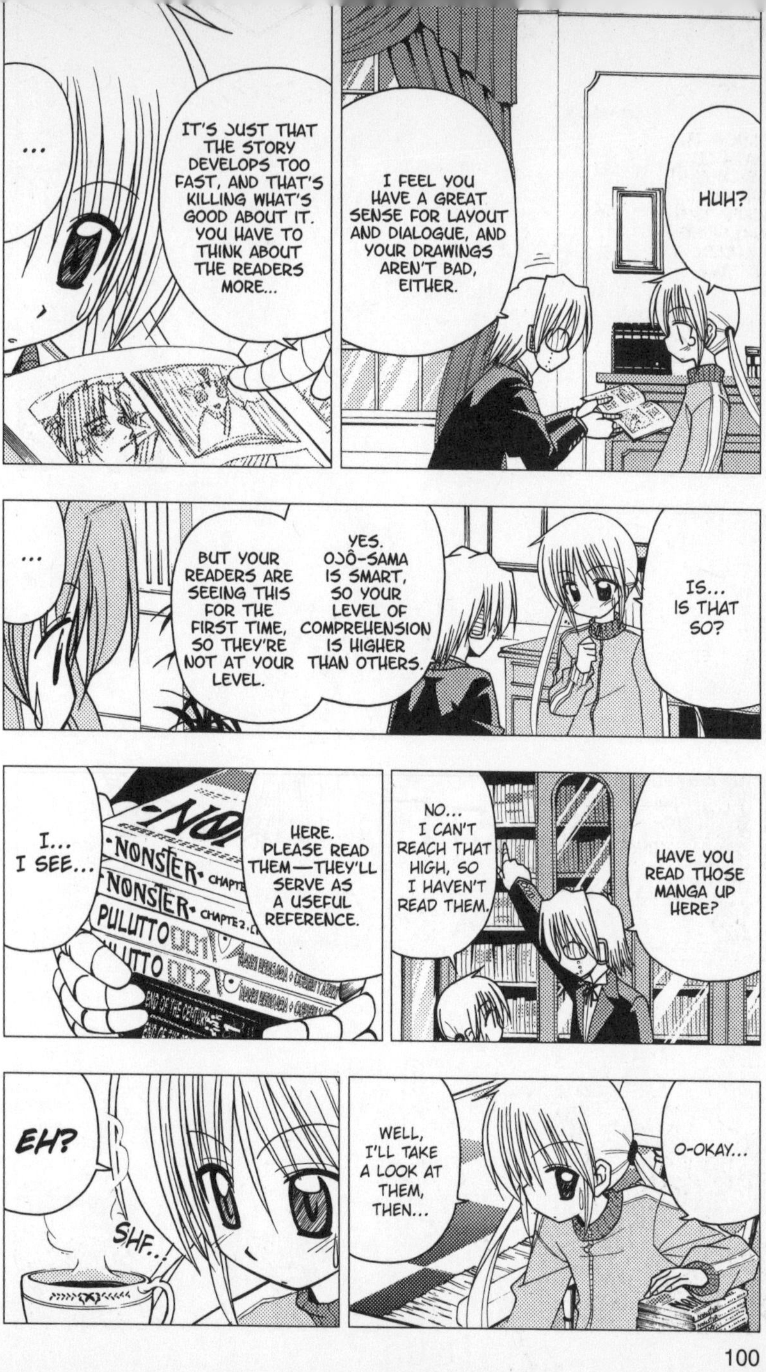
HUH?
I FEEL YOU HAVE A GREAT SENSE FOR LAYOUT AND DIALOGUE, AND YOUR DRAWINGS AREN'T BAD, EITHER.
IT'S JUST THAT THE STORY DEVELOPS TOO FAST, AND THAT'S KILLING WHAT'S GOOD ABOUT IT. YOU HAVE TO THINK ABOUT THE READERS MORE...
...
IS... IS THAT SO?
YES. OJÔ-SAMA IS SMART, SO YOUR LEVEL OF COMPREHENSION IS HIGHER THAN OTHERS.
BUT YOUR READERS ARE SEEING THIS FOR THE FIRST TIME, SO THEY'RE NOT AT YOUR LEVEL.
...
HAVE YOU READ THOSE MANGA UP HERE?
NO... I CAN'T REACH THAT HIGH, SO I HAVEN'T READ THEM.
HERE. PLEASE READ THEM—THEY'LL SERVE AS A USEFUL REFERENCE.
NONSTER
NONSTER
PULUTTO 001
PULUTTO 002
END OF THE CENTURY
I... I SEE...
O-OKAY...
WELL, I'LL TAKE A LOOK AT THEM, THEN...
EH?
SHF...

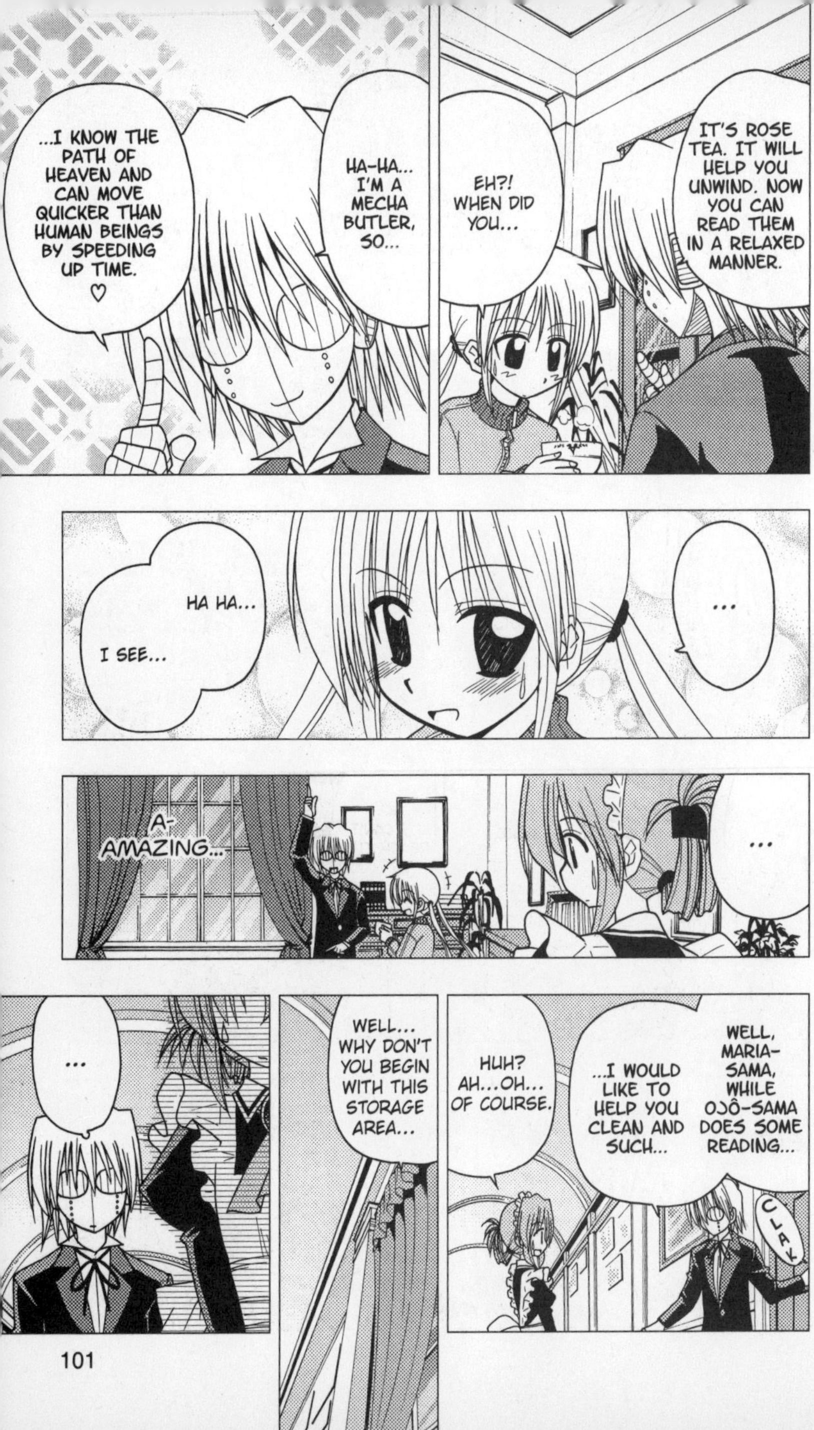
IT'S ROSE TEA. IT WILL HELP YOU UNWIND. NOW YOU CAN READ THEM IN A RELAXED MANNER.
EH?! WHEN DID YOU...
HA-HA... I'M A MECHA BUTLER, SO...
...I KNOW THE PATH OF HEAVEN AND CAN MOVE QUICKER THAN HUMAN BEINGS BY SPEEDING UP TIME. ♡
...
HA HA...
I SEE...
...
A-AMAZING...
WELL, MARIA-SAMA, WHILE OJÔ-SAMA DOES SOME READING...
...I WOULD LIKE TO HELP YOU CLEAN AND SUCH...
HUH? AH...OH... OF COURSE.
CLAK
WELL... WHY DON'T YOU BEGIN WITH THIS STORAGE AREA...
...

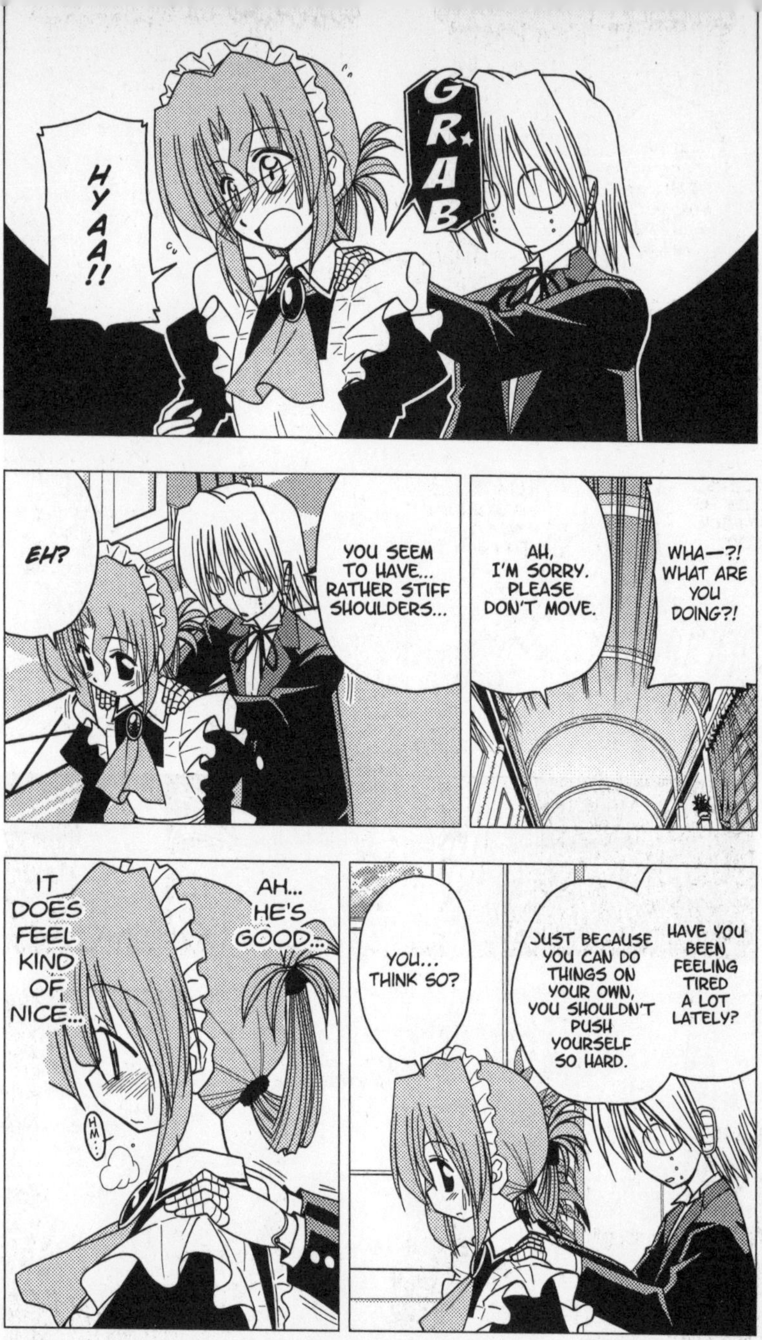
GRAB
HYAA!!
WHA—?! WHAT ARE YOU DOING?!
AH, I'M SORRY. PLEASE DON'T MOVE.
YOU SEEM TO HAVE... RATHER STIFF SHOULDERS...
EH?
HAVE YOU BEEN FEELING TIRED A LOT LATELY?
JUST BECAUSE YOU CAN DO THINGS ON YOUR OWN, YOU SHOULDN'T PUSH YOURSELF SO HARD.
YOU... THINK SO?
AH... HE'S GOOD...
IT DOES FEEL KIND OF NICE...
HM...

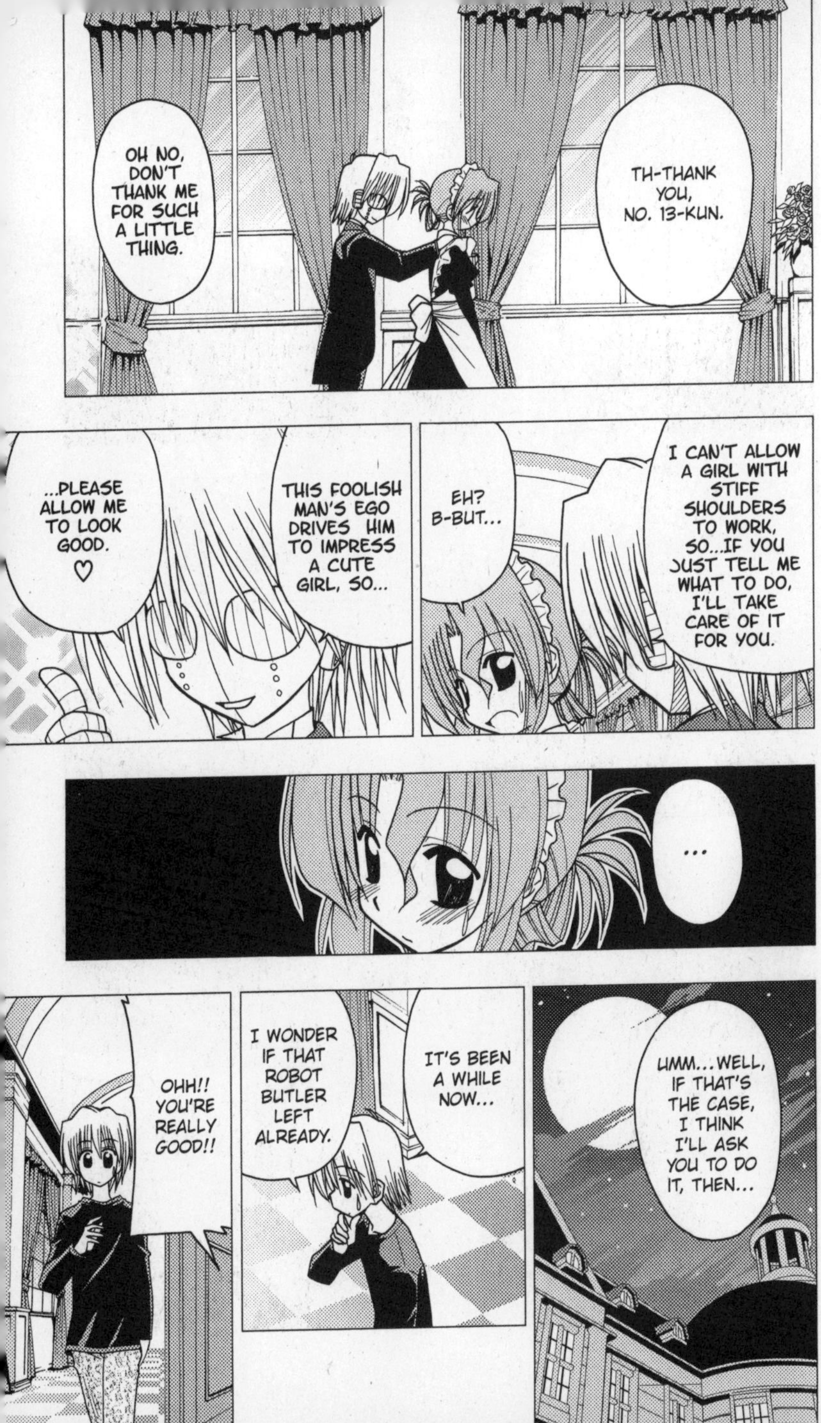
TH-THANK YOU, NO. 13-KUN.
OH NO, DON'T THANK ME FOR SUCH A LITTLE THING.
I CAN'T ALLOW A GIRL WITH STIFF SHOULDERS TO WORK, SO...IF YOU JUST TELL ME WHAT TO DO, I'LL TAKE CARE OF IT FOR YOU.
EH? B-BUT...
THIS FOOLISH MAN'S EGO DRIVES HIM TO IMPRESS A CUTE GIRL, SO...
...PLEASE ALLOW ME TO LOOK GOOD. ♡
...
UMM...WELL, IF THAT'S THE CASE, I THINK I'LL ASK YOU TO DO IT, THEN...
IT'S BEEN A WHILE NOW...
I WONDER IF THAT ROBOT BUTLER LEFT ALREADY.
OHH!! YOU'RE REALLY GOOD!!

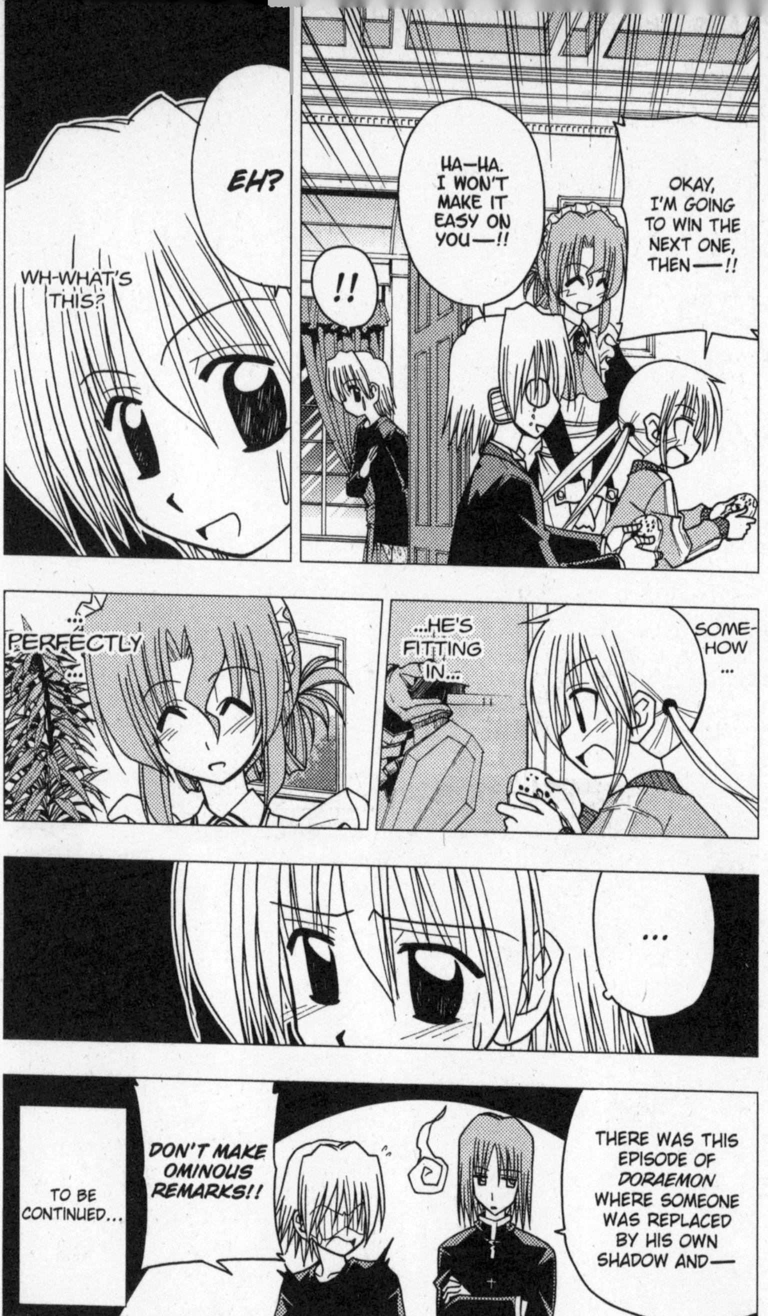
OKAY, I'M GOING TO WIN THE NEXT ONE, THEN—!!
HA-HA. I WON'T MAKE IT EASY ON YOU—!!
!!
EH?
WH-WHAT'S THIS?
SOME-HOW...
...HE'S FITTING IN...
...PERFECTLY...
...
THERE WAS THIS EPISODE OF *DORAEMON* WHERE SOMEONE WAS REPLACED BY HIS OWN SHADOW AND—
DON'T MAKE OMINOUS REMARKS!!
TO BE CONTINUED...

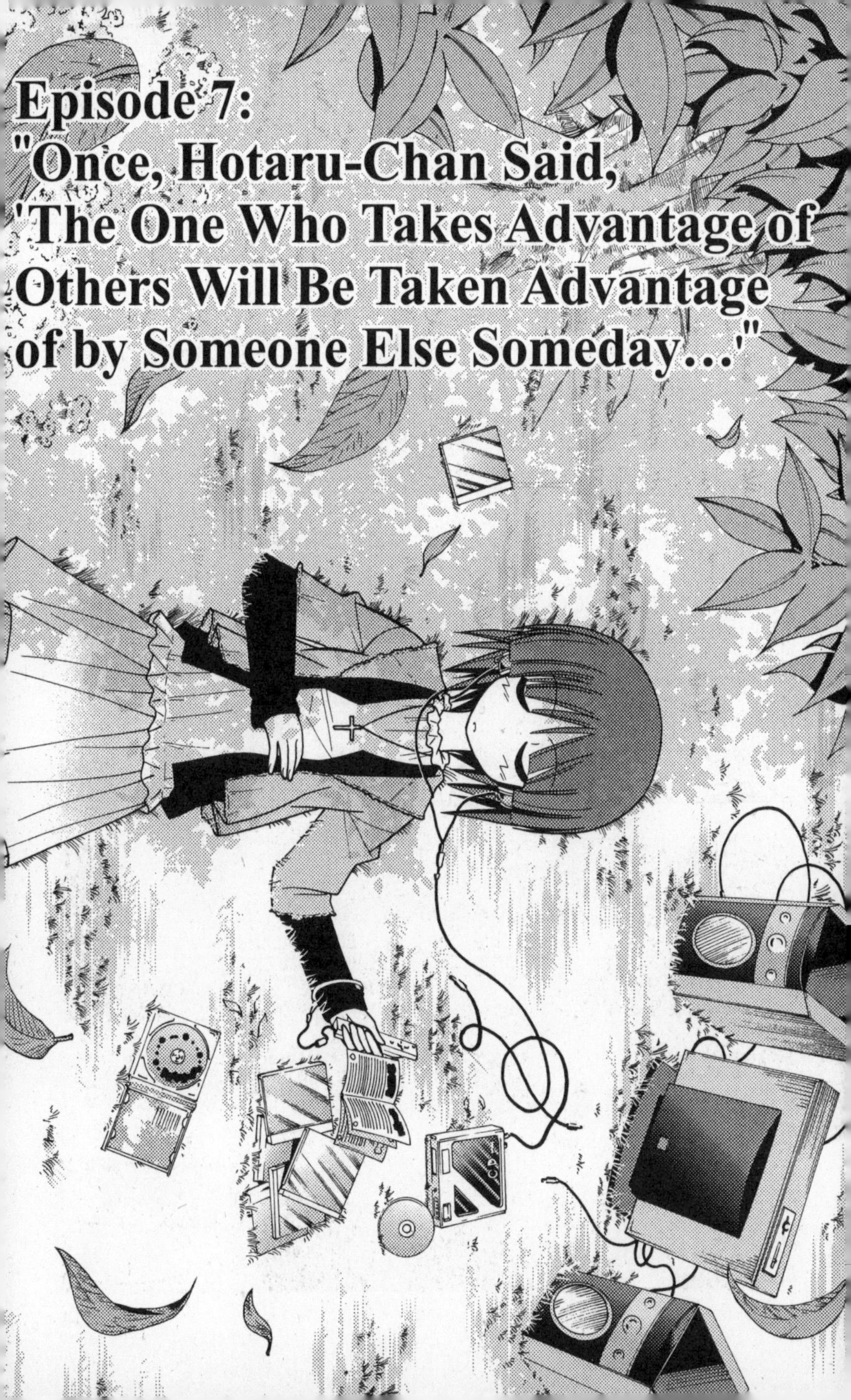
Episode 7:
"Once, Hotaru-Chan Said,
'The One Who Takes Advantage of
Others Will Be Taken Advantage
of by Someone Else Someday...'"

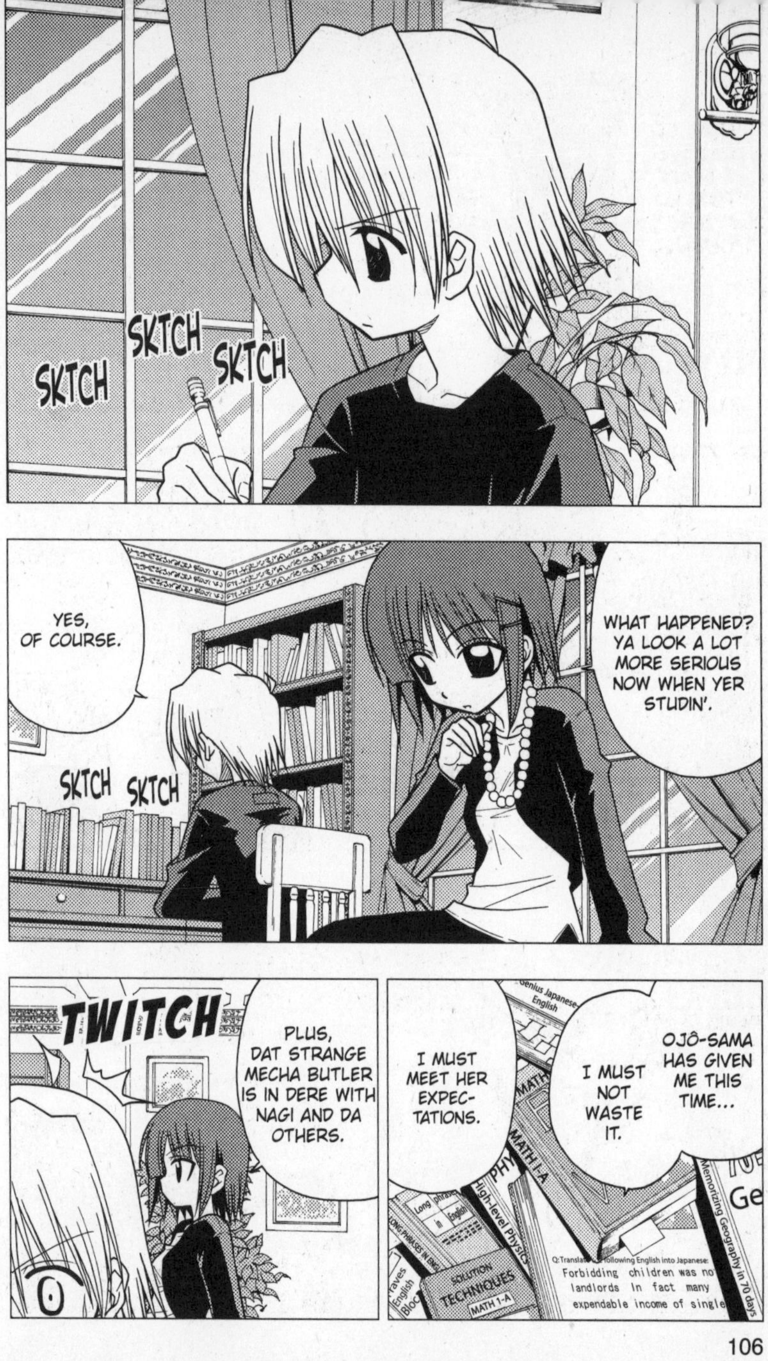
SKTCH
SKTCH
SKTCH
WHAT HAPPENED? YA LOOK A LOT MORE SERIOUS NOW WHEN YER STUDIN'.
YES, OF COURSE.
SKTCH
SKTCH
OJÔ-SAMA HAS GIVEN ME THIS TIME...
I MUST NOT WASTE IT.
I MUST MEET HER EXPECTATIONS.
Genius Japanese-English
MATH I-A
High-level Physics
Memorizing Geography in 70 days
SOLUTION TECHNIQUES MATH I-A
Forbidding children was not
landlords In fact many
expendable income of single
TWITCH
PLUS, DAT STRANGE MECHA BUTLER IS IN DERE WITH NAGI AND DA OTHERS.

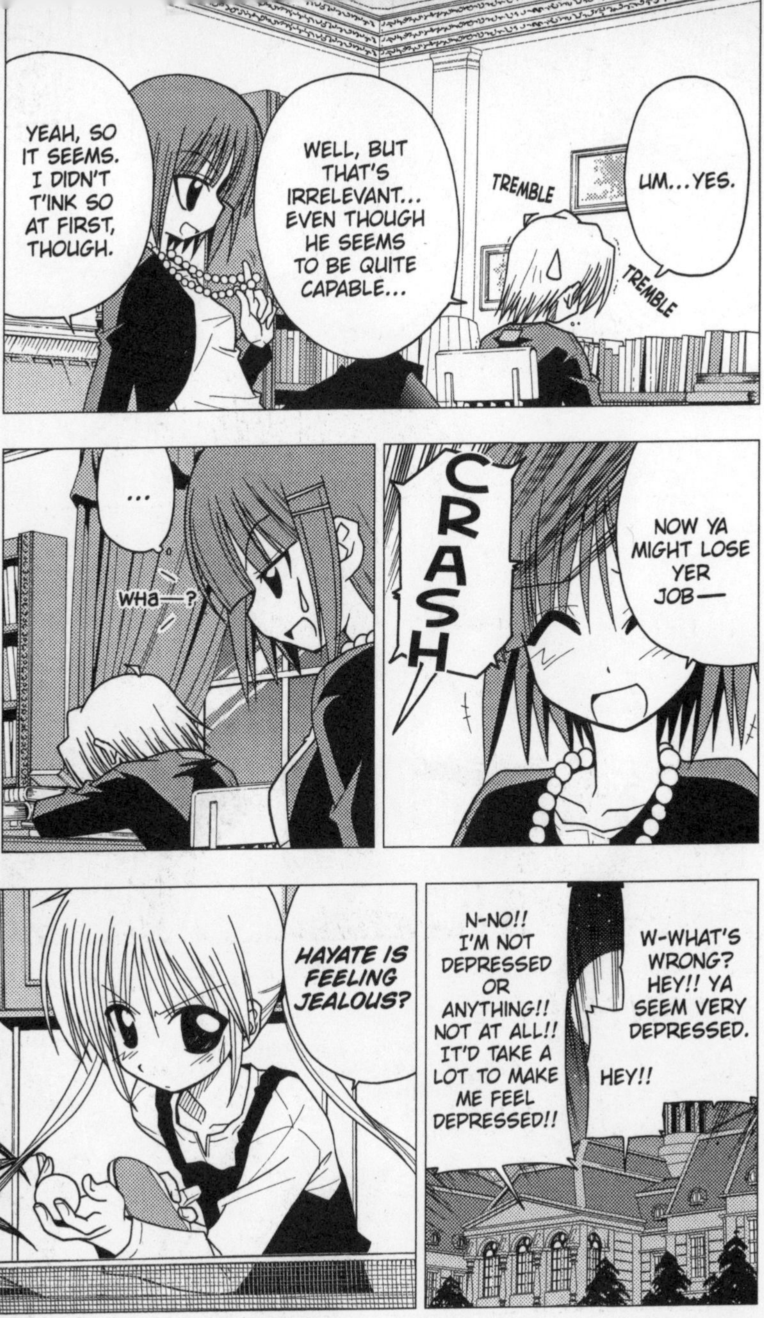
UM...YES.
TREMBLE
TREMBLE
WELL, BUT THAT'S IRRELEVANT... EVEN THOUGH HE SEEMS TO BE QUITE CAPABLE...
YEAH, SO IT SEEMS. I DIDN'T T'INK SO AT FIRST, THOUGH.
NOW YA MIGHT LOSE YER JOB—
CRASH
...
WHA—?
W-WHAT'S WRONG? HEY!! YA SEEM VERY DEPRESSED.
HEY!!
N-NO!! I'M NOT DEPRESSED OR ANYTHING!! NOT AT ALL!! IT'D TAKE A LOT TO MAKE ME FEEL DEPRESSED!!
HAYATE IS FEELING JEALOUS?

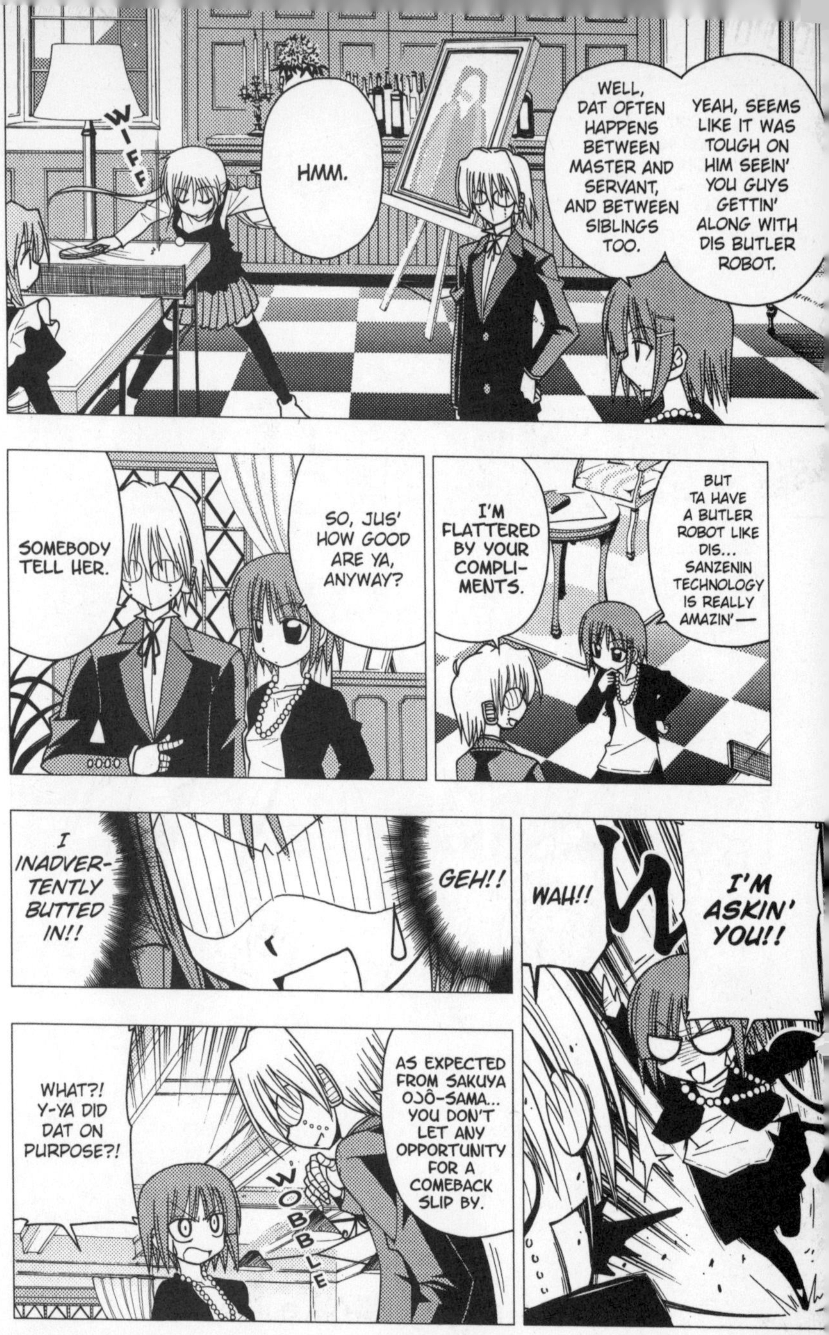
YEAH, SEEMS LIKE IT WAS TOUGH ON HIM SEEIN' YOU GUYS GETTIN' ALONG WITH DIS BUTLER ROBOT.
WELL, DAT OFTEN HAPPENS BETWEEN MASTER AND SERVANT, AND BETWEEN SIBLINGS TOO.
HMM.
WIFF
BUT TA HAVE A BUTLER ROBOT LIKE DIS... SANZENIN TECHNOLOGY IS REALLY AMAZIN'—
I'M FLATTERED BY YOUR COMPLI-MENTS.
SO, JUS' HOW GOOD ARE YA, ANYWAY?
SOMEBODY TELL HER.
I'M ASKIN' YOU!!
WAH!!
GEH!!
I INADVER-TENTLY BUTTED IN!!
AS EXPECTED FROM SAKUYA OJÔ-SAMA... YOU DON'T LET ANY OPPORTUNITY FOR A COMEBACK SLIP BY.
WOBBLE
WHAT?! Y-YA DID DAT ON PURPOSE?!

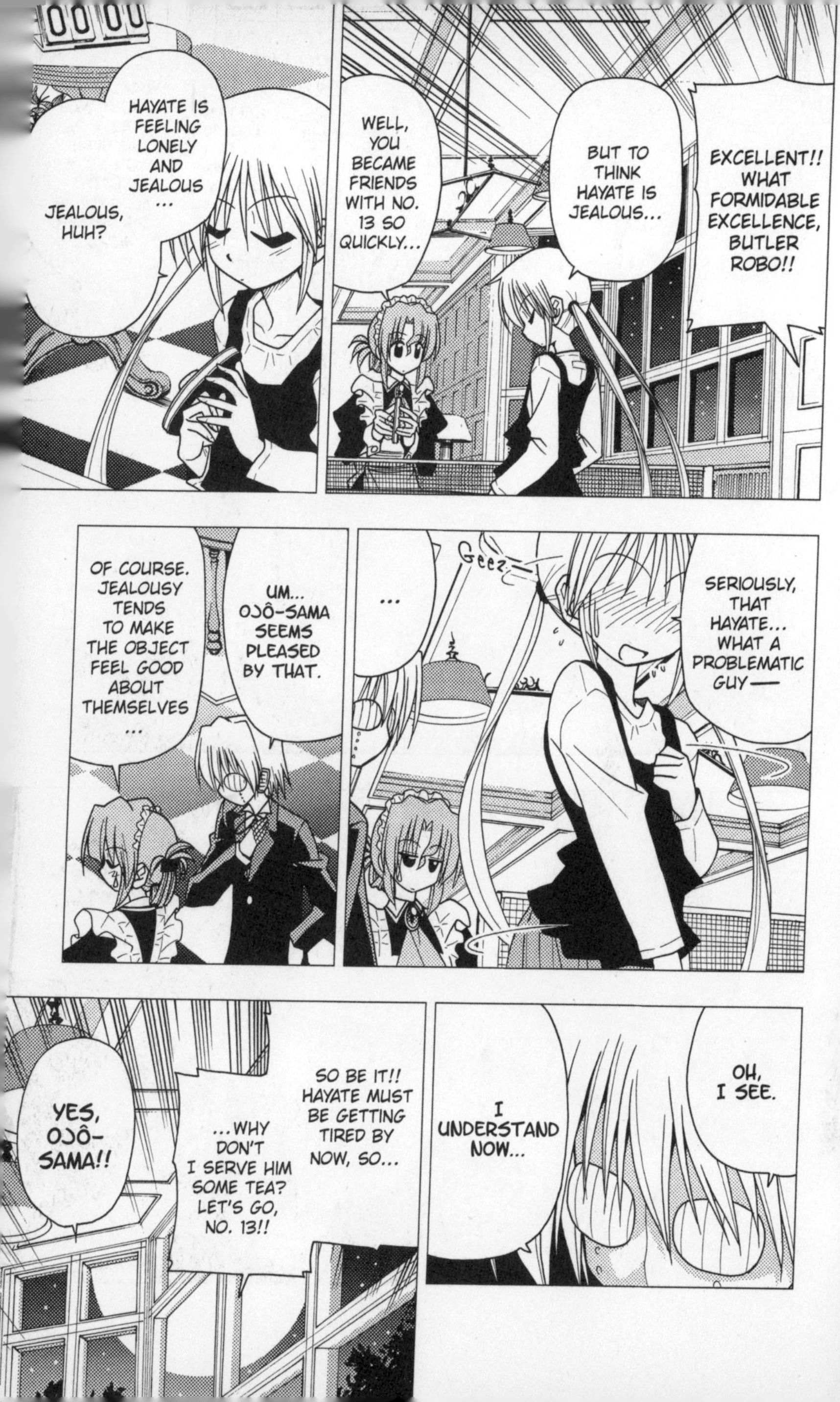
EXCELLENT!! WHAT FORMIDABLE EXCELLENCE, BUTLER ROBO!!
BUT TO THINK HAYATE IS JEALOUS...
WELL, YOU BECAME FRIENDS WITH NO. 13 SO QUICKLY...
00 00
HAYATE IS FEELING LONELY AND JEALOUS ...
JEALOUS, HUH?
SERIOUSLY, THAT HAYATE... WHAT A PROBLEMATIC GUY—
Geez
...
UM... OJÔ-SAMA SEEMS PLEASED BY THAT.
OF COURSE. JEALOUSY TENDS TO MAKE THE OBJECT FEEL GOOD ABOUT THEMSELVES ...
OH, I SEE.
I UNDERSTAND NOW...
SO BE IT!! HAYATE MUST BE GETTING TIRED BY NOW, SO...
...WHY DON'T I SERVE HIM SOME TEA? LET'S GO, NO. 13!!
YES, OJÔ-SAMA!!

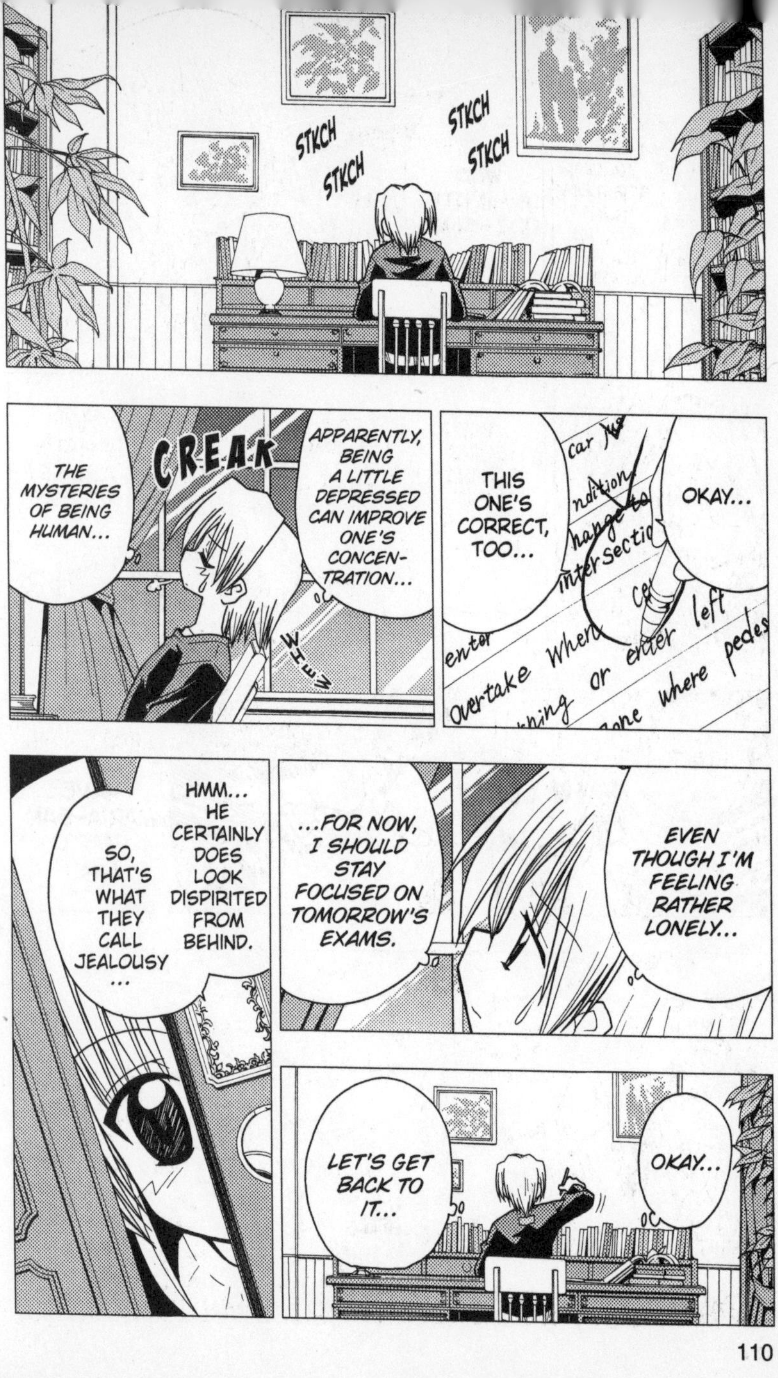
STKCH
STKCH
STKCH
STKCH
OKAY...
THIS ONE'S CORRECT, TOO...
APPARENTLY, BEING A LITTLE DEPRESSED CAN IMPROVE ONE'S CONCENTRATION...
CREAK
THE MYSTERIES OF BEING HUMAN...
WHEW
EVEN THOUGH I'M FEELING RATHER LONELY...
...FOR NOW, I SHOULD STAY FOCUSED ON TOMORROW'S EXAMS.
OKAY...
LET'S GET BACK TO IT...
HMM... HE CERTAINLY DOES LOOK DISPIRITED FROM BEHIND.
SO, THAT'S WHAT THEY CALL JEALOUSY...

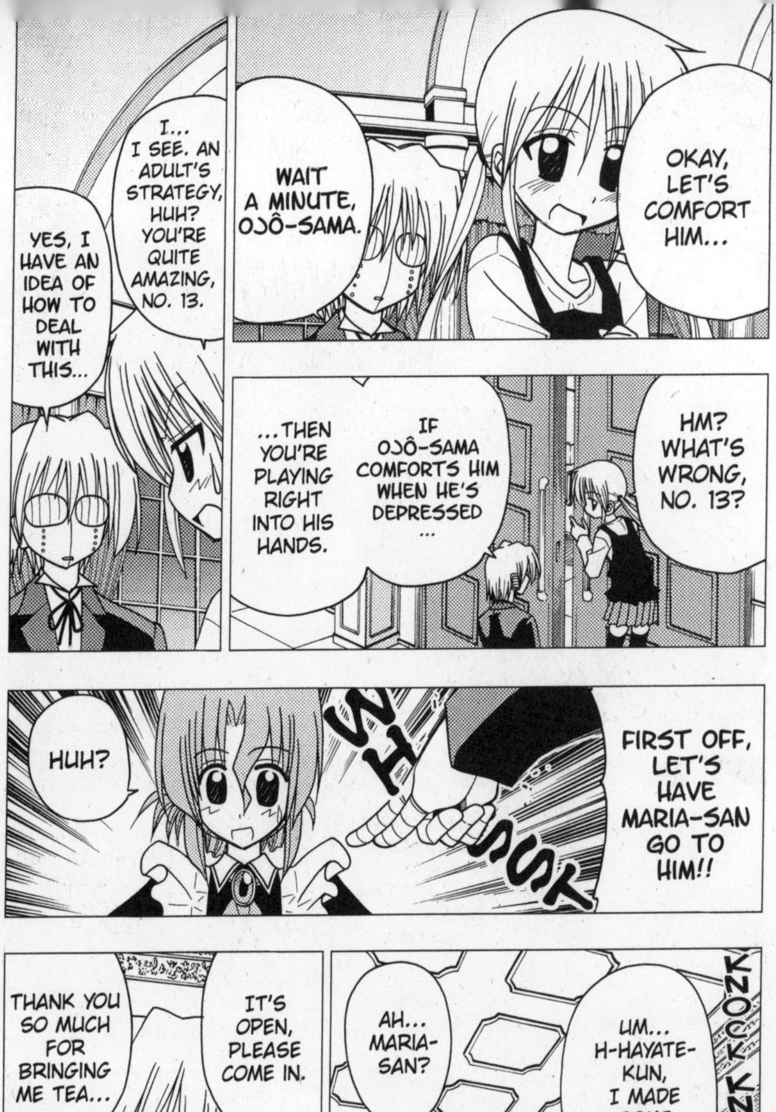
OKAY, LET'S COMFORT HIM...
WAIT A MINUTE, OJÔ-SAMA.
HM? WHAT'S WRONG, NO. 13?
IF OJÔ-SAMA COMFORTS HIM WHEN HE'S DEPRESSED ...
...THEN YOU'RE PLAYING RIGHT INTO HIS HANDS.
I... I SEE. AN ADULT'S STRATEGY, HUH? YOU'RE QUITE AMAZING, NO. 13.
YES, I HAVE AN IDEA OF HOW TO DEAL WITH THIS...
FIRST OFF, LET'S HAVE MARIA-SAN GO TO HIM!!
SWISH
HUH?
KNOCK KNOCK
UM... H-HAYATE-KUN, I MADE SOME TEA FOR YOU, SO...
AH... MARIA-SAN?
IT'S OPEN, PLEASE COME IN.
THANK YOU SO MUCH FOR BRINGING ME TEA...

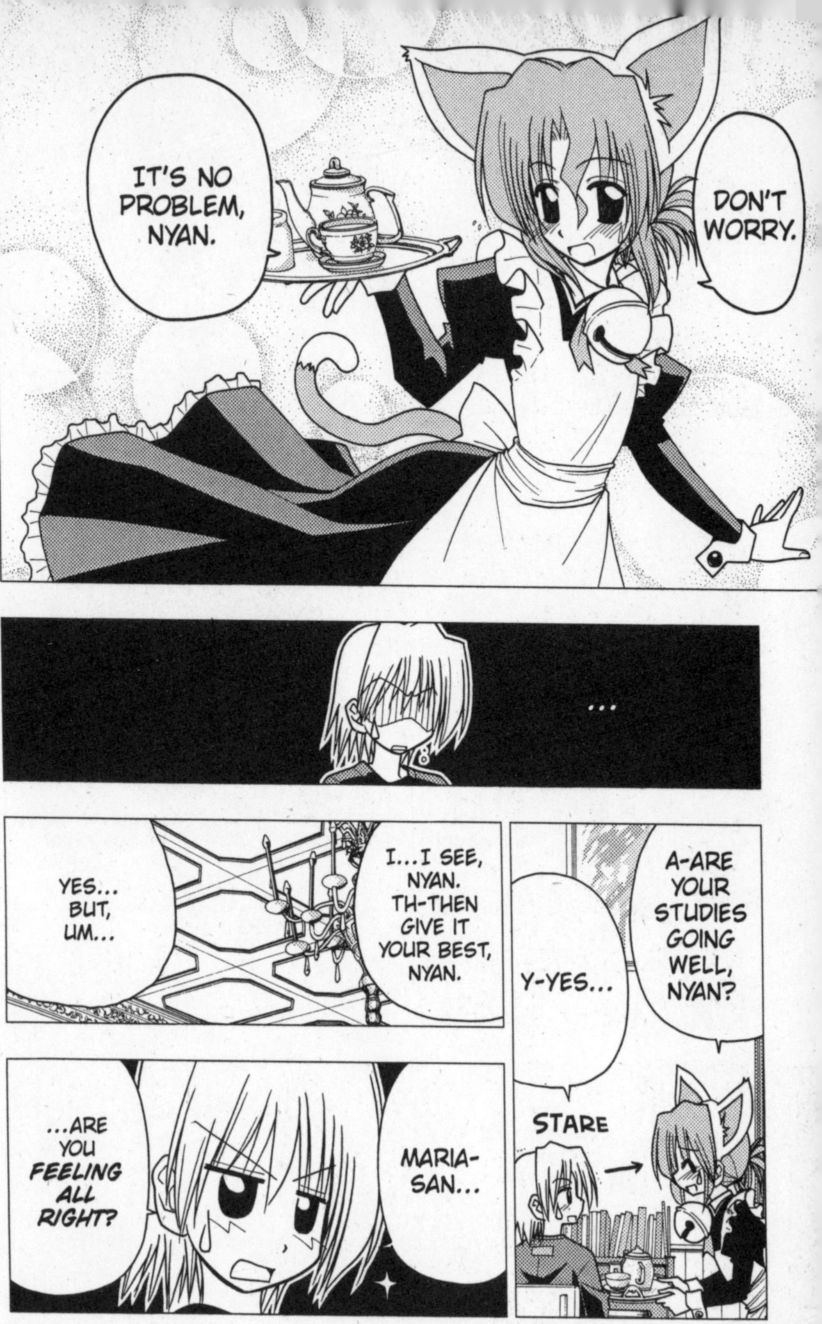
DON'T WORRY.
IT'S NO PROBLEM, NYAN.
...
A-ARE YOUR STUDIES GOING WELL, NYAN?
Y-YES...
STARE
I...I SEE, NYAN. TH-THEN GIVE IT YOUR BEST, NYAN.
YES... BUT, UM...
MARIA-SAN...
...ARE YOU FEELING ALL RIGHT?

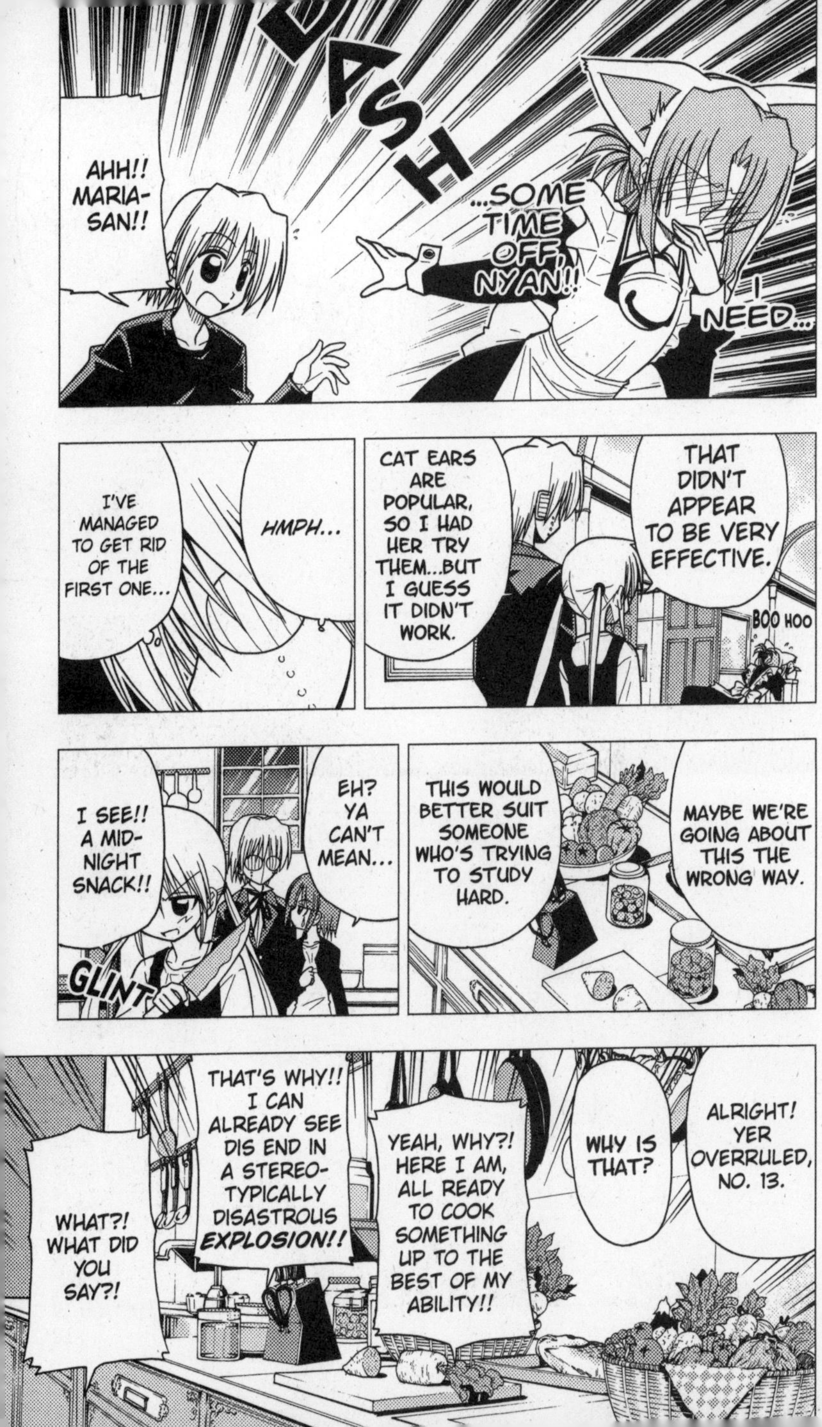
I NEED...
...SOME TIME OFF, NYAN!!
DASH
AHH!! MARIA-SAN!!
THAT DIDN'T APPEAR TO BE VERY EFFECTIVE.
BOO HOO
CAT EARS ARE POPULAR, SO I HAD HER TRY THEM...BUT I GUESS IT DIDN'T WORK.
HMPH...
I'VE MANAGED TO GET RID OF THE FIRST ONE...
MAYBE WE'RE GOING ABOUT THIS THE WRONG WAY.
THIS WOULD BETTER SUIT SOMEONE WHO'S TRYING TO STUDY HARD.
EH? YA CAN'T MEAN...
I SEE!! A MID-NIGHT SNACK!!
GLINT
ALRIGHT! YER OVERRULED, NO. 13.
WHY IS THAT?
YEAH, WHY?! HERE I AM, ALL READY TO COOK SOMETHING UP TO THE BEST OF MY ABILITY!!
THAT'S WHY!! I CAN ALREADY SEE DIS END IN A STEREO-TYPICALLY DISASTROUS *EXPLOSION!!*
WHAT?! WHAT DID YOU SAY?!

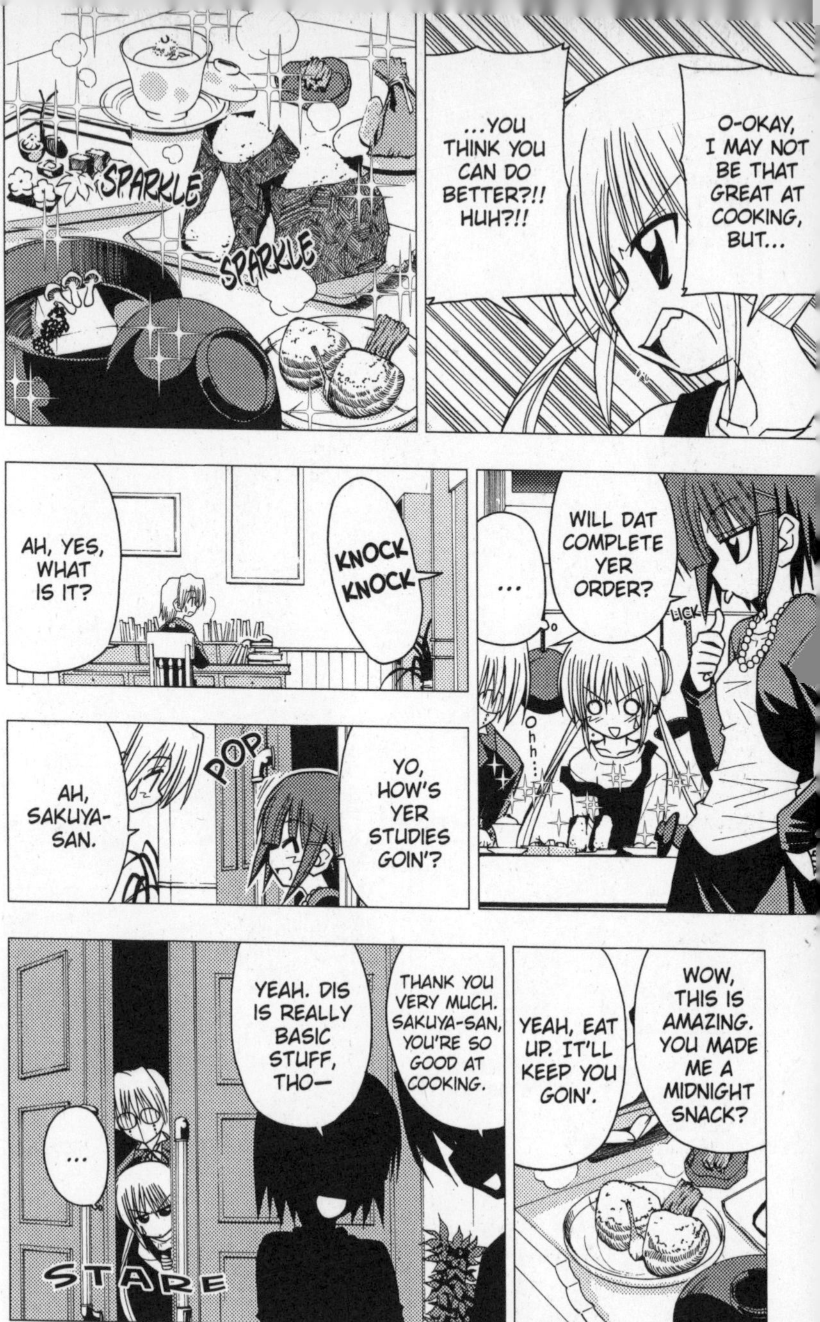
O-OKAY, I MAY NOT BE THAT GREAT AT COOKING, BUT...
...YOU THINK YOU CAN DO BETTER?!! HUH?!!
SPARKLE
SPARKLE
WILL DAT COMPLETE YER ORDER?
...
LICK
Ohh...
KNOCK KNOCK
AH, YES, WHAT IS IT?
YO, HOW'S YER STUDIES GOIN'?
POP
AH, SAKUYA-SAN.
WOW, THIS IS AMAZING. YOU MADE ME A MIDNIGHT SNACK?
YEAH, EAT UP. IT'LL KEEP YOU GOIN'.
THANK YOU VERY MUCH. SAKUYA-SAN, YOU'RE SO GOOD AT COOKING.
YEAH. DIS IS REALLY BASIC STUFF, THO—
...
STARE

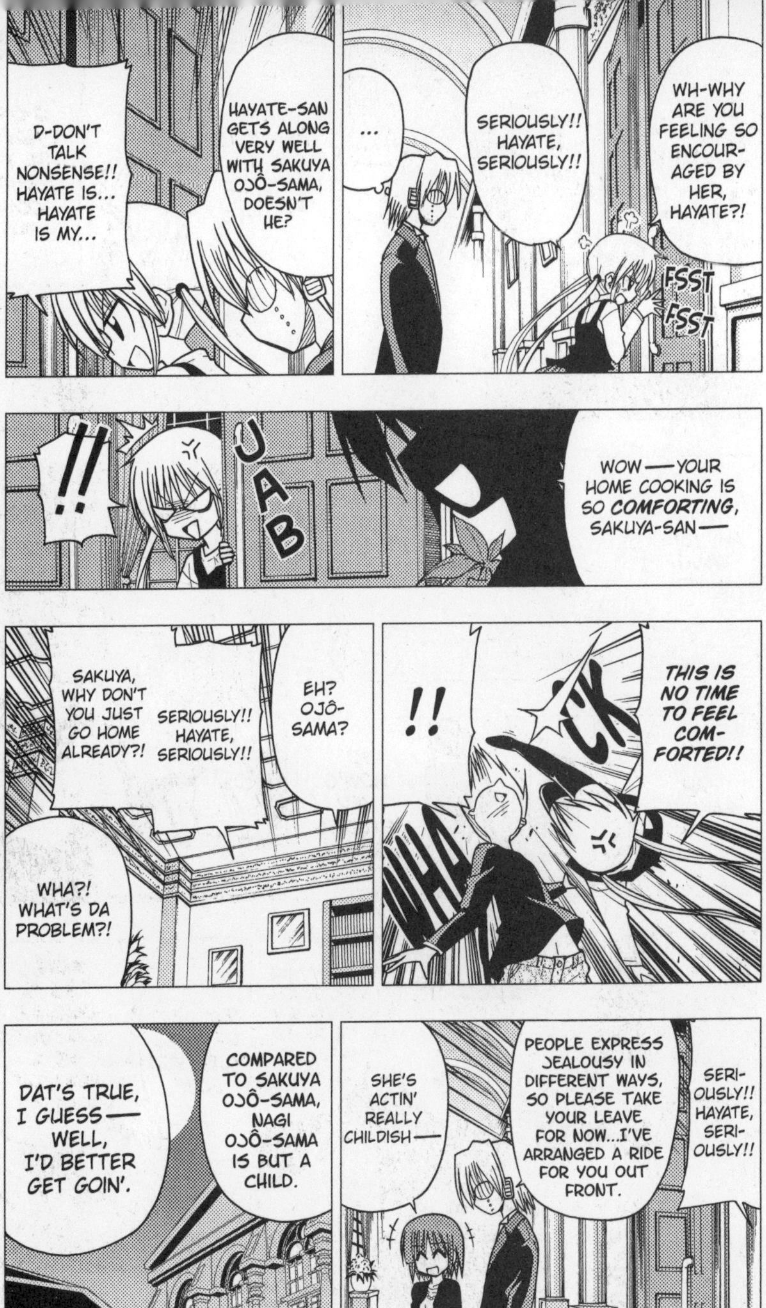
WH-WHY ARE YOU FEELING SO ENCOURAGED BY HER, HAYATE?!
FSST FSST
SERIOUSLY!! HAYATE, SERIOUSLY!!
...
HAYATE-SAN GETS ALONG VERY WELL WITH SAKUYA OJÔ-SAMA, DOESN'T HE?
D-DON'T TALK NONSENSE!! HAYATE IS... HAYATE IS MY...
WOW—YOUR HOME COOKING IS SO *COMFORTING*, SAKUYA-SAN—
JAB
!!
THIS IS NO TIME TO FEEL COMFORTED!!
CK
!!
WHA
EH? OJÔ-SAMA?
SERIOUSLY!! HAYATE, SERIOUSLY!!
SAKUYA, WHY DON'T YOU JUST GO HOME ALREADY?!
WHA?! WHAT'S DA PROBLEM?!
SERIOUSLY!! HAYATE, SERIOUSLY!!
PEOPLE EXPRESS JEALOUSY IN DIFFERENT WAYS, SO PLEASE TAKE YOUR LEAVE FOR NOW...I'VE ARRANGED A RIDE FOR YOU OUT FRONT.
SHE'S ACTIN' REALLY CHILDISH—
COMPARED TO SAKUYA OJÔ-SAMA, NAGI OJÔ-SAMA IS BUT A CHILD.
DAT'S TRUE, I GUESS—WELL, I'D BETTER GET GOIN'.

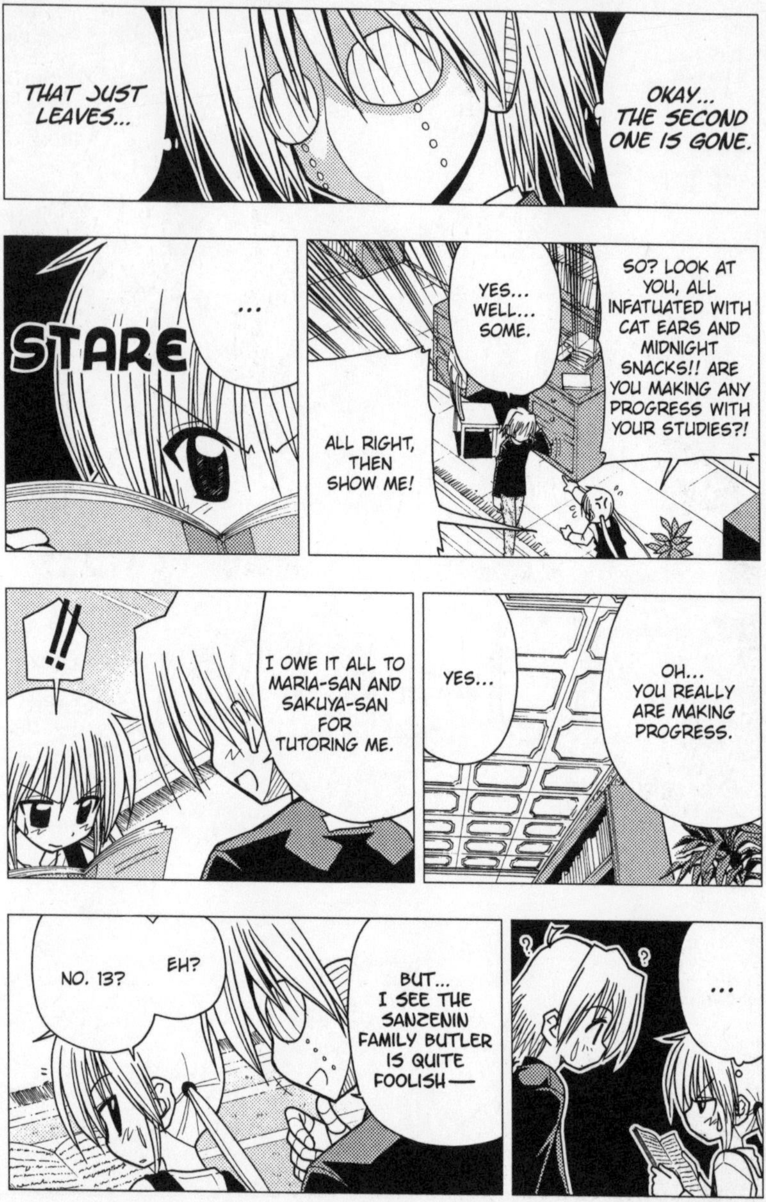
OKAY... THE SECOND ONE IS GONE.
THAT JUST LEAVES...
SO? LOOK AT YOU, ALL INFATUATED WITH CAT EARS AND MIDNIGHT SNACKS!! ARE YOU MAKING ANY PROGRESS WITH YOUR STUDIES?!
YES... WELL... SOME.
ALL RIGHT, THEN SHOW ME!
...
STARE
OH... YOU REALLY ARE MAKING PROGRESS.
YES...
I OWE IT ALL TO MARIA-SAN AND SAKUYA-SAN FOR TUTORING ME.
!!
...
BUT... I SEE THE SANZENIN FAMILY BUTLER IS QUITE FOOLISH—
EH?
NO. 13?

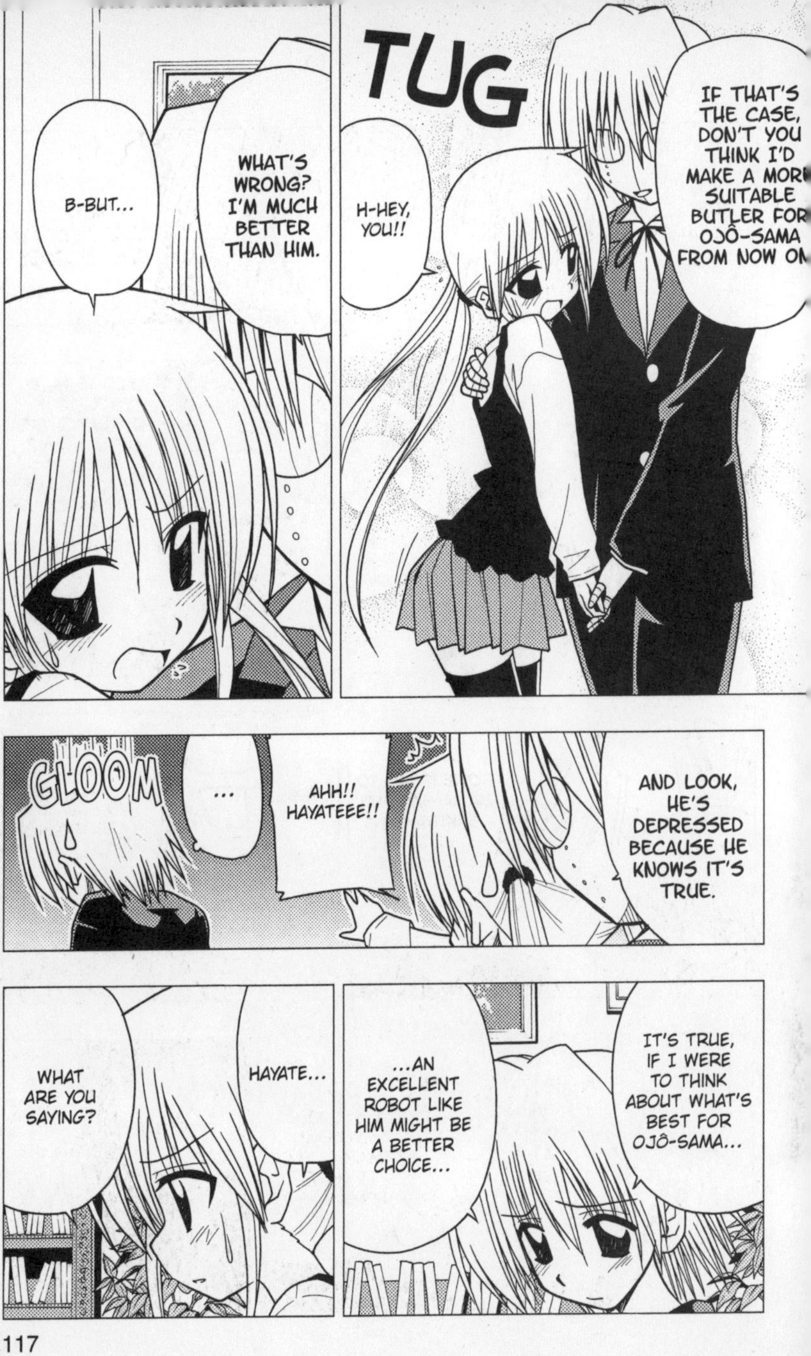
TUG
IF THAT'S THE CASE, DON'T YOU THINK I'D MAKE A MORE SUITABLE BUTLER FOR OJÔ-SAMA FROM NOW ON
H-HEY, YOU!!
WHAT'S WRONG? I'M MUCH BETTER THAN HIM.
B-BUT...
AND LOOK, HE'S DEPRESSED BECAUSE HE KNOWS IT'S TRUE.
AHH!! HAYATEEE!!
...
GLOOM
IT'S TRUE, IF I WERE TO THINK ABOUT WHAT'S BEST FOR OJÔ-SAMA...
...AN EXCELLENT ROBOT LIKE HIM MIGHT BE A BETTER CHOICE...
HAYATE...
WHAT ARE YOU SAYING?

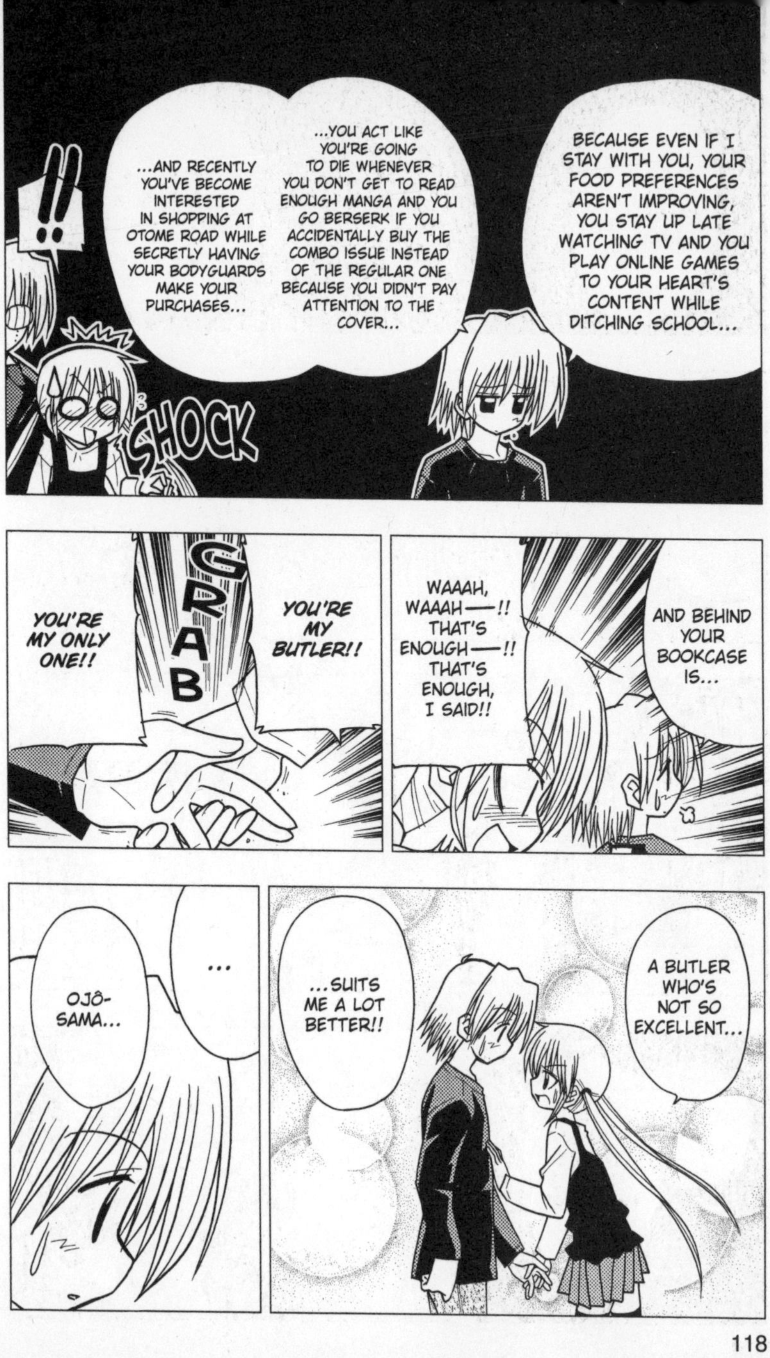
BECAUSE EVEN IF I STAY WITH YOU, YOUR FOOD PREFERENCES AREN'T IMPROVING, YOU STAY UP LATE WATCHING TV AND YOU PLAY ONLINE GAMES TO YOUR HEART'S CONTENT WHILE DITCHING SCHOOL...
...YOU ACT LIKE YOU'RE GOING TO DIE WHENEVER YOU DON'T GET TO READ ENOUGH MANGA AND YOU GO BERSERK IF YOU ACCIDENTALLY BUY THE COMBO ISSUE INSTEAD OF THE REGULAR ONE BECAUSE YOU DIDN'T PAY ATTENTION TO THE COVER...
...AND RECENTLY YOU'VE BECOME INTERESTED IN SHOPPING AT OTOME ROAD WHILE SECRETLY HAVING YOUR BODYGUARDS MAKE YOUR PURCHASES...
!!
SHOCK
AND BEHIND YOUR BOOKCASE IS...
WAAAH, WAAAH——!! THAT'S ENOUGH——!! THAT'S ENOUGH, I SAID!!
YOU'RE MY BUTLER!!
GRAB
YOU'RE MY ONLY ONE!!
A BUTLER WHO'S NOT SO EXCELLENT...
...SUITS ME A LOT BETTER!!
...
OJÔ-SAMA...

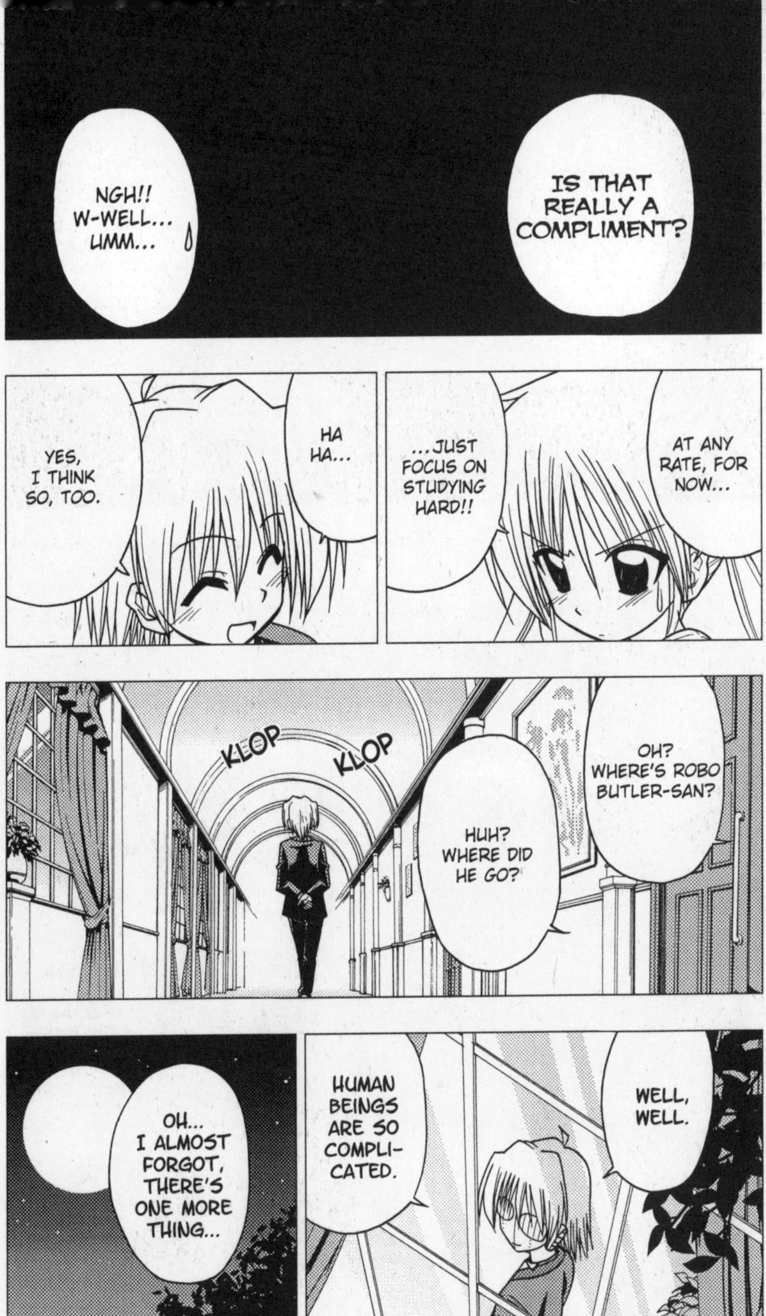
IS THAT REALLY A COMPLIMENT?
NGH!! W-WELL... UMM...
AT ANY RATE, FOR NOW...
...JUST FOCUS ON STUDYING HARD!!
HA HA...
YES, I THINK SO, TOO.
OH? WHERE'S ROBO BUTLER-SAN?
KLOP
KLOP
HUH? WHERE DID HE GO?
WELL, WELL.
HUMAN BEINGS ARE SO COMPLI-CATED.
OH... I ALMOST FORGOT, THERE'S ONE MORE THING...

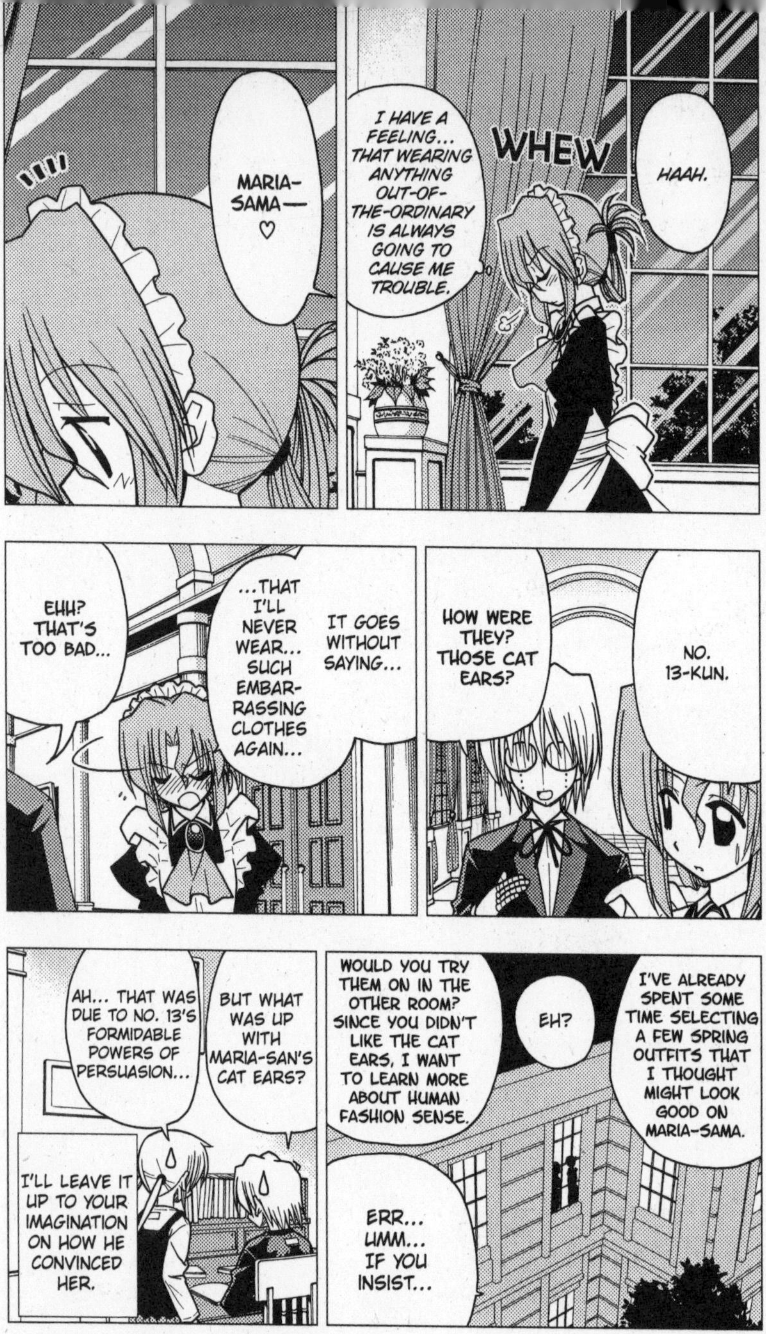
HAAH.
WHEW
I HAVE A FEELING... THAT WEARING ANYTHING OUT-OF-THE-ORDINARY IS ALWAYS GOING TO CAUSE ME TROUBLE.
MARIA-SAMA—♡
NO. 13-KUN.
HOW WERE THEY? THOSE CAT EARS?
IT GOES WITHOUT SAYING...
...THAT I'LL NEVER WEAR... SUCH EMBARRASSING CLOTHES AGAIN...
EHH? THAT'S TOO BAD...
I'VE ALREADY SPENT SOME TIME SELECTING A FEW SPRING OUTFITS THAT I THOUGHT MIGHT LOOK GOOD ON MARIA-SAMA.
EH?
WOULD YOU TRY THEM ON IN THE OTHER ROOM? SINCE YOU DIDN'T LIKE THE CAT EARS, I WANT TO LEARN MORE ABOUT HUMAN FASHION SENSE.
ERR... UMM... IF YOU INSIST...
BUT WHAT WAS UP WITH MARIA-SAN'S CAT EARS?
AH... THAT WAS DUE TO NO. 13'S FORMIDABLE POWERS OF PERSUASION...
I'LL LEAVE IT UP TO YOUR IMAGINATION ON HOW HE CONVINCED HER.

Episode 8:
"I Cried Out Loud on YOUR TUBE, and Now I Feel Great!"

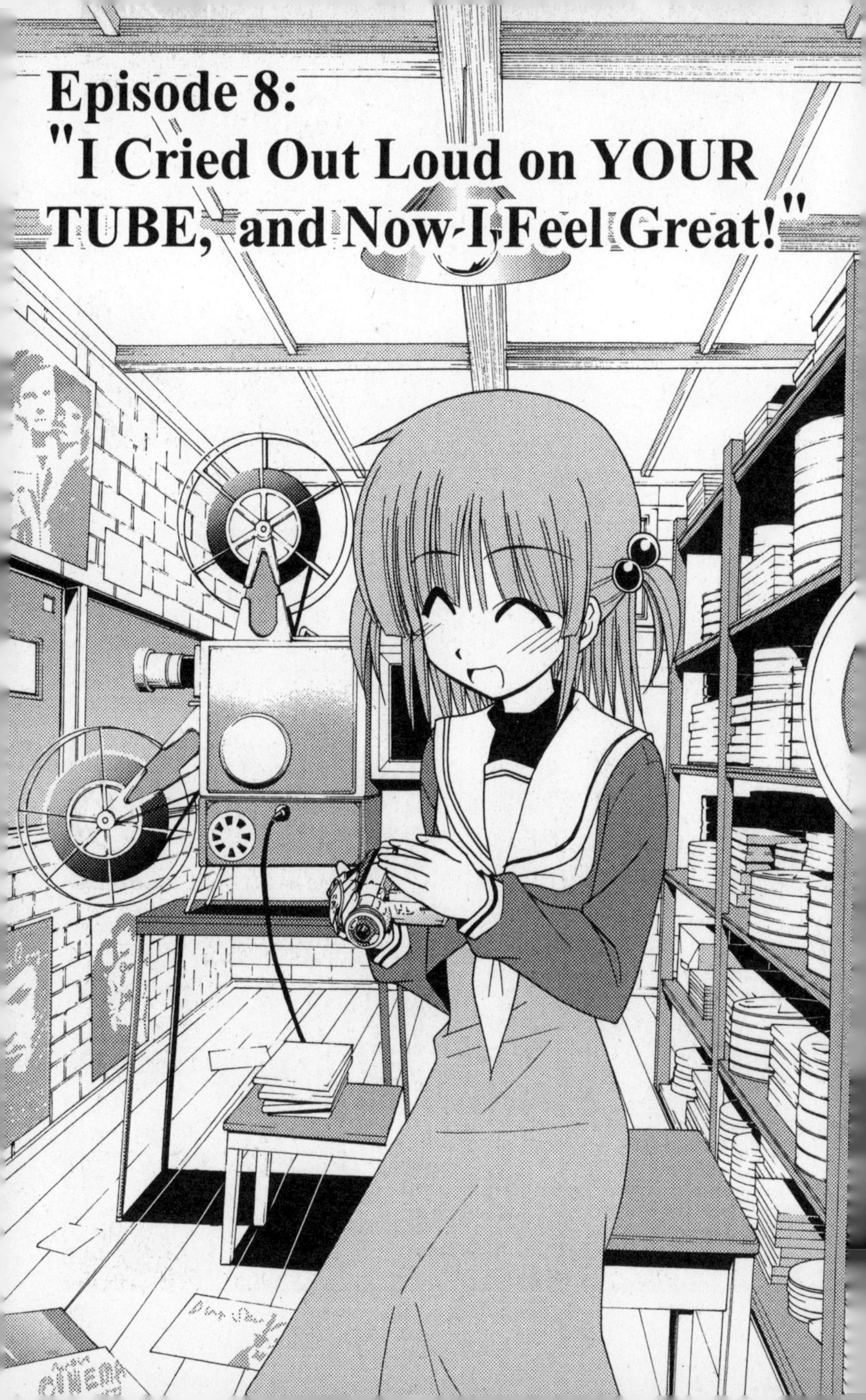

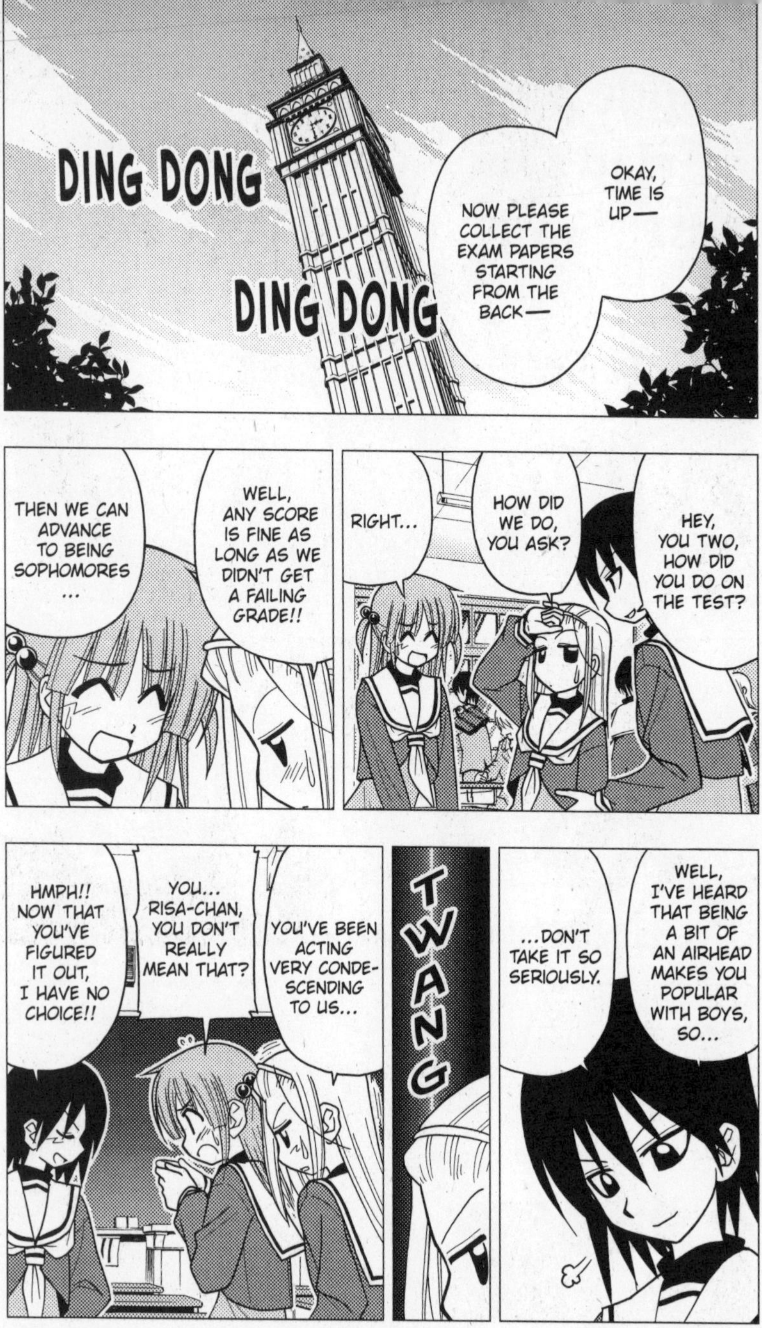
OKAY, TIME IS UP—
NOW PLEASE COLLECT THE EXAM PAPERS STARTING FROM THE BACK—
DING DONG
DING DONG
HEY, YOU TWO, HOW DID YOU DO ON THE TEST?
HOW DID WE DO, YOU ASK?
RIGHT...
WELL, ANY SCORE IS FINE AS LONG AS WE DIDN'T GET A FAILING GRADE!!
THEN WE CAN ADVANCE TO BEING SOPHOMORES ...
WELL, I'VE HEARD THAT BEING A BIT OF AN AIRHEAD MAKES YOU POPULAR WITH BOYS, SO...
...DON'T TAKE IT SO SERIOUSLY.
TWANG
YOU'VE BEEN ACTING VERY CONDE-SCENDING TO US...
YOU... RISA-CHAN, YOU DON'T REALLY MEAN THAT?
HMPH!! NOW THAT YOU'VE FIGURED IT OUT, I HAVE NO CHOICE!!

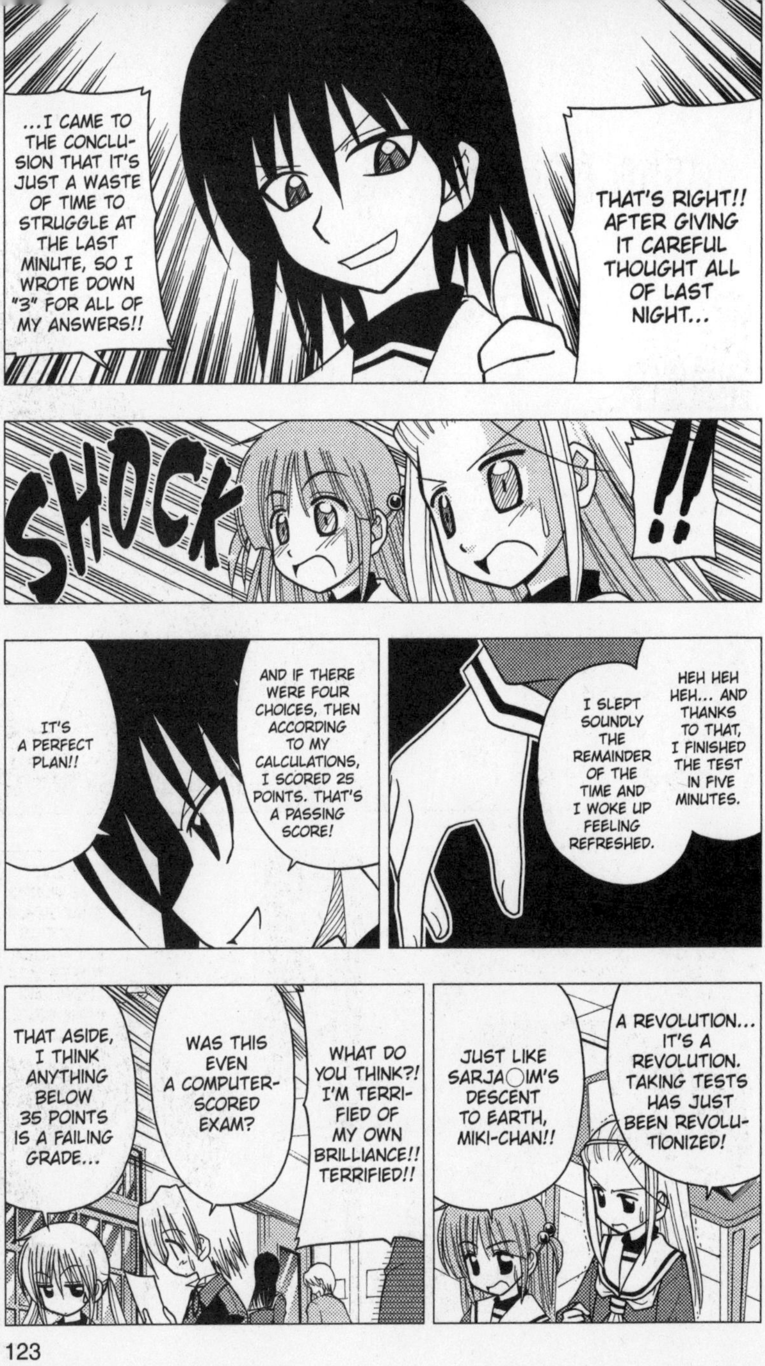
THAT'S RIGHT!! AFTER GIVING IT CAREFUL THOUGHT ALL OF LAST NIGHT...
...I CAME TO THE CONCLUSION THAT IT'S JUST A WASTE OF TIME TO STRUGGLE AT THE LAST MINUTE, SO I WROTE DOWN "3" FOR ALL OF MY ANSWERS!!
!!
SHOCK
HEH HEH HEH... AND THANKS TO THAT, I FINISHED THE TEST IN FIVE MINUTES.
I SLEPT SOUNDLY THE REMAINDER OF THE TIME AND I WOKE UP FEELING REFRESHED.
AND IF THERE WERE FOUR CHOICES, THEN ACCORDING TO MY CALCULATIONS, I SCORED 25 POINTS. THAT'S A PASSING SCORE!
IT'S A PERFECT PLAN!!
A REVOLUTION... IT'S A REVOLUTION. TAKING TESTS HAS JUST BEEN REVOLUTIONIZED!
JUST LIKE SARJA◯IM'S DESCENT TO EARTH, MIKI-CHAN!!
WHAT DO YOU THINK?! I'M TERRIFIED OF MY OWN BRILLIANCE!! TERRIFIED!!
WAS THIS EVEN A COMPUTER-SCORED EXAM?
THAT ASIDE, I THINK ANYTHING BELOW 35 POINTS IS A FAILING GRADE...

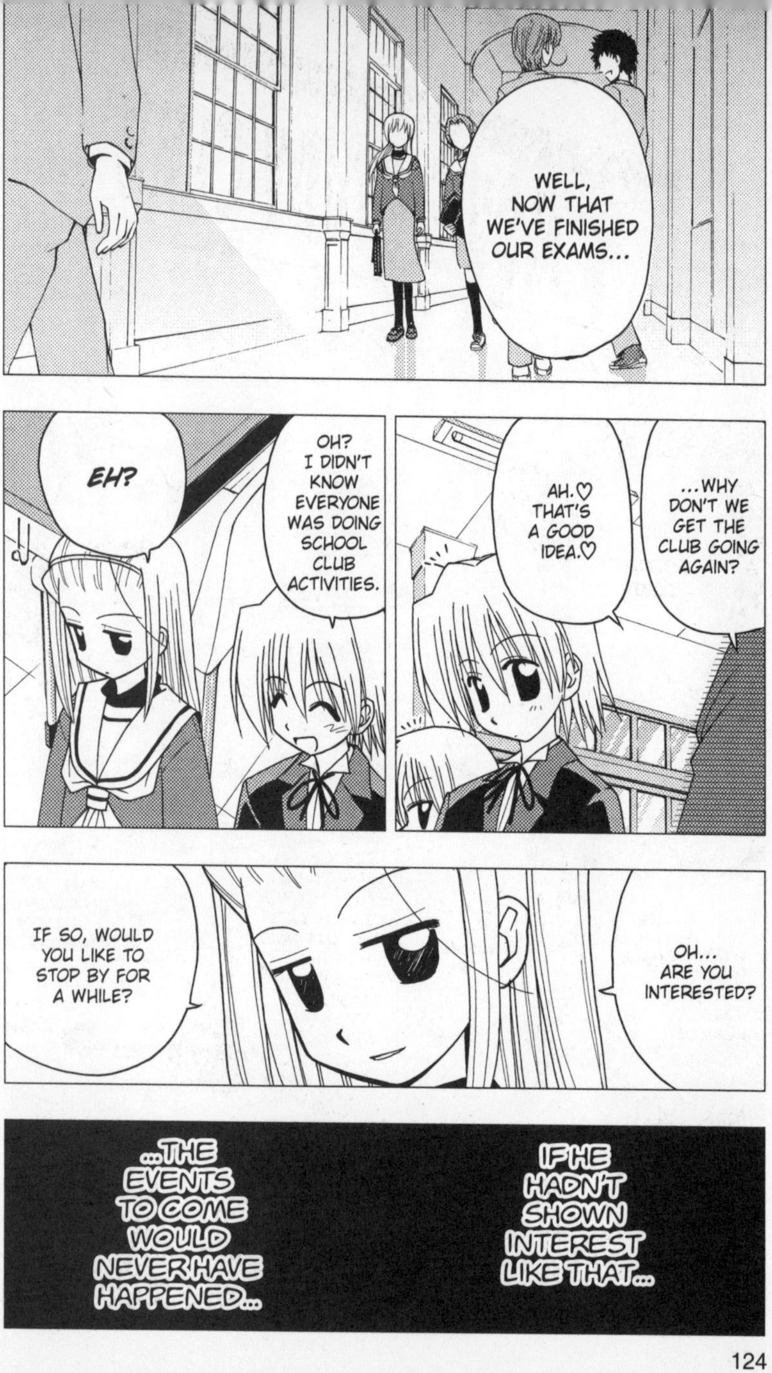
WELL, NOW THAT WE'VE FINISHED OUR EXAMS...
...WHY DON'T WE GET THE CLUB GOING AGAIN?
AH.♡ THAT'S A GOOD IDEA.♡
OH? I DIDN'T KNOW EVERYONE WAS DOING SCHOOL CLUB ACTIVITIES.
EH?
OH... ARE YOU INTERESTED?
IF SO, WOULD YOU LIKE TO STOP BY FOR A WHILE?
IF HE HADN'T SHOWN INTEREST LIKE THAT...
...THE EVENTS TO COME WOULD NEVER HAVE HAPPENED...

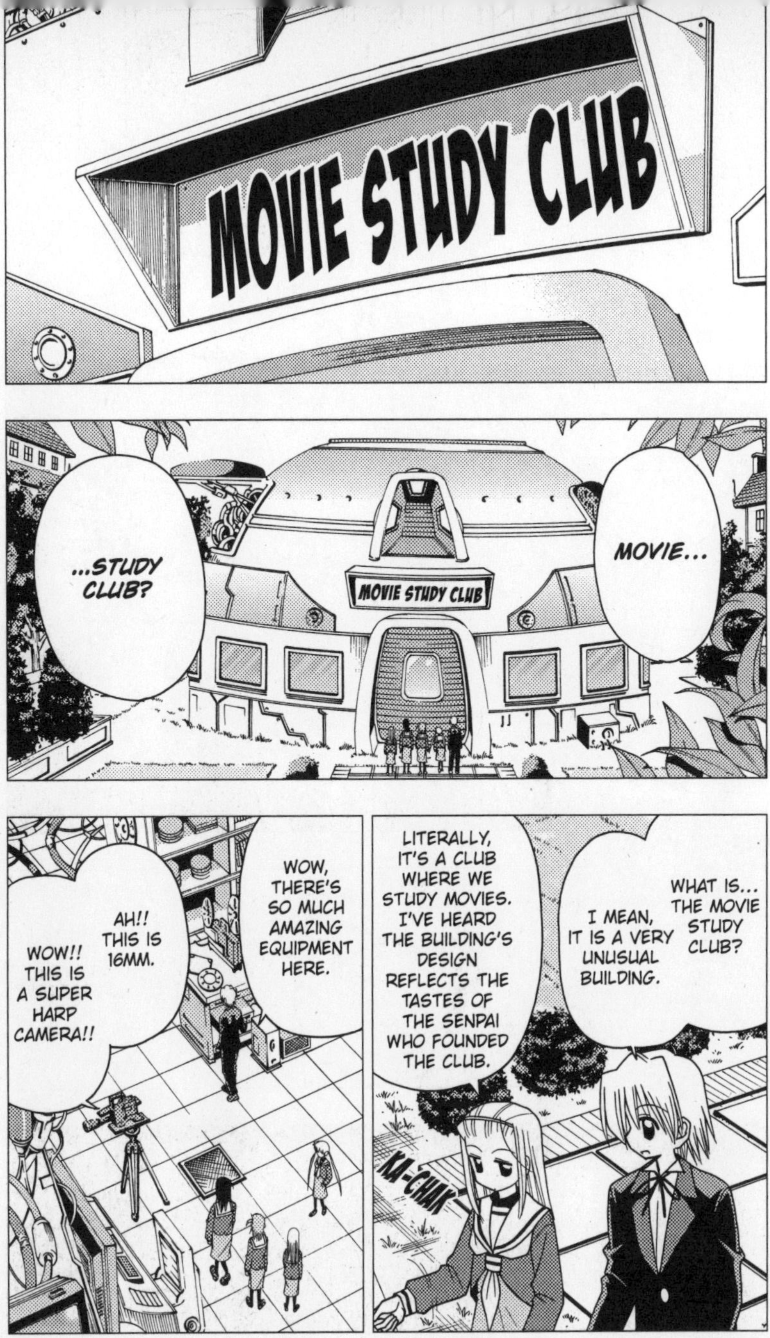
MOVIE STUDY CLUB
MOVIE...
...STUDY CLUB?
MOVIE STUDY CLUB
WHAT IS... THE MOVIE STUDY CLUB?
I MEAN, IT IS A VERY UNUSUAL BUILDING.
LITERALLY, IT'S A CLUB WHERE WE STUDY MOVIES. I'VE HEARD THE BUILDING'S DESIGN REFLECTS THE TASTES OF THE SENPAI WHO FOUNDED THE CLUB.
KA-CHAK
WOW, THERE'S SO MUCH AMAZING EQUIPMENT HERE.
AH!! THIS IS 16MM.
WOW!! THIS IS A SUPER HARP CAMERA!!

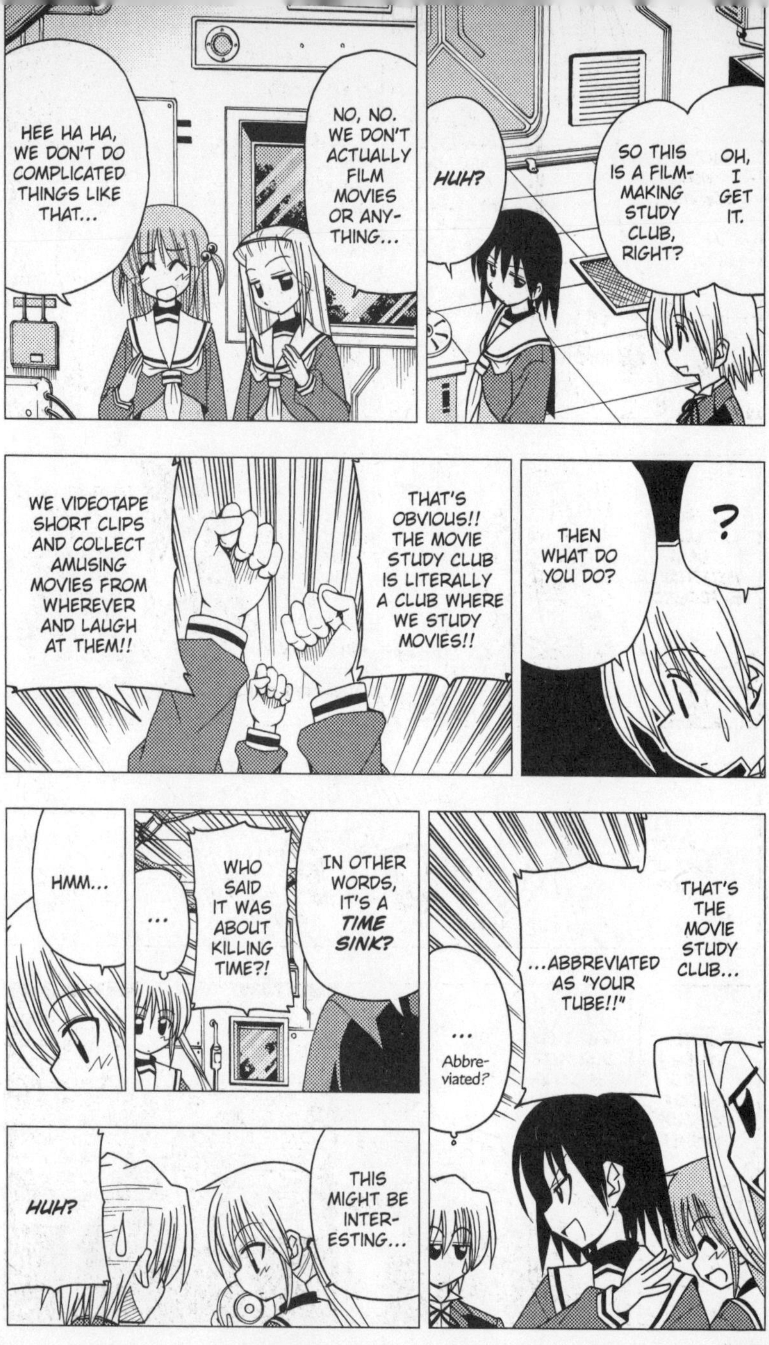
OH, I GET IT.
SO THIS IS A FILM-MAKING STUDY CLUB, RIGHT?
HUH?
NO, NO. WE DON'T ACTUALLY FILM MOVIES OR ANY-THING...
HEE HA HA, WE DON'T DO COMPLICATED THINGS LIKE THAT...
?
THEN WHAT DO YOU DO?
THAT'S OBVIOUS!! THE MOVIE STUDY CLUB IS LITERALLY A CLUB WHERE WE STUDY MOVIES!!
WE VIDEOTAPE SHORT CLIPS AND COLLECT AMUSING MOVIES FROM WHEREVER AND LAUGH AT THEM!!
THAT'S THE MOVIE STUDY CLUB...
...ABBREVIATED AS "YOUR TUBE!!"
... Abbre-viated?
IN OTHER WORDS, IT'S A *TIME SINK?*
WHO SAID IT WAS ABOUT KILLING TIME?!
...
HMM...
THIS MIGHT BE INTER-ESTING...
HUH?

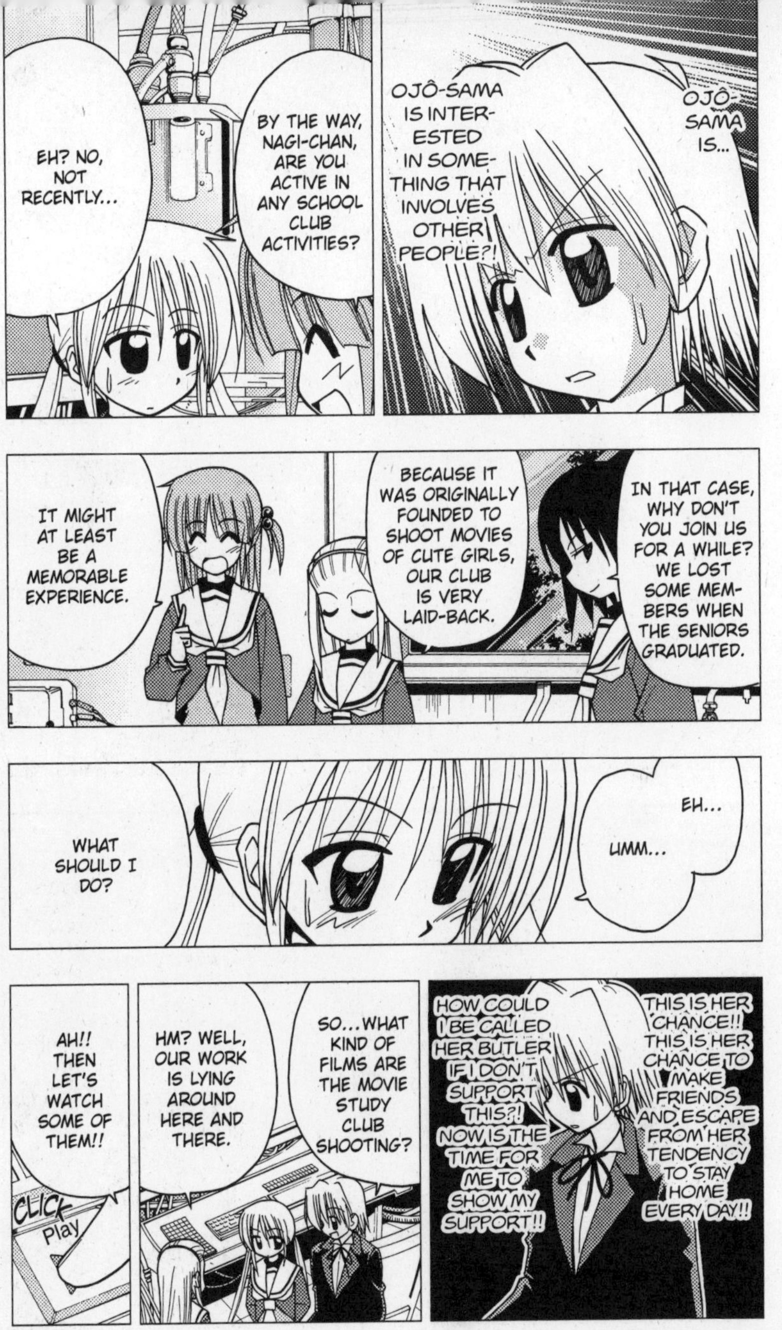
OJÔ-SAMA IS...
OJÔ-SAMA IS INTERESTED IN SOMETHING THAT INVOLVES OTHER PEOPLE?!
BY THE WAY, NAGI-CHAN, ARE YOU ACTIVE IN ANY SCHOOL CLUB ACTIVITIES?
EH? NO, NOT RECENTLY...
IN THAT CASE, WHY DON'T YOU JOIN US FOR A WHILE? WE LOST SOME MEMBERS WHEN THE SENIORS GRADUATED.
BECAUSE IT WAS ORIGINALLY FOUNDED TO SHOOT MOVIES OF CUTE GIRLS, OUR CLUB IS VERY LAID-BACK.
IT MIGHT AT LEAST BE A MEMORABLE EXPERIENCE.
EH...
UMM...
WHAT SHOULD I DO?
THIS IS HER CHANCE!! THIS IS HER CHANCE TO MAKE FRIENDS AND ESCAPE FROM HER TENDENCY TO STAY HOME EVERY DAY!!
HOW COULD I BE CALLED HER BUTLER IF I DON'T SUPPORT THIS?! NOW IS THE TIME FOR ME TO SHOW MY SUPPORT!!
SO...WHAT KIND OF FILMS ARE THE MOVIE STUDY CLUB SHOOTING?
HM? WELL, OUR WORK IS LYING AROUND HERE AND THERE.
AH!! THEN LET'S WATCH SOME OF THEM!!
CLICK
Play

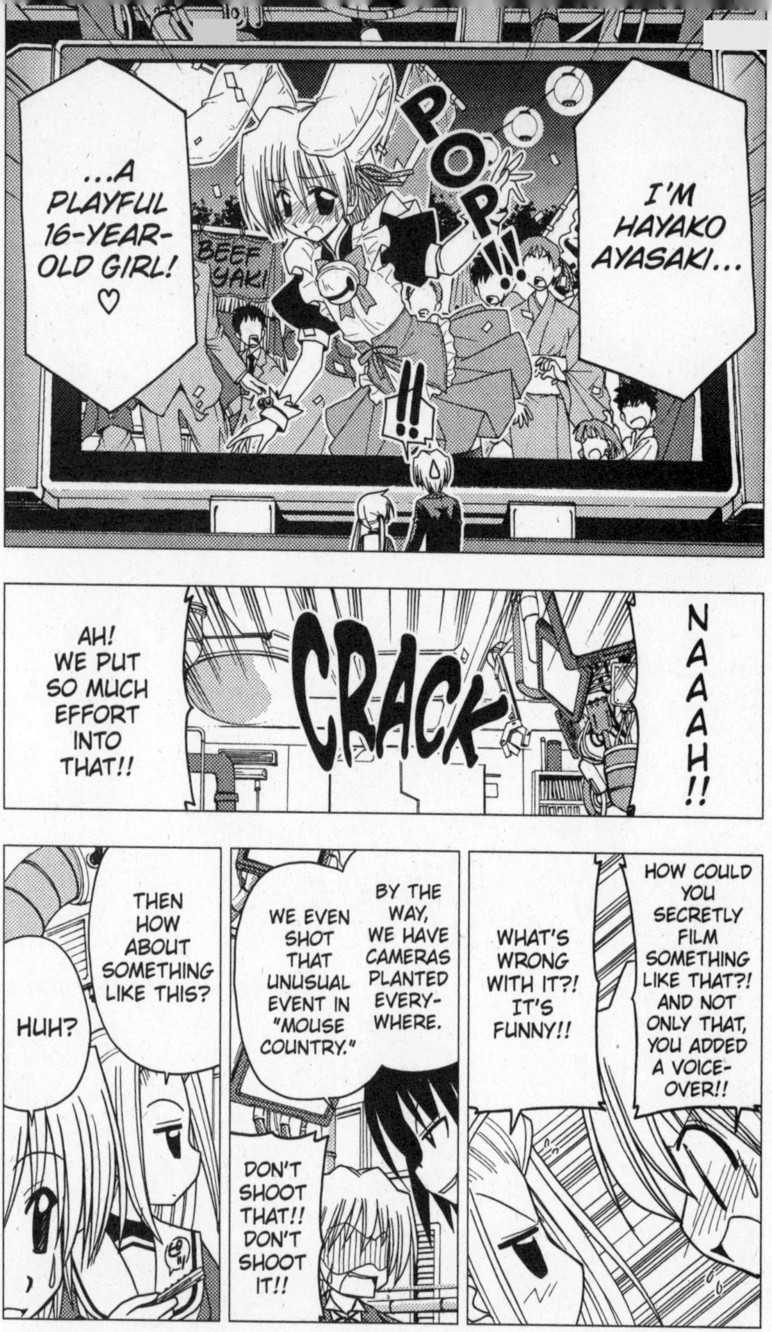
I'M HAYAKO AYASAKI...
POP!!
...A PLAYFUL 16-YEAR-OLD GIRL! ♡
BEEF YAKI
!!
NAAAAH!!
CRACK
AH! WE PUT SO MUCH EFFORT INTO THAT!!
HOW COULD YOU SECRETLY FILM SOMETHING LIKE THAT?! AND NOT ONLY THAT, YOU ADDED A VOICE-OVER!!
WHAT'S WRONG WITH IT?! IT'S FUNNY!!
BY THE WAY, WE HAVE CAMERAS PLANTED EVERYWHERE.
WE EVEN SHOT THAT UNUSUAL EVENT IN "MOUSE COUNTRY."
DON'T SHOOT THAT!! DON'T SHOOT IT!!
THEN HOW ABOUT SOMETHING LIKE THIS?
HUH?

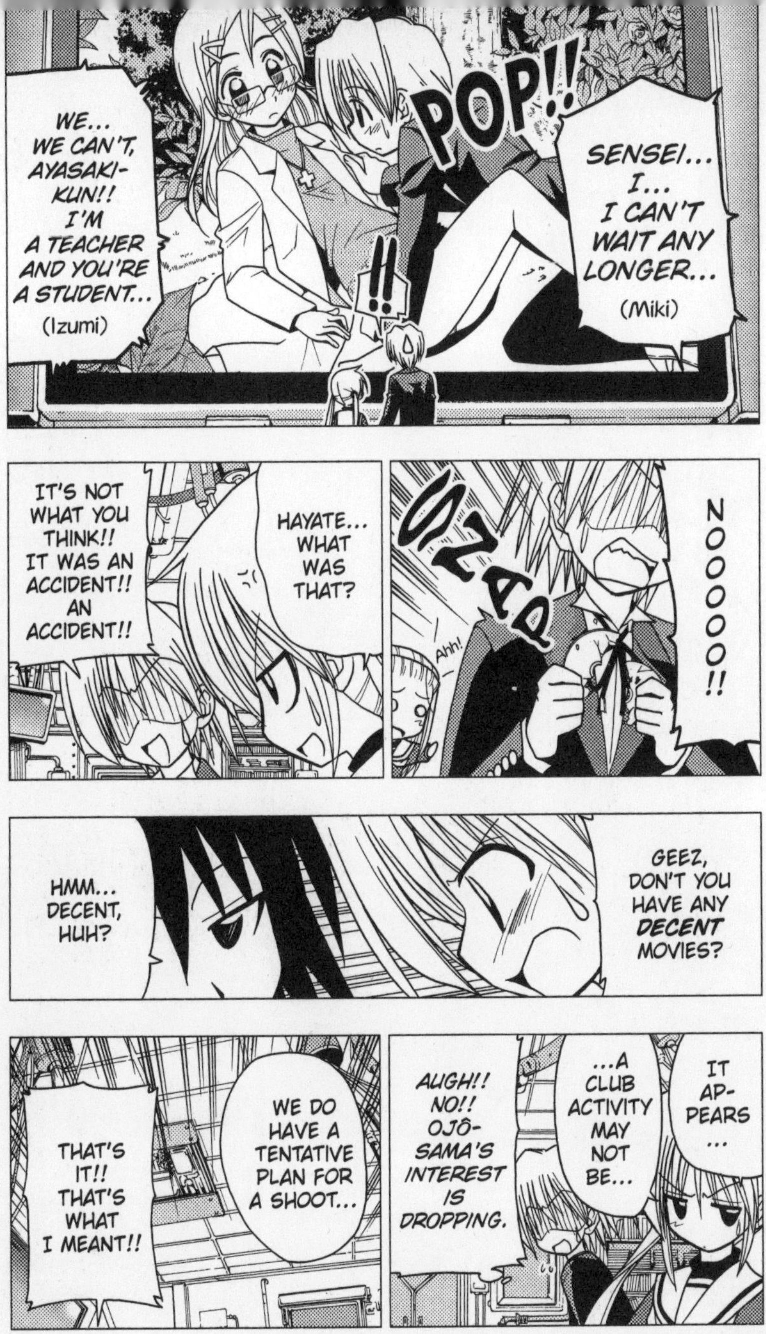
SENSEI... I... I CAN'T WAIT ANY LONGER... (Miki)
POP!!
!!
WE... WE CAN'T, AYASAKI-KUN!! I'M A TEACHER AND YOU'RE A STUDENT... (Izumi)
NOOOOOO!!
ZAP
Ahh!
HAYATE... WHAT WAS THAT?
IT'S NOT WHAT YOU THINK!! IT WAS AN ACCIDENT!! AN ACCIDENT!!
GEEZ, DON'T YOU HAVE ANY DECENT MOVIES?
HMM... DECENT, HUH?
IT AP-PEARS...
...A CLUB ACTIVITY MAY NOT BE...
AUGH!! NO!! OJÔ-SAMA'S INTEREST IS DROPPING.
WE DO HAVE A TENTATIVE PLAN FOR A SHOOT...
THAT'S IT!! THAT'S WHAT I MEANT!!

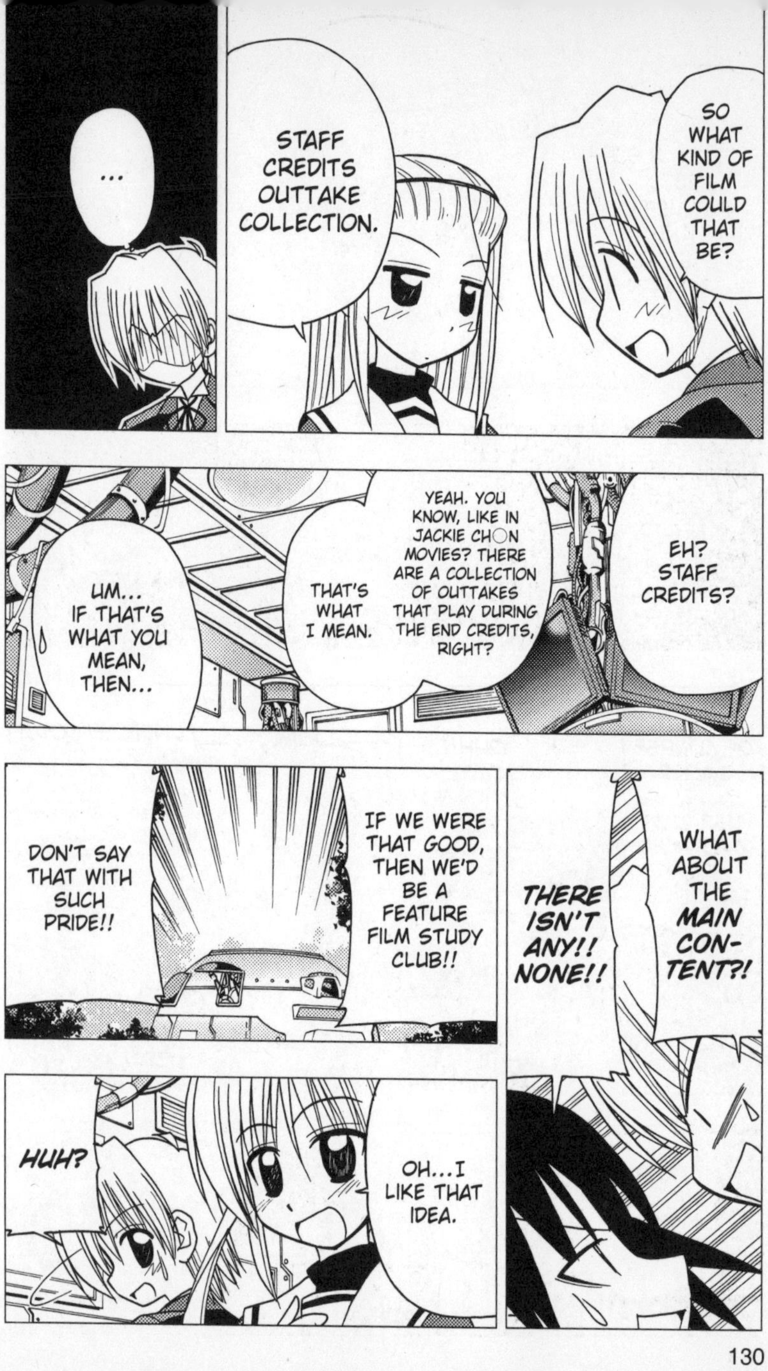
SO WHAT KIND OF FILM COULD THAT BE?
STAFF CREDITS OUTTAKE COLLECTION.
...
EH? STAFF CREDITS?
YEAH. YOU KNOW, LIKE IN JACKIE CH○N MOVIES? THERE ARE A COLLECTION OF OUTTAKES THAT PLAY DURING THE END CREDITS, RIGHT?
THAT'S WHAT I MEAN.
UM... IF THAT'S WHAT YOU MEAN, THEN...
WHAT ABOUT THE *MAIN CONTENT?!*
THERE ISN'T ANY!! NONE!!
IF WE WERE THAT GOOD, THEN WE'D BE A FEATURE FILM STUDY CLUB!!
DON'T SAY THAT WITH SUCH PRIDE!!
OH...I LIKE THAT IDEA.
HUH?

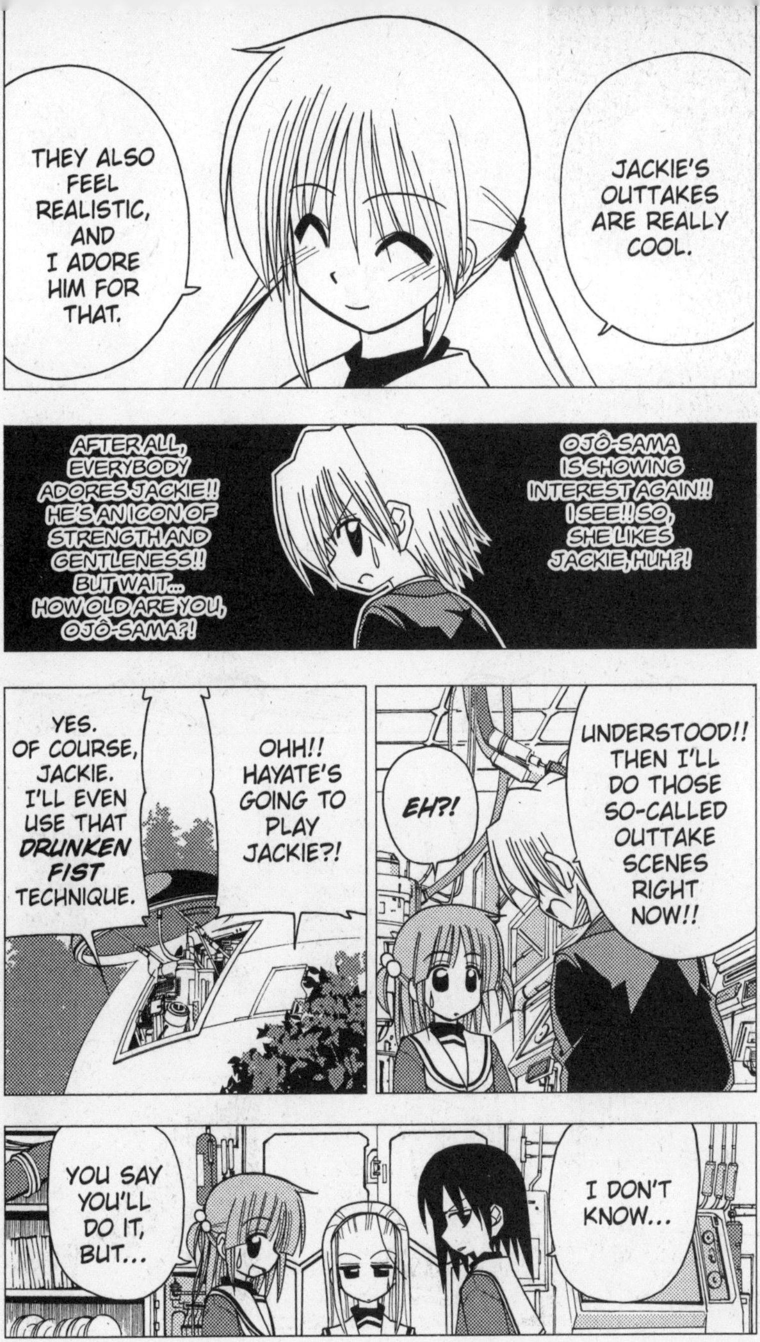
JACKIE'S OUTTAKES ARE REALLY COOL.
THEY ALSO FEEL REALISTIC, AND I ADORE HIM FOR THAT.
OJÔ-SAMA IS SHOWING INTEREST AGAIN!! I SEE!! SO, SHE LIKES JACKIE, HUH?!
AFTER ALL, EVERYBODY ADORES JACKIE!! HE'S AN ICON OF STRENGTH AND GENTLENESS!! BUT WAIT... HOW OLD ARE YOU, OJÔ-SAMA?!
UNDERSTOOD!! THEN I'LL DO THOSE SO-CALLED OUTTAKE SCENES RIGHT NOW!!
EH?!
OHH!! HAYATE'S GOING TO PLAY JACKIE?!
YES. OF COURSE, JACKIE. I'LL EVEN USE THAT ***DRUNKEN FIST*** TECHNIQUE.
I DON'T KNOW...
YOU SAY YOU'LL DO IT, BUT...

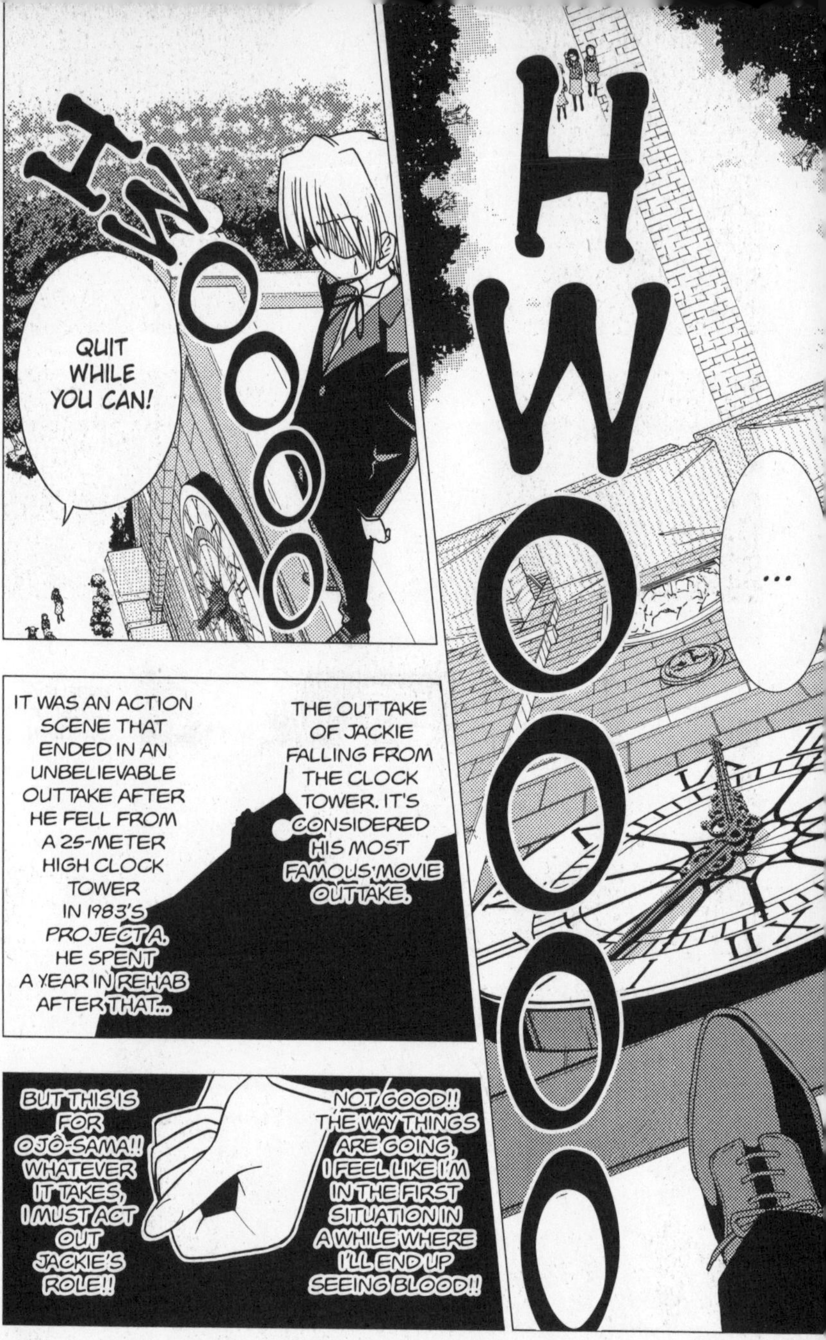
HWOOOOOO
...
HWOOOOOO
QUIT WHILE YOU CAN!
THE OUTTAKE OF JACKIE FALLING FROM THE CLOCK TOWER. IT'S CONSIDERED HIS MOST FAMOUS MOVIE OUTTAKE.
IT WAS AN ACTION SCENE THAT ENDED IN AN UNBELIEVABLE OUTTAKE AFTER HE FELL FROM A 25-METER HIGH CLOCK TOWER IN 1983'S PROJECT A. HE SPENT A YEAR IN REHAB AFTER THAT...
NOT GOOD!! THE WAY THINGS ARE GOING, I FEEL LIKE I'M IN THE FIRST SITUATION IN A WHILE WHERE I'LL END UP SEEING BLOOD!!
BUT THIS IS FOR OJÔ-SAMA!! WHATEVER IT TAKES, I MUST ACT OUT JACKIE'S ROLE!!

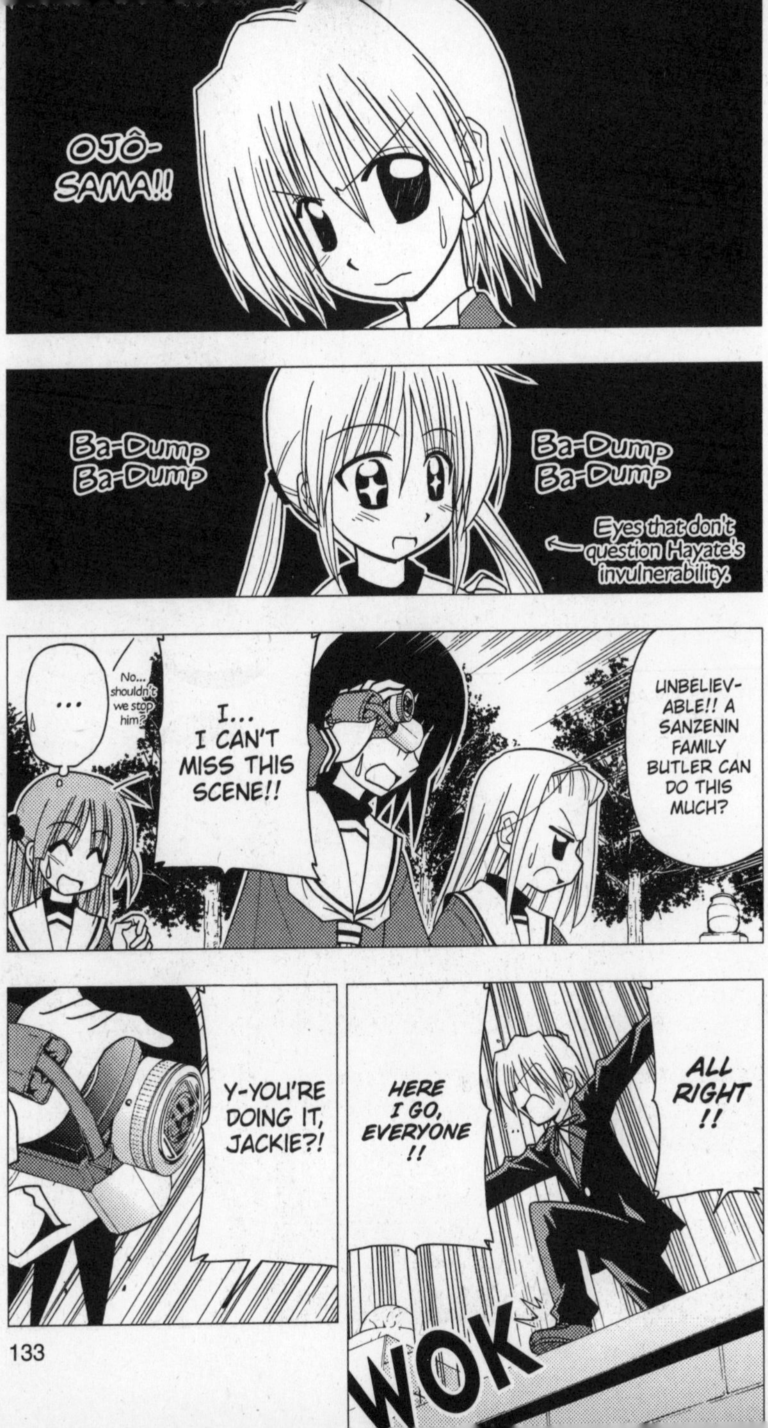
OJÔ-SAMA!!
Ba-Dump Ba-Dump
Ba-Dump Ba-Dump
Eyes that don't question Hayate's invulnerability.
UNBELIEV-ABLE!! A SANZENIN FAMILY BUTLER CAN DO THIS MUCH?
I... I CAN'T MISS THIS SCENE!!
...
No... shouldn't we stop him?
ALL RIGHT!!
HERE I GO, EVERYONE!!
WOK
Y-YOU'RE DOING IT, JACKIE?!

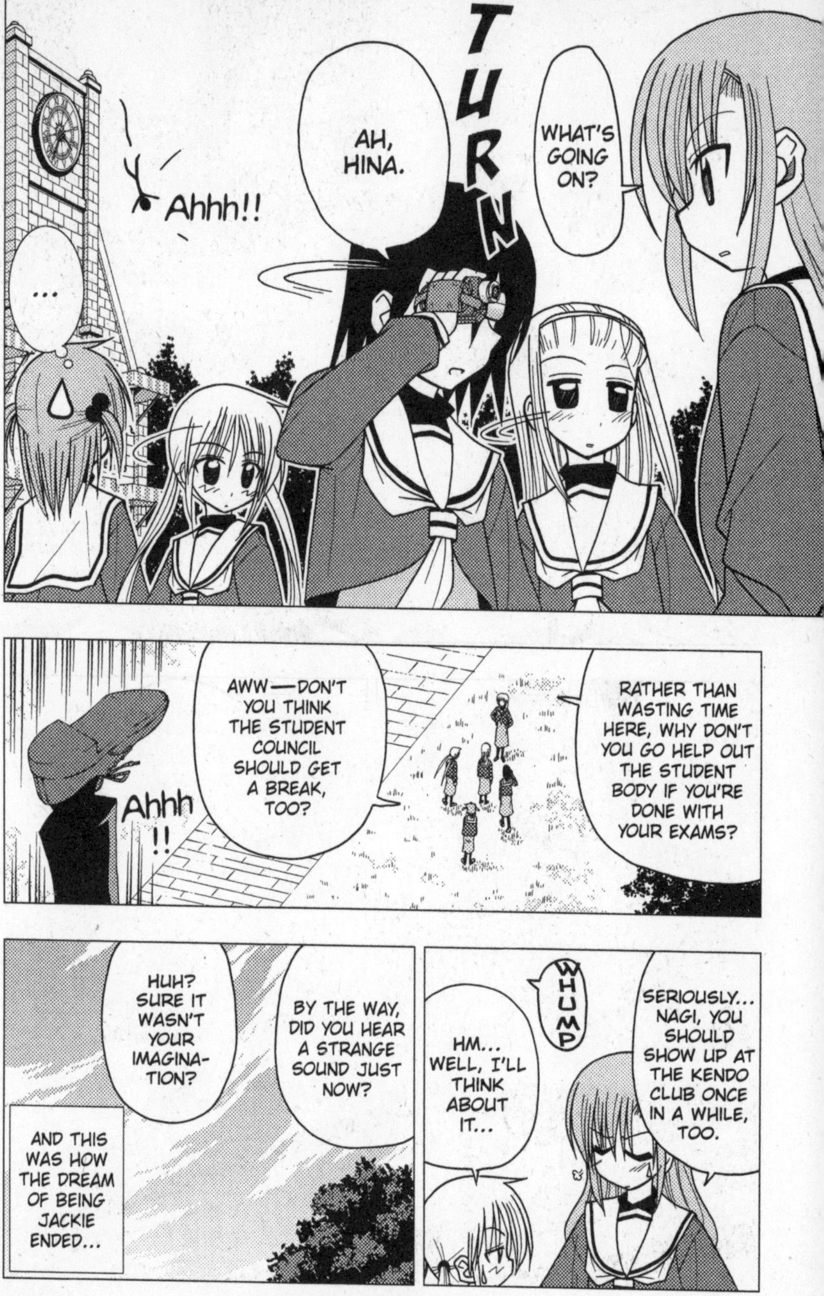
WHAT'S GOING ON?
TURN
AH, HINA.
Ahhh!!
...
RATHER THAN WASTING TIME HERE, WHY DON'T YOU GO HELP OUT THE STUDENT BODY IF YOU'RE DONE WITH YOUR EXAMS?
AWW—DON'T YOU THINK THE STUDENT COUNCIL SHOULD GET A BREAK, TOO?
Ahhh !!
SERIOUSLY... NAGI, YOU SHOULD SHOW UP AT THE KENDO CLUB ONCE IN A WHILE, TOO.
WHUMP
HM... WELL, I'LL THINK ABOUT IT...
BY THE WAY, DID YOU HEAR A STRANGE SOUND JUST NOW?
HUH? SURE IT WASN'T YOUR IMAGINA-TION?
AND THIS WAS HOW THE DREAM OF BEING JACKIE ENDED...

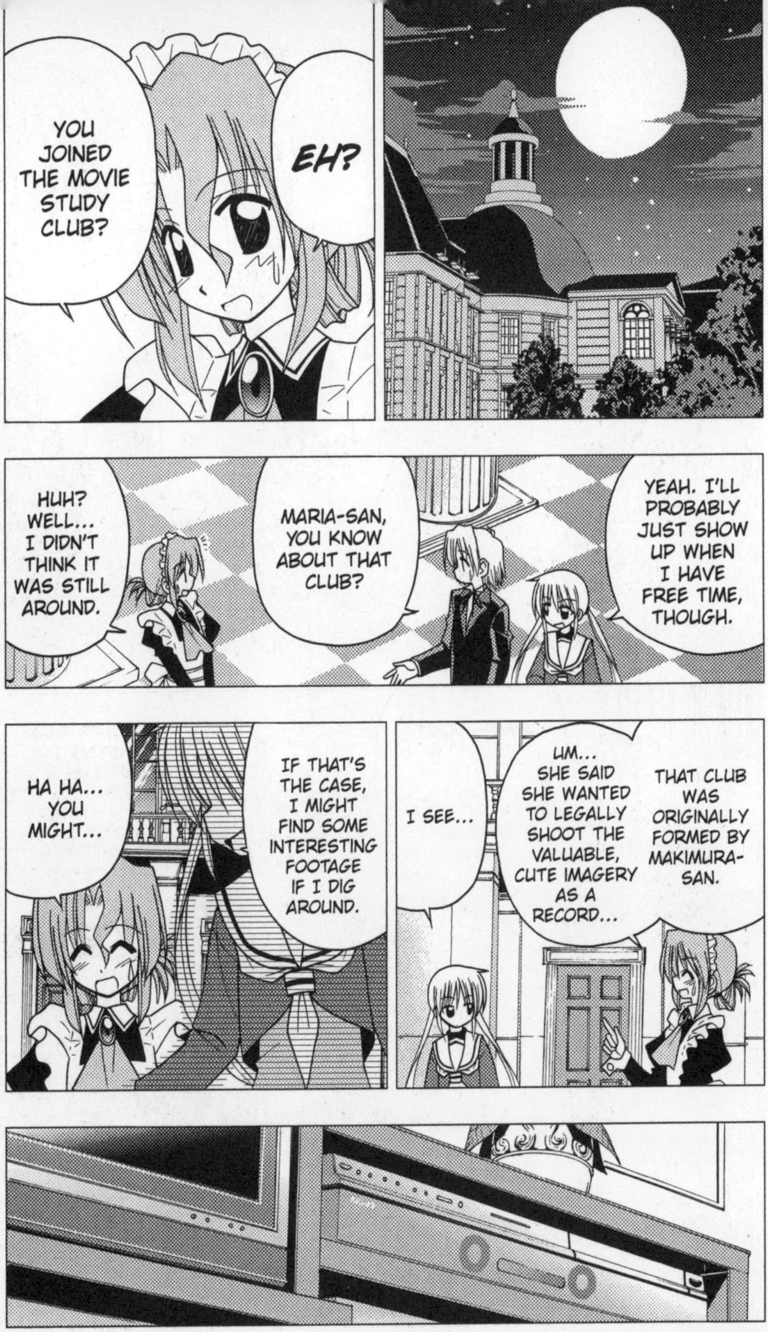
EH?
YOU JOINED THE MOVIE STUDY CLUB?
YEAH. I'LL PROBABLY JUST SHOW UP WHEN I HAVE FREE TIME, THOUGH.
MARIA-SAN, YOU KNOW ABOUT THAT CLUB?
HUH? WELL... I DIDN'T THINK IT WAS STILL AROUND.
THAT CLUB WAS ORIGINALLY FORMED BY MAKIMURA-SAN.
UM... SHE SAID SHE WANTED TO LEGALLY SHOOT THE VALUABLE, CUTE IMAGERY AS A RECORD...
I SEE...
IF THAT'S THE CASE, I MIGHT FIND SOME INTERESTING FOOTAGE IF I DIG AROUND.
HA HA... YOU MIGHT...

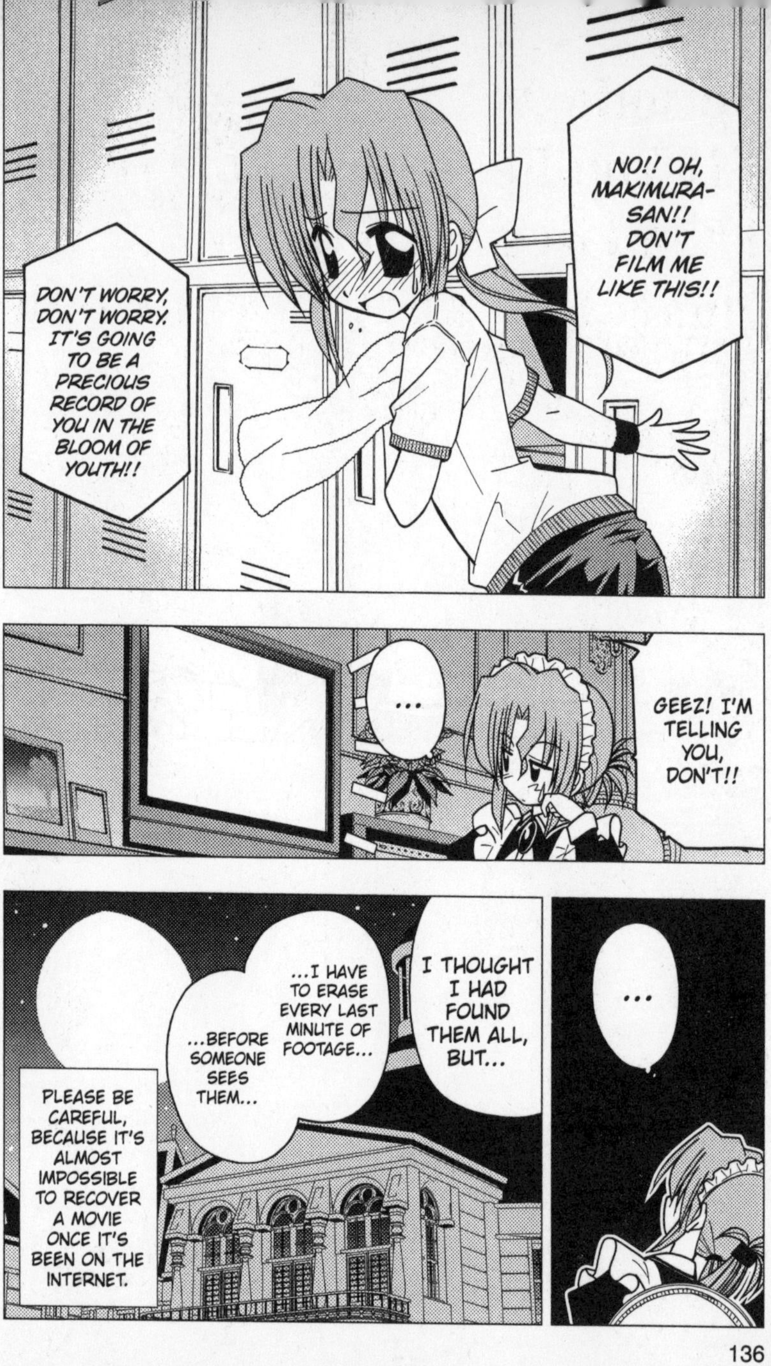
NO!! OH, MAKIMURA-SAN!! DON'T FILM ME LIKE THIS!!
DON'T WORRY, DON'T WORRY. IT'S GOING TO BE A PRECIOUS RECORD OF YOU IN THE BLOOM OF YOUTH!!
GEEZ! I'M TELLING YOU, DON'T!!
...
...
I THOUGHT I HAD FOUND THEM ALL, BUT...
...I HAVE TO ERASE EVERY LAST MINUTE OF FOOTAGE...
...BEFORE SOMEONE SEES THEM...
PLEASE BE CAREFUL, BECAUSE IT'S ALMOST IMPOSSIBLE TO RECOVER A MOVIE ONCE IT'S BEEN ON THE INTERNET.

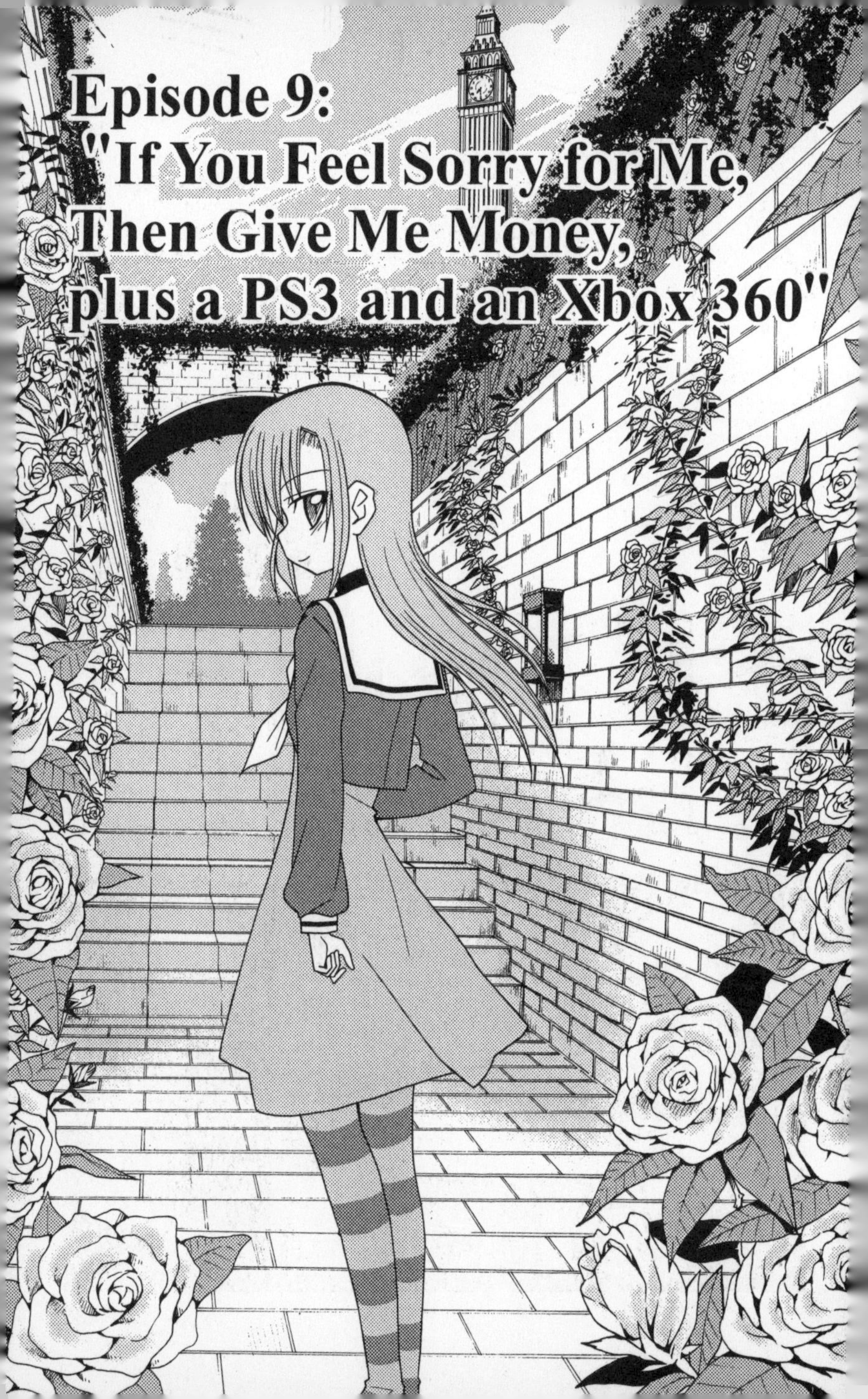
Episode 9:
"If You Feel Sorry for Me, Then Give Me Money, plus a PS3 and an Xbox 360"

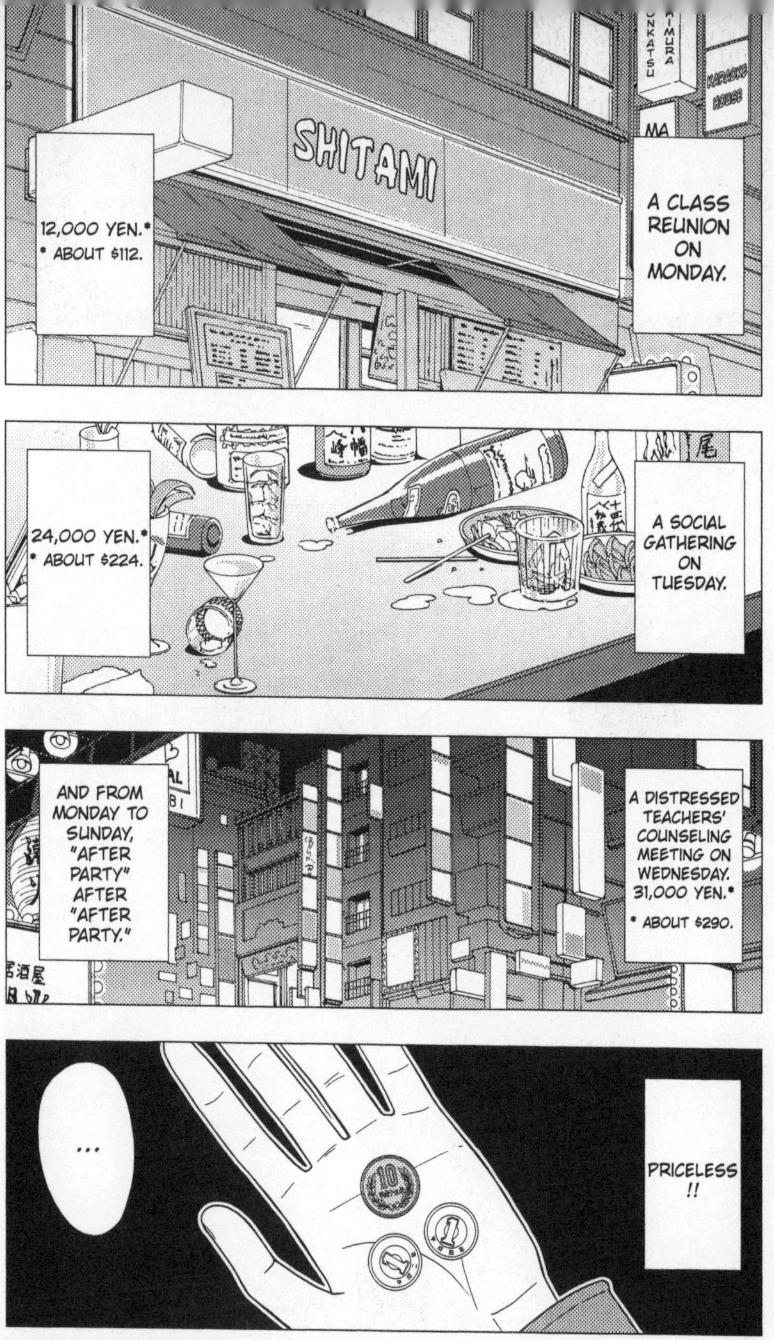
KARAOKE HOUSE
SHITAMI
A CLASS REUNION ON MONDAY.
12,000 YEN.*
* ABOUT $112.
A SOCIAL GATHERING ON TUESDAY.
24,000 YEN.*
* ABOUT $224.
A DISTRESSED TEACHERS' COUNSELING MEETING ON WEDNESDAY. 31,000 YEN.*
* ABOUT $290.
AND FROM MONDAY TO SUNDAY, "AFTER PARTY" AFTER "AFTER PARTY."
PRICELESS !!
...

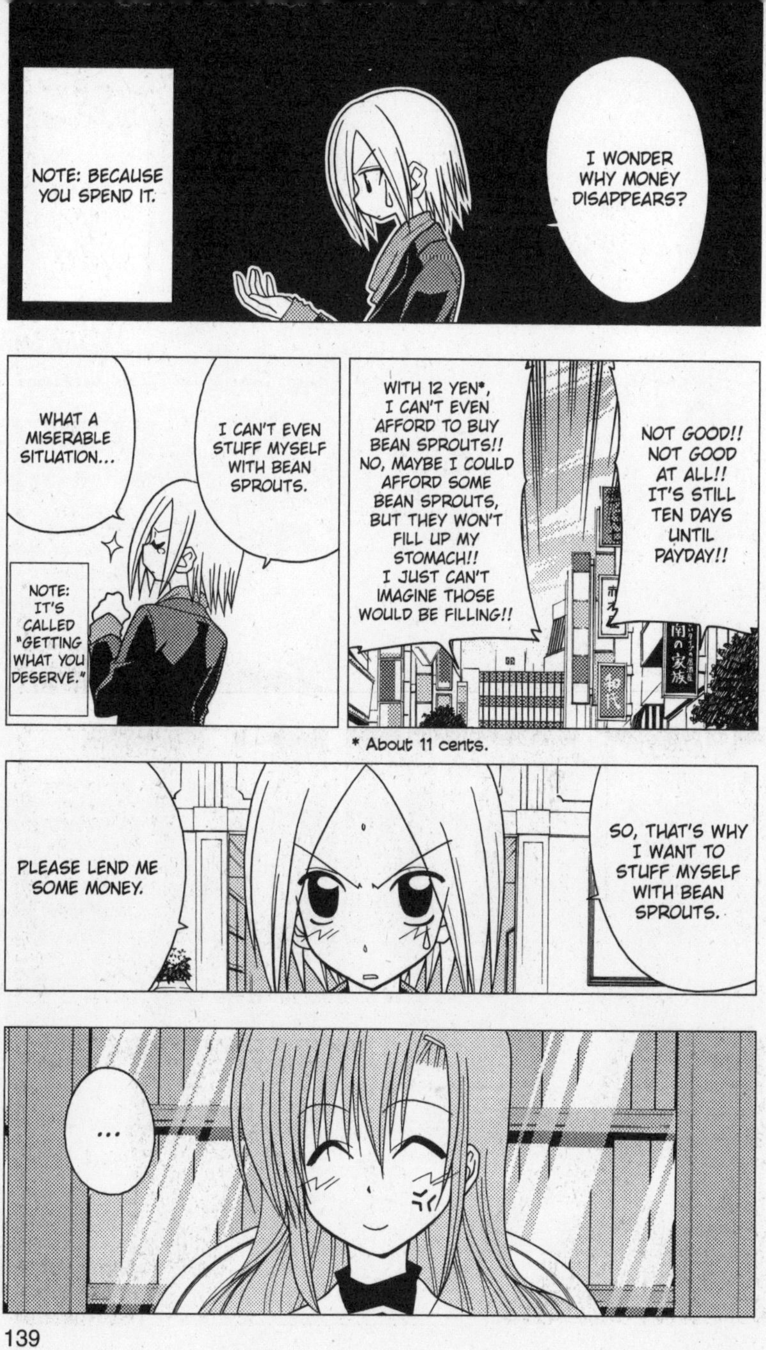
I WONDER WHY MONEY DISAPPEARS?
NOTE: BECAUSE YOU SPEND IT.
NOT GOOD!! NOT GOOD AT ALL!! IT'S STILL TEN DAYS UNTIL PAYDAY!!
WITH 12 YEN*, I CAN'T EVEN AFFORD TO BUY BEAN SPROUTS!! NO, MAYBE I COULD AFFORD SOME BEAN SPROUTS, BUT THEY WON'T FILL UP MY STOMACH!! I JUST CAN'T IMAGINE THOSE WOULD BE FILLING!!
I CAN'T EVEN STUFF MYSELF WITH BEAN SPROUTS.
WHAT A MISERABLE SITUATION...
NOTE: IT'S CALLED "GETTING WHAT YOU DESERVE."
SO, THAT'S WHY I WANT TO STUFF MYSELF WITH BEAN SPROUTS.
PLEASE LEND ME SOME MONEY.
...

* About 11 cents.

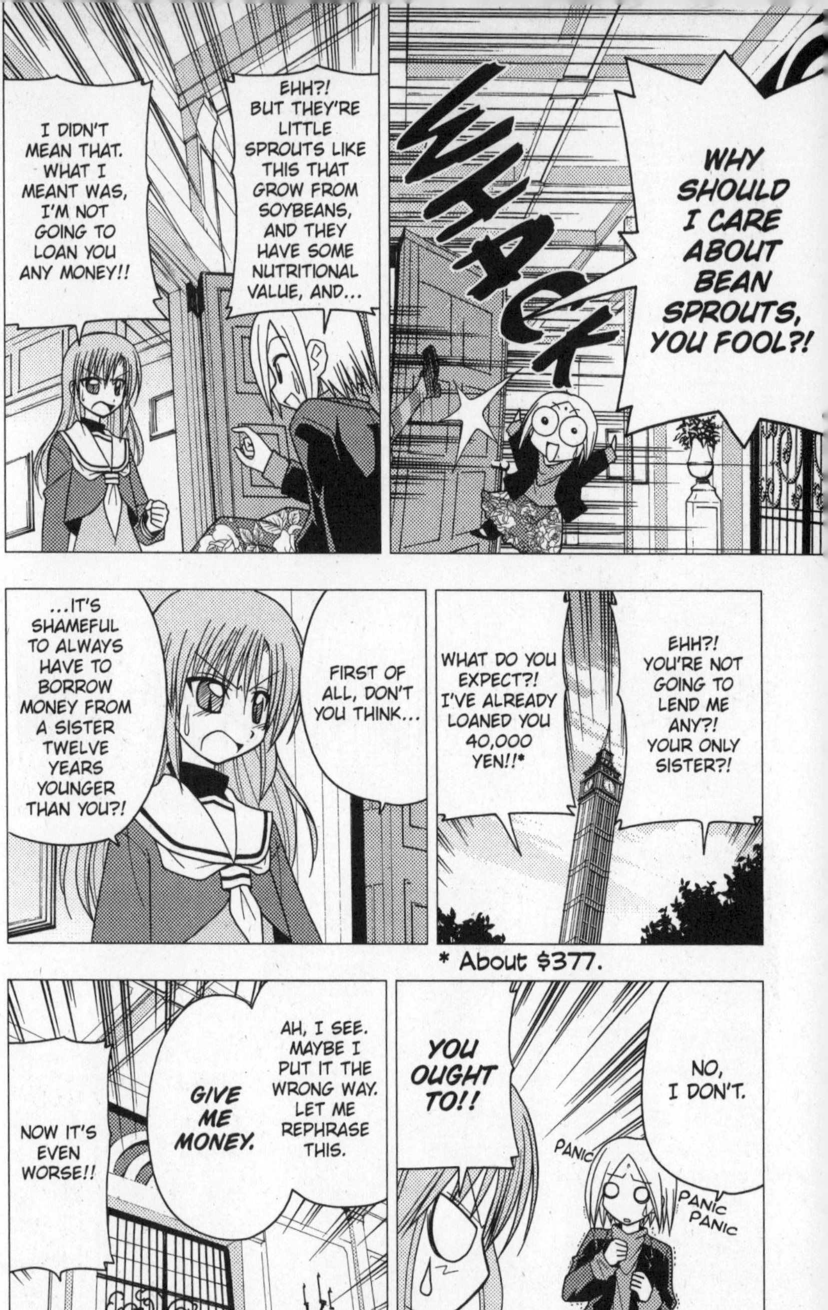
WHACK
WHY SHOULD I CARE ABOUT BEAN SPROUTS, YOU FOOL?!
EHH?! BUT THEY'RE LITTLE SPROUTS LIKE THIS THAT GROW FROM SOYBEANS, AND THEY HAVE SOME NUTRITIONAL VALUE, AND...
I DIDN'T MEAN THAT. WHAT I MEANT WAS, I'M NOT GOING TO LOAN YOU ANY MONEY!!
EHH?! YOU'RE NOT GOING TO LEND ME ANY?! YOUR ONLY SISTER?!
WHAT DO YOU EXPECT?! I'VE ALREADY LOANED YOU 40,000 YEN!!*
FIRST OF ALL, DON'T YOU THINK...
...IT'S SHAMEFUL TO ALWAYS HAVE TO BORROW MONEY FROM A SISTER TWELVE YEARS YOUNGER THAN YOU?!
NO, I DON'T.
YOU OUGHT TO!!
PANIC
PANIC PANIC
AH, I SEE. MAYBE I PUT IT THE WRONG WAY. LET ME REPHRASE THIS.
GIVE ME MONEY.
NOW IT'S EVEN WORSE!!

* About $377.

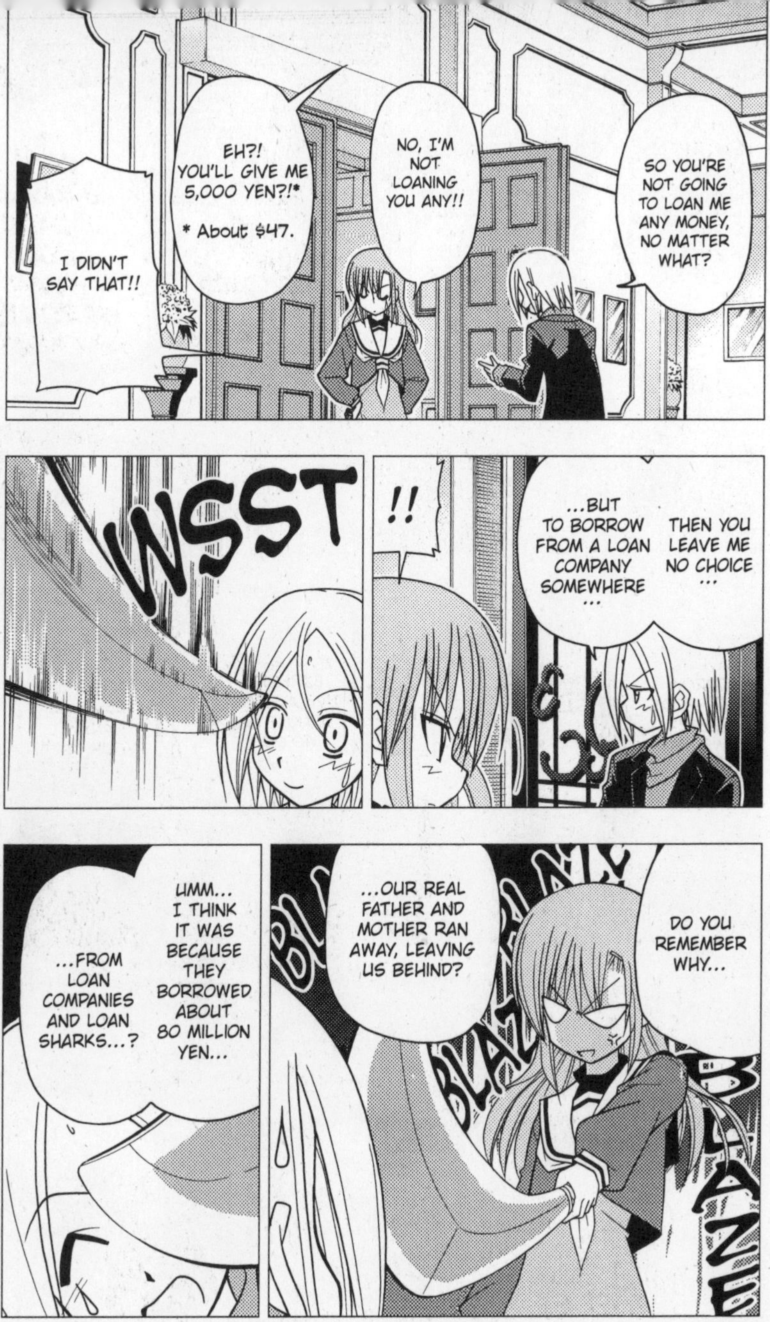
SO YOU'RE NOT GOING TO LOAN ME ANY MONEY, NO MATTER WHAT?
NO, I'M NOT LOANING YOU ANY!!
EH?! YOU'LL GIVE ME 5,000 YEN?!*
* About $47.
I DIDN'T SAY THAT!!
THEN YOU LEAVE ME NO CHOICE...
...BUT TO BORROW FROM A LOAN COMPANY SOMEWHERE...
!!
WSST
DO YOU REMEMBER WHY...
...OUR REAL FATHER AND MOTHER RAN AWAY, LEAVING US BEHIND?
UMM... I THINK IT WAS BECAUSE THEY BORROWED ABOUT 80 MILLION YEN...
...FROM LOAN COMPANIES AND LOAN SHARKS...?

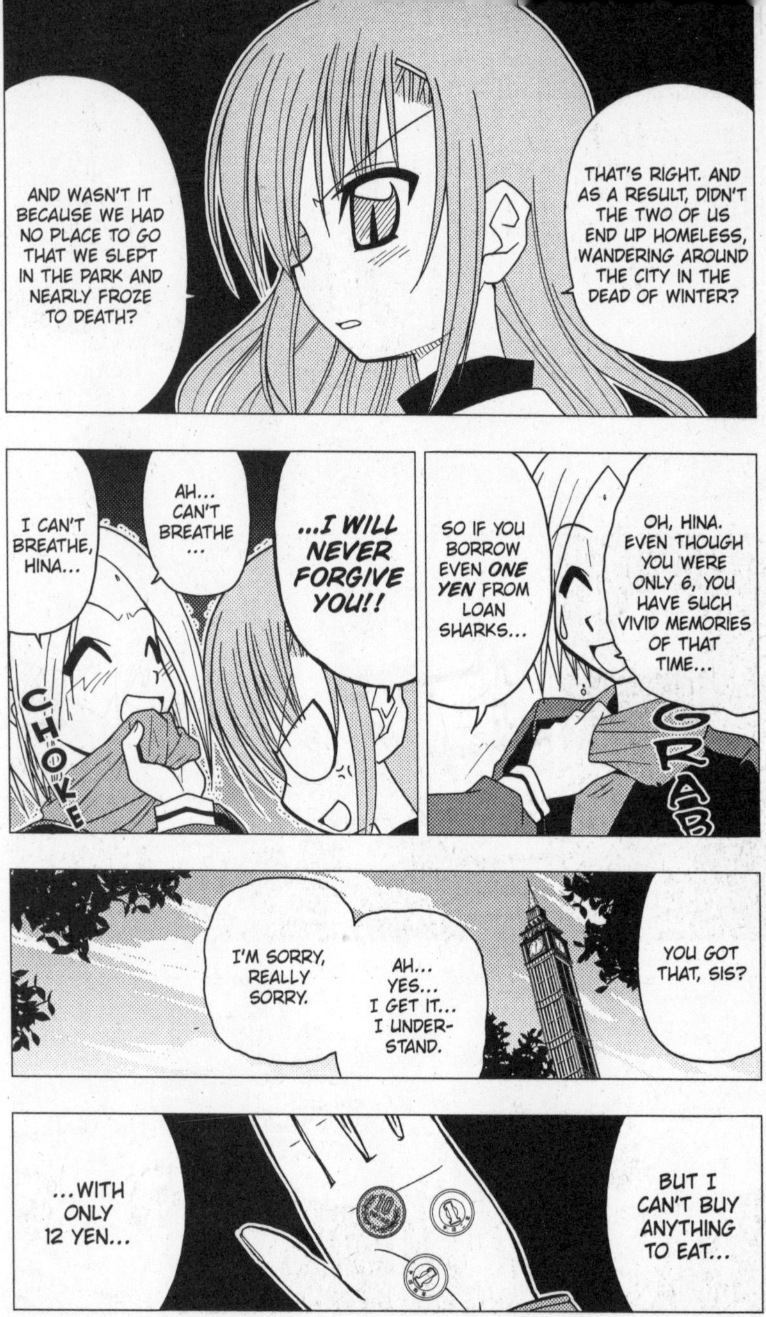
THAT'S RIGHT. AND AS A RESULT, DIDN'T THE TWO OF US END UP HOMELESS, WANDERING AROUND THE CITY IN THE DEAD OF WINTER?
AND WASN'T IT BECAUSE WE HAD NO PLACE TO GO THAT WE SLEPT IN THE PARK AND NEARLY FROZE TO DEATH?
OH, HINA. EVEN THOUGH YOU WERE ONLY 6, YOU HAVE SUCH VIVID MEMORIES OF THAT TIME...
SO IF YOU BORROW EVEN **ONE YEN** FROM LOAN SHARKS...
GRAB
...I WILL NEVER FORGIVE YOU!!
AH... CAN'T BREATHE...
I CAN'T BREATHE, HINA...
CHOKE
YOU GOT THAT, SIS?
AH... YES... I GET IT... I UNDERSTAND.
I'M SORRY, REALLY SORRY.
BUT I CAN'T BUY ANYTHING TO EAT...
...WITH ONLY 12 YEN...

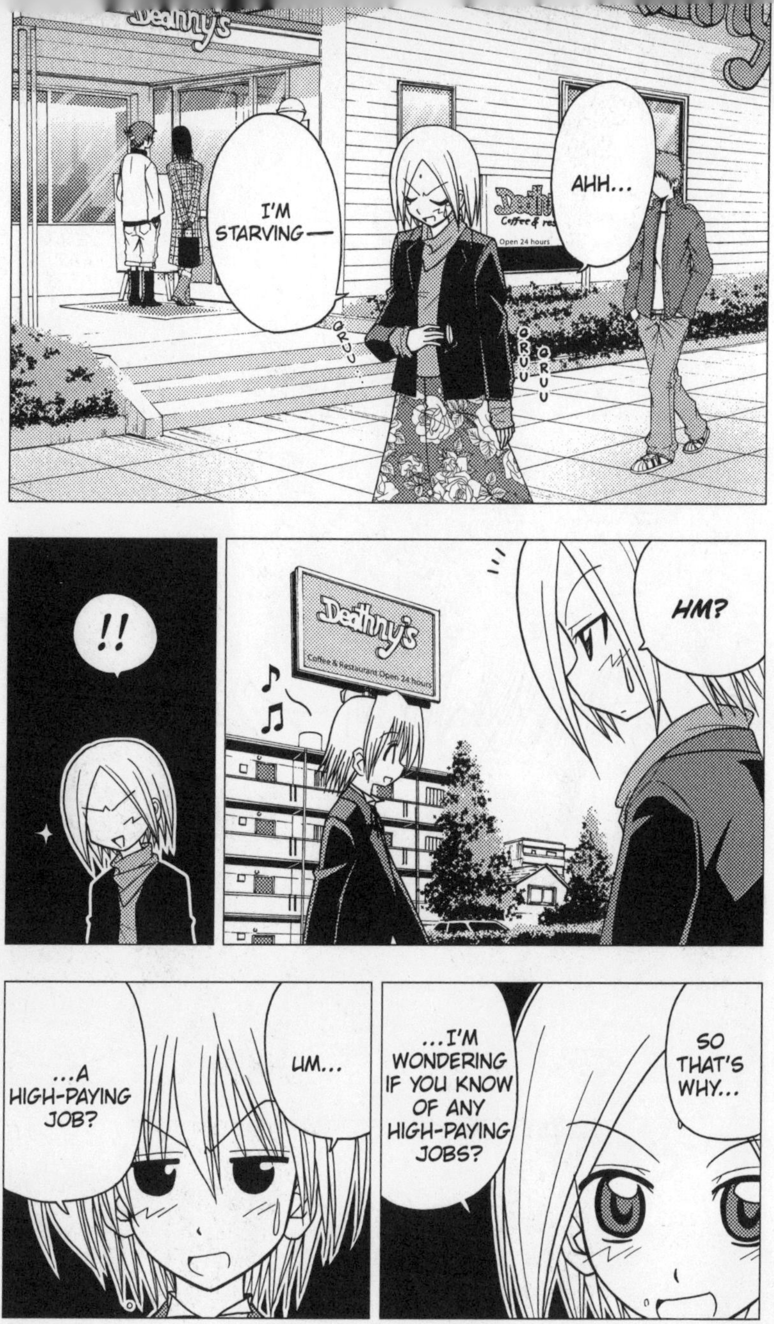
Deathny's
AHH...
Coffee & res
Open 24 hours
I'M STARVING—
GRUU
GRUU
GRUU
HM?
Deathny's
Coffee & Restaurant Open 24 hours
!!
SO THAT'S WHY...
...I'M WONDERING IF YOU KNOW OF ANY HIGH-PAYING JOBS?
UM...
...A HIGH-PAYING JOB?

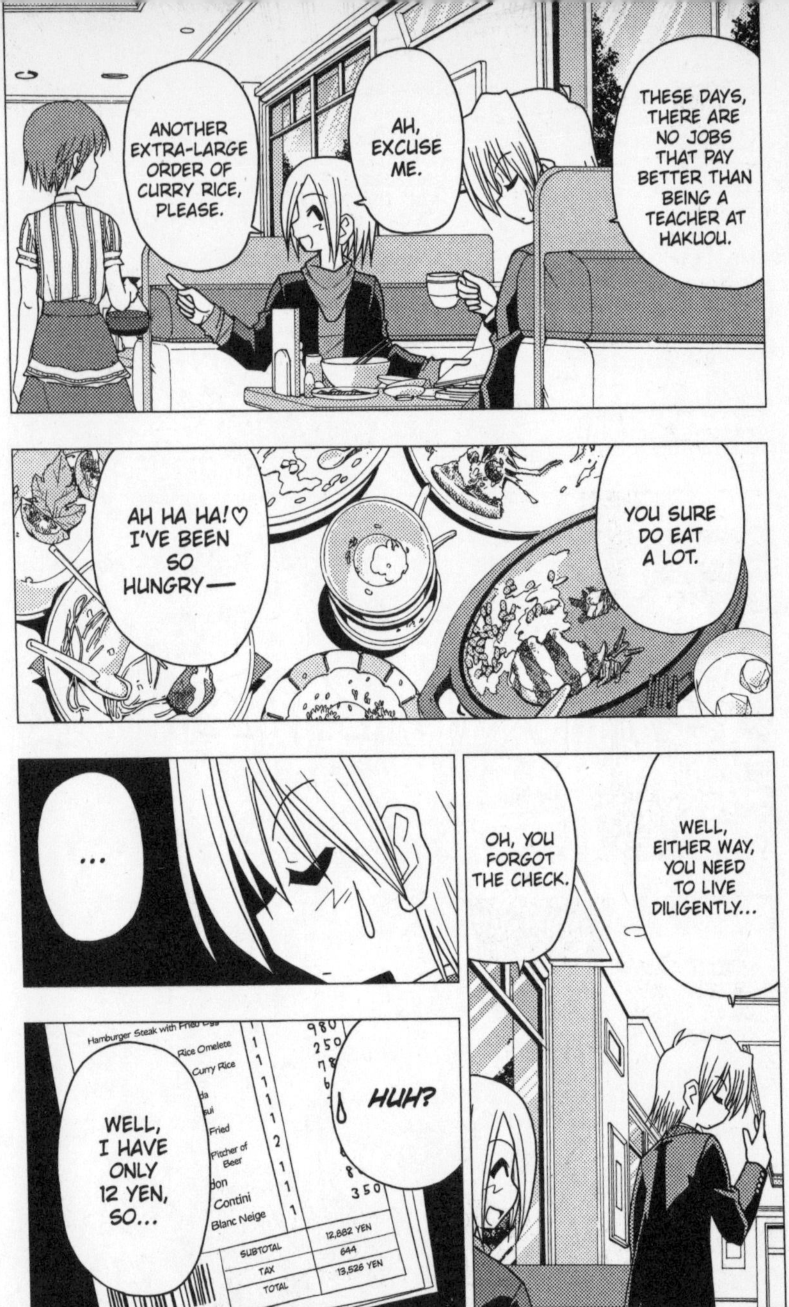
THESE DAYS, THERE ARE NO JOBS THAT PAY BETTER THAN BEING A TEACHER AT HAKUOU.
AH, EXCUSE ME.
ANOTHER EXTRA-LARGE ORDER OF CURRY RICE, PLEASE.
YOU SURE DO EAT A LOT.
AH HA HA!♡ I'VE BEEN SO HUNGRY—
WELL, EITHER WAY, YOU NEED TO LIVE DILIGENTLY...
OH, YOU FORGOT THE CHECK.
...
HUH?
WELL, I HAVE ONLY 12 YEN, SO...
Hamburger Steak with Fried Egg
Rice Omelete
Curry Rice
Pitcher of Beer
Contini
Blanc Neige
SUBTOTAL 12,882 YEN
TAX 644
TOTAL 13,526 YEN

* Bill comes to about $127.

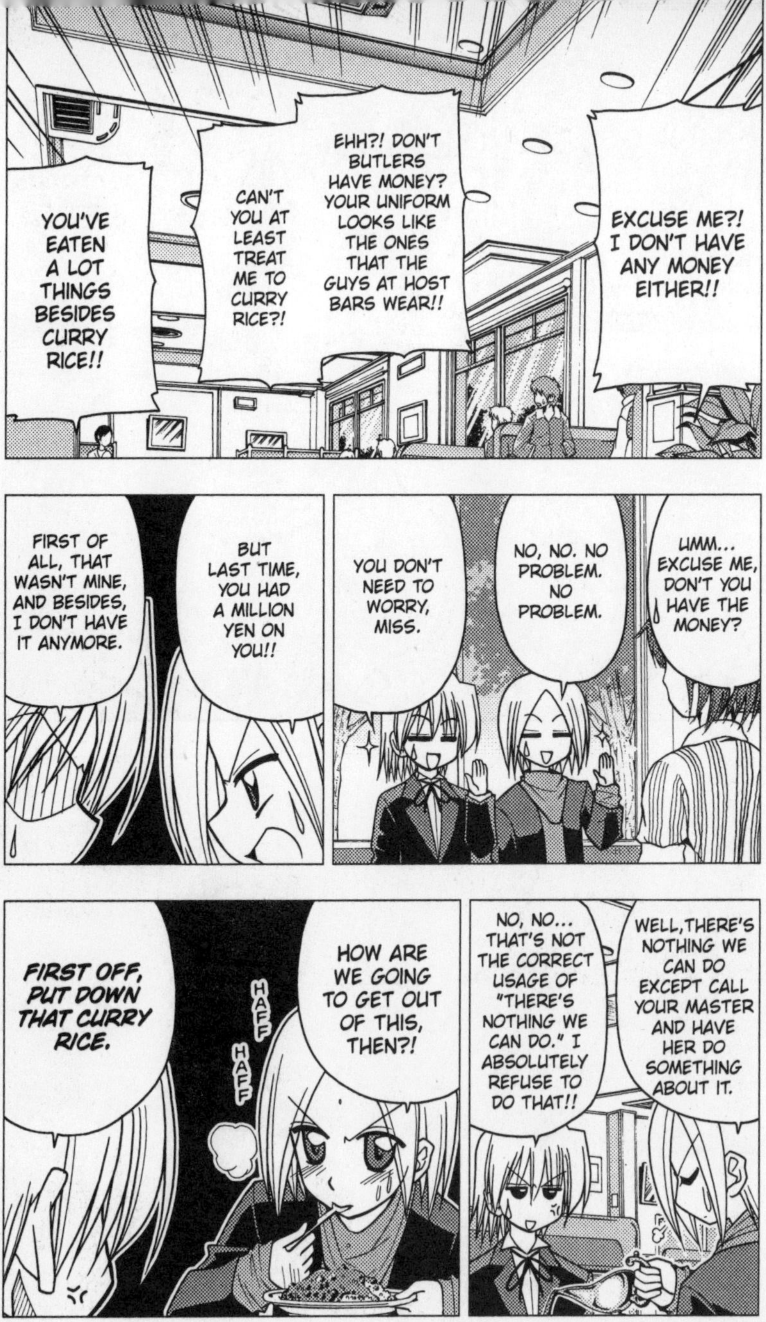
EXCUSE ME?! I DON'T HAVE ANY MONEY EITHER!!
EHH?! DON'T BUTLERS HAVE MONEY? YOUR UNIFORM LOOKS LIKE THE ONES THAT THE GUYS AT HOST BARS WEAR!!
CAN'T YOU AT LEAST TREAT ME TO CURRY RICE?!
YOU'VE EATEN A LOT THINGS BESIDES CURRY RICE!!
UMM... EXCUSE ME, DON'T YOU HAVE THE MONEY?
NO, NO. NO PROBLEM. NO PROBLEM.
YOU DON'T NEED TO WORRY, MISS.
BUT LAST TIME, YOU HAD A MILLION YEN ON YOU!!
FIRST OF ALL, THAT WASN'T MINE, AND BESIDES, I DON'T HAVE IT ANYMORE.
WELL,THERE'S NOTHING WE CAN DO EXCEPT CALL YOUR MASTER AND HAVE HER DO SOMETHING ABOUT IT.
NO, NO... THAT'S NOT THE CORRECT USAGE OF "THERE'S NOTHING WE CAN DO." I ABSOLUTELY REFUSE TO DO THAT!!
HOW ARE WE GOING TO GET OUT OF THIS, THEN?!
HAFF HAFF
FIRST OFF, PUT DOWN THAT CURRY RICE.

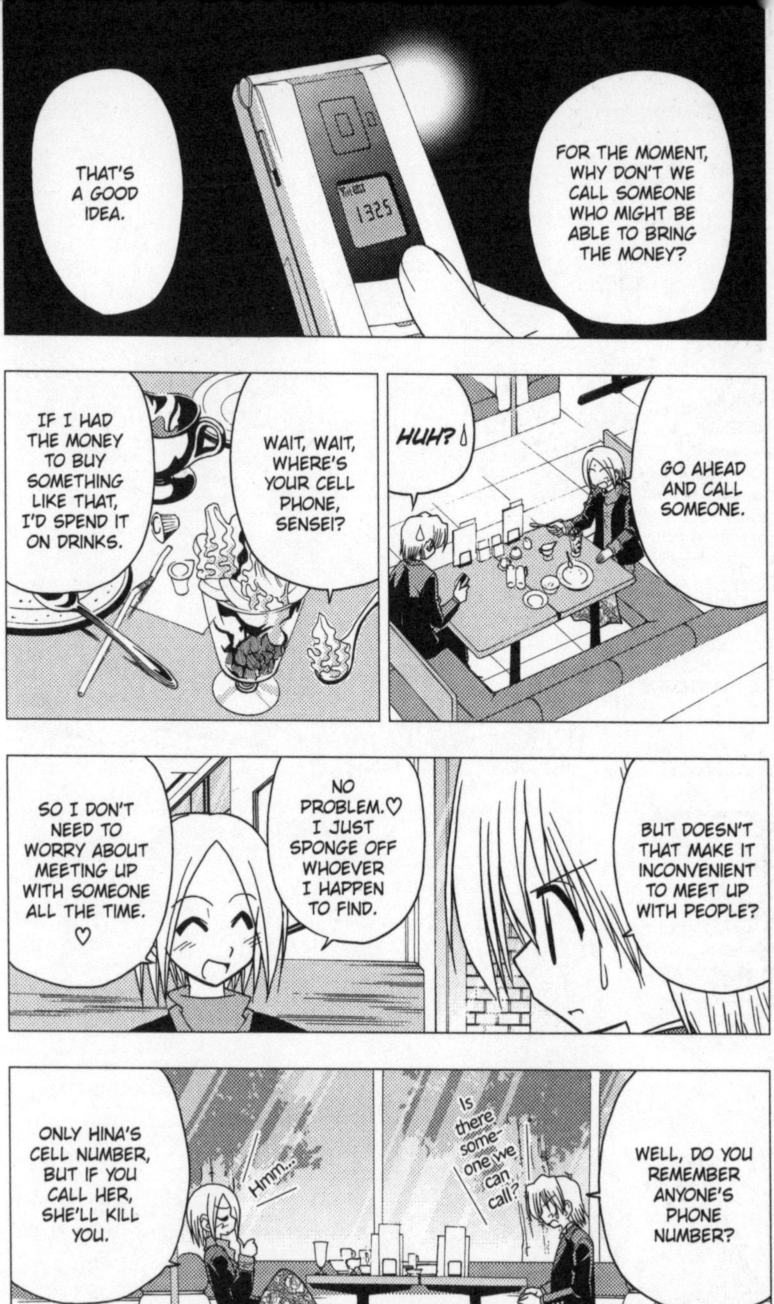
FOR THE MOMENT, WHY DON'T WE CALL SOMEONE WHO MIGHT BE ABLE TO BRING THE MONEY?
THAT'S A GOOD IDEA.
GO AHEAD AND CALL SOMEONE.
HUH?
WAIT, WAIT, WHERE'S YOUR CELL PHONE, SENSEI?
IF I HAD THE MONEY TO BUY SOMETHING LIKE THAT, I'D SPEND IT ON DRINKS.
BUT DOESN'T THAT MAKE IT INCONVENIENT TO MEET UP WITH PEOPLE?
NO PROBLEM.♡ I JUST SPONGE OFF WHOEVER I HAPPEN TO FIND.
SO I DON'T NEED TO WORRY ABOUT MEETING UP WITH SOMEONE ALL THE TIME. ♡
WELL, DO YOU REMEMBER ANYONE'S PHONE NUMBER?
Is there someone we can call?
Hmm...
ONLY HINA'S CELL NUMBER, BUT IF YOU CALL HER, SHE'LL KILL YOU.

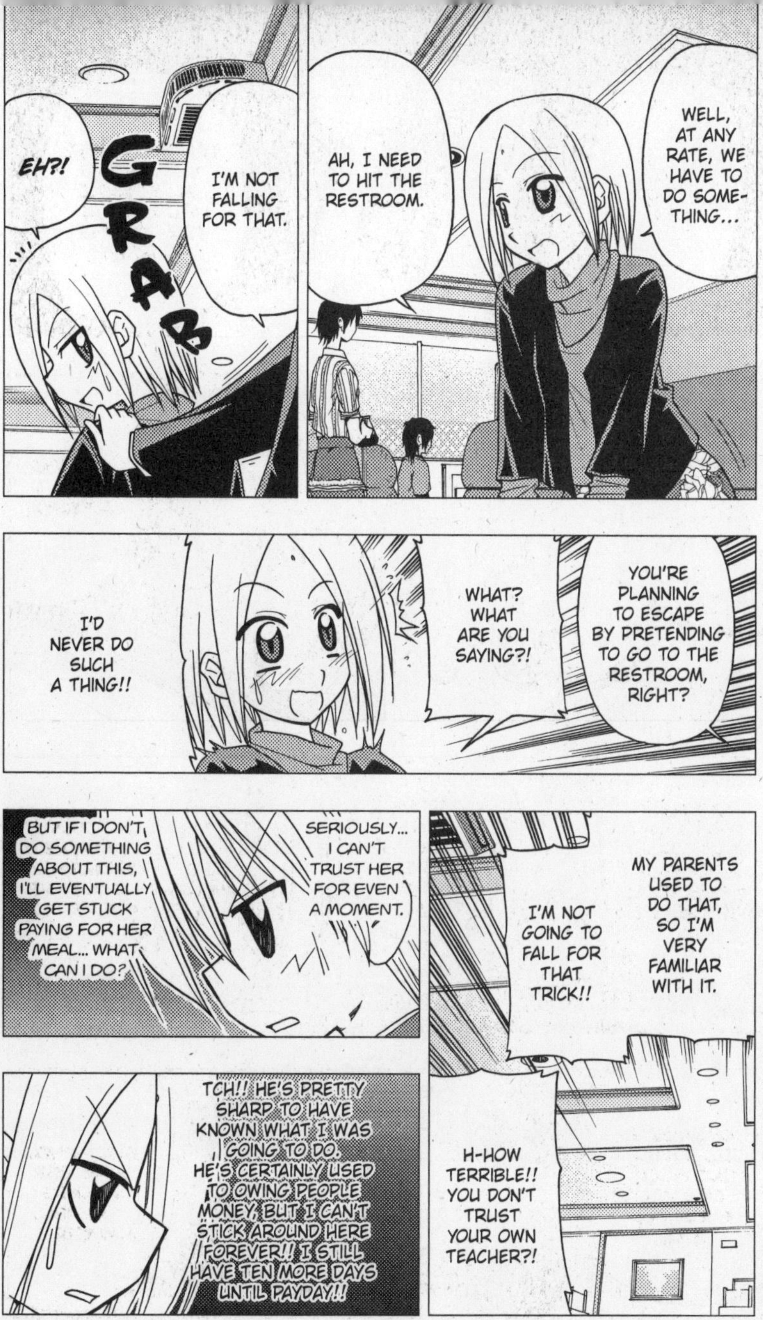
WELL, AT ANY RATE, WE HAVE TO DO SOME-THING...
AH, I NEED TO HIT THE RESTROOM.
I'M NOT FALLING FOR THAT.
GRAB
EH?!
YOU'RE PLANNING TO ESCAPE BY PRETENDING TO GO TO THE RESTROOM, RIGHT?
WHAT? WHAT ARE YOU SAYING?!
I'D NEVER DO SUCH A THING!!
MY PARENTS USED TO DO THAT, SO I'M VERY FAMILIAR WITH IT.
I'M NOT GOING TO FALL FOR THAT TRICK!!
SERIOUSLY... I CAN'T TRUST HER FOR EVEN A MOMENT.
BUT IF I DON'T DO SOMETHING ABOUT THIS, I'LL EVENTUALLY GET STUCK PAYING FOR HER MEAL... WHAT CAN I DO?
H-HOW TERRIBLE!! YOU DON'T TRUST YOUR OWN TEACHER?!
TCH!! HE'S PRETTY SHARP TO HAVE KNOWN WHAT I WAS GOING TO DO. HE'S CERTAINLY USED TO OWING PEOPLE MONEY, BUT I CAN'T STICK AROUND HERE FOREVER!! I STILL HAVE TEN MORE DAYS UNTIL PAYDAY!!

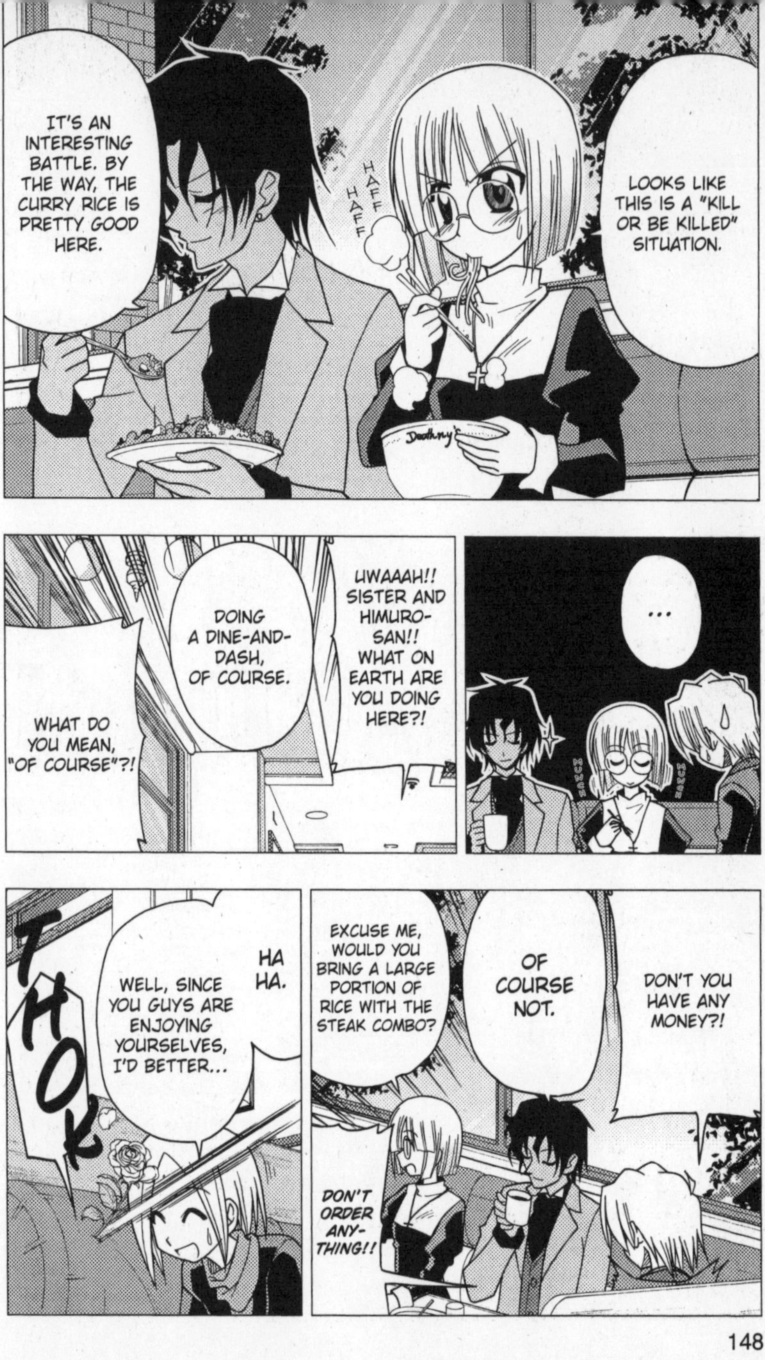
LOOKS LIKE THIS IS A "KILL OR BE KILLED" SITUATION.
HAFF HAFF
Deathny's
IT'S AN INTERESTING BATTLE. BY THE WAY, THE CURRY RICE IS PRETTY GOOD HERE.
...
MUNCH
MUNCH
UWAAAH!! SISTER AND HIMURO-SAN!! WHAT ON EARTH ARE YOU DOING HERE?!
DOING A DINE-AND-DASH, OF COURSE.
WHAT DO YOU MEAN, "OF COURSE"?!
DON'T YOU HAVE ANY MONEY?!
OF COURSE NOT.
EXCUSE ME, WOULD YOU BRING A LARGE PORTION OF RICE WITH THE STEAK COMBO?
DON'T ORDER ANYTHING!!
HA HA.
WELL, SINCE YOU GUYS ARE ENJOYING YOURSELVES, I'D BETTER...
THOK

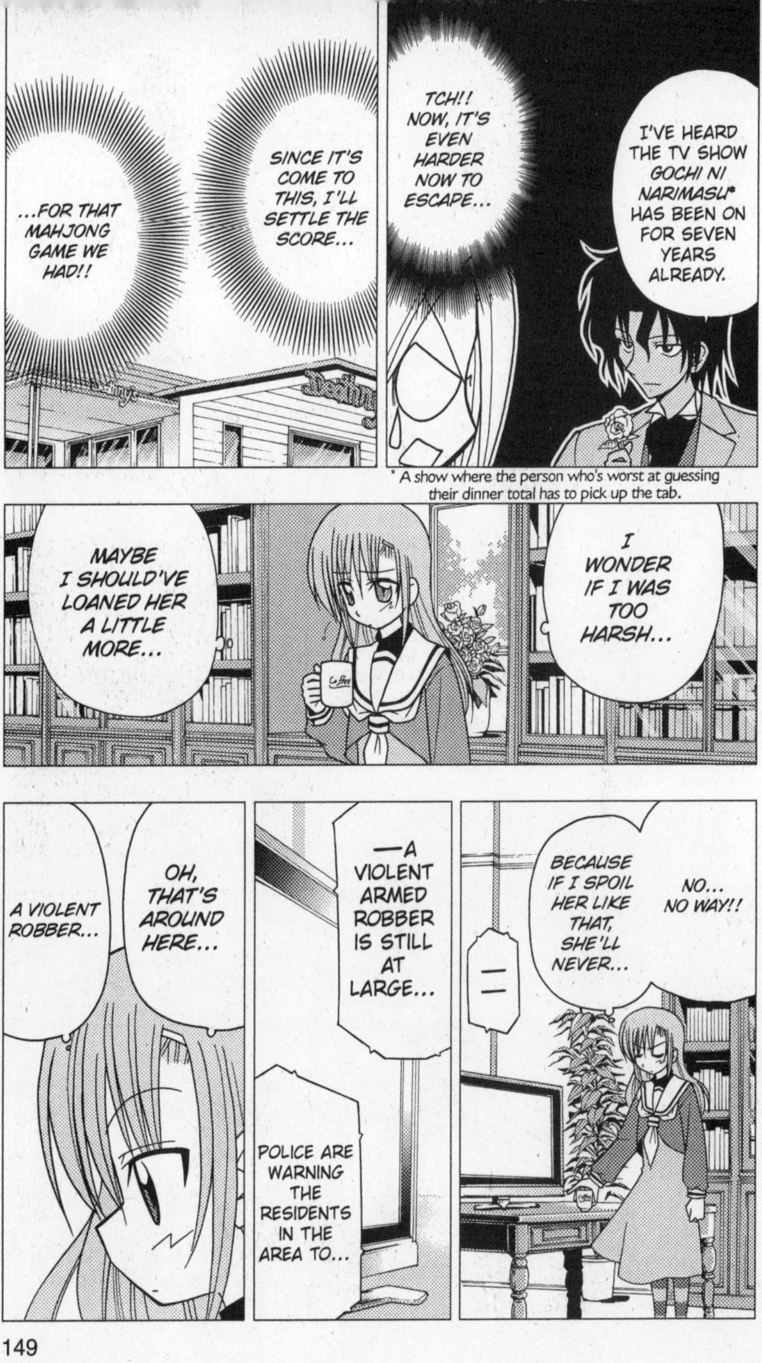
I'VE HEARD THE TV SHOW GOCHI NI NARIMASU* HAS BEEN ON FOR SEVEN YEARS ALREADY.
TCH!! NOW, IT'S EVEN HARDER NOW TO ESCAPE...
SINCE IT'S COME TO THIS, I'LL SETTLE THE SCORE...
...FOR THAT MAHJONG GAME WE HAD!!
I WONDER IF I WAS TOO HARSH...
MAYBE I SHOULD'VE LOANED HER A LITTLE MORE...
NO... NO WAY!!
BECAUSE IF I SPOIL HER LIKE THAT, SHE'LL NEVER...
— —
—A VIOLENT ARMED ROBBER IS STILL AT LARGE...
POLICE ARE WARNING THE RESIDENTS IN THE AREA TO...
OH, THAT'S AROUND HERE...
A VIOLENT ROBBER...

* A show where the person who's worst at guessing their dinner total has to pick up the tab.

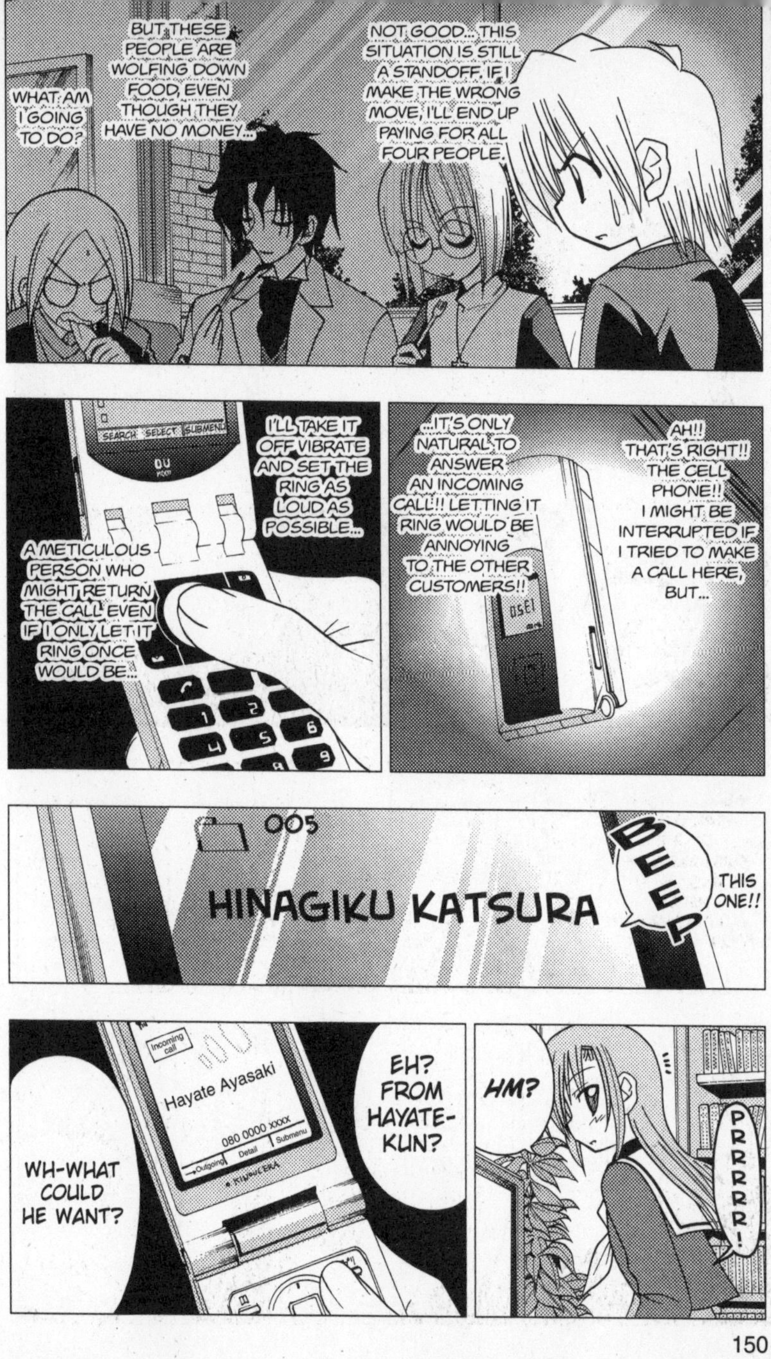
NOT GOOD... THIS SITUATION IS STILL A STANDOFF. IF I MAKE THE WRONG MOVE, I'LL END UP PAYING FOR ALL FOUR PEOPLE.
BUT THESE PEOPLE ARE WOLFING DOWN FOOD, EVEN THOUGH THEY HAVE NO MONEY...
WHAT AM I GOING TO DO?
AH!! THAT'S RIGHT!! THE CELL PHONE!! I MIGHT BE INTERRUPTED IF I TRIED TO MAKE A CALL HERE, BUT...
...IT'S ONLY NATURAL TO ANSWER AN INCOMING CALL!! LETTING IT RING WOULD BE ANNOYING TO THE OTHER CUSTOMERS!!
I'LL TAKE IT OFF VIBRATE AND SET THE RING AS LOUD AS POSSIBLE...
SEARCH SELECT SUBMENU
A METICULOUS PERSON WHO MIGHT RETURN THE CALL EVEN IF I ONLY LET IT RING ONCE WOULD BE...
THIS ONE!!
BEEP
005
HINAGIKU KATSURA
PRRRRR!
HM?
EH? FROM HAYATE-KUN?
Incoming call
Hayate Ayasaki
080 0000 xxxx
Outgoing Detail Submenu
WH-WHAT COULD HE WANT?

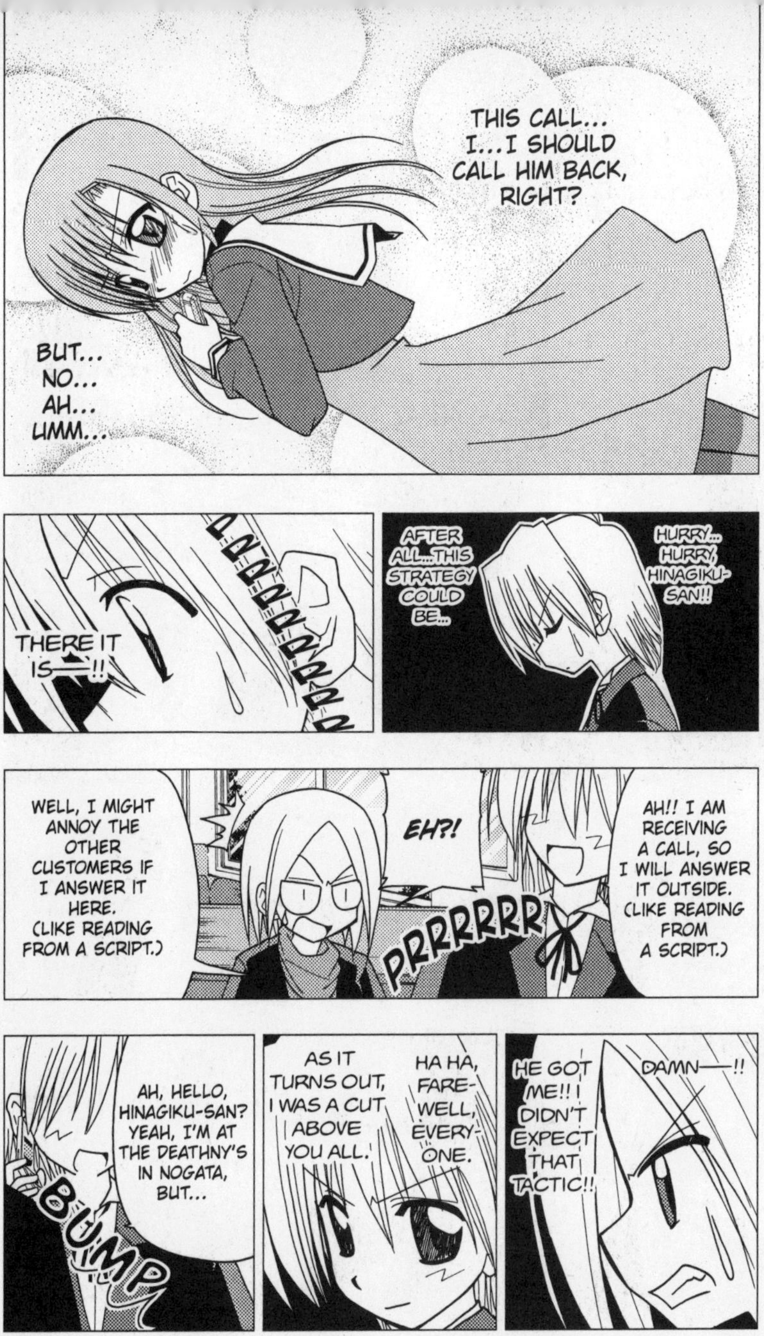
THIS CALL... I...I SHOULD CALL HIM BACK, RIGHT?
BUT... NO... AH... UMM...
HURRY... HURRY, HINAGIKU-SAN!!
AFTER ALL...THIS STRATEGY COULD BE...
THERE IT IS——!!
AH!! I AM RECEIVING A CALL, SO I WILL ANSWER IT OUTSIDE. (LIKE READING FROM A SCRIPT.)
EH?!
PRRRRRR
WELL, I MIGHT ANNOY THE OTHER CUSTOMERS IF I ANSWER IT HERE. (LIKE READING FROM A SCRIPT.)
DAMN——!!
HE GOT ME!! I DIDN'T EXPECT THAT TACTIC!!
HA HA, FARE-WELL, EVERY-ONE.
AS IT TURNS OUT, I WAS A CUT ABOVE YOU ALL.
AH, HELLO, HINAGIKU-SAN? YEAH, I'M AT THE DEATHNY'S IN NOGATA, BUT...
BUMP

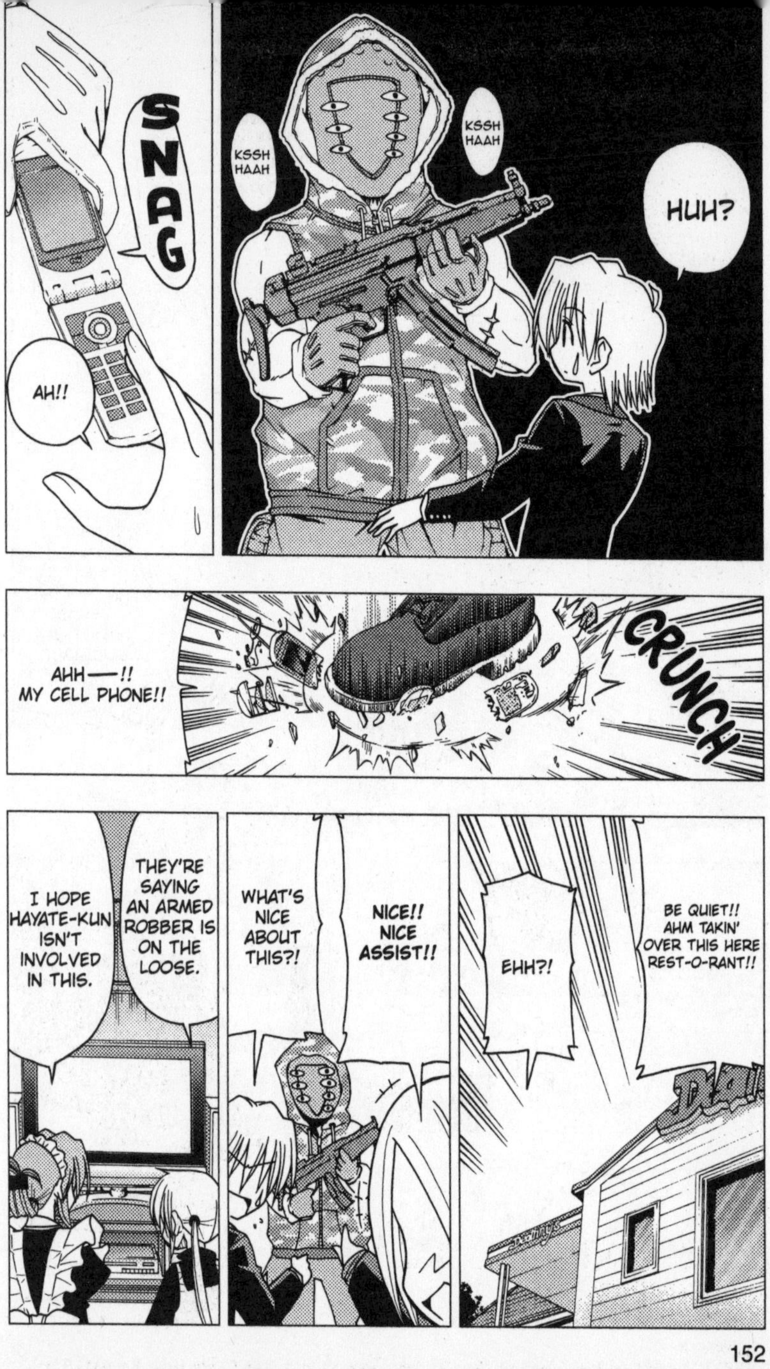
HUH?
KSSH HAAH
KSSH HAAH
SNAG
AH!!
CRUNCH
AHH—!! MY CELL PHONE!!
BE QUIET!! AHM TAKIN' OVER THIS HERE REST-O-RANT!!
EHH?!
NICE!! NICE ASSIST!!
WHAT'S NICE ABOUT THIS?!
THEY'RE SAYING AN ARMED ROBBER IS ON THE LOOSE.
I HOPE HAYATE-KUN ISN'T INVOLVED IN THIS.

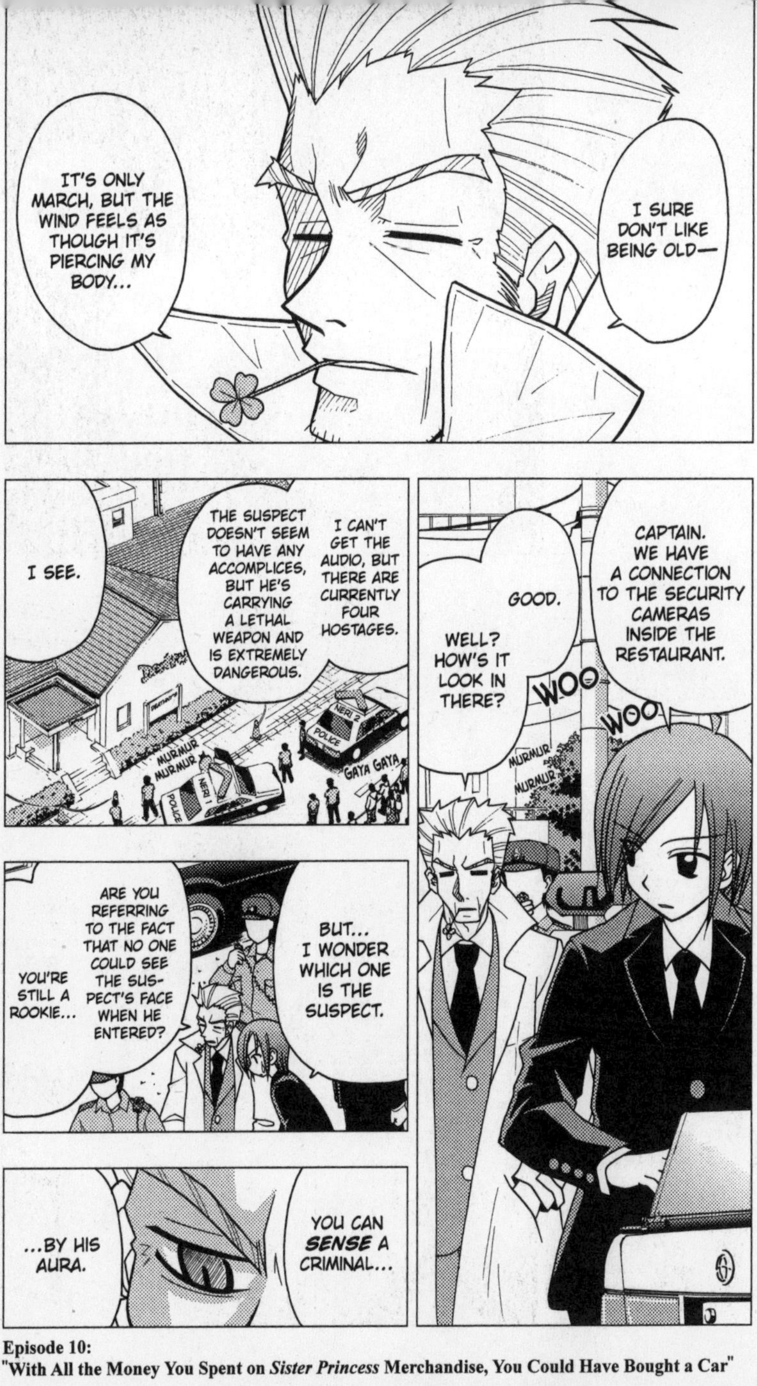
I SURE DON'T LIKE BEING OLD—
IT'S ONLY MARCH, BUT THE WIND FEELS AS THOUGH IT'S PIERCING MY BODY...
CAPTAIN. WE HAVE A CONNECTION TO THE SECURITY CAMERAS INSIDE THE RESTAURANT.
GOOD.
WELL? HOW'S IT LOOK IN THERE?
WOO
WOO
MURMUR
MURMUR
I CAN'T GET THE AUDIO, BUT THERE ARE CURRENTLY FOUR HOSTAGES.
THE SUSPECT DOESN'T SEEM TO HAVE ANY ACCOMPLICES, BUT HE'S CARRYING A LETHAL WEAPON AND IS EXTREMELY DANGEROUS.
I SEE.
POLICE
NERI 2
MURMUR
MURMUR
GAYA GAYA
NERI 1
POLICE
BUT... I WONDER WHICH ONE IS THE SUSPECT.
ARE YOU REFERRING TO THE FACT THAT NO ONE COULD SEE THE SUS-PECT'S FACE WHEN HE ENTERED?
YOU'RE STILL A ROOKIE...
YOU CAN *SENSE* A CRIMINAL...
...BY HIS AURA.

Episode 10:
"With All the Money You Spent on *Sister Princess* Merchandise, You Could Have Bought a Car"

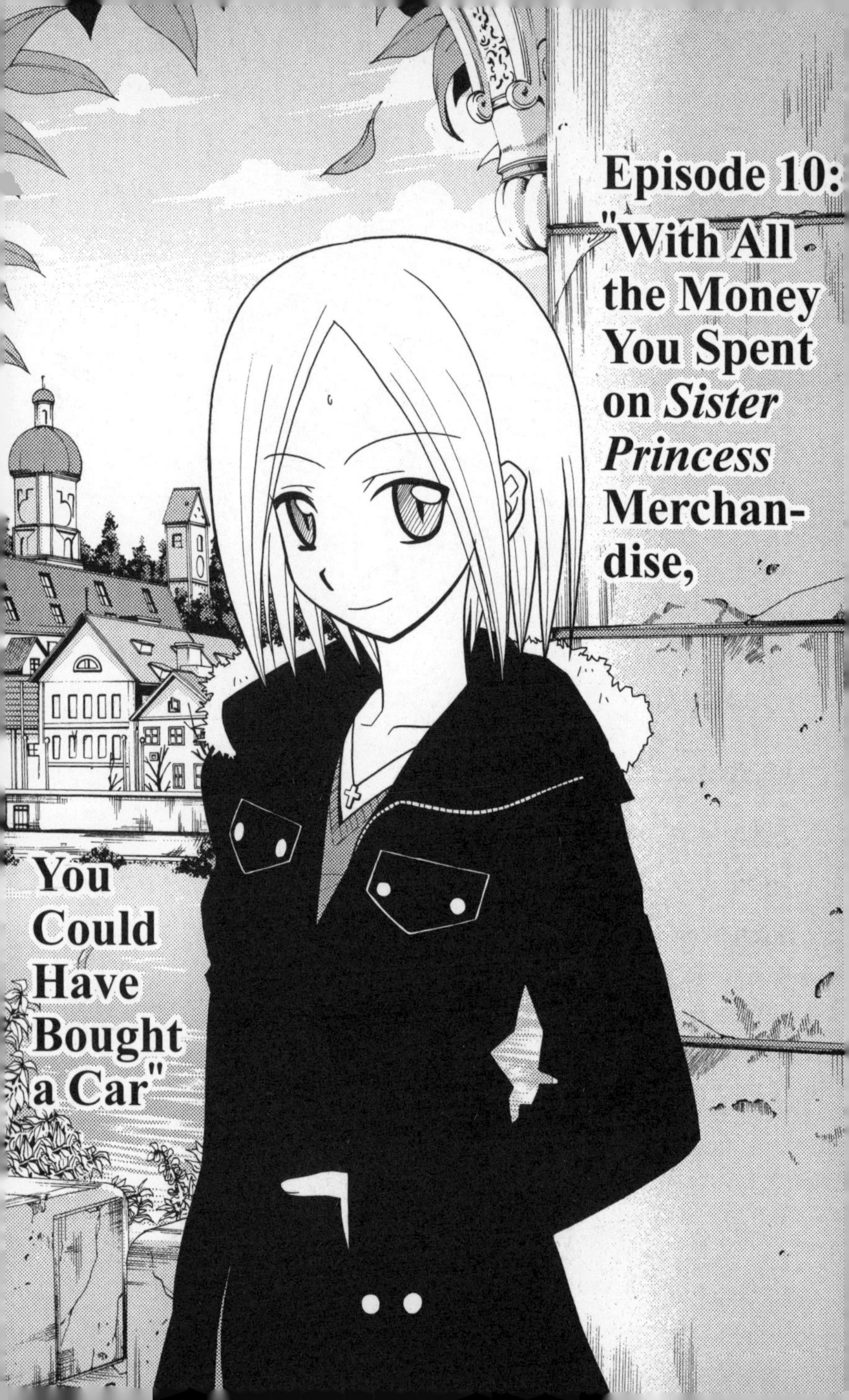
Episode 10:
"With All the Money You Spent on *Sister Princess* Merchandise,
You Could Have Bought a Car"

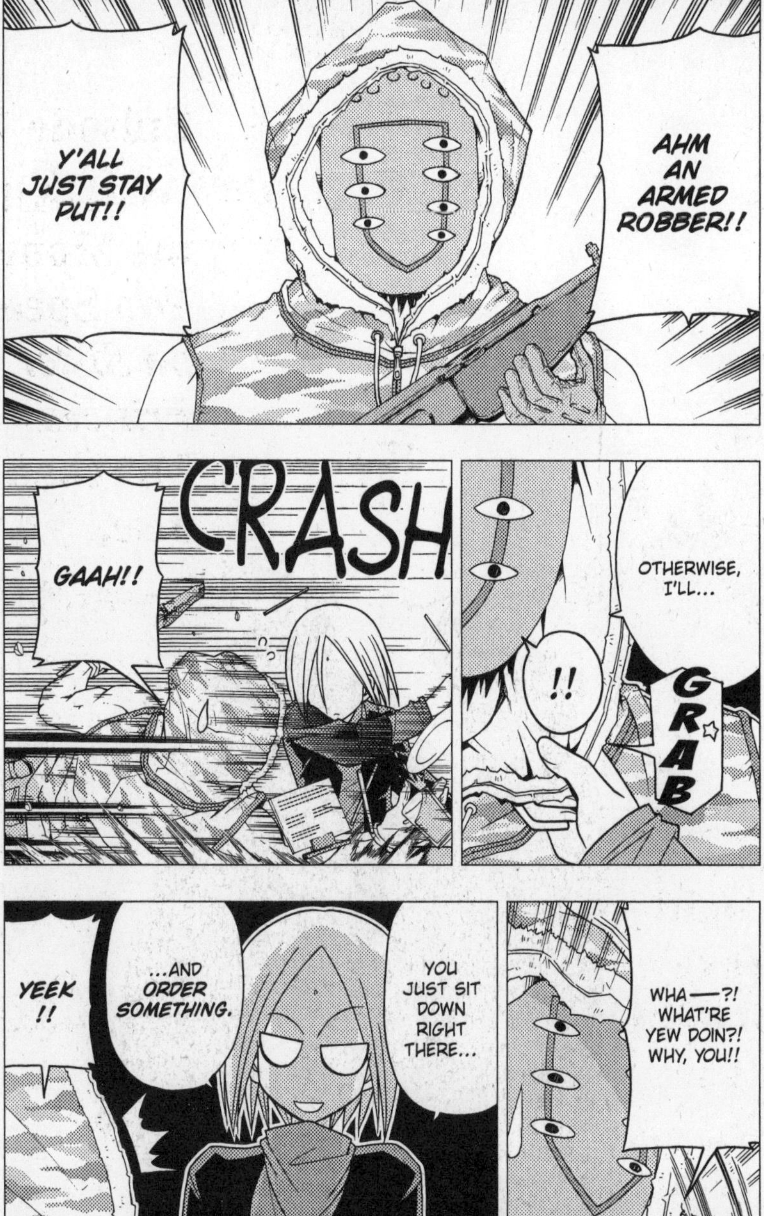
AHM AN ARMED ROBBER!!
Y'ALL JUST STAY PUT!!
OTHERWISE, I'LL...
!!
GRAB
CRASH
GAAH!!
WHA—?! WHAT'RE YEW DOIN?! WHY, YOU!!
YOU JUST SIT DOWN RIGHT THERE...
...AND ORDER SOMETHING.
YEEK !!

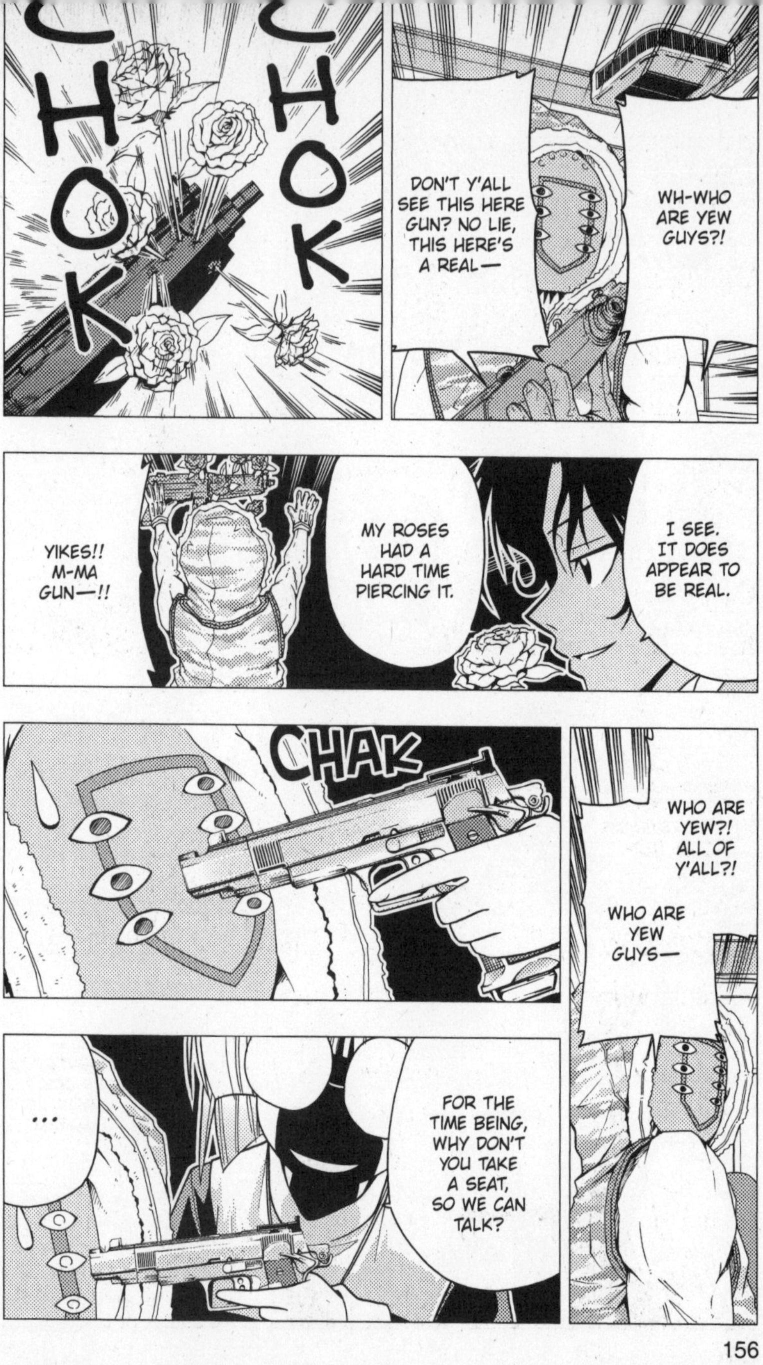
WH-WHO ARE YEW GUYS?!
DON'T Y'ALL SEE THIS HERE GUN? NO LIE, THIS HERE'S A REAL—
CHOK
CHOK
I SEE. IT DOES APPEAR TO BE REAL.
MY ROSES HAD A HARD TIME PIERCING IT.
YIKES!! M-MA GUN—!!
WHO ARE YEW?! ALL OF Y'ALL?!
WHO ARE YEW GUYS—
CHAK
FOR THE TIME BEING, WHY DON'T YOU TAKE A SEAT, SO WE CAN TALK?
...

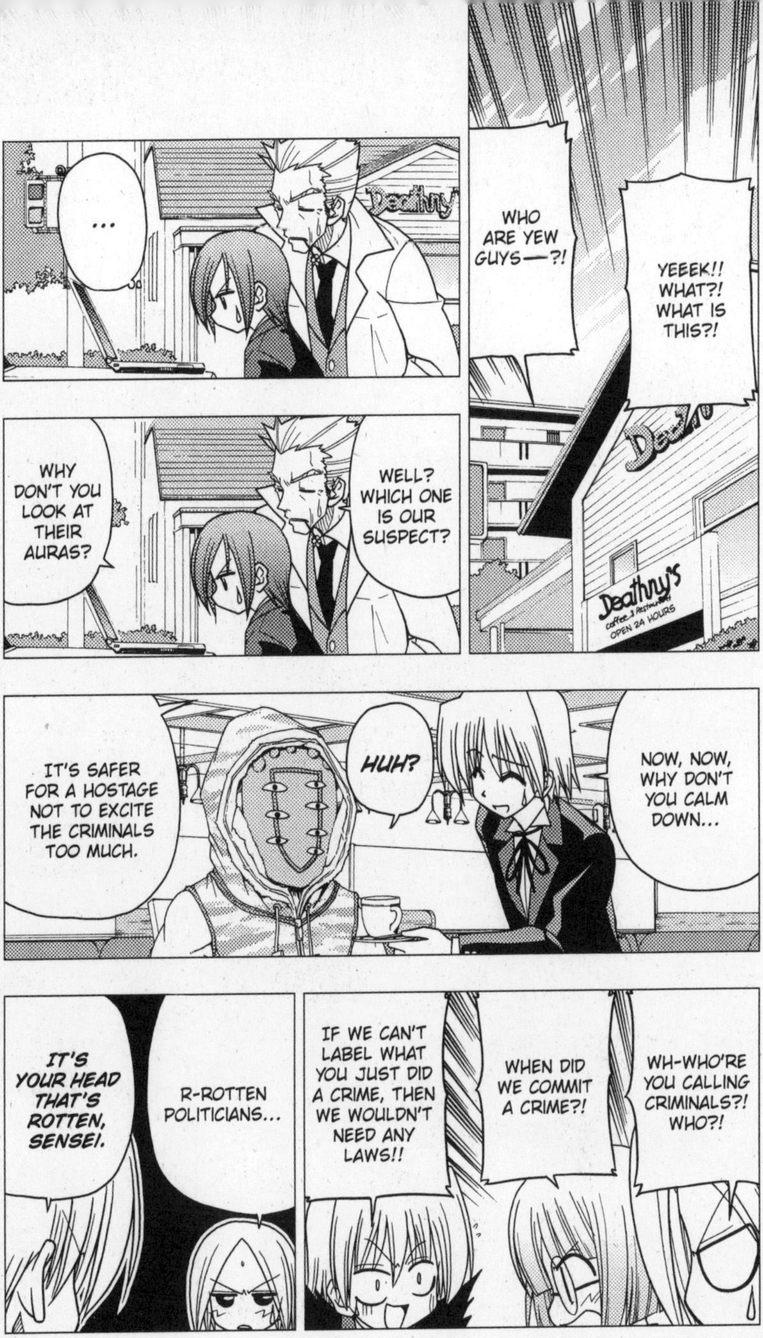
YEEEK!! WHAT?! WHAT IS THIS?!
WHO ARE YEW GUYS—?!
Deathny's
OPEN 24 HOURS
...
WELL? WHICH ONE IS OUR SUSPECT?
WHY DON'T YOU LOOK AT THEIR AURAS?
NOW, NOW, WHY DON'T YOU CALM DOWN...
HUH?
IT'S SAFER FOR A HOSTAGE NOT TO EXCITE THE CRIMINALS TOO MUCH.
WH-WHO'RE YOU CALLING CRIMINALS?! WHO?!
WHEN DID WE COMMIT A CRIME?!
IF WE CAN'T LABEL WHAT YOU JUST DID A CRIME, THEN WE WOULDN'T NEED ANY LAWS!!
R-ROTTEN POLITICIANS...
IT'S YOUR HEAD THAT'S ROTTEN, SENSEI.

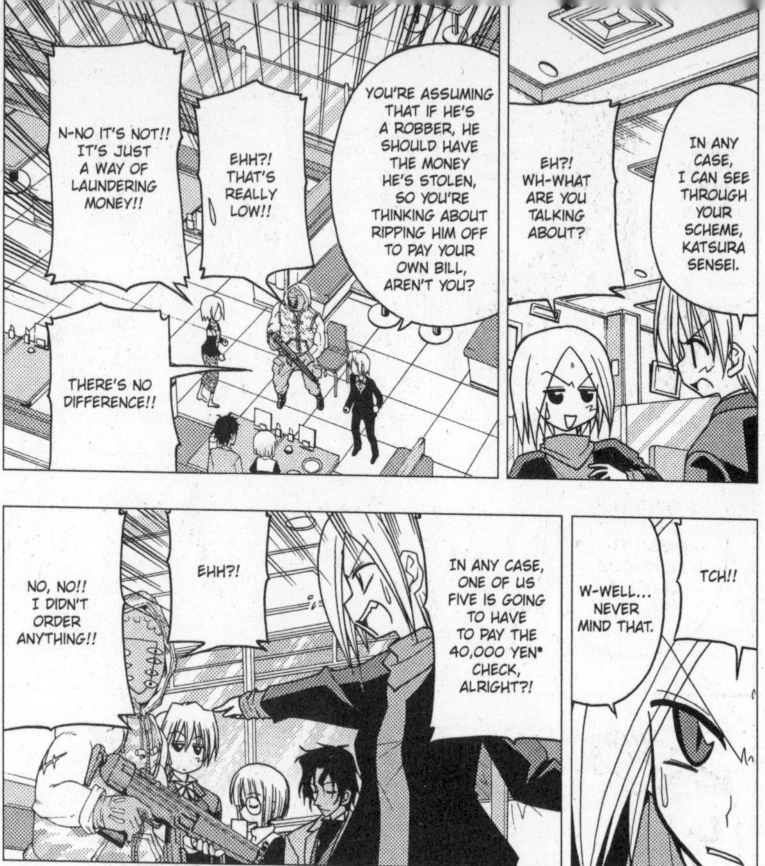
IN ANY CASE, I CAN SEE THROUGH YOUR SCHEME, KATSURA SENSEI.
EH?! WH-WHAT ARE YOU TALKING ABOUT?
YOU'RE ASSUMING THAT IF HE'S A ROBBER, HE SHOULD HAVE THE MONEY HE'S STOLEN, SO YOU'RE THINKING ABOUT RIPPING HIM OFF TO PAY YOUR OWN BILL, AREN'T YOU?
EHH?! THAT'S REALLY LOW!!
N-NO IT'S NOT!! IT'S JUST A WAY OF LAUNDERING MONEY!!
THERE'S NO DIFFERENCE!!
TCH!!
W-WELL... NEVER MIND THAT.
IN ANY CASE, ONE OF US FIVE IS GOING TO HAVE TO PAY THE 40,000 YEN* CHECK, ALRIGHT?!
EHH?!
NO, NO!! I DIDN'T ORDER ANYTHING!!

* About $375.

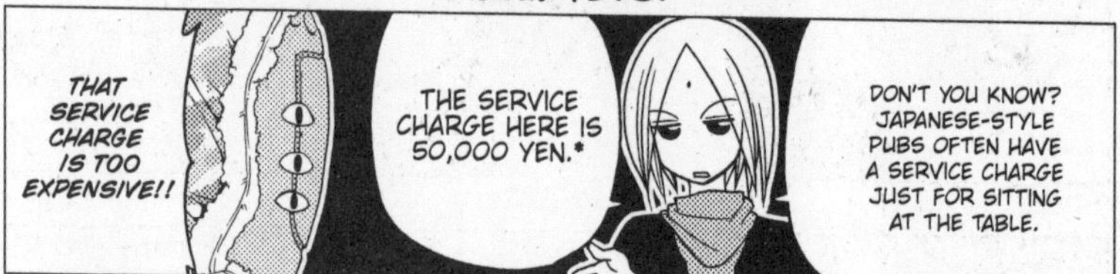
DON'T YOU KNOW? JAPANESE-STYLE PUBS OFTEN HAVE A SERVICE CHARGE JUST FOR SITTING AT THE TABLE.
THE SERVICE CHARGE HERE IS 50,000 YEN.*
THAT SERVICE CHARGE IS TOO EXPENSIVE!!

* About $468.

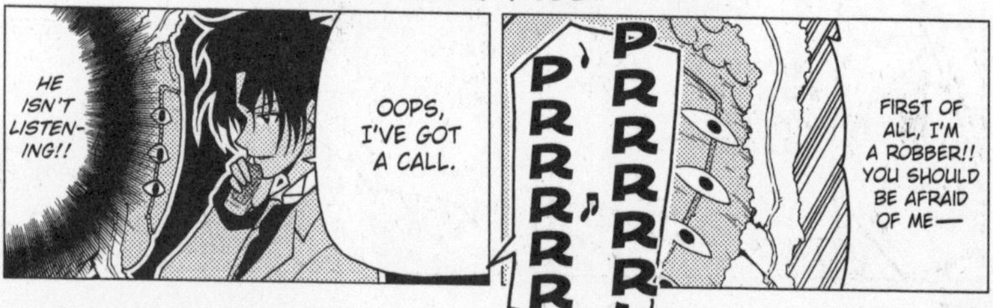
FIRST OF ALL, I'M A ROBBER!! YOU SHOULD BE AFRAID OF ME—
PRRRRR♪
PRRRRR♪
OOPS, I'VE GOT A CALL.
HE ISN'T LISTEN-ING!!

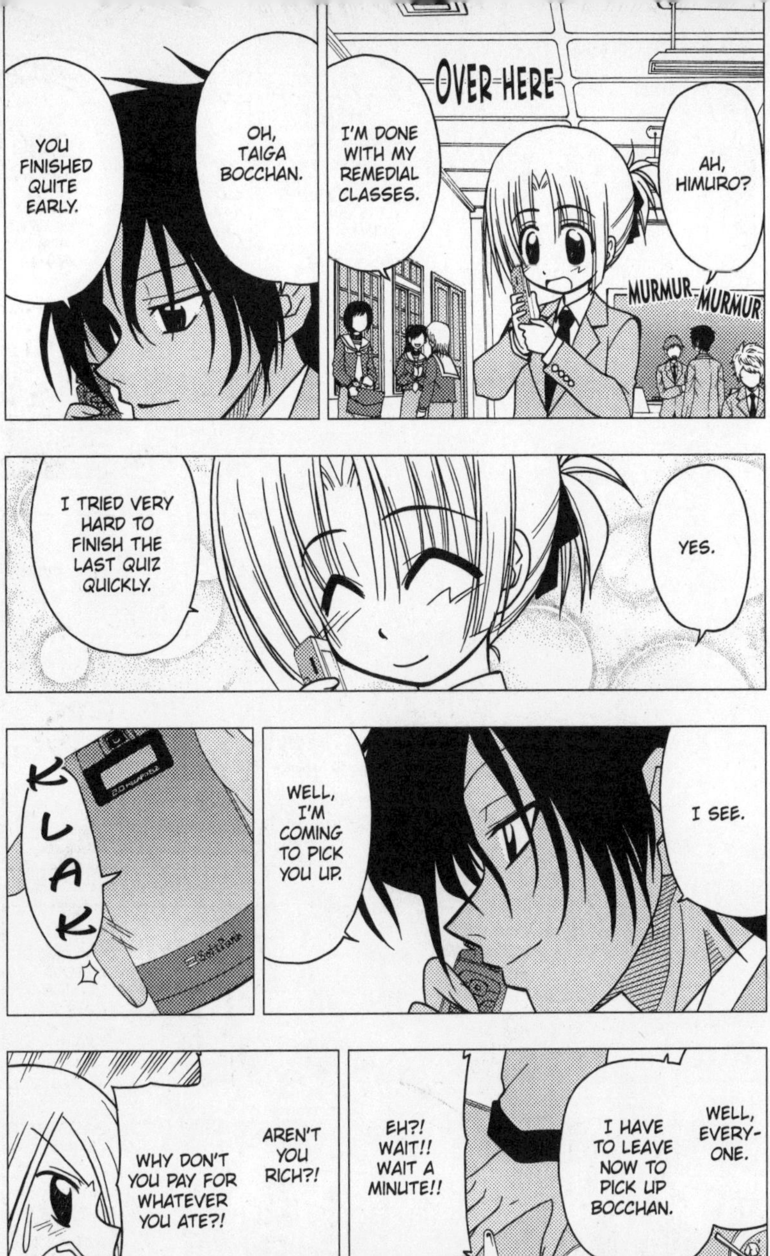
OVER HERE
AH, HIMURO?
MURMUR-MURMUR
I'M DONE WITH MY REMEDIAL CLASSES.
OH, TAIGA BOCCHAN.
YOU FINISHED QUITE EARLY.
YES.
I TRIED VERY HARD TO FINISH THE LAST QUIZ QUICKLY.
I SEE.
WELL, I'M COMING TO PICK YOU UP.
KLAK
WELL, EVERY-ONE.
I HAVE TO LEAVE NOW TO PICK UP BOCCHAN.
EH?! WAIT!! WAIT A MINUTE!!
AREN'T YOU RICH?!
WHY DON'T YOU PAY FOR WHATEVER YOU ATE?!

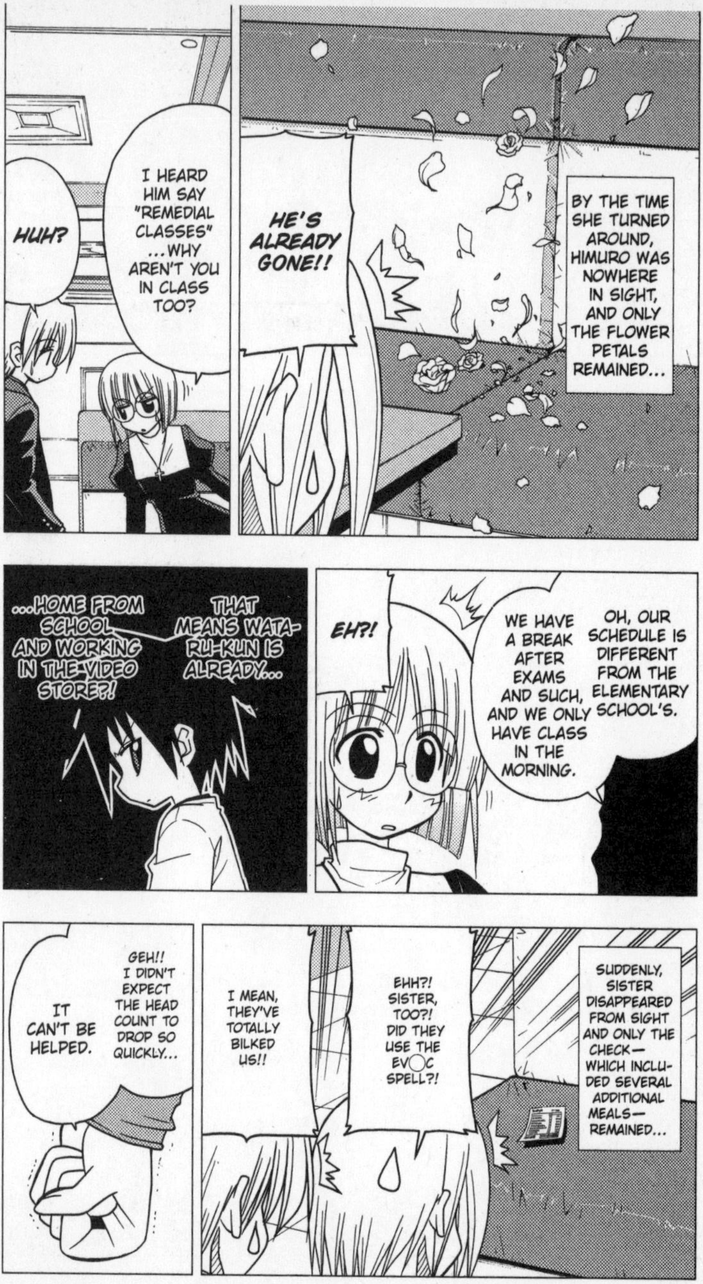

BY THE TIME SHE TURNED AROUND, HIMURO WAS NOWHERE IN SIGHT, AND ONLY THE FLOWER PETALS REMAINED...
HE'S ALREADY GONE!!
I HEARD HIM SAY "REMEDIAL CLASSES" ...WHY AREN'T YOU IN CLASS TOO?
HUH?
OH, OUR SCHEDULE IS DIFFERENT FROM THE ELEMENTARY SCHOOL'S.
WE HAVE A BREAK AFTER EXAMS AND SUCH, AND WE ONLY HAVE CLASS IN THE MORNING.
EH?!
THAT MEANS WATA-RU-KUN IS ALREADY...
...HOME FROM SCHOOL AND WORKING IN THE VIDEO STORE?!
SUDDENLY, SISTER DISAPPEARED FROM SIGHT AND ONLY THE CHECK—WHICH INCLU-DED SEVERAL ADDITIONAL MEALS—REMAINED...
EHH?! SISTER, TOO?! DID THEY USE THE EV◯C SPELL?!
I MEAN, THEY'VE TOTALLY BILKED US!!
GEH!! I DIDN'T EXPECT THE HEAD COUNT TO DROP SO QUICKLY...
IT CAN'T BE HELPED.

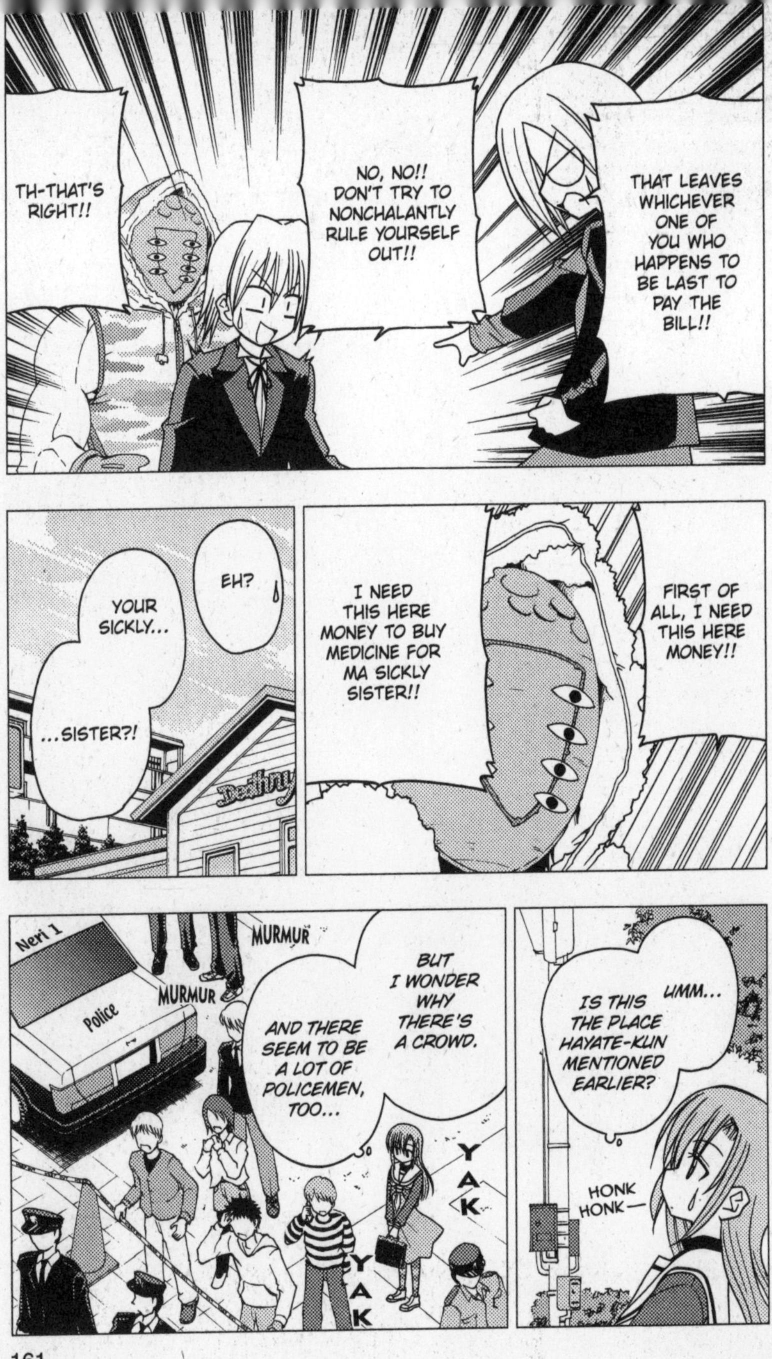
THAT LEAVES WHICHEVER ONE OF YOU WHO HAPPENS TO BE LAST TO PAY THE BILL!!
NO, NO!! DON'T TRY TO NONCHALANTLY RULE YOURSELF OUT!!
TH-THAT'S RIGHT!!
FIRST OF ALL, I NEED THIS HERE MONEY!!
I NEED THIS HERE MONEY TO BUY MEDICINE FOR MA SICKLY SISTER!!
EH?
YOUR SICKLY...
...SISTER?!
UMM...
IS THIS THE PLACE HAYATE-KUN MENTIONED EARLIER?
HONK HONK—
MURMUR
BUT I WONDER WHY THERE'S A CROWD.
AND THERE SEEM TO BE A LOT OF POLICEMEN, TOO...
MURMUR
Neri 1
Police
YAK YAK
YAK YAK

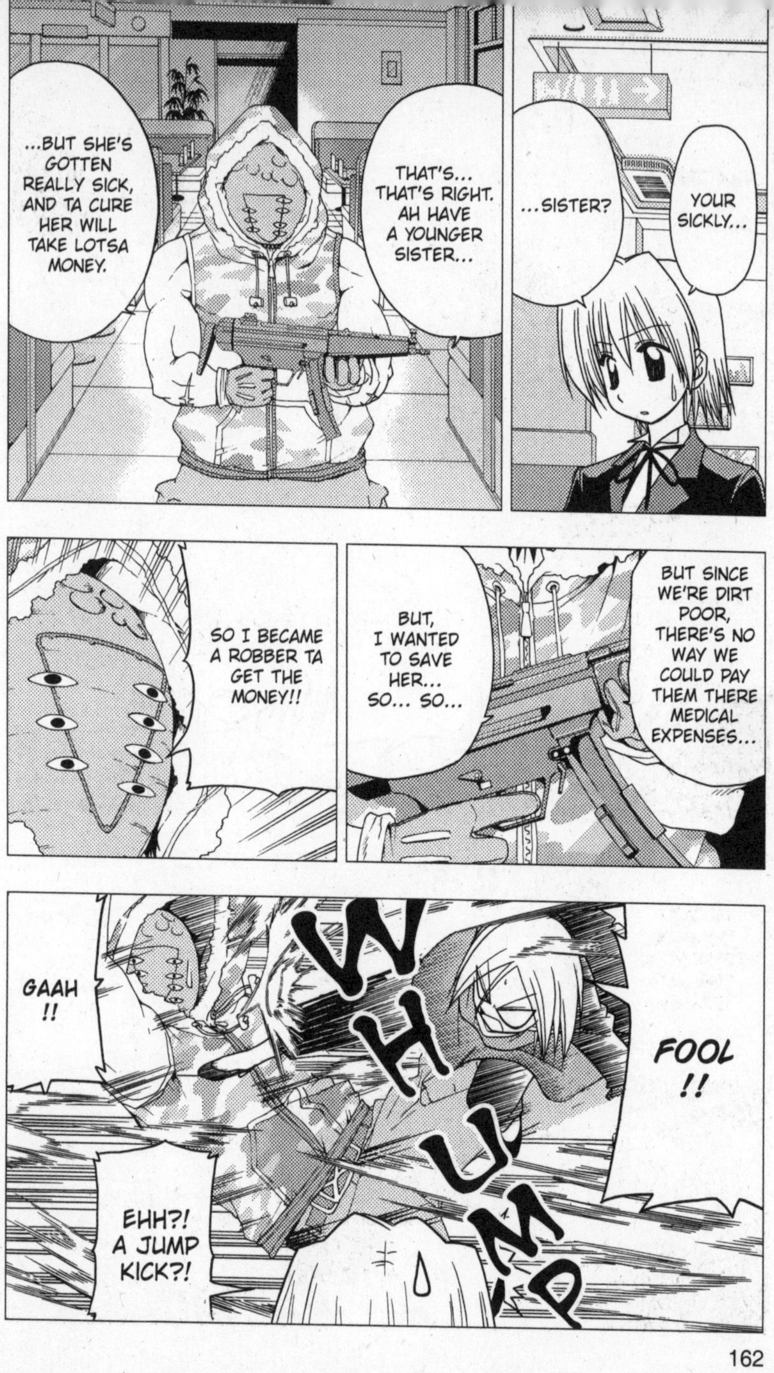
YOUR SICKLY...
...SISTER?
THAT'S... THAT'S RIGHT. AH HAVE A YOUNGER SISTER...
...BUT SHE'S GOTTEN REALLY SICK, AND TA CURE HER WILL TAKE LOTSA MONEY.
BUT SINCE WE'RE DIRT POOR, THERE'S NO WAY WE COULD PAY THEM THERE MEDICAL EXPENSES...
BUT, I WANTED TO SAVE HER... SO... SO...
SO I BECAME A ROBBER TA GET THE MONEY!!
FOOL !!
WHUMP
GAAH !!
EHH?! A JUMP KICK?!

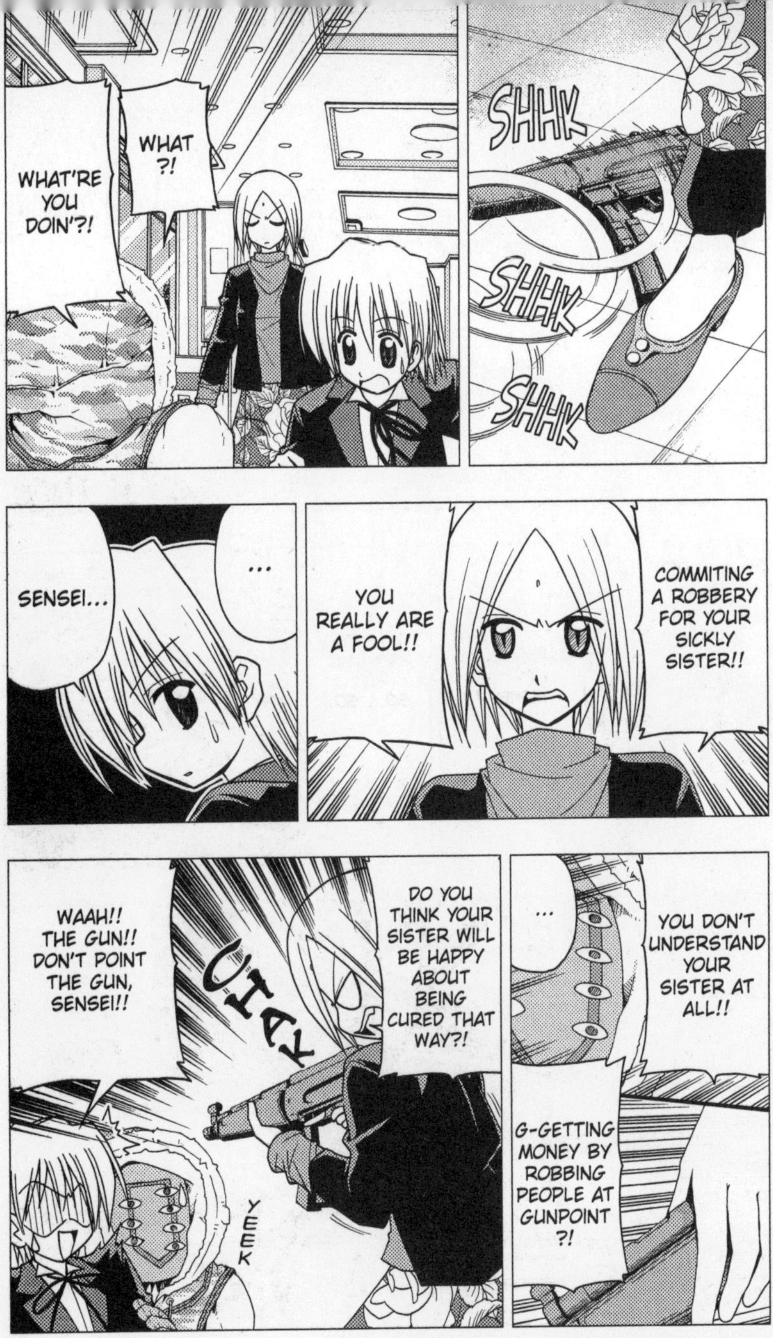
SHHK
SHHK
SHHK
WHAT ?!
WHAT'RE YOU DOIN'?!
COMMITING A ROBBERY FOR YOUR SICKLY SISTER!!
YOU REALLY ARE A FOOL!!
...
SENSEI...
YOU DON'T UNDERSTAND YOUR SISTER AT ALL!!
...
G-GETTING MONEY BY ROBBING PEOPLE AT GUNPOINT ?!
DO YOU THINK YOUR SISTER WILL BE HAPPY ABOUT BEING CURED THAT WAY?!
CHAK
WAAH!! THE GUN!! DON'T POINT THE GUN, SENSEI!!
YEEK

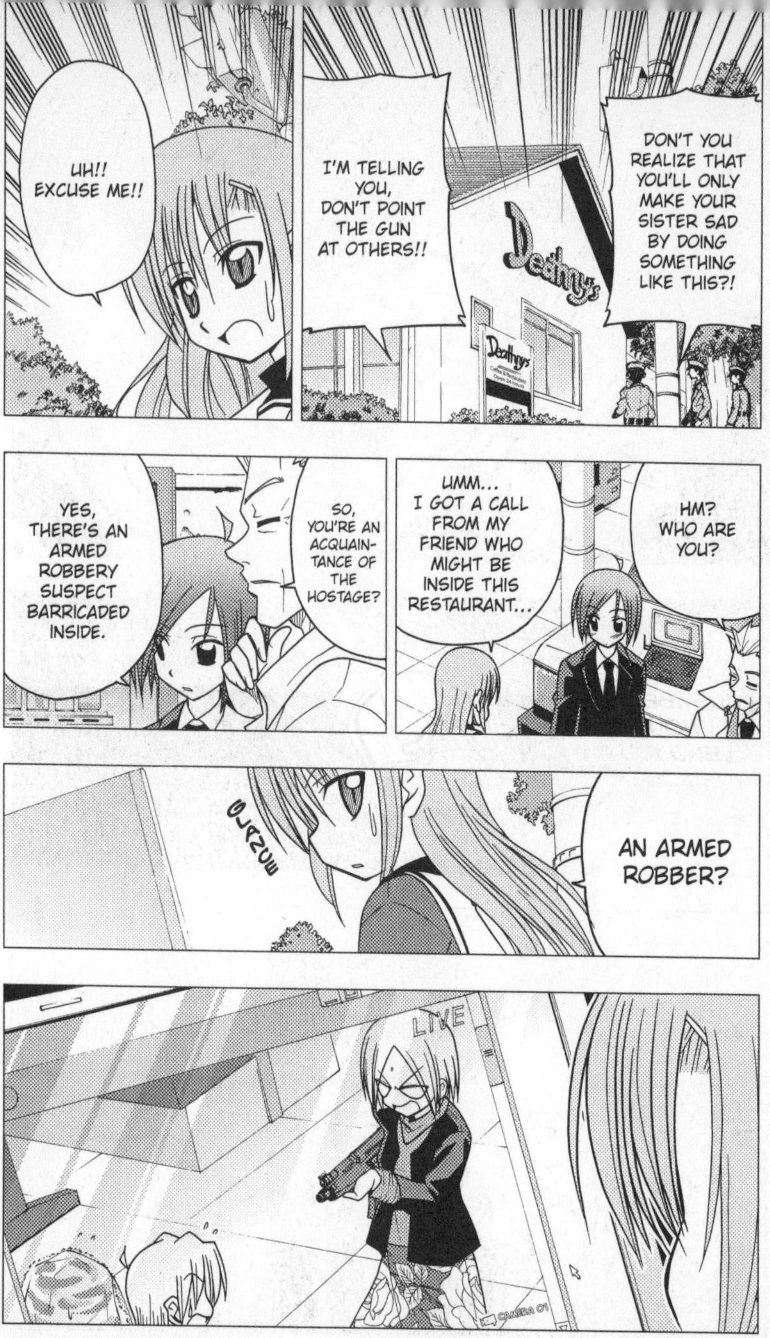
DON'T YOU REALIZE THAT YOU'LL ONLY MAKE YOUR SISTER SAD BY DOING SOMETHING LIKE THIS?!
I'M TELLING YOU, DON'T POINT THE GUN AT OTHERS!!
UH!! EXCUSE ME!!
HM? WHO ARE YOU?
UMM... I GOT A CALL FROM MY FRIEND WHO MIGHT BE INSIDE THIS RESTAURANT...
SO, YOU'RE AN ACQUAINTANCE OF THE HOSTAGE?
YES, THERE'S AN ARMED ROBBERY SUSPECT BARRICADED INSIDE.
AN ARMED ROBBER?
LIVE
CAMERA 01

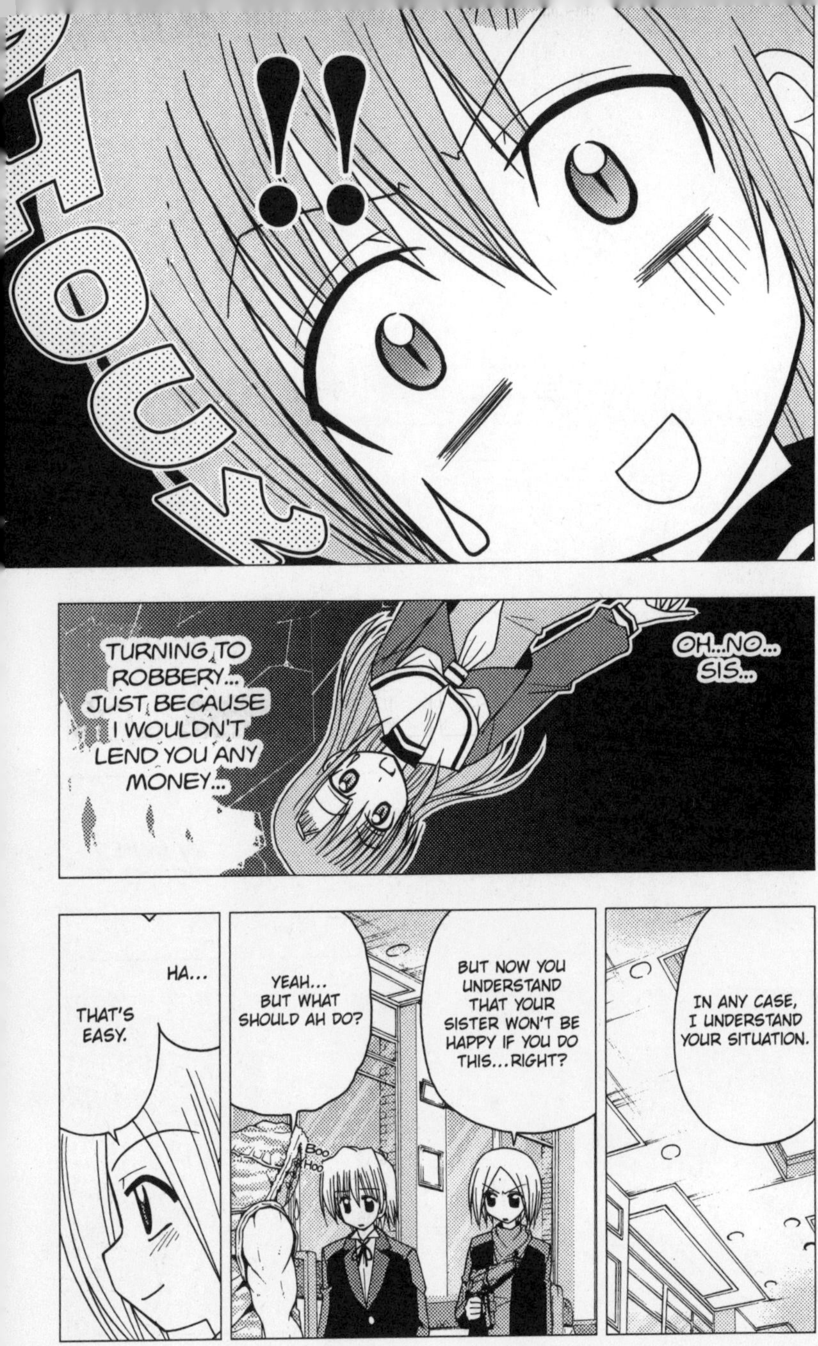
!!
OH...NO... SIS...
TURNING TO ROBBERY... JUST BECAUSE I WOULDN'T LEND YOU ANY MONEY...
IN ANY CASE, I UNDERSTAND YOUR SITUATION.
BUT NOW YOU UNDERSTAND THAT YOUR SISTER WON'T BE HAPPY IF YOU DO THIS... RIGHT?
YEAH... BUT WHAT SHOULD AH DO?
Boo Hoo
HA...
THAT'S EASY.

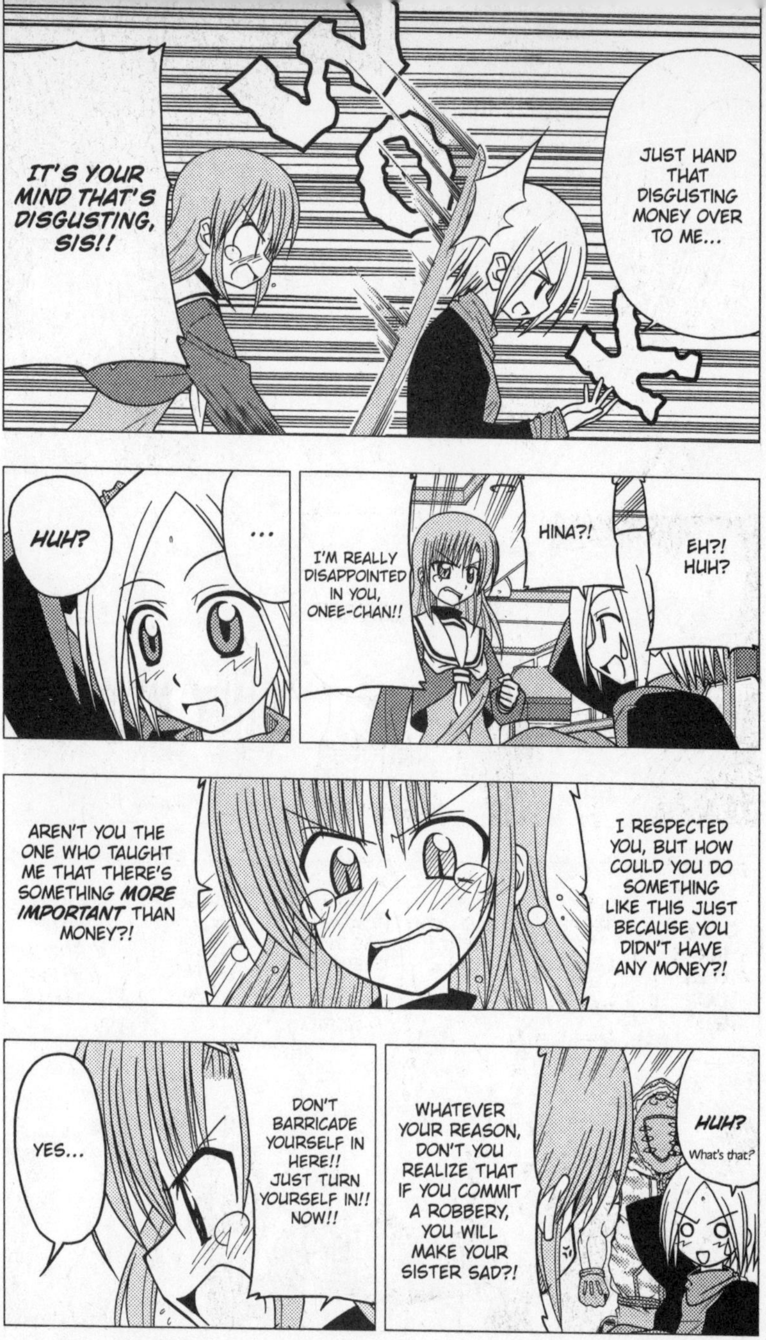
JUST HAND THAT DISGUSTING MONEY OVER TO ME...
IT'S YOUR MIND THAT'S DISGUSTING, SIS!!
EH?! HUH?
HINA?!
I'M REALLY DISAPPOINTED IN YOU, ONEE-CHAN!!
...
HUH?
I RESPECTED YOU, BUT HOW COULD YOU DO SOMETHING LIKE THIS JUST BECAUSE YOU DIDN'T HAVE ANY MONEY?!
AREN'T YOU THE ONE WHO TAUGHT ME THAT THERE'S SOMETHING MORE IMPORTANT THAN MONEY?!
HUH?
What's that?
WHATEVER YOUR REASON, DON'T YOU REALIZE THAT IF YOU COMMIT A ROBBERY, YOU WILL MAKE YOUR SISTER SAD?!
DON'T BARRICADE YOURSELF IN HERE!! JUST TURN YOURSELF IN!! NOW!!
YES...

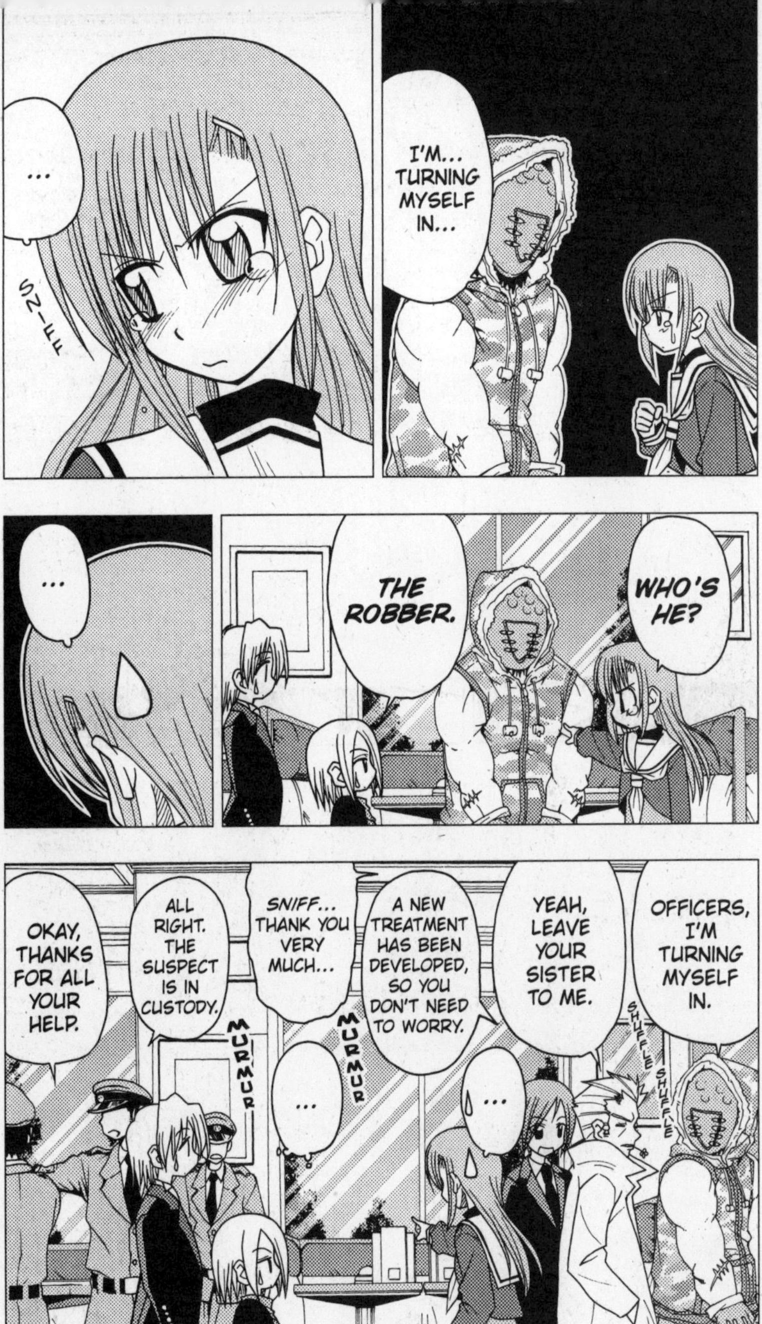
I'M... TURNING MYSELF IN...
...
SNIFF
WHO'S HE?
THE ROBBER.
...
OFFICERS, I'M TURNING MYSELF IN.
SHUFFLE
SHUFFLE
YEAH, LEAVE YOUR SISTER TO ME.
...
A NEW TREATMENT HAS BEEN DEVELOPED, SO YOU DON'T NEED TO WORRY.
MURMUR
SNIFF... THANK YOU VERY MUCH...
...
MURMUR
ALL RIGHT. THE SUSPECT IS IN CUSTODY.
OKAY, THANKS FOR ALL YOUR HELP.

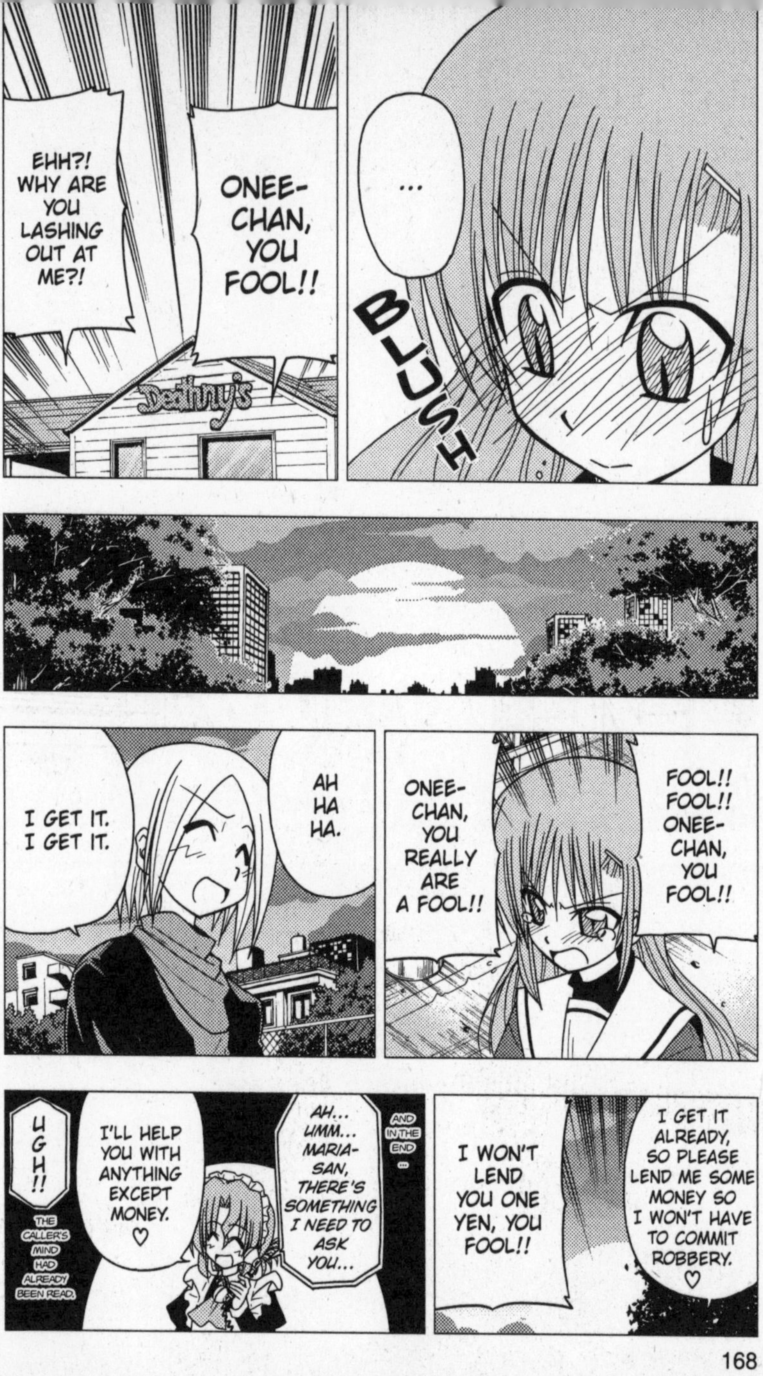
...
BLUSH
ONEE-CHAN, YOU FOOL!!
EHH?! WHY ARE YOU LASHING OUT AT ME?!
FOOL!! FOOL!! ONEE-CHAN, YOU FOOL!!
ONEE-CHAN, YOU REALLY ARE A FOOL!!
AH HA HA.
I GET IT. I GET IT.
I GET IT ALREADY, SO PLEASE LEND ME SOME MONEY SO I WON'T HAVE TO COMMIT ROBBERY. ♡
I WON'T LEND YOU ONE YEN, YOU FOOL!!
AND IN THE END...
AH... UMM... MARIA-SAN, THERE'S SOMETHING I NEED TO ASK YOU...
I'LL HELP YOU WITH ANYTHING EXCEPT MONEY. ♡
UGH!!
THE CALLER'S MIND HAD ALREADY BEEN READ.

Episode 11: "A Lonesome War"

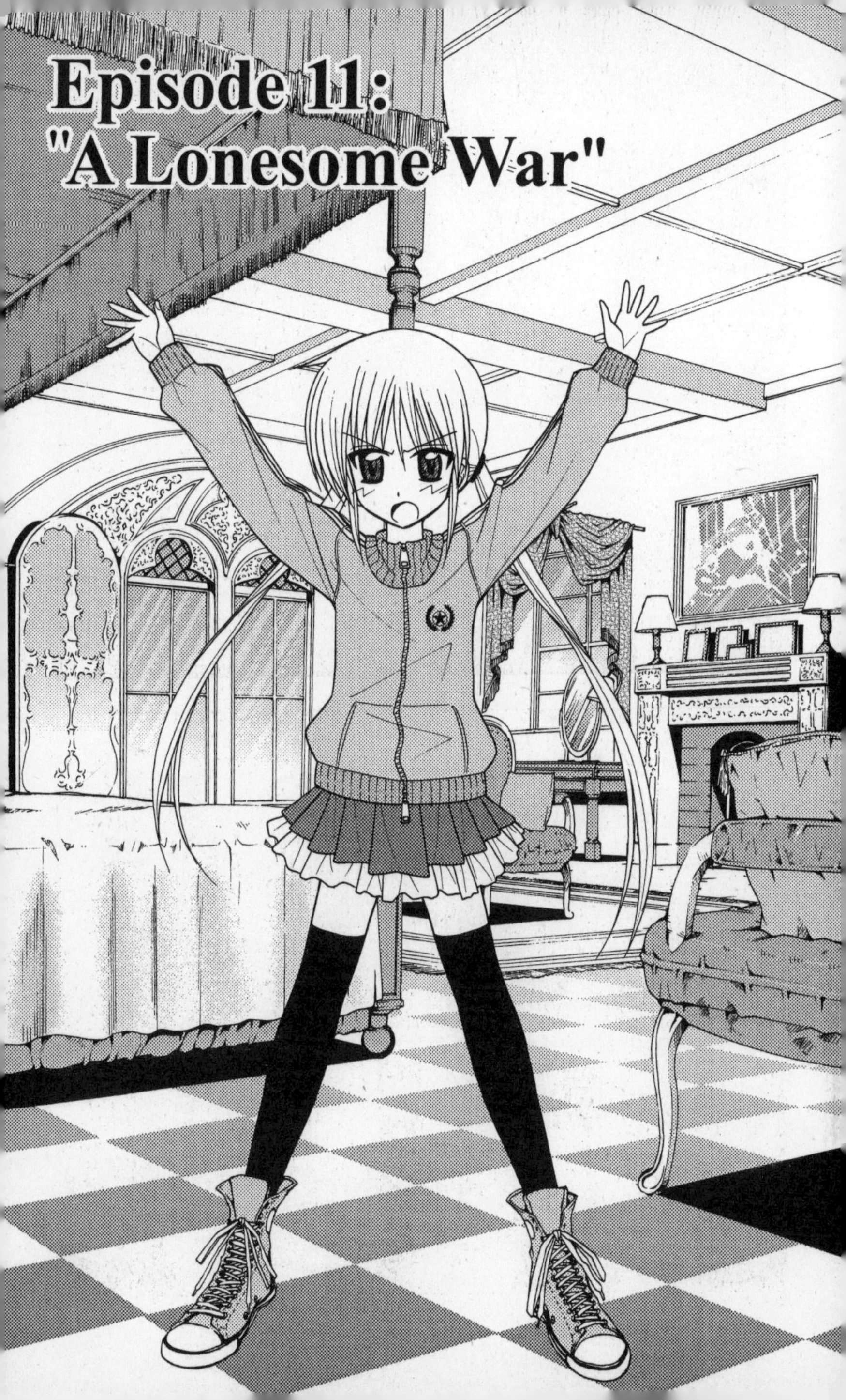

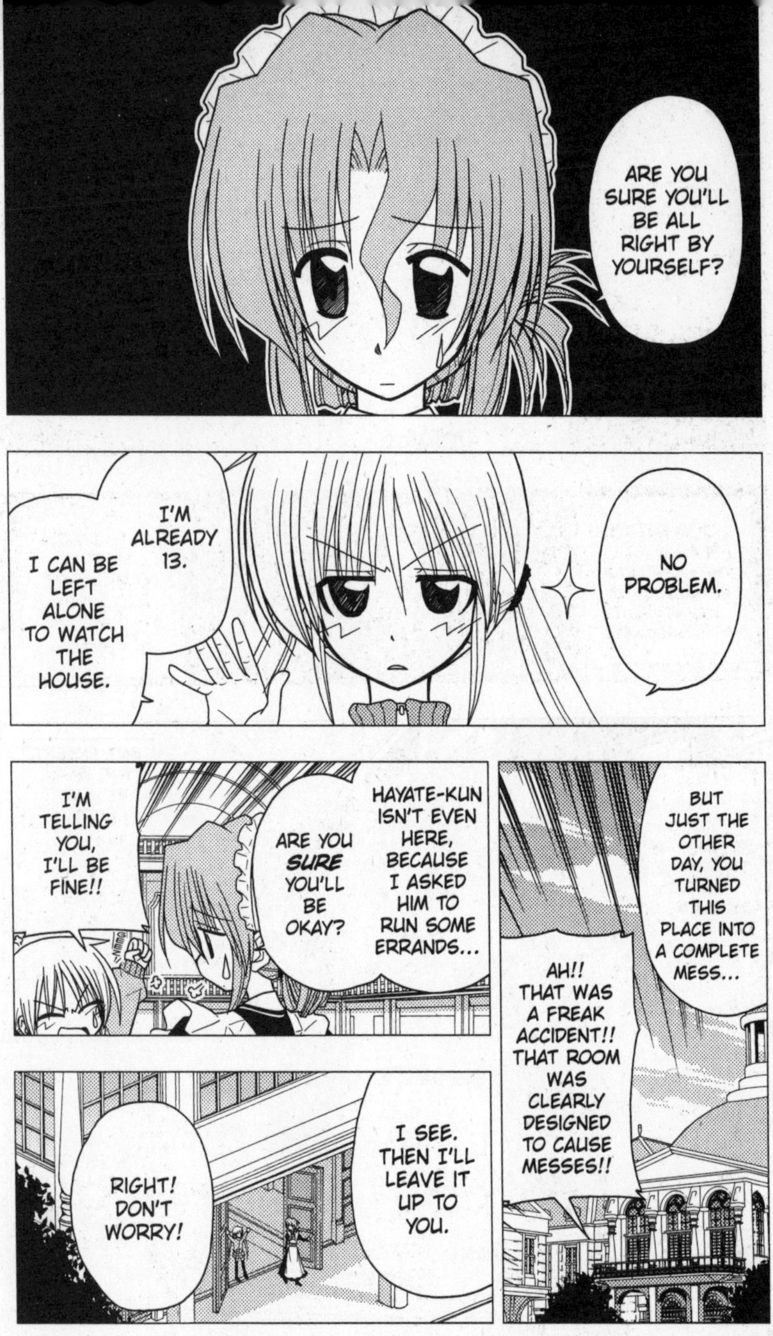
ARE YOU SURE YOU'LL BE ALL RIGHT BY YOURSELF?
NO PROBLEM.
I'M ALREADY 13.
I CAN BE LEFT ALONE TO WATCH THE HOUSE.
BUT JUST THE OTHER DAY, YOU TURNED THIS PLACE INTO A COMPLETE MESS...
AH!! THAT WAS A FREAK ACCIDENT!! THAT ROOM WAS CLEARLY DESIGNED TO CAUSE MESSES!!
HAYATE-KUN ISN'T EVEN HERE, BECAUSE I ASKED HIM TO RUN SOME ERRANDS...
ARE YOU *SURE* YOU'LL BE OKAY?
I'M TELLING YOU, I'LL BE FINE!!
I SEE. THEN I'LL LEAVE IT UP TO YOU.
RIGHT! DON'T WORRY!

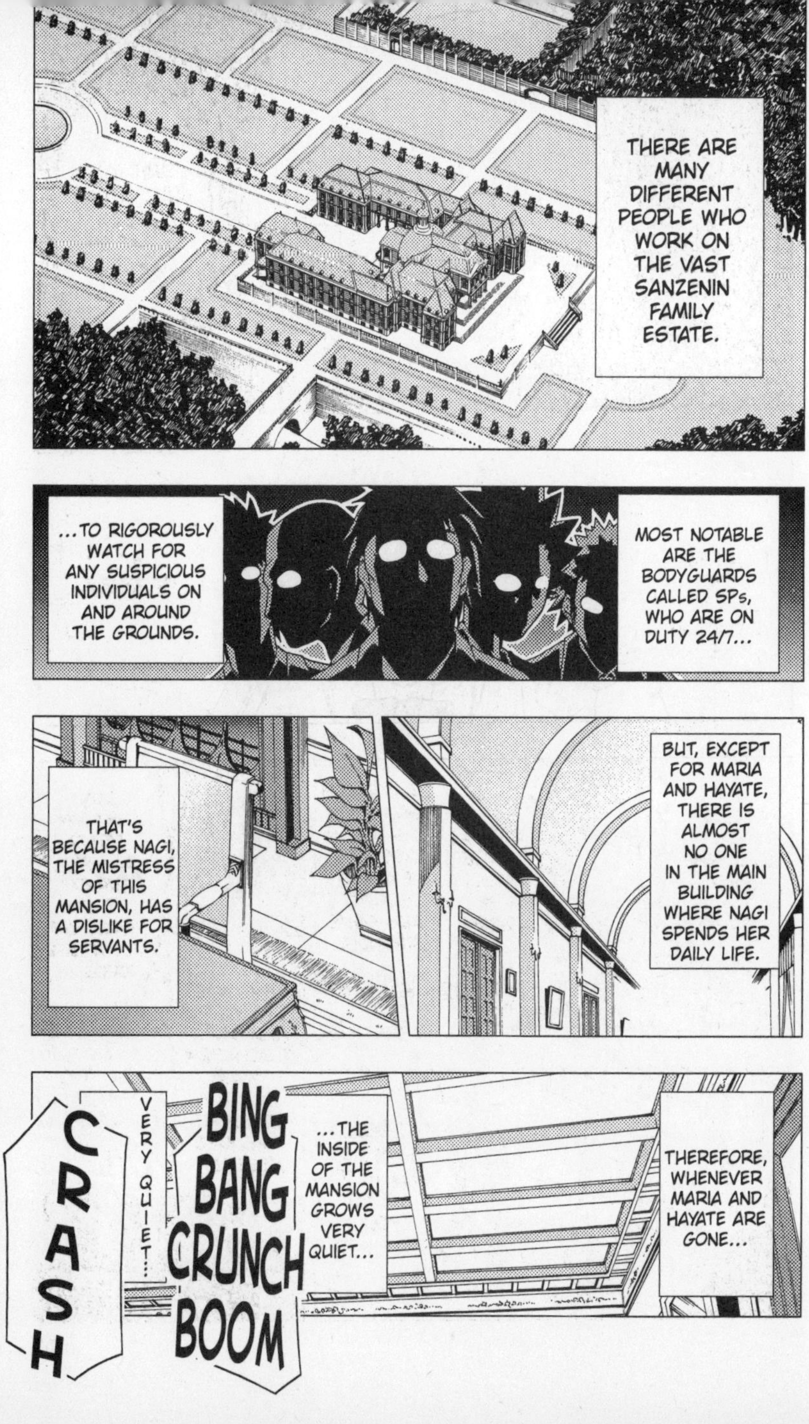
THERE ARE MANY DIFFERENT PEOPLE WHO WORK ON THE VAST SANZENIN FAMILY ESTATE.
MOST NOTABLE ARE THE BODYGUARDS CALLED SPs, WHO ARE ON DUTY 24/7...
...TO RIGOROUSLY WATCH FOR ANY SUSPICIOUS INDIVIDUALS ON AND AROUND THE GROUNDS.
BUT, EXCEPT FOR MARIA AND HAYATE, THERE IS ALMOST NO ONE IN THE MAIN BUILDING WHERE NAGI SPENDS HER DAILY LIFE.
THAT'S BECAUSE NAGI, THE MISTRESS OF THIS MANSION, HAS A DISLIKE FOR SERVANTS.
THEREFORE, WHENEVER MARIA AND HAYATE ARE GONE...
...THE INSIDE OF THE MANSION GROWS VERY QUIET...
BING BANG CRUNCH BOOM
VERY QUIET...
CRASH

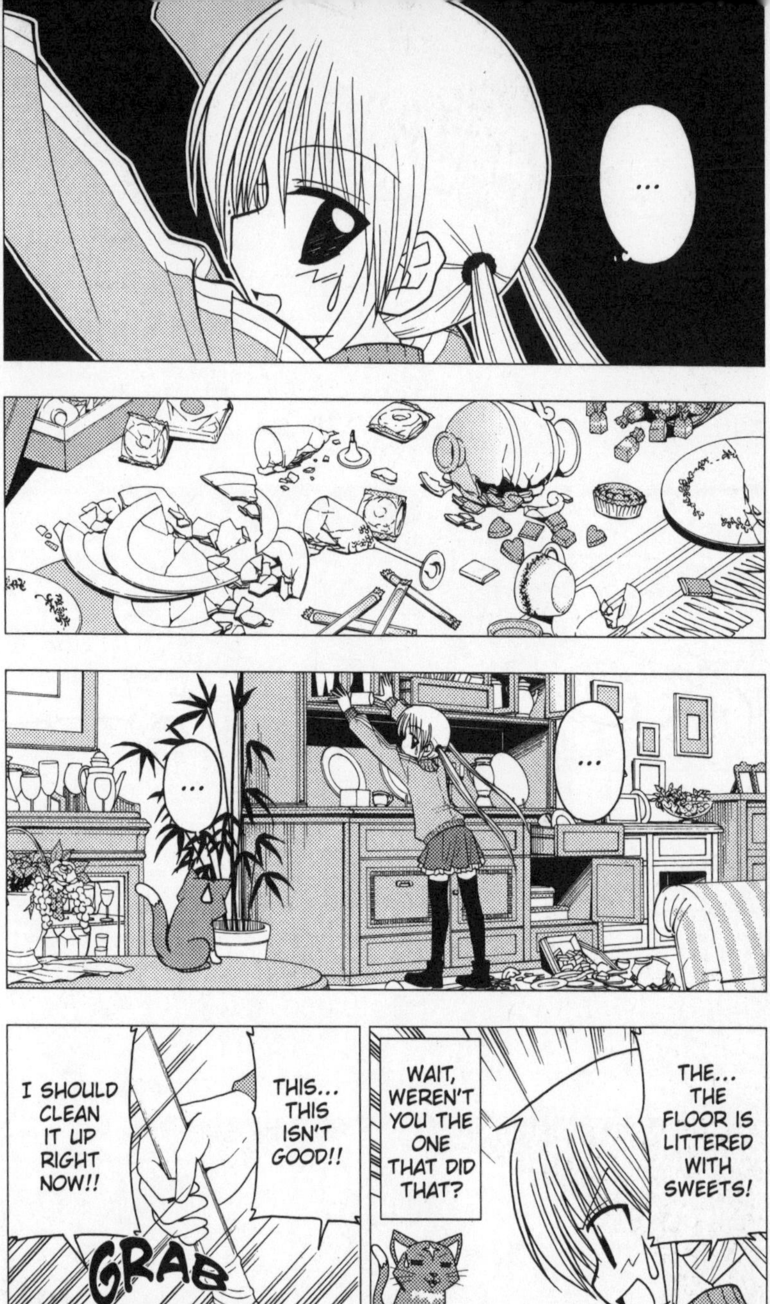
...
...
...
THE... THE FLOOR IS LITTERED WITH SWEETS!
WAIT, WEREN'T YOU THE ONE THAT DID THAT?
THIS... THIS ISN'T GOOD!!
I SHOULD CLEAN IT UP RIGHT NOW!!
GRAB

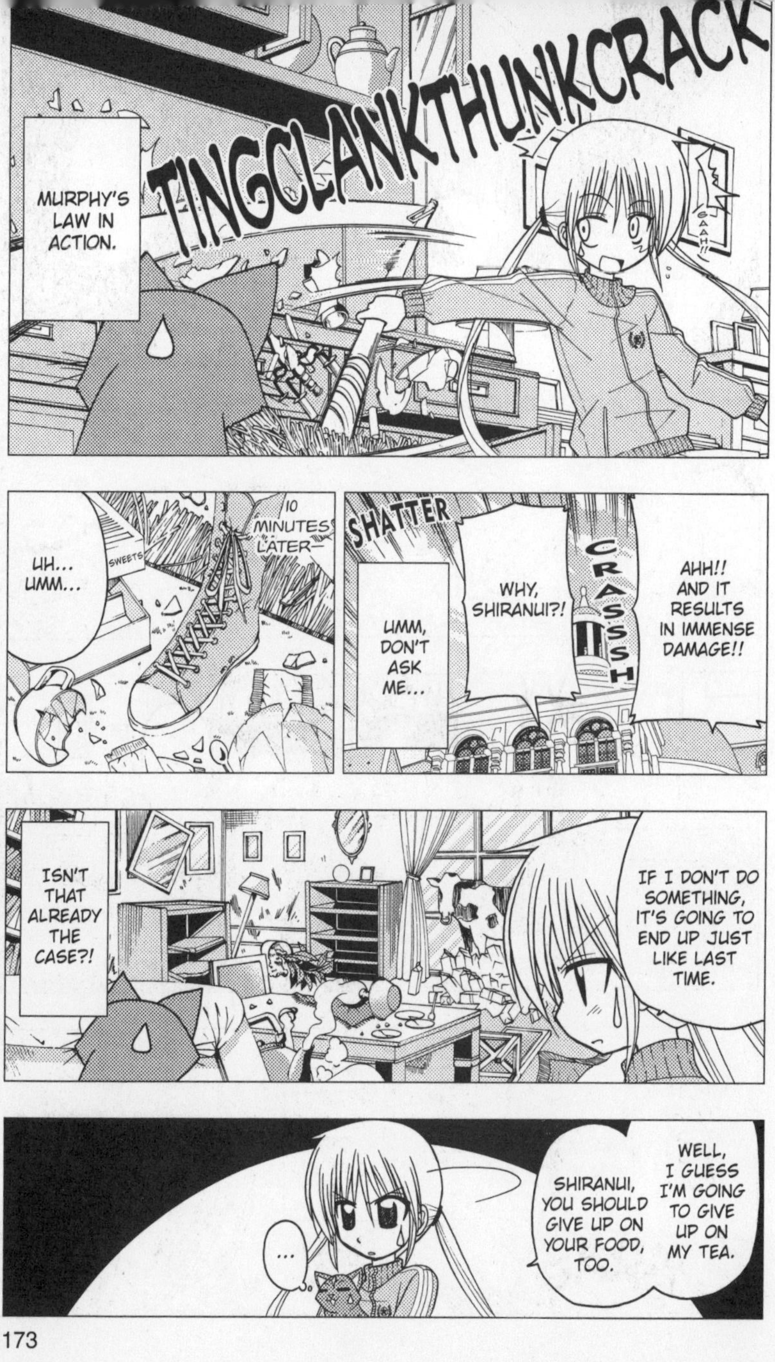
TINGCLANKTHUNKCRACK
GAAAH!!
MURPHY'S LAW IN ACTION.
SHATTER
CRASSH
AHH!! AND IT RESULTS IN IMMENSE DAMAGE!!
WHY, SHIRANUI?!
UMM, DON'T ASK ME...
10 MINUTES LATER—
SWEETS
UH... UMM...
IF I DON'T DO SOMETHING, IT'S GOING TO END UP JUST LIKE LAST TIME.
ISN'T THAT ALREADY THE CASE?!
WELL, I GUESS I'M GOING TO GIVE UP ON MY TEA.
SHIRANUI, YOU SHOULD GIVE UP ON YOUR FOOD, TOO.
...

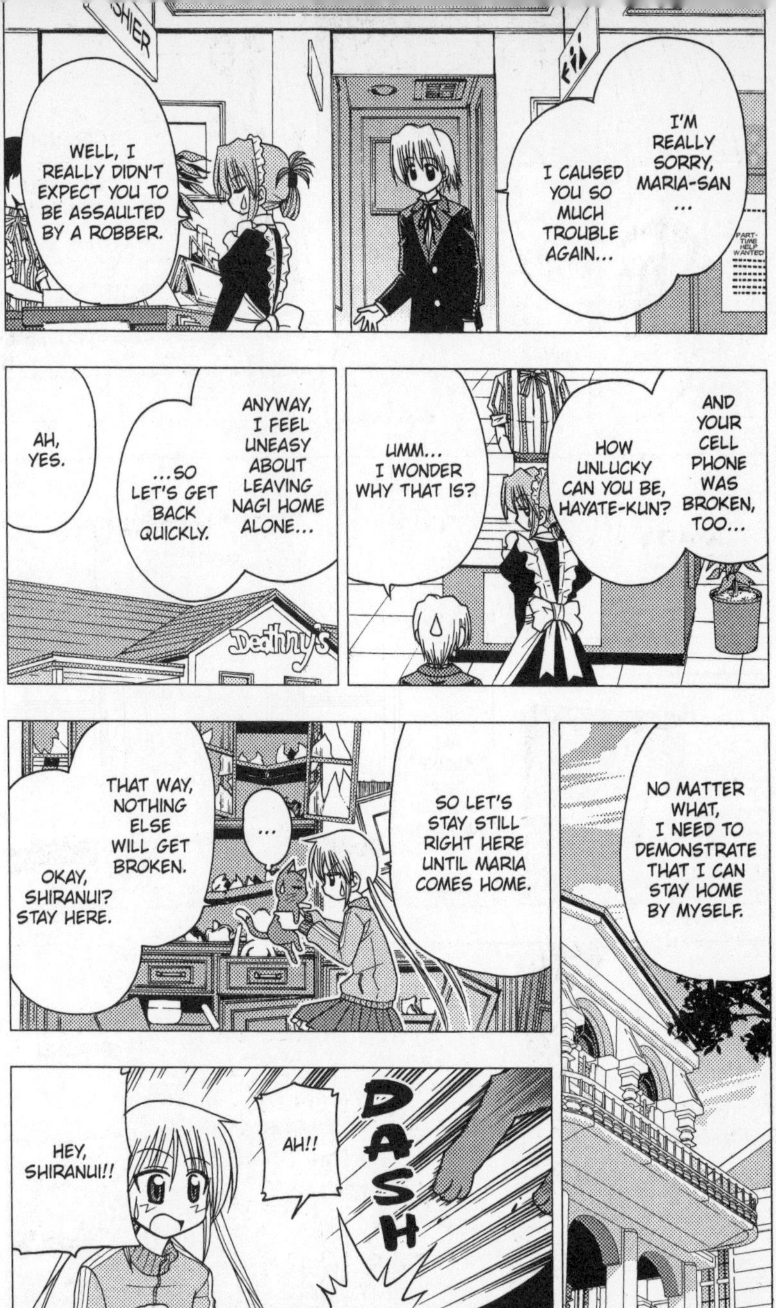
SHIER
PART-TIME HELP WANTED
I'M REALLY SORRY, MARIA-SAN...
I CAUSED YOU SO MUCH TROUBLE AGAIN...
WELL, I REALLY DIDN'T EXPECT YOU TO BE ASSAULTED BY A ROBBER.
AND YOUR CELL PHONE WAS BROKEN, TOO...
HOW UNLUCKY CAN YOU BE, HAYATE-KUN?
UMM... I WONDER WHY THAT IS?
Deathny's
ANYWAY, I FEEL UNEASY ABOUT LEAVING NAGI HOME ALONE...
...SO LET'S GET BACK QUICKLY.
AH, YES.
NO MATTER WHAT, I NEED TO DEMONSTRATE THAT I CAN STAY HOME BY MYSELF.
SO LET'S STAY STILL RIGHT HERE UNTIL MARIA COMES HOME.
...
THAT WAY, NOTHING ELSE WILL GET BROKEN.
OKAY, SHIRANUI? STAY HERE.
DASH
AH!!
HEY, SHIRANUI!!

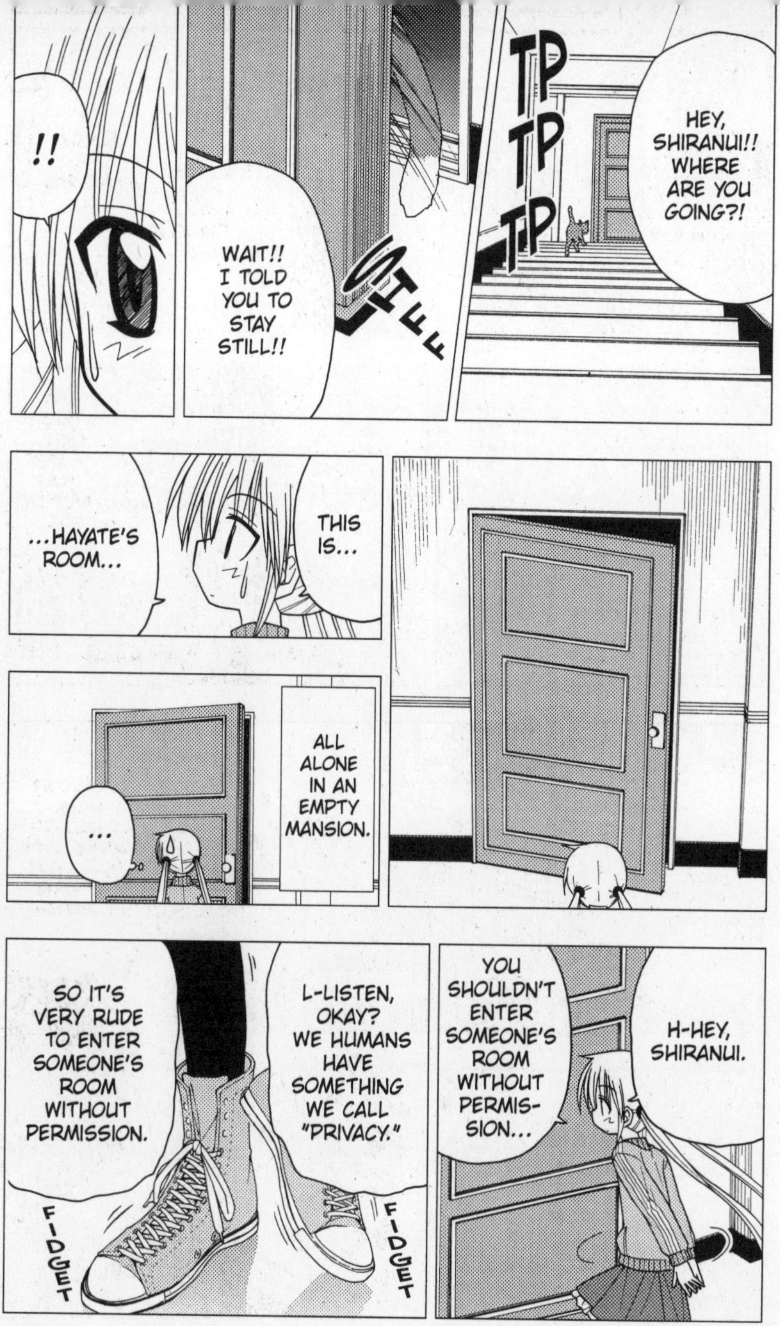
TP TP TP
HEY, SHIRANUI!! WHERE ARE YOU GOING?!
STIFF
WAIT!! I TOLD YOU TO STAY STILL!!
!!
THIS IS...
...HAYATE'S ROOM...
ALL ALONE IN AN EMPTY MANSION.
...
H-HEY, SHIRANUI.
YOU SHOULDN'T ENTER SOMEONE'S ROOM WITHOUT PERMIS-SION...
FIDGET
L-LISTEN, OKAY? WE HUMANS HAVE SOMETHING WE CALL "PRIVACY."
SO IT'S VERY RUDE TO ENTER SOMEONE'S ROOM WITHOUT PERMISSION.
FIDGET

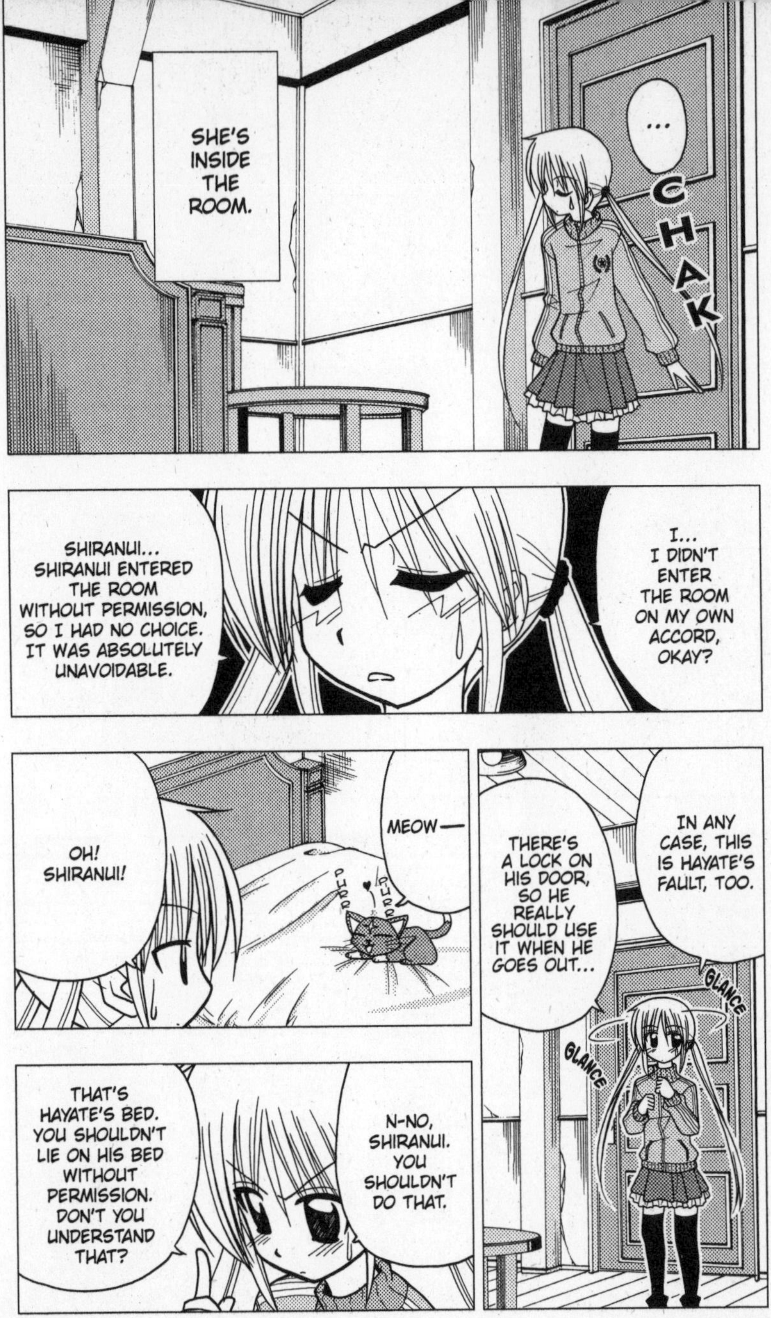
...
CHAK
SHE'S INSIDE THE ROOM.
I... I DIDN'T ENTER THE ROOM ON MY OWN ACCORD, OKAY?
SHIRANUI... SHIRANUI ENTERED THE ROOM WITHOUT PERMISSION, SO I HAD NO CHOICE. IT WAS ABSOLUTELY UNAVOIDABLE.
IN ANY CASE, THIS IS HAYATE'S FAULT, TOO.
THERE'S A LOCK ON HIS DOOR, SO HE REALLY SHOULD USE IT WHEN HE GOES OUT...
GLANCE
GLANCE
MEOW—
PURR
PURR
OH! SHIRANUI!
N-NO, SHIRANUI. YOU SHOULDN'T DO THAT.
THAT'S HAYATE'S BED. YOU SHOULDN'T LIE ON HIS BED WITHOUT PERMISSION. DON'T YOU UNDERSTAND THAT?

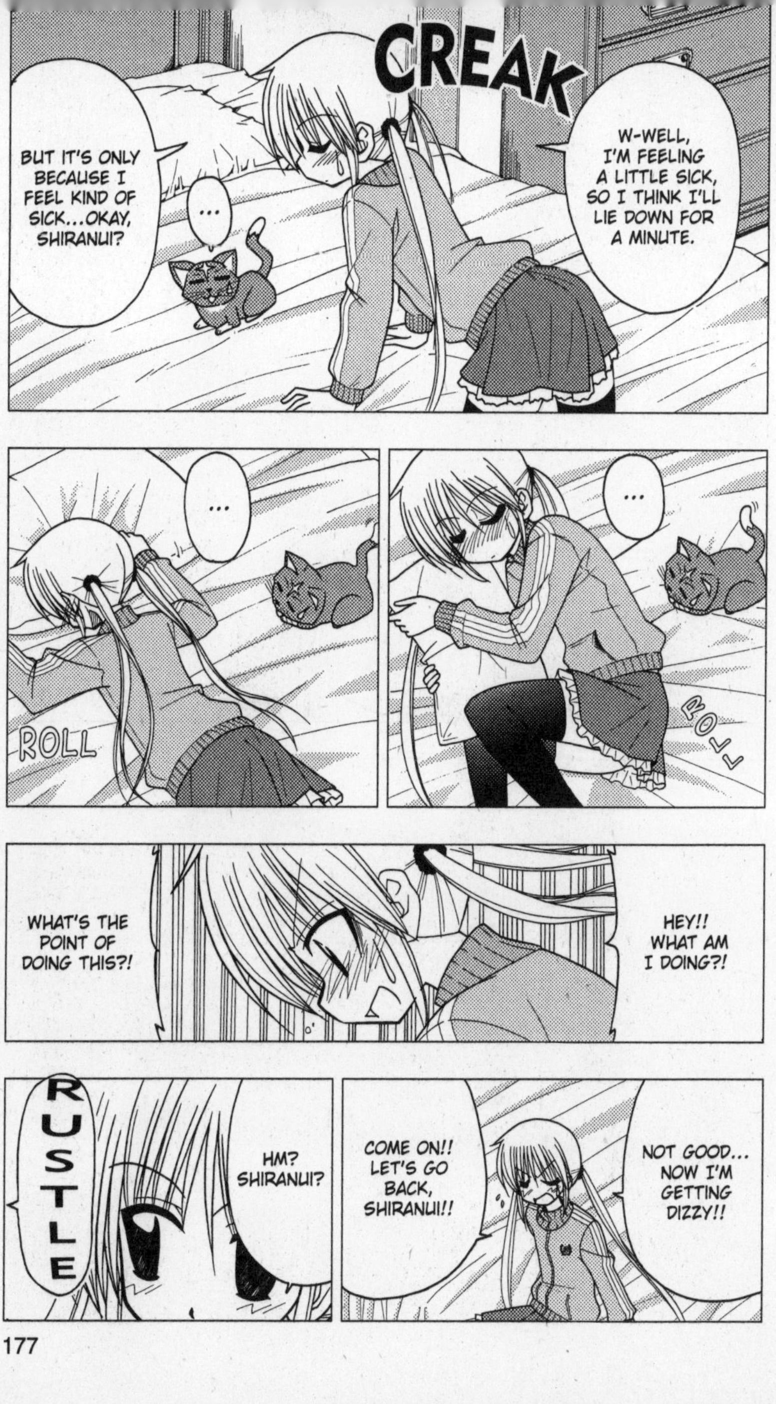
CREAK
W-WELL, I'M FEELING A LITTLE SICK, SO I THINK I'LL LIE DOWN FOR A MINUTE.
...
BUT IT'S ONLY BECAUSE I FEEL KIND OF SICK...OKAY, SHIRANUI?
...
ROLL
...
ROLL
HEY!! WHAT AM I DOING?!
WHAT'S THE POINT OF DOING THIS?!
NOT GOOD... NOW I'M GETTING DIZZY!!
COME ON!! LET'S GO BACK, SHIRANUI!!
HM? SHIRANUI?
RUSTLE

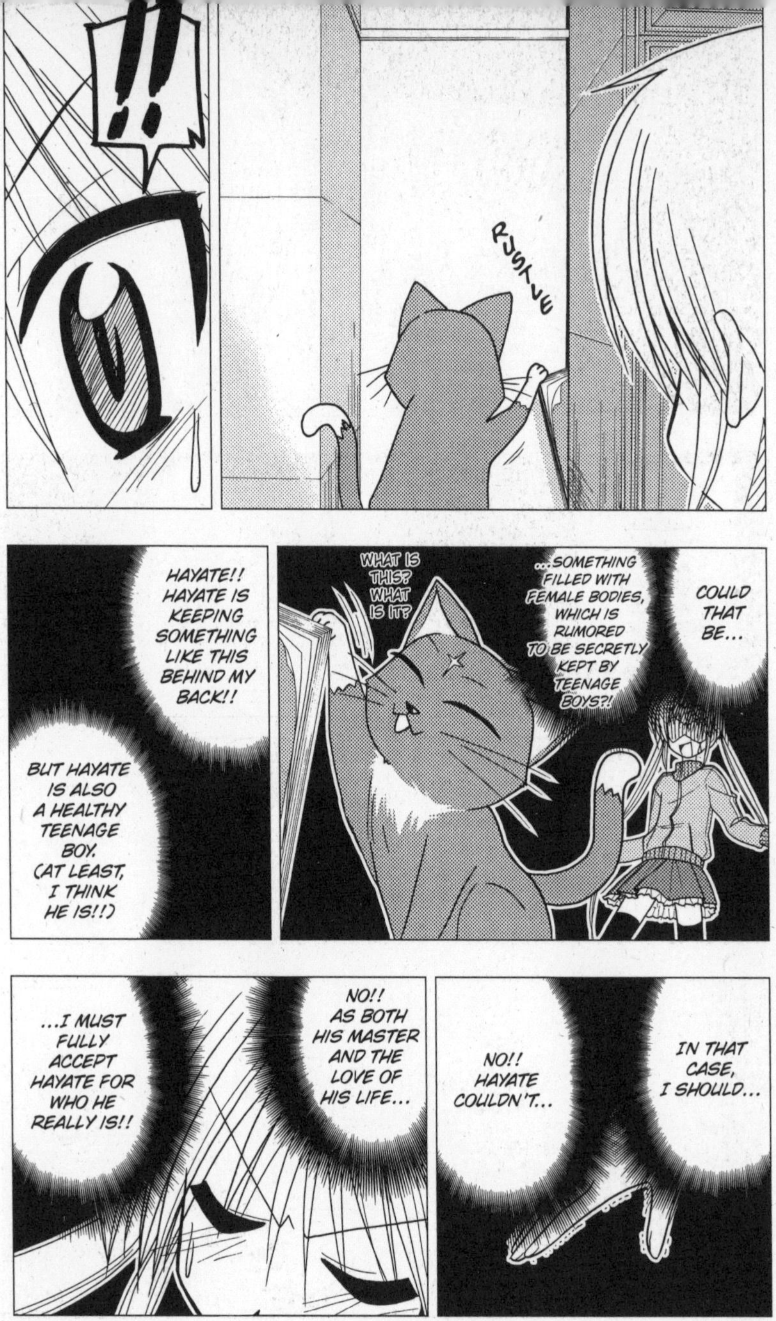
RUSTLE
!!
COULD THAT BE...
...SOMETHING FILLED WITH FEMALE BODIES, WHICH IS RUMORED TO BE SECRETLY KEPT BY TEENAGE BOYS?!
WHAT IS THIS? WHAT IS IT?
HAYATE!! HAYATE IS KEEPING SOMETHING LIKE THIS BEHIND MY BACK!!
BUT HAYATE IS ALSO A HEALTHY TEENAGE BOY. (AT LEAST, I THINK HE IS!!)
IN THAT CASE, I SHOULD...
NO!! HAYATE COULDN'T...
NO!! AS BOTH HIS MASTER AND THE LOVE OF HIS LIFE...
...I MUST FULLY ACCEPT HAYATE FOR WHO HE REALLY IS!!

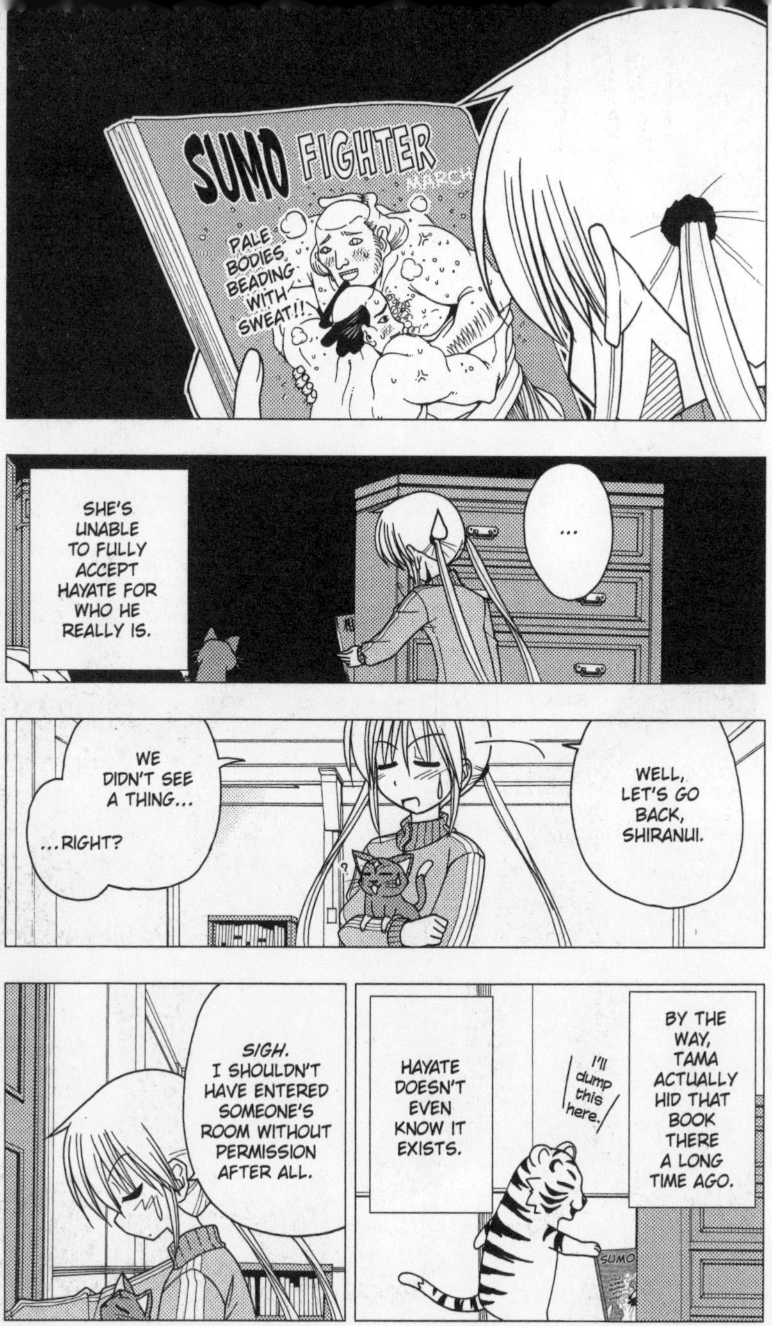
SUMO FIGHTER
MARCH
PALE BODIES BEADING WITH SWEAT!!
...
SHE'S UNABLE TO FULLY ACCEPT HAYATE FOR WHO HE REALLY IS.
WELL, LET'S GO BACK, SHIRANUI.
WE DIDN'T SEE A THING...
...RIGHT?
BY THE WAY, TAMA ACTUALLY HID THAT BOOK THERE A LONG TIME AGO.
I'll dump this here.
SUMO
HAYATE DOESN'T EVEN KNOW IT EXISTS.
SIGH. I SHOULDN'T HAVE ENTERED SOMEONE'S ROOM WITHOUT PERMISSION AFTER ALL.

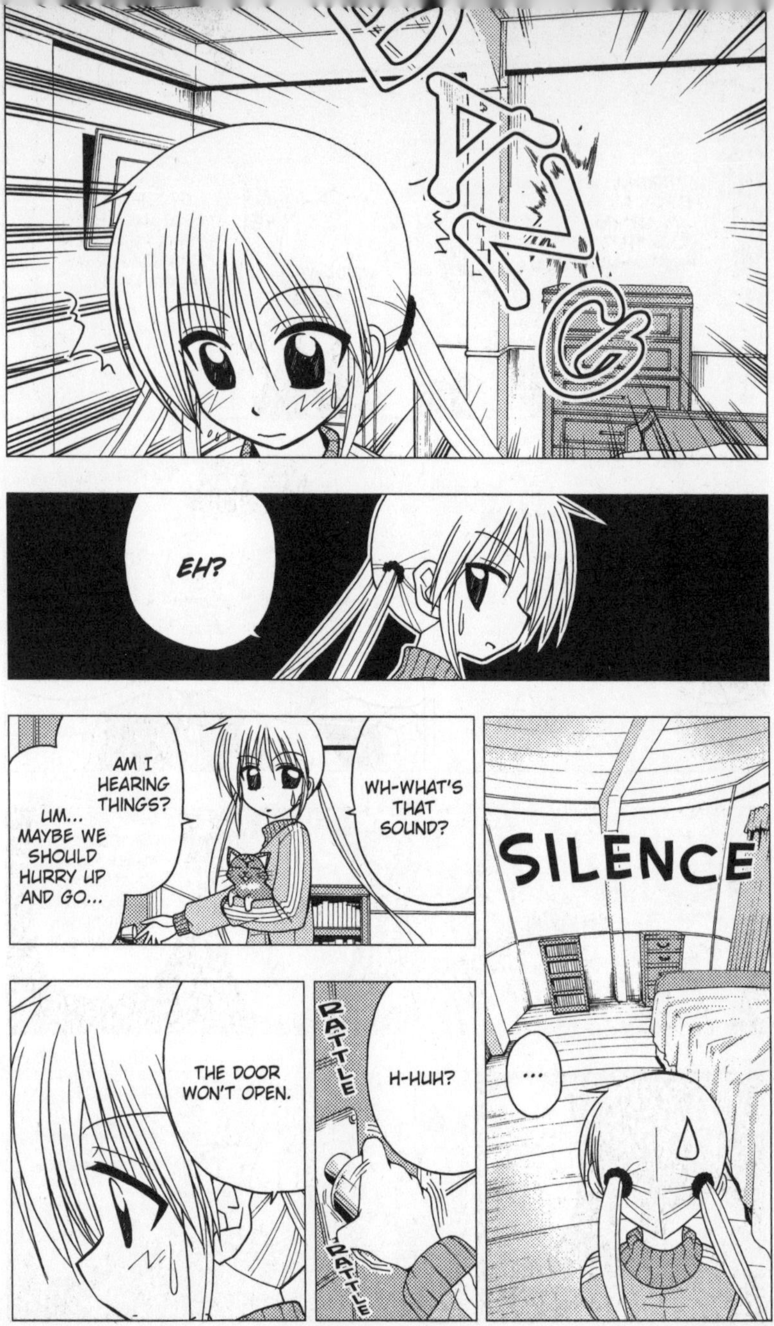
BANG
EH?
SILENCE
...
WH-WHAT'S THAT SOUND?
AM I HEARING THINGS?
UM... MAYBE WE SHOULD HURRY UP AND GO...
RATTLE
RATTLE
H-HUH?
THE DOOR WON'T OPEN.

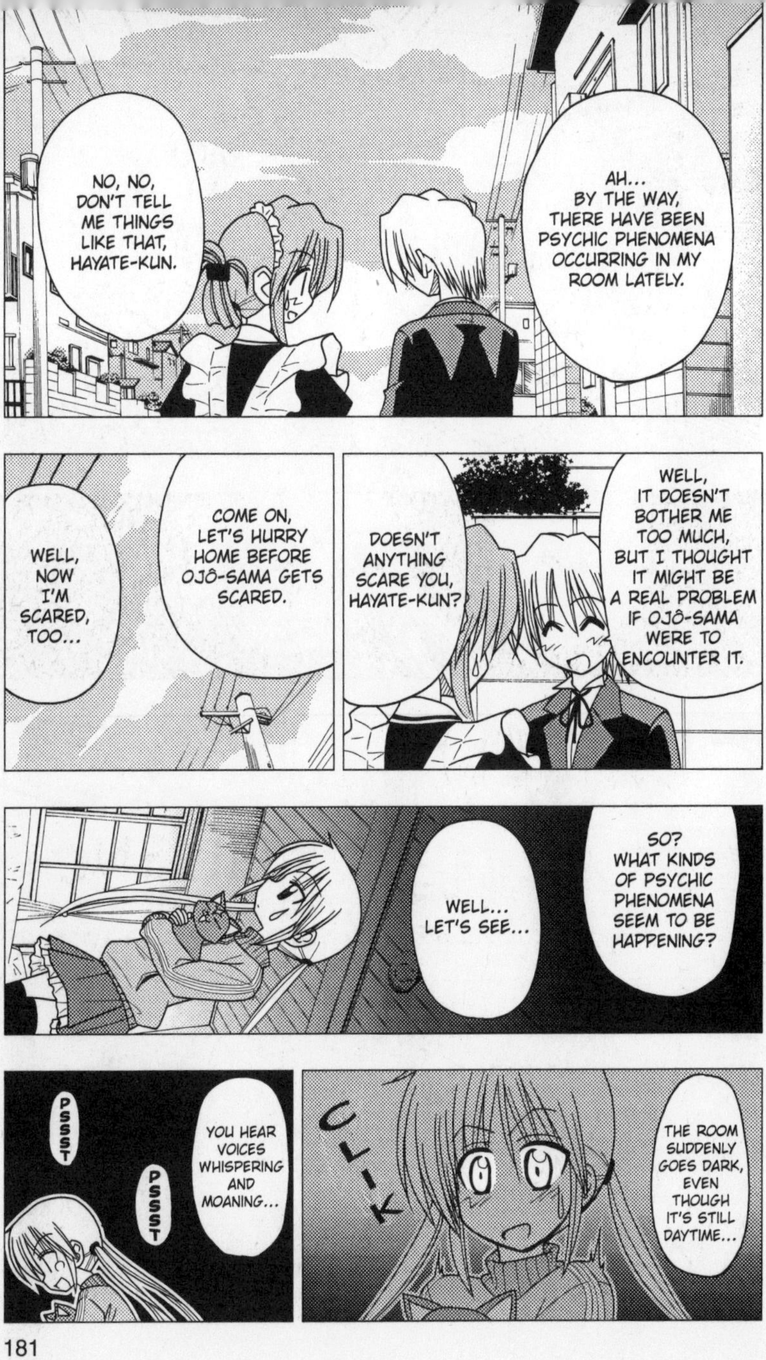
AH... BY THE WAY, THERE HAVE BEEN PSYCHIC PHENOMENA OCCURRING IN MY ROOM LATELY.
NO, NO, DON'T TELL ME THINGS LIKE THAT, HAYATE-KUN.
WELL, IT DOESN'T BOTHER ME TOO MUCH, BUT I THOUGHT IT MIGHT BE A REAL PROBLEM IF OJÔ-SAMA WERE TO ENCOUNTER IT.
DOESN'T ANYTHING SCARE YOU, HAYATE-KUN?
COME ON, LET'S HURRY HOME BEFORE OJÔ-SAMA GETS SCARED.
WELL, NOW I'M SCARED, TOO...
SO? WHAT KINDS OF PSYCHIC PHENOMENA SEEM TO BE HAPPENING?
WELL... LET'S SEE...
THE ROOM SUDDENLY GOES DARK, EVEN THOUGH IT'S STILL DAYTIME...
CLIK
YOU HEAR VOICES WHISPERING AND MOANING...
PSSST
PSSST

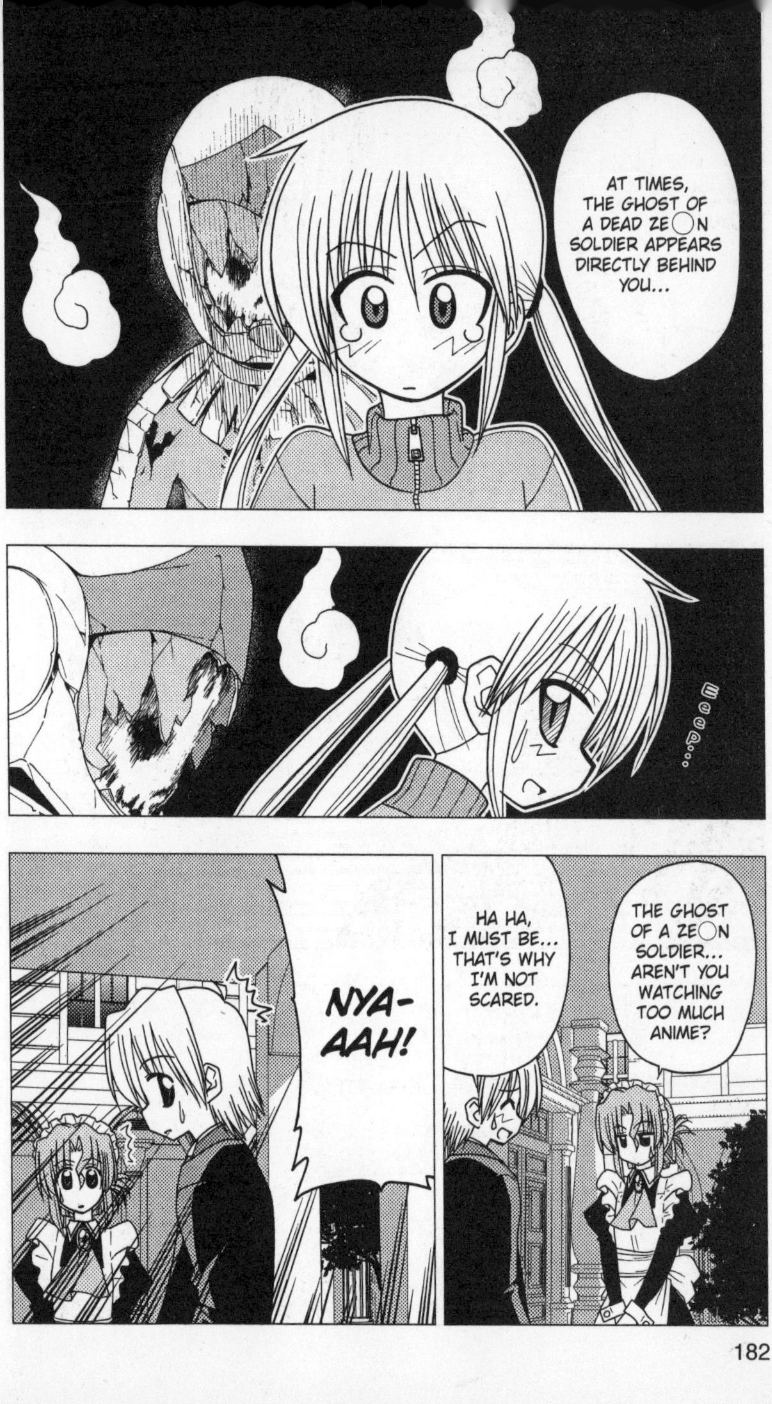
AT TIMES, THE GHOST OF A DEAD ZE◯N SOLDIER APPEARS DIRECTLY BEHIND YOU...
Eeep...
THE GHOST OF A ZE◯N SOLDIER... AREN'T YOU WATCHING TOO MUCH ANIME?
HA HA, I MUST BE... THAT'S WHY I'M NOT SCARED.
NYA-AAH!

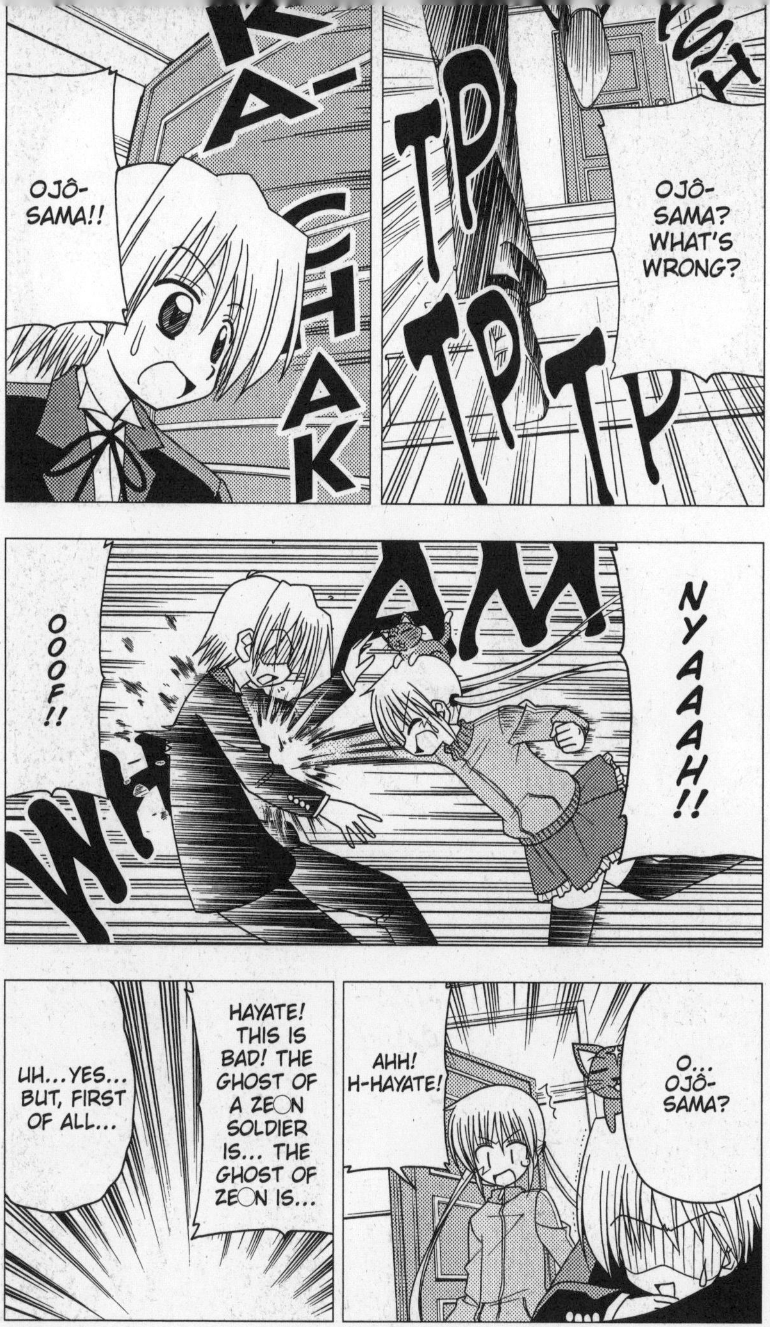
TP TP TP TP
OJÔ-SAMA? WHAT'S WRONG?
KA-CHAK
OJÔ-SAMA!!
NYAAAAH!!
OOOF!!
O... OJÔ-SAMA?
AHH! H-HAYATE!
HAYATE! THIS IS BAD! THE GHOST OF A ZE◯N SOLDIER IS... THE GHOST OF ZE◯N IS...
UH...YES... BUT, FIRST OF ALL...

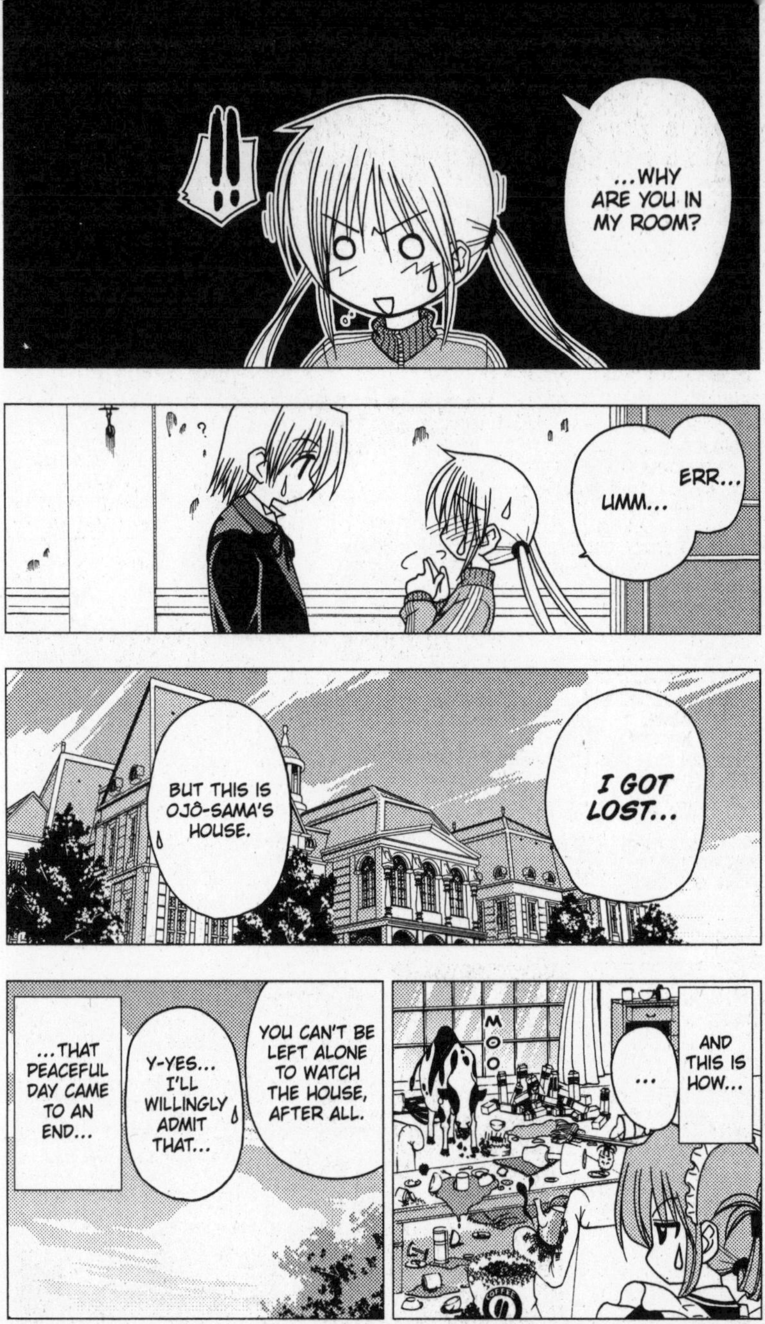
...WHY ARE YOU IN MY ROOM?
!!
ERR...
UMM...
I GOT LOST...
BUT THIS IS OJÔ-SAMA'S HOUSE.
AND THIS IS HOW...
...
MOO
YOU CAN'T BE LEFT ALONE TO WATCH THE HOUSE, AFTER ALL.
Y-YES... I'LL WILLINGLY ADMIT THAT...
...THAT PEACEFUL DAY CAME TO AN END...

TO BE CONTINUED

- HAYATE THE COMBAT BUTLER -

BONUS PAGE

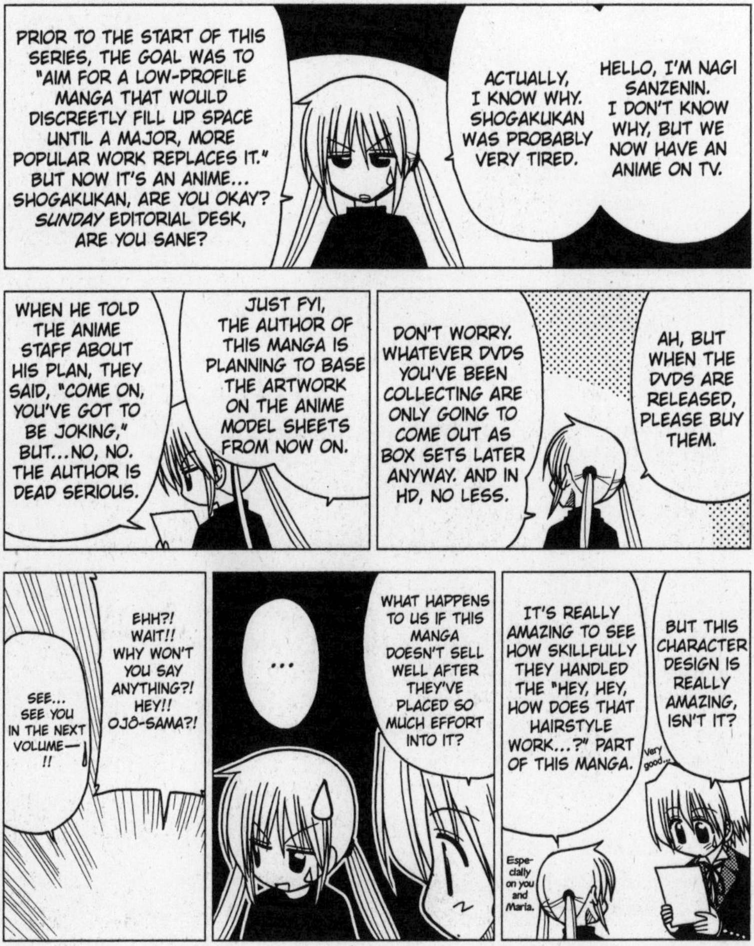

HELLO, I'M NAGI SANZENIN. I DON'T KNOW WHY, BUT WE NOW HAVE AN ANIME ON TV.
ACTUALLY, I KNOW WHY. SHOGAKUKAN WAS PROBABLY VERY TIRED.
PRIOR TO THE START OF THIS SERIES, THE GOAL WAS TO "AIM FOR A LOW-PROFILE MANGA THAT WOULD DISCREETLY FILL UP SPACE UNTIL A MAJOR, MORE POPULAR WORK REPLACES IT." BUT NOW IT'S AN ANIME... SHOGAKUKAN, ARE YOU OKAY? *SUNDAY* EDITORIAL DESK, ARE YOU SANE?
AH, BUT WHEN THE DVDS ARE RELEASED, PLEASE BUY THEM.
DON'T WORRY. WHATEVER DVDS YOU'VE BEEN COLLECTING ARE ONLY GOING TO COME OUT AS BOX SETS LATER ANYWAY. AND IN HD, NO LESS.
JUST FYI, THE AUTHOR OF THIS MANGA IS PLANNING TO BASE THE ARTWORK ON THE ANIME MODEL SHEETS FROM NOW ON.
WHEN HE TOLD THE ANIME STAFF ABOUT HIS PLAN, THEY SAID, "COME ON, YOU'VE GOT TO BE JOKING," BUT...NO, NO. THE AUTHOR IS DEAD SERIOUS.
BUT THIS CHARACTER DESIGN IS REALLY AMAZING, ISN'T IT?
Very good...
IT'S REALLY AMAZING TO SEE HOW SKILLFULLY THEY HANDLED THE "HEY, HEY, HOW DOES THAT HAIRSTYLE WORK...?" PART OF THIS MANGA.
Especially on you and Maria.
WHAT HAPPENS TO US IF THIS MANGA DOESN'T SELL WELL AFTER THEY'VE PLACED SO MUCH EFFORT INTO IT?
...
EHH?! WAIT!! WHY WON'T YOU SAY ANYTHING?! HEY!! OJŌ-SAMA?!
SEE... SEE YOU IN THE NEXT VOLUME—!!

PROFILE

[Age]
28

[Birthday]
January 9th

[Blood Type]
A

[Family Structure]
Father, Mother, Older sister, Grandfather, Grandmother

[Height]
166 cm

[Weight]
56 kg

[Strengths/Likes]
Gundam plastic models, figures, Yukiji.

[Weaknesses/Dislikes]
Alcohol. Women who are selfish, headstrong, and out of control.

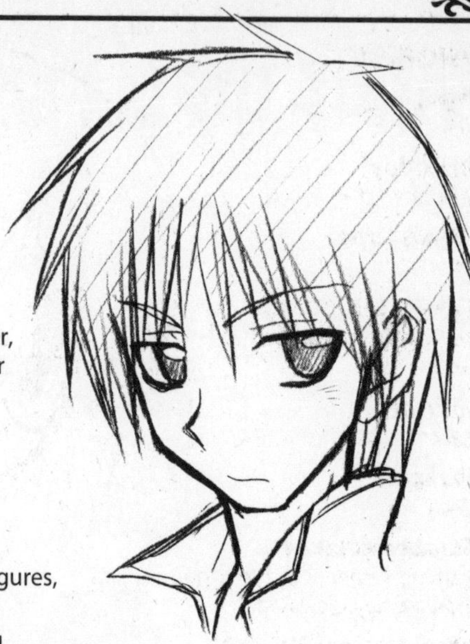

KYONOSUKE KAORU

According to my original plan, he was supposed to deal with various things at school along with the white-haired male teacher who is seen talking with Nagi (Vol. 4, pg. 67) one page before Kaoru's first appearance in the story.

But then, I realized that I was placing him in an awkward situation…

Actually, I was also having a hard time drawing him.

He's Yukiji's childhood friend, an elementary school classmate who fell for her back when she used to be cute. Out of habit, those feelings remain to this day…

He focuses on making Gundam plastic models every day as a way to help bury his sadness over the fact that she's not so cute as an adult…

He had a marriage interview with Saki-san in this volume, and the pair unexpectedly seemed to enjoy each other's company.

Well, since both of them are so single-minded, I doubt this could develop into a relationship…

But still, I wonder if the day might come when he and Yukiji are able to become close friends?

Umm… I really can't imagine that happening…

PROFILE

[Age]
19

[Birthday]
February 1st

[Blood Type]
AB

[Family Structure]
Mother, Grandfather
(Godfather)

[Height]
163 cm

[Weight]
53 kg

[Strengths/Likes]
Training, ramen, cute younger
boys, money, sleeping.

[Weaknesses/Dislikes]
Lies.

SONIA SHAFLNARZ

Sister is a character I had planned out to the smallest detail involving the Sanzenin family inheritance, but her character development has been a bit difficult to manage. Even so, I really want to do more with this character.

Since there are many nice characters in this manga, it's surprisingly useful to have some antisocial "bad guy" types.

Sister, Yukiji, Himuro, and in some ways even Hayate can be considered antisocial types of characters. I think it would be interesting to see the development of a very evil-minded battle between all of them.

This type of character works surprisingly well with Himuro, so I think we'll see more scenes from now on where she's together with Himuro.

Of course, since neither of them have any interest in each other, I don't think there's even the slightest chance for it to develop into a relationship…

As an author, I have a lot of things I want to do involving Saki-san and Sister, but that seems to stray too far from the main plot, so stories like that are not going to appear any time soon.

Hmm…

SO! HERE WE ARE!

HAYATE THE COMBAT BUTLER HAS NOW MADE IT TO THE 10TH VOLUME.

IT'S MOVED INTO THE DOUBLE DIGITS!

WHAT DO YOU THINK?

THANKS TO YOUR SUPPORT, THIS MANGA IS BEING MADE INTO AN ANIMATED TV SHOW. THANK YOU VERY MUCH.

BEFORE I STARTED ON THIS SERIES, I THOUGHT TO MYSELF,
"I WISH I COULD MAKE THIS MANGA GOOD ENOUGH TO BE AN ANIME,"
BUT IT'S UNBELIEVABLE THAT MY WISH ACTUALLY CAME TRUE.

SURPRISING THINGS CAN HAPPEN UNEXPECTEDLY IN OUR LIVES.

TO PURSUE MY DREAM OF BECOMING A COMIC ARTIST, I COMPETED FOR VARIOUS MANGA AWARDS, BUT I JUST DIDN'T HAVE ANY LUCK WITH THOSE WHATSOEVER. I WAS REJECTED REPEATEDLY AND NEVER ENDED UP WINNING ANYTHING AT ALL.

HATING MY OWN LACK OF TALENT, I WORKED AS ANOTHER ARTIST'S ASSISTANT FOR FIVE YEARS, AND AT TIMES I SPENT OVER A YEAR DRAWING JUST 32 PAGES OF MANGA.

(AND AFTER ALL THAT WORK, I WAS ELIMINATED IN THE SECOND ROUND. WHAT DO YOU THINK OF THAT?)

BUT I TRULY FEEL THAT ONE CAN COME THIS FAR JUST BY WORKING EARNESTLY.

AS YOU CAN SEE, YOU CAN GET BY SOMEHOW. IT DOESN'T MATTER, ESPECIALLY FOR A MANGA ARTIST.

IN ANY CASE, I LEARNED THAT WHAT'S IMPORTANT IS TO NEVER GIVE UP AND TO KEEP ON DRAWING, SO I TOO WILL CONTINUE TO WORK HARD AT DRAWING.

IT IS MY INTENTION TO CONTINUE WITH IT AGAIN THIS YEAR, UNTIL ALL THAT'S LEFT OF MY PASSION ARE ASHES!

SO, I WOULD BE GRATEFUL FOR YOUR SUPPORT FOR MY MANGA AND ANIME!

AND PLEASE GO VISIT WEB SUNDAY, TOO!

WELL, I'M LOOKING FORWARD TO SEEING YOU ONCE AGAIN IN VOLUME 11!

SEE YA—☆

HTTP://WEBSUNDAY.NET/

Wataru and Sakuya— The After-Hina Matsuri Night Festival

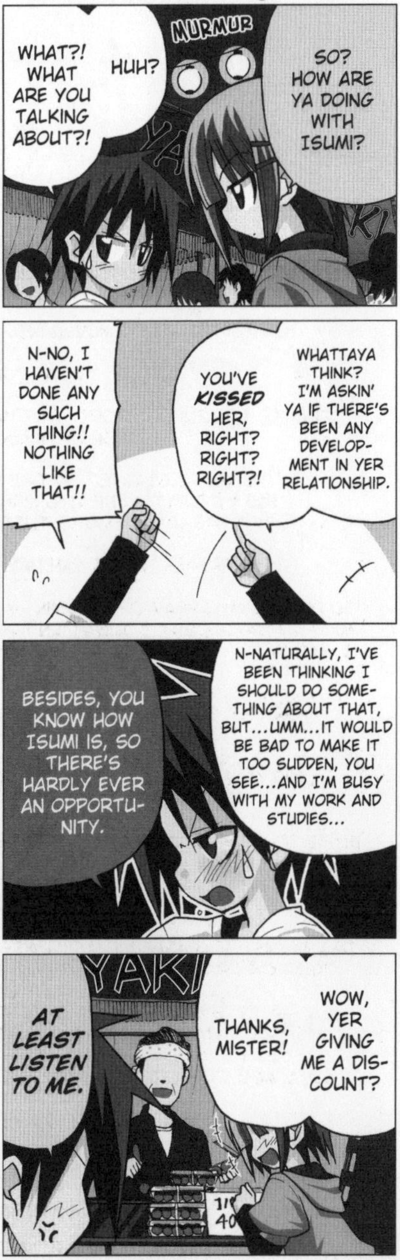
SO? HOW ARE YA DOING WITH ISUMI?
MURMUR
HUH?
WHAT?! WHAT ARE YOU TALKING ABOUT?!
WHATTAYA THINK? I'M ASKIN' YA IF THERE'S BEEN ANY DEVELOP-MENT IN YER RELATIONSHIP.
YOU'VE *KISSED* HER, RIGHT? RIGHT? RIGHT?!
N-NO, I HAVEN'T DONE ANY SUCH THING!! NOTHING LIKE THAT!!
N-NATURALLY, I'VE BEEN THINKING I SHOULD DO SOME-THING ABOUT THAT, BUT...UMM...IT WOULD BE BAD TO MAKE IT TOO SUDDEN, YOU SEE...AND I'M BUSY WITH MY WORK AND STUDIES...
BESIDES, YOU KNOW HOW ISUMI IS, SO THERE'S HARDLY EVER AN OPPORTU-NITY.
YAKI
WOW, YER GIVING ME A DIS-COUNT?
THANKS, MISTER!
AT LEAST LISTEN TO ME.

The Person Who Can't Spot a Lie...

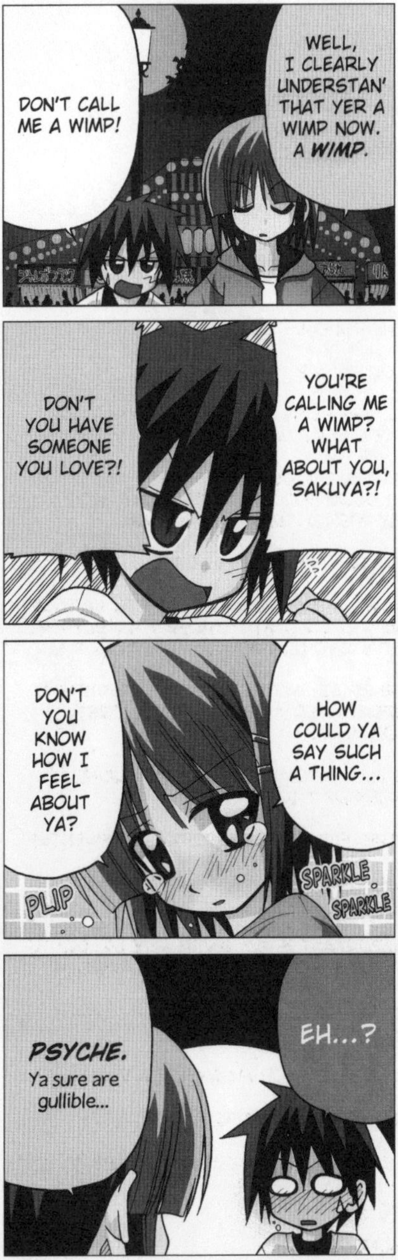
WELL, I CLEARLY UNDERSTAN' THAT YER A WIMP NOW. A *WIMP*.
DON'T CALL ME A WIMP!
YOU'RE CALLING ME A WIMP? WHAT ABOUT YOU, SAKUYA?!
DON'T YOU HAVE SOMEONE YOU LOVE?!
HOW COULD YA SAY SUCH A THING...
DON'T YOU KNOW HOW I FEEL ABOUT YA?
SPARKLE
SPARKLE
PLIP
EH...?
PSYCHE.
Ya sure are gullible...

- HAYATE THE COMBAT BUTLER -

-OPTION THAT SENDS YOU DIRECTLY TO A BAD END-

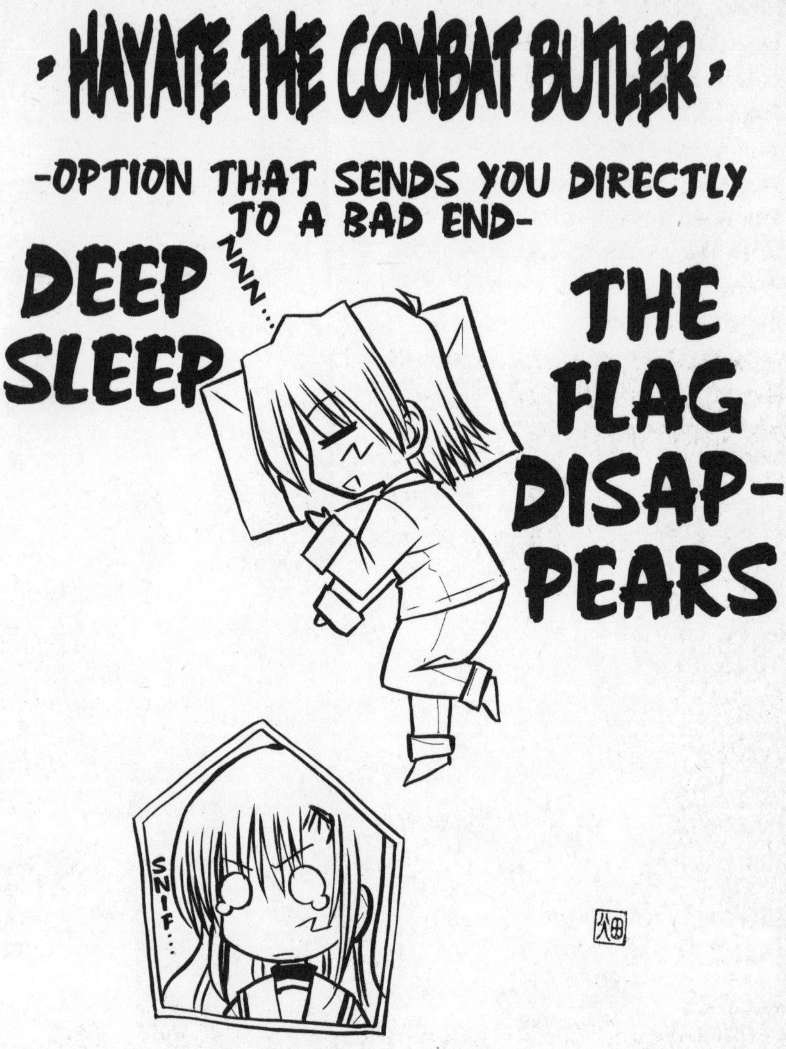
DEEP SLEEP
ZZZ...
THE FLAG DISAP-PEARS
SNIF...